ISBN 978-1-330-53297-3
PIBN 10074888

# METHODIST

# QUARTERLY REVIEW.

## 1877.

VOLUME LIX.—FOURTH SERIES, VOLUME XXIX.

D. D. WHEDON, LL.D., EDITOR.

NEW YORK:
NELSON & PHILLIPS.
CINCINNATI: HITCHCOCK & WALDEN.
1877.

# CONTENTS OF VOLUME LIX.—1877.

## JANUARY NUMBER.



## APRIL NUMBER.

## JULY NUMBER.



## OCTOBER NUMBER.

METHODIST

QUARTERLY REVIEW.

JANUARY, 1877.

## ART. I.—LANGUAGE AND HISTORY.

THE new science of Linguistics has been, like every other, forcibly impressed into the service of skepticism. Its parents and best friends declare that this is not a voluntary enlistment, and they demand its release from an enforced service. The moment is a favorable one for setting forth some of the reasons why language is not a lantern to search obscure regions of history, or a witness to an immeasurable length of human development, or even a safe instructor in the growth of human ideas. The moment is favorable, because the philosophy of human progress is once more in the foreground, after having been for some years overshadowed by physical science. We once more definitely recognize the necessity of reasoning together. A few bald physical facts no longer assume to set aside logic and render philosophy contemptible. Many who were recently bewildered by the unexpected phosphorescence of bogs that had long lain in darkness, perceive once more that the sun is still the light of the earth and lord of our skies. The facts of development, whatever they may be, must be lightened upon out of the understanding, and their value estimated by the processes of human logic. The significance of a fact is to be gathered by a painfully minute attention to all its surroundings, and by a more laborious study of its relations to the whole world of knowledge and the entire government of the reason. We cannot declare that evolution lies in the vast abyss opened under

us by theorists on the testimony of rocks alone—making their supposed *ipse dixit* final. There are laws of interpretation, comparison, evidence. The very language of nature requires an interpreter. And every utterance must be analyzed, correlated with other sayings, and used, when sifted of all doubts, with the caution and discretion essential to all sound inference.

No new and royal road to truth has been opened by scientific discoveries. We must use our judgments, compare our knowledge, and, at last, we must *philosophize* upon it. New facts *may* confute old philosophies, but it must be in fair battle. Victory cannot be gained by marching off in the opposite direction, or by a flanking march. The camp of philosophy must be captured, for its equipments and its camping-grounds are necessary to the hostile forces. These general truths are more fully appreciated than they were a few years ago. The sober second thought is *regnant.* Agassiz gave evolution five years in which to run its course. Are we witnessing at the end of two of those years the first flagging of that spirited racer?

The time to examine the ground upon which we stand has come, and language must be asked for its exact testimony concerning the history of man on the earth. The purpose of the present article is to strip that testimony of three false interpretations. It is unfairly used to teach that *man has been for a very long time upon the earth;* that *it is itself older than recorded time;* that *it is an authority for the history of venerable ideas*—ideas so old as to have no date in history. The last false interpretation is more important than it seems, and the too hasty acceptance of it by some scholars may cause great mischief. Language, like other human faculties and arts, had a foundation in our original endowments, an elaboration in practice and experience, and has been the subject of a wide range of modifications. Its beginnings are nowhere recorded except in Genesis; its early growths are more completely lost than any others that have sprung out of the nature of man. Its present (and recent) condition, varieties, and laws of change, are our best field for its study, and we have not gone over a hundredth part of this. Speech habits in the historical period are imperfect guides in the unknown times when men first spoke. Admitting that they began as our children do, this will not help us to understand their learning to talk without an

older generation to teach them. There are growths, such as the demonstrative roots, which have no analogies in historical experience; we cannot compare the process of their development with our own changes of words. Terms that have kept for a long time a common base of signification in widely-branched classes of tongues shed no light on the growth of ideas; for the secondary meanings, not the primary, need to be one, (for the argument,) and the survival of the original base makes it unsafe to reason that the secondary sense has been in use at any particular unknown time. The root *pu* (pure, purge) has to this day a higher and a lower sense; we dare not infer the higher sense merely from the wide diffusion of the root. Language is, as a growth, a child of the intellect, not of the lip.* There is abundant proof, to be sure, that lip-change (unnoticed by the ear) has led to intellectual change, and *vice versa;* but we must seek in mental processes for the evolution of every thing that dignifies speech. An optative mood is not a matter of articulation; a mental process comes to permanence by seizing upon an articulation for a house; but the process must have gone on, and the process must continue to go on. There is, then, a study of intricate mental processes, rather than of mouthfuls of vocalized air, at the bottom of every linguistic investigation. How old is language? means, How old is the human intellect? If we had any certain means of determining at what age, or in what necessities, or by what stimulations of desire, man's intellect accomplishes any great step forward, we might use it in language; we have no such time-rate or thought-gauge. We must be content in this field to take all the helps from without, to adjust the knowledge we obtain about speech as well as we can to the generally received chronologies and systems of philosophy. Language is a servant and a minister—a most useful one, but still a servant. Language has no ascertainable chronology of itself, much less of man and his other institutions. These thoughts will be explained more fully in the following pages.

I. Does language assert a high antiquity for human history? The most instructive aspect of this question is presented in

* "No language is a *mere* collection of words; and Locke, in all that he has written about *words*, has offered no proof that any system of *syntax* is ultimately due to sensible ideas."—*Farrar: Origin of Language*, p. 162.

the institutional character of language. It is a human habit, a custom, an institution. We may waive all questions concerning the origin of language; however they may have begun to talk, historical men have been talkers; and their speech, so far as it can be traced backward, has always been subject to the general conditions that surround habits. Among these conditions are those of change. There is a permanent and a changeable element in man's development. In language this permanent element is that man talks;* the changeable element is that he talks differently in different times and lands. He changes his language though he does not cease to talk. In this respect, lingual habits resemble others that rise to the dignity of institutions. They rest upon a permanent base, and they rise from it in diverse and changing structures.

For example: Man is political; some form of government is essential to his social expression; but this habit or institution runs into large diversity, and is, indeed, subject to subtle variation wherever human vitality works with any freedom. So in language; the permanent base remains, the superstructure undergoes perpetual change. The relations of the sexes furnish another example. The institution of marriage has its base in sex difference; its vast range of diversity, and its subtle and complex changefulness, are due to the power of man over his habits. Manifestly the base or permanent element is worth nothing for historical research. Its definition, as unchanging, imports that it is useless as a key to change, or an explanation of a mutable order of things. And in history we are concerned with what changes. Something happens to a people. We shall not explain it by saying that they have a speech, were addicted to government, and were of two sexes. But if we know that their government was a monarchy, their speech Aryan, their marriage Monogamic, we may be a little helped to understand the change. As a rule, however, the inferences we base on such an amount of information concerning institutions want trustworthiness. Modern historical

* The people who do not talk always turn out to be talkers. The last time it was publicly stated that the Veddahs of Ceylon have no language, Max Muller had the matter investigated. It turned out, as it has always done in other cases, that there was plenty of language, and very good language, too; "Many of the words are mere corruptions of Sanskrit."—*Chips*, vol. iv, p. 342.

writing has sought to give value to its work by penetrating far more deeply into the changeful side of institutions. How bald the old generalizations—"Sparta was a kingdom and Athens a republic"—compared with the minute description of the mechanism of these governments furnished us by modern histories! When we deal with institutions as parts of a national life, we need to know them somewhat intimately before we make them the grounds of inferences, the explanations of political changes; and, as a rule, the more nearly our knowledge approaches completeness the more useful it becomes; nay, it is possible that the last day's work may upset all the reasonings of former study.*

If we consider the changeful character of language, we shall find abundant reason for desiring minute information before we build a house of inference upon it. The story of the science of language is full of false inferences, set up one day to be pulled down the next. Some of these failures are the fruits of stupendous egotism in the self-conceited authors of them;† but many more were very sincere guesses at truth, fortified by a deal of misplaced learning. Nor have we a right to reason that here and now the danger of error has been removed. Our knowledge, as we shall presently show, wants as signally as ever the minuteness that will warrant sound inference.

The incompleteness of a linguistic test of historical facts is somewhat greater than that arising from the use of other institutions in the same way. Marriage has been cast into a few simple molds, and has always indicated, with some definiteness, a few other social habits. Government is commonly of such a public and ostentatious character that some of its lines surviving are the first signs of national wreck. Religion tends to more stability, even in the variable factors, than any other

* The theory that language is an institution should be credited to Prof. Whitney. Prof. Max Müller makes faces at it, but gives no sound reason for rejecting it.

† The description by Plato is still applicable to a good deal of theorizing: "I have not a bad notion which come into my head only this moment. I believe that the primeval givers of names were undoubtedly like too many of our modern philosophers, who, in their search after the nature of things, are always getting dizzy from going round and round, and moving anyhow; and this appearance, which arises out of their own internal condition, they suppose to be a reality of nature."—*Cratylus*, i, 650.

outgrowth of the mind and heart of man. But language is subtle in its changefulness, and very wide differences spring from narrow bases. About forty characters, or sounds, run into endless combinations, and the combining law may be so subtle as to require the finest discrimination for its discovery. Take a classification: Let the three forms, *New town*, *Newton*, and *Naples*, stand for a morphological classification of languages. The student's first trouble is that any civilized tongue will furnish him, as English has done, with the types by which he is to distribute them into classes.

But let us imagine ourselves testing historical statements by some other institution. Let us say that we have undertaken to unravel a tangled story of the British Kelts. It occurs to us to settle the matter of the Arthurian legends by an appeal to the governmental habits of the people. We shall be at once reminded that we do not know the details of the governmental institutions except through the legends. The general information derived from other sources is worthless for our purpose; the legends assert certain details concerning which we have no other information. We should require to know so much as to need no help from our test in order to know the test. Equally true would be the statement when applied to language. When we have so mastered our test as to be able to use it, we should no longer need it. The completeness of knowledge required implies a like completeness in our knowledge of the life of the people concerned.

It is time to remind the reader that an institution is not merely something set up—it is something grown. It is a result of vital ongoings and interflows of sap between root and branch—of reactions between men and their institutions. The heart of a people, as well as the brain of a people, takes form in the institution. But who can read it backward and spell out the fine type in which love and loyalty, inveterate hatreds and obdurate evils, write themselves into page and volume? The sublimest ongoings of human life come to record in a complexity that baffles our skill in discrimination, and makes it doubtful whether the keenest intellect with the richest furnishing has ever unraveled the making of even one human institution. Sir John Lubbock's attempt to trace the least complicated one—that one in which the permanent factor is

confessedly largest—the institution of marriage, was made with great learning and no common critical faculty. But who would stake his fortune on the soundness of the results?

We take language as a test of history, and must begin by confessing that a bald grammar and a fractional dictionary, containing a tenth, perhaps, of the whole vocabulary, are our whole lingual equipment. We do not know one word for certain of the popular speech; a few pieces of a literary or political sign-book are pretentiously styled a language, and asked to tell what dead witnesses have left unsaid. The whole business is a splendid delusion. We fancy that, because language is penetrative, subtly pervasive, common carrier for all vital functions in society, concerned, with every thing, and used, like the tub of Diogenes, for every purpose, forsooth we can learn it from a bit of lexicon, and there learn all its associated activity.

The truth is that we must know the whole of the language, and that when we know the whole of it there will be no historical questions; for in mastering the whole of the language we shall have studied every thought, custom, and emotion which it described. The amazing self-conceit that can build hypotheses of grave concernment on linguistic data appears when we recall our ignorance of the *spoken* dialects even of the Greeks and Romans. The test of language applied to the mutations of the Roman Constitution is nearly worthless because the book speech in which those changes come to record is a very imperfect display of the thoughts and conflicts, the interests and passions, which led to change. We need the popular terms in which wrath and prejudice recorded themselves. Imagine the difficulties of our political history, so short and made in such perfect sunlight, if we had not those epitomes of political life, our slang terms "Loco-foco," "Barnburner," "Silver Gray," "Kitchen Cabinet," etc. All that and all its correlatives are hopelessly dead with the dead popular speech of the whole ancient world. When now and then a poet like Aristophanes has stooped to these vulgar forms, he has enriched us not a little in suggestion; but the suggestion is always vague, and stimulative of the imagination rather than guiding to the judgment. The writer once conceived the task of writing the history of the little Republic of Genoa. He had before him the finest

extant collection of social documents in the records of the Bank of St. George. This bank combined the functions of the modern bank with those of a Custom-House, a Probate Court, and a "Safety Deposit." For centuries its books threw a clear and strong light upon the social customs and personal vicissitudes of the whole people. But a very early lesson in that magnificent presence was that lexicons were practically useless. The perfect comparison of this vast collection of records was a preliminary task—the labor of a life-time—for understanding this polyglot and dialectic tongue. And if all that had been done, there remained to lament an irretrievable loss of the figures under many a term—a sharp and terse sense had gone with the life that wrought these terms.

We only feebly comprehend, even when we distinctly think it, how new is our one speech for all the people. Most civilized peoples are dialectic to this day. Lovers at Naples and Milan woo in different tongues; the mother-tongue is different in every valley of Italy; and, in less measure, the same is true all over the old world. Even in England, the dialect vocabulary is as large as the literary. Beyond Rome and Athens we plunge into an impenetrable fog because the popular speech is utterly unknown to us. How vast must be the presumption that attempts to correct the testimony of the Scriptures by the chance-found fragments of contemporaneous speech!

How pale and cold is the image of a past life which we recover by the fullest lights of history!* When all aids have conspired, much of the liveliness of Grote's History comes from transferring the vital consciousness of Englishmen to the shores of the Ægean. We fail to catch the difference of tone, of atmosphere, and fancy that by broadening the kinship of our na-

* Of these nations, [early Semitic,] with the single exception of the Israelites, we have, properly speaking, no history. Their manners and customs, [a little,] their religion, the succession of their sovereigns, are known to us. But we have no continuous series of events; although the knowledge of them is fuller, through the investigations of the last fifty years, than in former times, yet it is still shadowy, fragmentary, mythical. They are like the figures seen in the dream of Sardanapalus, as depicted by the modern poet; here a mighty hunter, or conqueror, like Nimrod, or Sesostris, or Sennacherib, there a fierce and voluptuous queen like Semiramis—yet

"All along
Of various aspects, but of one expression."

—*Dean Stanley's Lectures on the History of the Jewish Church*, Third Series, p. 52.

ture we may think and feel like a Spartan or a Cretan of the ancient world. It is pure conjecture, and the best history becomes entertaining historical romance. The subtle organs of its life have perished, and we are left to shrewd guesses, filled in with our own temper and desire.

No doubt, then, it may be all true that language would disclose all secrets—if we had it. But, for antiquity proper, we have scarcely a shred of that language which enshrined the molding emotions and aspirations of social existence. We can only shrewdly guess what words the people spoke in the cities of Egypt, of Babylon, or even in Jerusalem. Their *ipsissima verba* died with their generations and are hopelessly lost. Look at the vast labor of the early English Text Society over the English speech between the years 1200 and 1600, and who of us that has followed these arduous toils with most satisfaction feels any assurance that we have more than grazed the popular consciousness of medieval England? So little of what Englishmen of those centuries said has been preserved, and so much of our treasure wants the color and ring of the ancient metal, that we distrust our glossaries as a counterfeiting of the coin of the dead.

The Elamites could not have been Semitic, because some memorials from beyond the Tigris belong to the Elamites, and the language disproves the statement in Genesis. So says, in substance, a bright scholar in the British Museum. Probably he had not stopped to think of the wildness of his conjecture. 1. There is no clear proof that the original Elamites either remained in the region or emigrated from it. 2. There is no proof that they ever settled the particular city whose ruins have come to light. 3. There is no reason to believe that all the descendants of Shem continued to speak a Semitic dialect, but the contrary. 4. If an Elamite city were conquered by an Aryan tribe, the official language might become Aryan, and only that survive in records. 5. It is presumptuous to assume that the records were found *in situ*—that is, upon the ground where the history was made to which they refer. These statements are made very broad, to answer for many cases. If we have any reason to doubt the Semitic blood of the Elamites of the prophets, our doubts depend on other evidence than that of language. The language of the region in

question may have changed a dozen times between Chedorlaomer and Cyrus; and there is, probably, not the faintest evidence as to what language the people at any time spoke.* Of the State dialect, at different epochs, fragments may survive, but the more or less permanent people have left no sign.

It ought not to be necessary to record over again one caution, which, happily, we have near reminders of. We every day speak of "The Indians," preserving, against our knowledge, the error of the early discoverers of this land. An accident has given us a false name, but we go on using it because it is a small inconvenience to change. If a name can be so bald a lie in our mouths, what may it not have been in the older and less instructed world? Every ancient people was known to itself by one name, to its neighbors by another. A conquest might fasten the nickname on the people; a misconception of the name, or a translation of it, or both, might give rise to a third or fourth. Popular vanity might trace the national lineage to a false source, just as kings acquired divine descent. Blunders in names alone would confuse many a chapter of ancient history *did we depend on language for our information.*

To these observations must be added a suggestion upon a much-neglected theme. The migrations of the ancient world, especially of the earlier ages of man, are almost a sealed book. Language is absolutely worthless as a key, for several reasons:

The *status* after any given set of movements, say those which followed Babel, has, probably, been altogether changed in the next century, and successive changes have washed out the landmarks of each other. Race lines settled at last into some permanence; but the border lines, except when boldly defined by sea or mountain, remained dim and wavering. In the mutations, race and language ceased alike to be pure-blooded. Semitic blood took up Aryan speech, and *vice versa;* the races mingled more or less, and the entangled lines will never be separated and straightened by study of royal monumental literature.

* The terms *Elam* and *Elamite* in the Prophetic Books set up no claim to ethnological or linguistic accuracy. Persia is still called Persia after greater changes. But there is no difficulty in supposing that the original Semitic stock continued to dwell in the old lands, though it did not govern. Perhaps the most confusing race mixtures belong to this very region.

The facility with which people change their speech is too often overlooked. ,We say English without taking in the vast breadth of the term. We cannot half read Chaucer even with a dictionary. To comprehend him would require the labor of a life-time. The author usually styled Caedmon is even less comprehensible, although his scriptural themes take away nine tenths of the difficulties. An unintelligible English may be heard by taking a half-day's journey from London. The body of the North French people have, probably, spoken Keltic, German, and French within a period which is short compared with the periods of antiquity to which linguistic tests are applied. In Britain several dialects of Keltic, English, Danish, Latin, and French, with variations, making an aggregate of twenty diverse tongues, have been spoken since the time of Julius Cesar. The intercommunicating body of Englishmen spoke Danish, English, and French successively within the compass of a century and a half. The body of the Jewish people probably changed their tongue at least three times in eight centuries. Whenever we deal with long reaches of time, we are compelled to take account of this instability of speech as a cause of apparent race confusions, as a *possible* index of the change that arrests our attention. For the causes of these changes in tongue are almost always violent. As we approach the infant world, the instability of speech increases under the double action of migrations and violence—both of which act in earlier human history with vastly greater force than in our modern and properly historical period. We must know by other tests before language can render us more than hypothetical aid; intimate knowledge it cannot give us.

II. It has been fancied that language asserts for itself a high antiquity. The inquiry necessary to establish this proposition has some difficulties in common with those in other branches of knowledge that face the same question. Whenever we dispassionately consider any problem of time as related to the earth or to human development, we are menaced into diffidence by the want of a time-measure of growth. All that we have are for such small uses that it is like dipping the Atlantic dry with a pint cup to apply them. A measure of time is not a gauge of eternity; and high antiquity is only another name for what is practically eternity. A rate of deposit for mud at

the mouth of a river will be differently calculated by different men. The delta of the Mississippi has been formed in a relatively brief period, or in an eternity of time, accordingly as you credit different scientists.

But throwing out all such cases, and presuming that exact measure is possible in all such cases, how do you apply the unit of measure so obtained to the vaster problem presented by rivers that ceased to flow before man beheld them? In your measure the conditions of the problem, made up by natural selection out of a vast body of possible conditions, are all neatly outlined before your eyes. In the other case you cannot know the actual conditions that played around the event and shaped its progress. And the moment you assert for this unknown movement—of which nothing survives but its result—"a high antiquity," you definitely declare its growth to be beyond the reach of human calculation. But, whatever view be taken of this reasoning, it will remain true that time-measures are not exact enough to render effective service to any theory.

In language this defect is peculiarly striking. We know next to nothing of the conditions of early linguistic growth. What we know exactly on the subject of such growth in general, we know only from our own lingual habits, and those of our contemporaries and immediate predecessors on the earth. This knowledge is not adapted to furnish any time-measure, for the simple reason that we are not making language *ab initio*—we have it and are changing it. We cannot so much as begin an inference as to the rate of progress among men making language. If we add to our exact knowledge of contemporary change the whole body of historical learning in this science, we are still without a time-measure; for our historical knowledge terminates before we reach the original makers of speech.*

It may, perhaps, be affirmed that classification of languages

* Some hold that the power of inventing names still exists. I think the concept under the words is in confusion. When the French people said *plon plon*, they had some imitative notion under it, but it is not agreed what it was. Nonsensical combinations of sounds are not names, and imitative vocalization is not now like original name-giving—it is working a vein long since discovered, not finding gold. The *materials* of nicknames are always old. On the other side of this subject see Farrar, "Origin of Language," p. 70.

enables us to penetrate very far before the historical period. Some have thought so, and there are under classification *theories* that require a "high antiquity." The theories are, however, only hypotheses benevolently treated because they promote work. The genetic classification has called forth some of these theories. But this classification lends but little aid to those who would see far down the ancient abyss. It deals with only a small part of human tongues; it is very incomplete, and uncertainly made out over portions of its best traveled territory, and what it says about time and growth cannot well be translated until the witness has established his own personality. Make out your classification before you marshal its divisions on the plains of eternity.

Other theories are employed hypothetically to explain the perplexing problem presented by a morphological classification which assumes that Chinese is a primary stratification, Turkish a secondary, and English a tertiary. We should be helped to understand a hundred matters that drive us to despair if we only knew the time-gauge of language. How long did men speak with naked roots? How long did they combine without breaking up the separate structure of roots? Why, at the outset, these questions are balked by the fact, assumed in the hypothesis, that some people have been talking in bare roots through all the ages of man. Given as an hypothesis that modern Chinese is the infant prattle of the antique world, how long does it take a language to get into the secondary stage? Given an English language whose ancestors and congeners have been in the tertiary stage from the earliest moment in time when they are known to us, what is the time-measure for the rate of change in human speech?

The amount of time required to change *vak* into *vaks*, to develop an optative, or to form demonstrative roots, is just a shrewd guess—and probably can never be any thing more. Those processes are not now going on, or if they are, *ex-hypothesi* they are proceeding so slowly that we cannot sense the motion. We imagine that we should be greatly helped in tracing these processes of formation if we knew how fast they proceeded; and wherever such an imagination plays there will be time theories. Trying them with the other facts may stimulate observation, as scaffolds help in constructing houses;

but the scaffold will come down if the building is ever finished. Our vision is for time, not for eternity; and to assume an immense antiquity for any thing is to put its growth beyond the domain of exact knowledge. It is the fashion just now to use indefinite time as scaffolding around the temple of the new knowledge; a large number of difficult questions looked to be accessible from that staging. It had to be tried; its philosophy was left for later consideration. Various groups of investigators have tried, with more or less self-satisfaction, the eternity solution. "You cannot affirm that this might not have happened in ten billions of years." No; on that hypothesis you would negative nothing, for all your knowledge only qualifies you the better to anticipate unknown and imponderable conditions in the awful abyss opened under the given theory. But this is not science—this asserting that one or another thing might happen in a billion of years. The other assertion is equally true—you cannot know *that* it would come about as your theory makes it. There are indications that the reaction has begun. It is not a pleasant confession to make, that science is impossible—that we cannot connect our actual knowledge by verifiable general propositions; and it is beginning to be perceived that to send all growth back into the bosom of eternity is to rob us of all means of verifying it, and correctly formulating its laws.

In language enough work remains to be done with the portion of the field that all agree lies in the historical period; and most linguistic students are content to explore these fresher tracts of growth. We may yet find within them some of the treasure we cannot expect to raise from the bottomless gulf of innumerable centuries. If the truth is in that awful well we shall never find it; possibly it may be sparkling in brooks that babble past our own doors. A noticable discontent with the mystery surrounding afar-off growth is one of the most cheerful signs in linguistic writings. We retain a chance of obtaining a full round science of speech so long as this group of scholars reject hypothesis that would vail their science with despair; for when it shall be definitely admitted that every essential principle of growth pushes its roots into an indefinite past, it will be as definitely admitted that linguistic science is impossible. If plurals, optatives, and demonstrative roots are

children of eternity, we shall never know how they were born into human speech.

Every question sought to be solved by a vast antiquity has a humble fellow justly entitled to the same honours. It is said that Aryan and Semitic speech broke away from each other a very long time ago—the unity of human speech cannot be maintained, in the face of the differences in these groups, except on the hypothesis of the very high antiquity of human speech. To this it might be said that unity may not require that Aryan and Semitic speech should be branches of an older speech in such definite mode as Greek and English meet in ancient Aryan. A very early separation—early in development, though it were only five thousand years ago—would probably bequeath no permanent, more common, traits than those which exist. But passing this simple explanation, which is worth more working than it has had, compare the great fact in question with a relatively small one. Our American languages are to be furnished with congeners, and to be traced out on a time-plane. Granting that the congeners are easily found, how long a time did the development of the special characteristics of these languages consume? The question is an inviting one in many aspects; but it is started here only to suggest—if we are so disposed, we may invent eternities at pleasure as explanations of linguistic mysteries.*

There remains in this branch of our subject one important consideration. In language we are dealing with processes in the human mind. All the physical difficulties to be overcome in men are too inconsiderable to be considered. A plural or an optative requires a mental process for its development. Now, how long does it take men to reach this process and go

* Max Müller, "Chips," vol. iv, page 340, says: "Every one of these languages is the growth of thousands *and thousands* of years, [*one thousand* would suffice,] the workmanship of millions and millions of human beings. If they were now preserved they might hereafter *fill the most critical gaps in the history of the human race.* At Rome, at the time of the Scipios, hundreds of people might have written down a grammar and dictionary of the Etruscan language, of Oscan or Umbrian; but there were men then, as there are now, who shrugged their shoulders and said, 'What can be the use of preserving these barbarous, uncouth idioms?'" We make the quotation for a double purpose, to show the value of these American dialects, and to point out the way in which this scholar gets into trouble. The words we have italicised are rhetorical exaggerations; he does not believe what they teach.

through with it? One may guess; but he cannot know that men must have talked ten thousand years first. It is much more probable that it was reached soon than that it remained for ages a far-off event. How long does it take men to invent any thing? A simple theory is that it took them until, in a kind of dumb consciousness, they needed it. Ten thousand years has been assumed for the invention of a bow and arrow. The guesser had to shut off a ready retort by assuming an accelerated rate of speed for ages of invention that found steam and telegraph in a single generation. But the moment one mentions a varying rate of progress, or a principle of increasing velocities, we are at liberty to conjecture anything—especially that the rate of motion may have been swifter up to bows and arrows. In the presence of an imperious need the intellect moves more rapidly than in the languid atmosphere of satisfying abundance.* If it be the first step which costs—and in language this is greatly true—one may infer that the dumb consciousness that works in speech worked out its inventions with great rapidity. It is perfectly possible that all the chief diversities in speech were reached soon as a consequence of separations that occurred early in human time, and the infant recollection lost the common speech habits as it lost the sense of brotherhood. So, on the other hand, the great lines of resemblance were formed by more enduring association, fixing some abiding habits, in fellowship with vast ranges of variation, such as pervade the Turanian family. More permanent associations gave birth to more numerous common habits, having a less numerous company of variations, such as we witness in Aryan languages. Still closer life blossomed into those symmetrical forms which run through the Semitic group.

There is nothing in any of these hypotheses which hints at a longer human speech history than our common chronology authorizes. Some wonderful growths have unfolded into surpassing completeness in brief periods. All the modern Latin

* As we are no longer obliged to create language, we have entirely lost a crowd of processes which tended to its elaboration. But among the early races there was a delicate tact enabling them to seize on those attributes which were capable of supplying them with appellatives. ... "They saw a thousand things at once, and, indeed, their language-creating faculty mainly consisted in a power of seizing upon relations."—*Farrar:* "*Origin of Language,*" 1860, page 68. How long did it require to make a language under such a head of steam?

tongues are examples. Granted that Italian was not made by Dante, or by a preceding generation of poets, a vast development occurred in a relatively simple speech in the space of a single century. It is a barely possible hypothesis that Italian, Provençal, French, and Spanish, were ancient modes of Latin; but if this were granted for truth, it would remain true that they shot into a luxuriant growth with astonishing rapidity. It is cheerfully admitted that Neo-Latin does not help us in matters which these tongues received by inheritance; they do, however, bear witness to a considerable velocity, under a supreme necessity, in the mental machinery which manufactures linguistic inventions.

Intending to treat this problem cautiously and as fully as our space permits, we turn to a question or two involving the time-measure. The one about Aryan and Semitic divergence —a divergence so wide as to have left small traces of unity— is it not as satisfactorily explained by the theory of an early separation as by that of vast ages of growth? If these languages grew apart, they would, more probably, be totally unlike if their infant growth were apart. A hundred years, then, would efface resemblances that thousands of years would not efface after speech-habits had been formed.

The whole range of diversity, and all the questions that arise under that head, are best reserved for further study; but if we must theorize we shall do well to exhaust the theory of varying degrees of association and separation. Intricate questions may be at least helped to settlement by the fact that inhabit ants of neighboring valleys of Italy cannot now understand each other, and by the fellow-fact that their speech is essentially one. In low stages of culture, and under separation, men go on speaking substantially alike, and yet are unable to master the differences in each other's speech. Put the same men under culture, under the pressure of multiplying social activities, and they will diverge more rapidly, or one speech will sink into servile relations to the other, according to the nature of their associations, whether near or remote—that of equals, or of master and servant.

In short, let it be clearly said no body of knowledge is of so little direct service to other bodies of knowledge, and none needs so much help from others as linguistics. If history could

give a clear account of human migrations, early and late; of the state of culture among the makers of dialects that died and made no sign; of the actual speech of every group of men from the first, linguistics could soon work out some of its problems. These are questions upon which it has no certain knowledge. If anthropology had reached definite conclusions about savagery and the growth of various social habits, other linguistic questions would be settled. Changeable words are unsafe guides in these wildernesses of knowledge.

III. Another class of historical inquiries, on which language is supposed to throw a calcium light, deserves to be considered. Words, we are told, reveal mental states in far-off men. Take the discussion concerning θεος and *deus*.* So prepossessed are a class of students with the theory that the word is the sign of the existence of the thing, that to derive these two words from different roots has been thought to assume an atheistic stage in early Greek thought. They lost their *deva*, and for some time were godless; they recovered God, and invented a new name for him. So the logic runs. It is highly probable that the apparent fact under doubt may be no fact at all—the two words may yet be helped to an understanding of their common parentage. But admitting that they are not the same word, why interpose an atheistic period between the use of *deva* and θεος? Both may have existed side by side, and Greek alone of the surviving Aryan dialects may have preserved one of the two. Such a poverty as the atheistic hypothesis implies seems a gratuitous assumption. But the real reason for the hypothesis lies deeper. It is, that theory which undertakes to verify ancient ideas by means of words. Often the antiquity of the word itself is questionable, oftener we know nothing of its ancient meaning, oftenest we have only unsatisfactory evidence that *the people* used the word at all. Certain roots, it may be granted, must have been widely used; other derived

* The general reader will find a long discussion of this subject in Müller's fourth volume of "Chips." Note A, page 227. He concludes, I think, the loss in Greek of the Aryan word for god, and its replacement by another word nearly identical in form, but totally distinct in origin, should be left for the present an open question in "Comparative Philology." The grammatical discussion does not touch the question of a "*loss*;" it is only as to whether θεος and *deus* have the same origin. I cannot see why three fourths of a question should be surrendered without argument.

forms may owe their preservation to a small fraction of a people.

Now there are just two roads by which we may find a word in ancient use. One is its preservation in different stocks. The same word in Greek and German witnesses to its use before the separation of these races. The other road is its use in literature. This last is worth nothing as a proof of popular ideas. By neither road—and this is most important—do we reach the ancient popular sense. Now take this word *deva*. It is supposed to prove theism in the Aryan race.

We must begin with remembering that the only tolerably satisfactory evidence for an Aryan race at all is that furnished by the affinities of various dialects grouped under that term.* Pure blood is the most mythical of myths. We must also distinguish between the fact that theistic conceptions have existed among Hindus, Greeks, Romans, and Germans. We know this on other evidence than that of language. We must also discriminate between the ideas of our time and those of the far-off world we are seeking to describe. The word *deva* alone, after these considerations have been weighed, does not prove very much. The admiration for the brightness of the heavens which breaks out in the word must have been mixed with other emotions before it could speak a religious dialect, and these other emotions, coming in by various channels from Jewish sources, may have merely used the nearest or handiest word for a shrine. The word itself witnesses to a time of darkness—before any thing more than the brightness of the heavens was meant by it—and some other evidence must explain how the greater glory of God came to be expressed by the term.

The root *pu* (in *purus*, *purificare*, *pure*, *purify*) has been cited as an example of the light words give us upon early ideas. *Pœna* is thought to be derived from this root, and hence an inference that before the civil ideas about ransom, the notion of a purgation, to be effected by punishment, existed in the Aryan mind, and was the soil out of which the civil conceptions sprang—that, in other words, our Aryan ancestors were religious before they had the civil institution of punish-

* Max Müller says: "It is but too easily forgotten that if we speak of Aryan and Semitic families, the ground of classification is language and language only." —"*Chips from a German Workshop*," vol. iv, p. 211.

ment. Now, we may believe these things on other and better evidence, of which there is a good deal, but the religion of the root *pu* is too small a foundation for such a house. Remembering for what different concepts we even now use the word *purge*, we may get a good hold of caution in reasoning from the most ancient *pu* to the modern religious sense of *pure*, or the most distant association in moral ideas. For is it not a most provokingly neutral root? We speak to-day of pure Alderney, pure lead, pure wine, and pure malignity; and we could easily show that the word has always required help to express religious ideas.* The early history of punishment is beset with some difficulties, and the help of a word is too readily accepted by the despairing student. We must be much wiser in both branches of knowledge—words and early primitive ideas—before the word *pœna* can be of the smallest service. Etymology is a delusion and a snare.

These examples might be multiplied indefinitely. We have not yet reached this subject in linguistic investigation. In lines where unbroken ranks of writers fill the spaces to be investigated, we might proceed with ease if we were always careful enough to question each rank as we pass up. But outside of the Hebrew people and the Bible no line of writers stretches to the flood. The mutations of words, both in form and contents, cannot be traced except painfully and uncertainly. Before we assume meanings in antiquity we must account more satisfactorily for a vast number of phonal variations. The moment a linguistic doctrine is asked to bear the load of an important historical explanation it breaks down under the weight. As in the case of θεος and *deus*, we fall through into the glottological discussion which never gets finished. In etymology, things that look most alike are really the most unlike; and until the phonal foundations are laid, the superstructure of meanings and derivations must be mostly fabricated of ingenious conjectures. It must not be forgotten how difficult it is to treat linguistic change as a growth. Ascoli,

* The tendency to fly too high is illustrated in the common practice of assigning the meaning of milkmaid to the original of *daughter*. Ascoli pricks a bubble, assigning to the original root the sense "one that gives milk" It is as innocent of sentiment as the word *heifer*. (See *Glottologia*, note to § 36.) The sentiments we associate with the word may have existed; the point is that this term does not show that they existed.

whose work in the field of phonal derivation commands the admiration of all linguistic students, distinctly recognizes the health and sickness of speech, the physiological and the pathological facts. Changes produced by accidents and violences lie under puzzles of a most perplexing character. To explain them we need to know a tract of history whose records are lost. At a critical point in the investigation of the original *Sk* of the Aryan speech—the pre-Sanskrit *Sk*—Ascoli turns to historical data for a guide, and on the threshold of that investigation writes these scholarly words:—

We shall see in this investigation how vain . . . are the expectations of those who hope to see all comparative grammar reduced to a series of synoptical tables containing simple and exclusive equations which will enable us to make an easy progress, through a simple mechanism of alphabetic harmonies, across all times and countries, up to the primitive forms. All the pathological phenomena, from the very nature of them and because they imperfectly coincide with the general phases, must be vigorously excluded from this magic picture,* [of alphabetical harmonies.]

In other words, exact linguistic knowledge fails precisely at the point where history asks aid, and the two sister-knowledges mournfully cry for help to each other at the same point in human progress. The problem being to account for pathological facts, for changes suffered by a sound, and thence to draw a safe theory of etymological changes in derivations, we must take account of the fact that the Aryan tongues are mixed in India with Dravidic dialects. First theory: The Dravidic is the aboriginal tongue; Aryan peoples conquered Northern and Central India. This theory is supported by some facts of literature and history; enough to justify us in tentatively accepting it, not enough to found upon with entire certainty—it will not do to forget that the theory is tentative. Second theory: A class of changes in Aryan, not otherwise explicable, must be due to the contact of the two tongues (Dravidic and Aryan) in the region occupied simultaneously by both. Professor Ascoli admits that, despite this theory, the pillars of Hercules are before him. Every thing like chronology is excluded from the examination unless we are willing to work upon Mosaic data. With that we lack precision, but are assigned serviceable

* The translation is not literal, but faithfully preserves the thought of the Milanese scholar. (See *Corsi di Glottologia*, § 4 L)

limits within which to search. The theory of indefinite time is unfathomable and yields no ore. We are compelled, in the next place, to compare living Dravidic with dead Aryan forms. Had we the dead Dravidic we could attain some accuracy, perhaps; but the *popular* speech that survives cannot be taken for the popular speech of four thousand years ago. It must be remembered, too, that it is not a case of Ariovistus receiving, not giving, hostages; for Aryan must have modified Dravidic in the process of receiving modifications. What, then, if the very facts of coincidence were the result of Aryan influence upon Dravidic? What is it that authorizes us to assume that the Dravidic sounds stood, before the Aryans came, as they now stand thousands of years later? It is an effort to measure the unseen shadow of one moving cloud by that of another projected from the same skies a thousand years later. One part of the theory is perfectly sound, that which assigns pathological facts to contacts with other tongues, and when history has told us what these tongues were we can *know;* till then we must be content, and the scholars are content, to *search*, following every lead of hypothesis and fainting not, however many may yield no precious ores. Indeed, none can be altogether empty; and the small dust swept together will make ingots of precious gold. The evil is that the scholar's hypothesis is the rhetor's truth; Ascoli guesses, and pursues his guess with a temperate enthusiasm. Some careless rhetor calls the guess a discovery, and boils over with excess of heat. It would be well if rhetors and theorists would leave linguistic scholars to complete their tasks in peace; and we may all take it for granted that discovering the foundations of human history is not the office of this branch of research.

It has been carelessly assumed that the interjectional and imitative theory of the origin of language opens a vast depth of time under the growth of speech. It is pure assumption. If we know any thing about imitative processes in sounds, we know that they defy all theories of a rate of progress. The process is now going on, and has always been going on, in a narrow region of speech. Supposing that from that narrow base all the rest has sprung, we cannot guess how long the distance may be between an imitation of a cry and the loss of all notion of imitation in the modified word. If Tennyson still

writes "clouds did *transe* the sky," and the word *trance* takes hold on Latin uses of *transire* to mean death—the old literal and the more modern refined use subsisting side by side—what law of progress from material to intellectual meanings can we hope to discover? If this movement is so subtle, how can we hope to make a time-space between an imitative sound and a derivative of it that has no hint of imitation? But in point of fact, the imitative theory is only an ingenious hypothesis, incapable of demonstrative proof, or of those rational inferences which are often accepted in place of demonstration. It cannot be said that it accounts for all the facts; it might be stretched to account for a hundredth part of them, but other facts reject the explanation. At some early period men began to use devices in their speech. They distinguished different meanings by variations in musical accent, by graduated vowels, by consonantal change. The slender capacities of imitation would cease to be relied upon when the devices of the intellect began to be used, and all existing non-imitative language probably sprung from these devices. It is only conjecture that imitation ever sufficed one generation of our ancestors; it is as reasonable to believe that imitation is now just what it always has been—that is, one only of the modes in which men convey their impressions. We must go outside of language for a basis of the imitative theory. A theorist draws out upon a time-chart a set of ages of stone, iron, bronze—a scheme of human arts—and infers that the speech of his first men was a meager set of cries because he has arbitrarily endowed them with an imperfect and obstructed intellectual activity. His "ages" are fanciful creations, and his notions about the intellectual caliber of early men are simply gratuitous. If one chooses to believe him, there is no law against such a mighty exercise of faith; but none of the facts lend the least support to the theory. At last it is a question of the "smartness" of Adam and his children. Assuming that they had no experience, how bright, quick, inventive, were they? The primeval man of an immeasurable antiquity is a dreadfully dull and slow fellow, and his antiquity rests upon that assumption about his intellect. Nothing that we know authorizes us to teach that generation after generation passed away before any of the devices of the brain entered into the forma-

tion of words. Just so soon as one device—a vowel variation, for example, (as *ba, bo, bu*)—had been, however accidentally, invented, it would naturally expand in use. Other devices, when hit upon, would also grow. The vowel device *seems* about as easily formed as the imitative one. Indeed, imitation *would produce vowel change*, and even a dull brain would probably notice it very soon. It should be noticed that a "smart" man at last turns up in these everlasting-growth theories. A Cadmus must be had. Will any one suggest a reason, based on lingual facts, for waiting ten thousand or fifty thousand years for him? There is absolutely nothing in language to suggest an indefinite, but vastly long, age of men too obtuse of ear to notice the variation of natural sounds, and too slow of invention to use vowel variation. We should reject the imitative theory, except as a possible first lesson in sounds; it is not the base under existing human speech—this rises upon a simple set of devices fabricated out of the simplest capacities of the voice.

Much higher up, language is a question of intellectual culture. The speech of Milton never exists among savages—they have no use for it. The law may be reasonably extended to the earliest times—in fact, theorists unconsciously apply this law to primeval life. A miserable, degraded, dull-eyed, and thick-headed autochthon needs only to bawl and screech. But be good enough to admit that even such an autochthon would notice the difference between bawling and screeching, and that when he had, however unconsciously, noted the difference, he would screech for one purpose and bawl for another. His first lesson in imitation would in this process be transformed into the use of a vocal device—the brain of this imaginary autochthon would have taken charge of the speech-making process. Who shall prove that early men were such autochthons? Who shall prove that they could not tell the difference between bawling and screeching? Who shall make us certain that their growth, keeping pace with their needs, did not produce *all* the intellectual devices which lie at the base of simple words? *

* The student may profitably consult "Lessons from Nature," by St. George Mivart, chapter iv, and Mr. Tylor's "Primitive Culture." I am not aware, however, that any writer has made before me the point that imitative language must have been in man a schoolmaster in vocal devices.

# ART. II.—RECENT ORIGIN OF MAN.

[SECOND ARTICLE.]

*The Recent Origin of Man, as Illustrated by Geology and the Modern Science of Prehistoric Archæology.* By JAMES C. SOUTHALL. Philadelphia: J. B. Lippincott & Co. London: Trübner & Co. 1875.

## THE MAMMOTH.

CHAPTER XX is devoted to a great number of interesting facts about the mammoth, showing its comparatively recent date. Mr. Prestwick, the celebrated English authority, though still desirous to keep up a high antiquity for man, says: "I do not, for my part, see any geological reasons why the extinct mammalia should not have lived down to comparatively recent times, possibly not farther back than eight or ten thousand years." And in another place he remarks, that "the evidence seemed to me as much to necessitate the bringing forward of the great extinct animals toward our time, as the carrying back of man in geological time."

Mr. Southall has gathered in chapter xx a large collection of facts about the relations of extinct animals in general, and the mammoth in particular, to historic times. He copies from the Smithsonian works the sketch of the big Elephant Mound of Grant County, Wis., which seems to show that the mound builders had a knowledge in some way either of the elephant, the mastodon, or the tapir. Some of the discoveries detailed, though appearing in reputable scientific publications, are distrusted or discredited by scientific men. The connection of human and mastodon relics near Charleston, S. C., is one case. The deposits here are so thin and superficial that it is very difficult to be sure that there is no mixture of different ages, the more so, as the bones of the ordinary ox and the domestic hog are found also, neither of which were ever indigenous to this continent, and must, therefore, be specimens introduced by the modern settlers.

Mr. Southall, in common with many others, quotes the alleged discovery of human relics in Missouri, by Dr. Kock, when he exhumed the great mastodon now in the British Museum, and whose account of finding the bones, and the flint arrowhead *under one of them*, is current among European scientists as good authority. It has long been known to western

scientific men that Dr. Kock, through a good collector of specimens, was grossly ignorant of strict science, and, what is worse, utterly reckless of truth in his statements. The ground where he found the skeleton is totally different from what he stated; the thirteen or fourteen feet of different strata described, as overlying the skeleton, have no existence whatever, it being found close to the surface in swamp muck. The men who assisted him in exhuming it say the pit was not drained nor bailed out; but they worked up to their waists in water, groping at the bottom for the bones in such a way as to give no chance to know whether an arrowhead belonged to the time of the bones, or fell in while working.

More recently the "American Journal of Science" has analized Koch's pamphlets, and exposed their recklessness and ignorance. Professor Hoy, of Wisconsin, years ago exposed the falsity of the statements before the Chicago Academy of Science. Mr. Southall seems inclined to think that the mammoth survived later than the Pluvial Period, which may be true in some regions. One of the most singular discoveries bearing on this point is detailed in chapter xxxiv, taken from M. Desor's account of Siberian antiquities in the *Matèriaux pour l'Histoire de l'Homme*, 1873. The relics

Consist of a number of articles in bronze obtained by a Russian engineer, M. Lapatine, from the Tartars in the neighborhood of Krasuojarsk, on the southern frontier of Siberia. The objects mentioned are two poniards, two hatchets, six knives, a pair of scissors, a file, a bridle bit, and five buckles. Most of these articles are coated with a beautiful brown patina; others are covered with a green patina, similar to that observed on the antiquities found in the ancient European tombs. Their antiquity, we are told, is beyond question. They are far superior to, and entirely different from, the utensils and weapons in use among the Tartars; they have nothing in common with the classic forms, nor with those of the prehistoric epochs of Europe; nor are they Chinese nor Hindu. That they are the product of an indigenous civilization seems to be confirmed by the tombs, which are found in great numbers on the banks of the Yenisei, and which Pallas refers to an ancient people no longer in existence, but whose culture is attested by a funeral *mobilier* quite complete, which is composed in part of the same objects as those under consideration.

After stating that many of these bronzes represent very elegantly various animals, as the fox, eagle, etc., Mr. Southall

gives good engravings of them, and calls attention to one which appears to represent the Siberian mammoth. Mr. Southall is confident of the representation; but M. Desor, apparently staggered by the idea of a mammoth in the Bronze Period, while he acknowledges the resemblance, is disposed to think it accidental, and that the image represents only a freak of the artist's fancy. It certainly looks far more like a real mammoth than the tangled set of scratches found on a fragment of tusk in a European cave, and generally accepted as a contemporary picture of the animal. M. Desor thinks that the civilization shown by these bronzes was too elevated to exist in the present Siberian climate, and brings geological facts to prove that the great lowland regions must have been submerged, in which case "the northern slope of the Altai would enjoy a much more temperate climate." M. Desor puts in the invariable French proviso that this submergence must be "slow," but without adducing any proof of the slowness. Mr. Southall brings the following facts to show the submergence and its rapidity.

M. Dupont, of Belgium, adverting to the strange association in quaternary Europe of species characteristic both of cold and warmer climates, for instance, the reindeer and the hippopotamus, says that the hippopotamus proves the absence of cold winters, and the northern species show equally the absence of hot summers; in other words, the climate was much more equable than now; "but," continues M. Dupont, "it is the north-east wind which brings the cold in winter and the heat in summer, a double effect of a great plain in that direction. It is necessary, then, to seek the explanation of the climate of the quaternary epoch in the absence of those lands, and *the presence of a great sea to the north-east of Europe.*"

Ermann, in his "Travels in Siberia," says:

The ground in Yakutsk, the internal condition of which was found in sinking M. Shergin's well, consists, to the depth of at least one hundred feet, of strata of loam, fine sand, and magnetic sand. They have been deposited from waters which at one time, *and it may be presumed suddenly*, overflowed the whole country as far as the Polar Sea. In these deepest strata are found twigs, rocks, and leaves of trees of the birch and willow kinds. Everywhere throughout these immense alluvial deposits are now lying the bones of antediluvian quadrupeds along with vegetable

remains. In the lower valley of the Lena . . . and at both sides of the mouth of this river, are found the teeth and bones of mammoths, rhinoceroses, and other quadrupeds, and even whole carcases . . . As we go nearer to the coast the deposits of wood below the earth, and also the deposit of bones which accompany the wood, increase in extent and frequency. Here, beneath the soil of Yakutsk, the trunks of birch-trees lie scattered only singly; but, on the other hand, they form such great and well-stored strata under the tundras, between the Lena and the Indigirka, that the Yukogirs never think of using any other fuel than fossil wood. . . . In the same proportion the search for ivory grows continually more certain and productive from the banks of the lakes in the interior to the hills along the coast of the Icy Sea. Both these kindred phenomena attain the greatest extent and importance at the farthest chain of islands above mentioned, which are separated from the coast by a strait about one hundred and fifty miles wide, of very moderate depth. Thus in New Siberia lie hills two hundred and fifty or three hundred feet high, formed of drift wood. . . . Other hills on the same island, and on Kotélnoi, are heaped up to an equal height with skeletons of pachyderms, bisons, etc., which are cemented together by frozen sand, as well as by strata of ice. It is only in the lower strata of the New Siberian wood-hills that the trunks have that position which they would assume in swimming or sinking undisturbed. On the summit of the hills they lie flung upon one another in the wildest disorder, forced upright in spite of gravitation, and with their tops broken off, or crushed, as if they had been thrown with great violence from the south on a bank and then heaped up. Now a smooth sea, covering the tops of these hills on the islands, would, even with the present form of the interjacent ground, extend to Yakutsk, which is but two hundred and seventy feet above the sea. But before the latest deposits of mud and sand had settled down, and had raised the ground more than one hundred feet, the surface of such a sea as we have supposed would have reached much farther up, even to the cliffs in the valley of the Lena. So it is clear that at the time when the elephants and trunks of trees were heaped up together, one flood extended from the center of the continent to the farthest barrier existing in the sea as it now is.

## Recent Changes in Physical Geography.

Lyell fought a successful battle against the "catastrophists," and showed that many of these changes were better accounted for by more moderate forces, acting through long periods of time. From the time of this victory Sir Charles was disposed to carry his idea to excess, and to require enormous periods of time to be accepted in almost all circumstances as a substitute for force. When the claims for a great human antiquity arose, these long periods were found to be magnificent supports to the theories of such antiquity, and accordingly their authors have adopted a set of phrases, which have become almost a scientific cant, to express their opinion. At every recital of a denudation, or submergence, or silting up, or an upheaval, they almost invariably prefix the adjective "slow," or the phrase "inconceivably slow," often without giving a particle of proof of the supposed slowness; and throw in a liberal supply of exclamations, such as "What an enormous antiquity!" in discussions where no great lapse of time has been shown. This unscientific looseness and ready assumption is becoming tiresome, and it is none the less reprehensible because indulged in by some very eminent men. We want more facts and fewer conjectures. As Mr. Southall says:—

> It is assumed that it is unphilosophical to admit any more violent energies than those which existing operations present. It is assumed that the glacial epoch is separated from our days by a vast cycle of time; it is assumed that the physical geography of the earth has not been substantially modified for tens, or hundreds, or thousands of years; it is assumed that it requires long ages to effect the extinction of a fauna; it is assumed that elevations and subsidences of land have occurred at the rate of two and a half feet in a century; it is assumed that the rivers of to-day are the same streams with the same volume of water which existed at the close of the glacial period; it is assumed that it requires the sequence of innumerable centuries to effect a transition from a harsh to a temperate climate; it is assumed that because no great river-horses, or huge proboscisticus, or powerful carnivores, roam in our age through civilized Europe, a long and protracted period must have intervened since the hippopotamus wallowed in the marshes of the Thames, and the cave lion roared on the Mendip Hills.

There is, perhaps, some excuse for the proneness to these and other assumptions among European minds. When a man, inured from birth to the elaborate and refined civilization of

England and France, digs up a flint arrowhead or a rotten canoe, he gets a glimpse of a mode of life so different from any thing in the range of his experience, that he feels as though no figures could exaggerate the greatness of its antiquity. The American is in different circumstances. We have been shot at with flint arrowheads, and have paddled hundreds of miles through the forests in aboriginal canoes. These things are familiar to us, and we can only smile at the assumption that they necessarily belong to the dim ages which vanished a million years ago. In respect to physical geography, a large portion of the changes known to history have been rapid. Mr. Southall says:—

> According to Chinese and Japanese accounts, several volcanoes have risen from the bed of the sea on the coasts of Japan and Corea during the historical period. In the year 1007 a roar of thunder announced the appearance of the volcano of Toinmoura on the south of Corea, and after seven days a mountain four leagues in circumference appeared, towering up to the height of one thousand feet. The Japanese affirm that the celebrated Fusi Yama, the highest mountain in Japan, was upheaved in a single night from the sea twenty-one centuries and a half ago. In the Santorin group of the Ægean Sea quite a number of new islands have been upheaved in the historic period, one of them as lately as 1867.

In 1819 a great earthquake occurred in Hindostan. The village and British part of Sindree were permanently submerged, together with two thousand square miles of territory. At last accounts only some of the highest points of the masonry projected above the waves. Another piece of territory fifty miles long was by the same earthquake elevated some ten feet. The natives at the place, when they observed the elevation, gave it the name of *Ullah Bund*, the Mound of God. Still more recently another, a large area in that region, appears to have sunk, and another to have been elevated, converting Sindree Lake into a salt marsh. (Lyell.) In the year 1812 a tremendous series of earthquakes, continuing for weeks or months, occurred in the region around New Madrid on the Mississippi. A change of level was effected so suddenly that at one place the river for a little while reversed its course, and ran up stream. Lakes twenty miles long were formed in an hour, and a region seventy-five miles long and thirty miles

wide is now known as the Sunk Country. In the years 1826 and 1827 a succession of earthquakes so changed the level of the land along a coast in New Zealand that the sealers could no longer recognize the locality; and a hull of a vessel, supposed to be the "Active," lost some thirty years previously, was found two hundred yards inland, with a tree growing through its bottom. (Lyell.) At another earthquake in the same group, in 1855, a tract of land equal to four thousand square miles is believed to have been raised from one to nine feet.

In 1772 the volcano Papandayang, in the island of Java, had a great eruption, by which its summit sunk, or lost in some way four thousand feet of its height.

The famous earthquake in Lisbon is well known, by which prodigious physical effects were suddenly produced. Sixty thousand persons were destroyed in six minutes, the quay of the city sunk into an almost fathomless abyss, and the shock was felt from North America to Sweden. In Peru, in 1746, a tremendous earthquake destroyed Lima, and sunk a part of the coast of Callas, so as to convert it into a bay. On the Scandinavian coasts raised beaches occur whose history shows that *if the elevation was uniform* it occurred at the rate of two and a half feet in a century.

Sir Charles Lyell assumes that is to be reckoned as uniform; and some distinguished geologists have even taken that as a general measure of continental elevation, by which they might calculate the rates of submergence and emergence of other regions. Now at the time this estimate was made there was no evidence to show whether the rise had been uniform or not; the "uniformitarian" hypothesis was a sheer assumption, the only thing known being that certain points long ago known to be lower are now found higher. More recently a Norwegian geologist, from careful examination of the coast, declares that the elevation took place by comparatively rapid successive movements separated by intervals of rest or of slower action. It is well known, also, that the movement was very much greater at some points than others. Ermann mentions ("Travels in Siberia") that a lake near the Ural sunk two hundred and ninety-one feet between 1795 and 1812. The raised beach on the Frith of Forth, in Scotland, has risen about twenty-six feet since the time of the Romans. If this were

uniform, the motion would be about nineteen inches in a century; but observations since 1810 show elevations which, if uniform, are at the rate of four feet and a half in a century. The Hydrographic Office at Washington publishes a notice that the Gulf Stream islands, discovered in the Arctic seas, near Nova Zembla, in 1872, are on the spot where the Dutch navigators found a sand bank under one hundred and eight feet of water three hundred years ago.

Mr. Southall in this chapter details a great number of other physical changes occurring in the surface of the earth during historical times, but it is not necessary to recapitulate them. Lyell and his followers, in their contest against the "catastrophists," naturally reacted to an opposite extreme, and tried to exclude rapidly-acting forces almost entirely from geology. A candid examination of the facts adduced by Mr. Southall shows that this extreme is as unscientific as the one it superseded. The great problems of geology will never be successfully solved by such easy patent methods. Some changes have been produced by moderate causes acting through long periods of time, but it is now clear that others have resulted from forces acting with unusual energy in much shorter periods. The difficult task is, therefore, imposed on scientific men of distinguishing one from the other, and combining time and force in such a way as to give a true history. We must work patiently through these perplexing investigations, and in the mean time be more careful not to announce crude, ill-digested conclusions.

### Relations of Stone, Bronze, and Iron.

Chapter xxiii is devoted to the above topic. Mr. Southall admits that particular tribes have used stone before bronze, and bronze before iron; but he denies that any general division of *past time* into three ages of stone, bronze, and iron can correctly be made. Some tribes are in the Stone Age now, and many others are using stone and iron at the same time. Even in Western Europe, where this distinction is chiefly applied, the Bronze Age is often absent, and, when present, generally the bronze and stone implements were used together, while it is also clear that long after iron was introduced stone implements were still common. In a general way it is true that

stone is earlier than bronze, and bronze than iron; but they are very much mixed, and sometimes inverted, as in the ruins of Troy, where Schliemann found a Stone Age later than bronze and iron both. A similar mixture was found in Mexico and Peru, whose inhabitants used both bronze and stone habitually, and a bronze cell was found in one of the oldest Egyptian pyramids; while flint implements were found in European dlolmens and *tumuli*, dating as late as the fourth and fifth centuries. The Chinese annals show that stone weapons were used in that country at least as late as between A. D. 964 and 1279. Stone axes, (chi-fou,) stone knives, (chi-t'ao,) a stone sword, (chi-kien,) and a stone agricultural implement, (chi-jin,) are also mentioned.

In the ancient monarchies of the valley of the Euphrates the metals were well known. Rawlinson says ("Five Great Monarchies," vol. i, pp. 119, 120) that in the very first age of Babylonia a civilized people used stone and metallic implements together. "In the Chaldean plain the tombs and ruins have yielded knives, hatchets, arrowheads, and other implements both of flint and bronze . . . chains, nails, fish-hooks, etc., of the same metal . . . leaden pipes, and jars, . . . armlets, bracelets, and finger-rings of iron." * Under the great stone bulls of Nineveh, which had never before been disturbed, Mr. Place found knives of black flint, along with "bracelets and necklaces of carnelian, emerald, amethyst, and other hard stones polished and fashioned in the shape of beads, and the heads of animals." †

The Ethiopians of the Upper Nile in the time of Xerxes had attained a high civilization, yet their contingent to Xerxes's army used stone arrow-points and horn javelin-heads, a striking case of flint implements being used while bronze and iron were well known: the Stone, Bronze, and Iron Ages all together:—

In the magnificent tomb discovered near the ancient Panticapæum, in the Tauric Chersonese, the flint implements again appear. The tomb found under a burial mound (*tumulus*) one hundred and sixty-five feet in diameter belonged to one of the early kings. It contained a shield of gold, a gilded quiver, a

* Smith's "Ancient History of the East," p. 375.

† *Congrès d'Anthropologie et d'Archäol.*, 1867, p. 118.

sword with a curiously embossed hilt, metal knives with carved ivory handles, statuettes, bronze cauldrons, and a hundred and twenty pounds' weight of gold jewelry.

Rosallini, the companion of Champollion and other explorers, stated long ago that knives and other articles of flint have repeatedly been found in the tombs by the side of the Egyptian mummies. At the meeting of the *Institut Egyptian*, May 19, 1870, M. Mariette Bey expressed himself as follows:—

> The fact that there are found (in Egypt) flints worked by the hand of man cannot be contested. . . . The flints in question do not go back to the age of stone. They belong to the historic age of Egypt. . . . In all historic antiquity, even to the time of the Ptolemies, flints were worked on this plateau. . . . With the flints they made knife-blades, which they fixed in handles of wood. One finds them even among the Greeks. These knives are sometimes toothed in the form of a saw. In the third place they made lance-heads.

In Abyssinia the Bogos still use both flint and iron for implements. M. Leemans says that an ancient Buddhist temple in Java, which was erected about A. D. 700, has its walls covered with bass-reliefs. These beautiful sculptures show perforated flint implements with wooden handles, and pile dwellings. Herodotus says that the Scythians east of the Caspian, at the time they defeated Cyrus, used gold and brass freely about their weapons and armor; but "they use neither iron nor silver, which, indeed, their country does not produce." According to this the eastern Scythians were in the Bronze Age, when Cyrus was in the Iron Epoch.

These are specimens of the facts adduced. Mr. Southall has given numerous others, and they show conclusively the extensive use of stone with both bronze and iron, not only down to the Middle Ages, but even to our day.

Possibly some future archæologist will puzzle himself over the millions of gun-flints used and lost by all armies fifty years ago. There has been an inexcusable flippancy and carelessness in assuming too sharp a distinction between the Stone and Metal Ages, and in assigning a locality, often imperfectly explored, to one or the other age, according to whether the excavators happened or not to light on any remaining pieces of

metal. The use of metals probably goes in some regions, back of the great deluge of the *loess* and *Terre a Brique*, into the Palæolithic Period, and has continued ever since. It is inconceivable how nations of prodigious antiquity came to be so firmly attached to the use of stone.

Mr. Southall has done an important service in this chapter in showing that extensive work in hewn stone implies the possession of metallic tools, and that tribes using stone only never execute them. It is possible that he carries the application of the principle too far, however, as it is clear to any one acquainted with the soft coral rocks, and porous, frothy lavas existing in many Pacific islands, where stone works exist, that there would be no insuperable difficulty in splitting and hammer-dressing these friable blocks with wooden wedges and stone hammers. The statement that the coral blocks in Tahiti were "polished" must be inaccurate, as coral rocks are all porous, and do not admit of polish. It is said, however, that an ancient extensive work of great blocks of hewn stone exist near Hilo, on Hawaii, and that the material was a "*dark, vitreous basalt*, faced and polished on every side."

There seems to be reason to doubt these assertions. Basalt is not "vitreous." Professor H. M. Lyman, of Chicago, is a native of Hawaii, and visited the ruins. He says he thinks the blocks are not basaltic, but lavas of other kinds, worked without iron tools, which he thinks quite practicable. Dr. S. L. Andrews, of Romeo, Mich., and for many years a missionary on Hawaii, says that the chiefs of the islands positively had large blocks of lava worked out by the natives with stone tools and an oppressive exaction of labor. The lavas are frequently fissured in such a way as to admit of blocks being got out without iron, and their vesicular friable character allows of hammer-dressing into almost any form.

## Ruins of Troy.

Our author calls attention to the fact that Dr. Schliemann's discoveries in ancient Troy show a history completely subversive of the theory that a stone age must be considered always older than one of metal. Down at the lowest stratum was a city believed to be older than the Troy of Homer. Here

were evidences of wealth and civilization, with a mixture of bronze and stone implements. Above this was the Homeric city of classical fame. Here were all the evidences of still greater wealth and power, with abundance of gold, bronze, copper, elegant pottery, etc., together with many stone weapons. It will be remembered also in this connection that the Homeric poems speak of iron. Above this there was a stratum where the relics are ruder and poorer, and the inhabitants, though more modern than the Trojans, left no metal at all, the implements being purely of stone and other non-metallic substances. The next stratum shows stone implements also, and metal again appears. Finally, above all are the modern deposits, where relics of all sorts occur. We see therefore, then, at Troy a stone age succeeded to a luxurious age of gold and bronze.

In chapters xxi and xxii the author discusses the absence of Palæolithic remains from Egypt, as well as from the north of England, Scotland, Ireland, Denmark, Norway, and Sweden.

There appears to have been no Palæolithic Period among the inhabitants of Egypt. M. Delanoüe, however, thinks he found evidence of such a period in a local river terrace on a hillock at Fatira, thirty meters above the recent floods of the Nile. The fact that there was a beautiful instrument of polished flint among the relics would seem, however, by ordinary rules, to place them in the Neolithic stage of life. The height above the modern waters has led M. Delanoüe to think that an enormous period must have elapsed to cut down the river valley since that day so as to lower the flood level thirty meters. The facts are these: In ancient historic times the rock barrier, which in some places stretched across the valley, obstructed the flow at inundation times sufficiently to make temporary lakes. Pharaoh Amenemes III., and other kings of the twelfth dynasty, left records of the flood levels on the rocks, showing a lowering of twenty-seven feet since their time. It must be remembered that when the barrier was higher, and the rush of water swifter down the slope, the cutting would be more rapid, for the erosive action of rivers, according to engineers, is in proportion to the velocity. At this rate of erosion, the time of the higher level water could never reach back a tenth part of the time supposed necessary by anthropologists to touch the Palæo-

lithic Age. It is well known that streams which, like the Nile, carry a large amount of fine, gritty sediment, rasp away projecting rocks in their course much more rapidly than clear-water streams. Any traveler in the Alps may verify this by comparing the great depth of rock cutting effected by the muddy streams issuing from glaciers, with the shallow depressions made by brooks collected from spring water. Another point is to be considered. Most oriental travelers are of the opinion that the rainfall there, even as late as two or three thousand years ago, was much greater than now. If this was true of the Nile, the fact would account both for the water being higher than now with a given amount of obstruction, and would cause a more rapid rasping down of the barrier itself: for, according to civil engineers, the rapidity of erosion of a river bottom is directly as the depth of the water.

Mr. Southall is, therefore, clearly of the opinion that there was no proper Palæolithic Period among the Egyptians, though they made stone implements, and often rude ones, even down to the Ptolemaic Age. The reason of this absence of a proper Palæolithic stage, Mr. Southall finds in the probability that the very first immigrants into the valley of the lower Nile were civilized men.

### The Peat Mosses.

The peat of the Somme was discussed in the chapter on the ethnology of that valley. The other parts of Europe are also very interesting, and have furnished an important series of facts and relics. Among the best studied are the peat beds of Denmark. These occupy hollows in the surface of the Bowlder Drift, and no Palæolithic remains are found in them. They are considered by archæologists to reach nearly or quite back to the beginning of the Neolithic Age. Mr. Hudson Tuttle thinks this peat is twenty-two thousand years of age; Sir Charles Lyell thinks that it may be sixteen thousand years; Steenstrup puts it at a *minimum* of four thousand; and Professor Worsade at not less than three thousand. As a matter of fact these calculations were based on no accurate *data*, and show their utter looseness by their contradictory results. The estimates of great antiquity rest on these facts. The lower parts of the peat beds contain trunks of Scotch fir, (*Pinus sylvestris*,) which has fallen in from the margin. This tree no longer grows in

Denmark. With the firs are found polished stone implements. Above the firs the peat contains oak logs, and with them very elegant and elaborate bronze articles occur, such as could hardly precede the Christian era. In the most modern peat beech logs and iron relics occur, and the beech is said to be superseding the oak in the country. The argument is that two changes in the prevailing timber imply great, and very slow, changes of climate. To Americans who have seen the pine swept out of regions equal to half a dozen Denmarks in half a life-time, the argument seems puerile; and even if the climate, and not the demands of the lumber trade, was the cause, we do not know that such a change requires any enormous antiquity. The data are too vague. Danish bronzes, similar to those of the peat bogs, are found in Ireland belonging to the period of the Danish invasion, A. D. 827; and there seems nothing tangible in these bogs to show an antiquity of more than three thousand years.

Marlot says the fir has not grown in Denmark in the Historic Period. This does not seem well proved, but amounts to nothing because the Historic Period in that peninsula does not reach back beyond the tenth century of our era. Cesar said this fir did not grow in England in his day, yet he was mistaken. Logs of it ninety feet long have been found in the peat with Roman remains, cut by the Roman general Ostorius in Vespasian's, reign. These relics were in Yorkshire. The Scotch fir, then, grew in England after Cesar's day, but is now only found north of the Scottish border. If this change occurred in England in less than eighteen hundred years, why should the same thing require fifteen or twenty thousand years in Den mark?

It is not easy to see why, in defiance of well-known facts, many archæologists so exaggerate the slowness of peat growth. Here are a few of the facts collected by Mr. Southall from various sources:—

There is on the Earl of Arran's estate, in Scotland, a primeval bog and forest, which makes it apparent that the pine, oak, and beech were not successive, but contemporaneous *at different levels*; the bog growing as well as the trees, (thus overtaking the upper species last.) Holes cut in the peat of this estate filled up at the rate of three inches a year.

Professor Worsaae says that woolen cloth was found with the aboriginal relics of the Danish peat. This shows commerce abroad, or the raising of sheep at home, at a time not probably enormously remote.

Where the Roman general Ostorius cut the forest of Scotch firs in Yorkshire, the Hatfield Moss has since grown over an area of ninety thousand acres. At the bottom of the peat, many feet down, Roman axes and knives, with the stumps of Scotch fir, oak, etc., etc., were found. Many of the trunks were hewn, bored, chopped, and split; and rails, wedges, bars, pieces of chain, horses' skulls, axes, and coins of the Roman emperors, were found.

In Kincardine Moss, Scotland, Roman coins, etc., were found, and also a Roman military road-bed of timber, over which eight feet of peat had accumulated. At Gröningen a coin of the Emperor Gordian, A. D. 237, was found under thirty feet of peat. In the Jura Mountains old iron furnaces are found, with Roman and Gallic coins of two thousand years or less of age. Over one of these furnaces twenty feet of peat had accumulated. In Derbyshire a grazier perished on a bog in a snow-storm. Twenty-eight years after his body was found three feet deep in the peat. In the "Natural History of Stafford," it is stated that coins of Edward IV. have been found eighteen feet down in the peat. Sir Charles Lyell states that at Lagore, in Ireland, relics of stone, bronze, and iron are found under fifteen feet of peat.

In the seventeenth century the Earl of Cromarty described to the Royal Society the origination of a new peat bog, which in less than fifty years covered up the trunks of trees fallen on it, and was thick enough to be cut for fuel.

From all these and many other facts, it is evident that the rate of peat growth is not slow enough to be a proof of any enormous period of human antiquity.

### The Mud of the Mississippi.

The Mississippi River rolls to the Gulf of Mexico a mass of mud and sand of prodigious volume. General Humphrey, of the United States Army Engineers, while making the survey of the river, had elaborate observations kept up for a year at various points to determine the amount of this sediment. He

makes it equal to a stratum one foot in depth over an area of about two hundred and seventy square miles every year. The river annually cuts away great areas of its banks, and deposits immense tracts of mud and sand in other places.

Such rapid changes produce many interesting phenomena, and have led to various efforts to determine the antiquity of the deposits. In digging for the gas-works in New Orleans, the skeleton of a "Red Indian" was found, according to Dr. Dowler, at the depth of sixteen feet, and beneath four successive layers of cypress forest. Dr. Dowler endeavored to get an estimate of the general rate of mud accretion on the delta where New Orleans stands, and then assuming it to be both correct and uniform, estimated that it would require fifty-seven thousand years to deposit the sixteen feet of material above the skeleton. Lyell partly approves the calculation. Now General Humphrey, in his elaborate survey, came to the conclusion that the whole ground of New Orleans and the surrounding country, down to the depth of about forty feet, was only four thousand four hundred years old.

Mr. Fontaine, Mr. Hurlbut, and others, state that owing to the enormous rapidity with which the river changes its course, articles lost in the life-time of men now living are, in many places, buried one hundred feet deep. Dr. Andrews saw cottonwood saplings on the banks, with only seven rings of annual growth, over whose original roots the inundations had deposited three feet of clay. There are streets in New Orleans now where the water flowed a hundred feet deep sixty years ago. Mr. Fontaine gives an amusing statement that information reached the New Orleans Academy of Sciences that a piece of wood has been found at Port Jackson deeper down than Dr. Dowler's "Red Indian," and at a considerable distance from the river, and, moreover, showing workmanship by a high order of tools. Some members of the academy investigated the relic and found it to be the gunwale of a Kentucky flat-boat. Mr. F. remarks as follows on the action of the Mississippi River:—

By undermining and engulfing its banks with every thing upon them, logs tangled in vines and bedded in mud, cypress stumps, Indian graves, and modern works of art, are suddenly swallowed up and buried at all depths by its waters, from ten to one hundred

and eighty-seven feet. The deep channel then works its way from them, and leaves them beneath a deep soil of inconceivable fertility, which quickly produces above them a dense forest.

### The Mud of the Nile.

The Nile much resembles the Mississippi, both in its magnitude, in its great annual overflows, in its prodigious quantities of sediment, and in its disposition to erode its banks and precipitate into its abysses ancient and modern articles alike. Mr. Horner, indorsed to some extent by Sir John Lubbock, has fallen into Dr. Dowler's New Orleans blunder. That is to say, he assumes that when any article is found below the surface, it is purely because the general level of the valley has risen by that amount, by the gradual accretions of the sediment of the overflows. The calculation was as follows: Nine feet four inches of sediment have accumulated around the obelisk at Heliopolis and the statue of Rameses at Memphis. Now the obelisk "is believed" to be about four thousand one hundred and fifty years of age, and the statue of Rameses is thought to date from his reign, about three thousand two hundred years ago. Dividing the measure of the accretion by the number of years, Mr. Horner concludes that the rate of accretion has been about three and a half inches in a century. He also found a piece of pottery thirty-nine feet below the surface, and applying the three and a half inch century-measure to that depth, he concluded that the pottery "had been buried thirteen thousand years."

Mr. Horner seems to make no account of other monuments, as the temple of Denderch, for example, where a much greater accretion has occurred in half the time, but falls headlong into the same trap with Dr. Dowler and the "Red Indian." A writer in the "London Quarterly Review" sets the whole thing in its true light, by calling attention to the fact that Sir Robert Stephenson found in the Delta, at Damietta, at a greater depth than was ever reached by Mr. Horner, a brick bearing upon it the stamp of Mehemet Ali. Mr. Saville also states that in the deepest boring at the foot of the statue of Rameses II. there was found pottery fancied to be "Palæolithic," but stamped with the Grecian honeysuckle. Mr. Horner and an Egyptian officer made over ninety excavations in two lines across the valley, and in most of them found frag-

ments of burnt brick at greater depths than the piece of pottery above mentioned. Now, as burnt bricks were rarely used in Egypt until the time of the Romans, it seems probable that most of these fragments do not antedate the beginning of commerce with Rome. The Romans, who possessed unlimited forests, could burn and ship bricks to Egypt, when the latter country, being destitute of timber, could not often afford the immense expense of fuel for the kilns. The "Anthropological Review," which has certainly no prejudice against long periods, pronounces Mr. Horner's evidence "preposterous," and thinks it is to be regretted that Sir Charles Lyell "should have thought it worth while to notice such absurdities."

### The Cones of the Tinière.

This locality has been made the basis of another calculation, which, by the approval of Lyell, Lubbock, and the European archæologists generally, has become famous, and is much esteemed as a proof of human antiquity. As the statement is brief, and can scarcely be further condensed, we quote it entire from Mr. Southall:—

> At the eastern extremity of the Lake of Geneva, at the city of Villeneuve, the torrent of the Tinière descends abruptly from the mountains. It brings down annually a certain amount of gravel, which has been deposited in the form of a half-cone upon the plateau on the border of the lake. The apex of the cone rests against the side of the mountain, and the base extends in a semicircle around the mouth from which the torrent descends. A railroad cutting has exposed a section of one of the cones nearly to its base. Four feet from the top were found Roman relics, at ten feet were found bronze implements, and at nineteen feet Professor Marlot found stone implements. The entire depth of the cone is thirty-two feet six inches. Some two or three hundred years ago the increase of the cone was stopped by confining the torrent between stone walls. This leaves about fourteen hundred or fifteen hundred for the Roman period. In this time about four feet of gravel (as the calculation runs) were deposited, or about three and a half inches in a century. From this *datum* Marlot calculates that the antiquity of the bronze relics is about three thousand eight hundred years, that of the stone relics about six thousand four hundred years, and that of the whole cone about ten thousand years.

Dr. Andrews has demolished this calculation. He says, ("American Journal of Science," March, 1868:)—

It is with great hesitation that I question the conclusions of a European *savant*, made respecting his own country; but having twice examined these cones with great care, and followed the torrent a mile into the mountains to study its appearance and actions, I cannot avoid the conclusion that there is a very singular mathematical error in estimating the age of the cones, and an omission of several important geological facts, which vitiate the whole calculation. The nature of the mathematical error will be made obvious by a few facts. The gravel cones of Switzerland are very numerous, and the principle of their formation easily understood.

On the supposition that the torrent brings down about the same amount of gravel every year, it will readily be seen that the first year's deposit will be upon the plateau in a conical heap of no great breadth, but considerable height. The second year's gravel, however, will be spread over the entire surface of the first, and being wider, it must be much thinner. The third year's accretion will be broader and thinner still; and so on to the last. It follows that the superficial annual layers are always the thinnest, because the broadest. Now, if Marlot is correctly quoted, he first derives his scale of from three and three tenths to four inches' increase per century from the superficial layers where they are thinnest, and then applies it without modification to the interior, where the annual accretions are much thicker. His unit of measure is therefore too small, and exaggerates the total age. It is perfectly plain that the true method is to take the cubic contents of the strata, whose age is known, and compare the amount with the cubic contents of the whole cone; or, in plain language, if the annual rainfall and gravel wash has been uniform, then as the quantity of gravel in the layers deposited since the Roman conquest is to the quantity in the whole cone, so is the time required for the deposit of those layers to the time required for the formation of the whole cone.

The revised *data* and calculation would be as follows: Height of apex, 38 feet. Radius of base, 900 feet. Cubic feet in the strata deposited since the Roman conquest, 5,283,205. Time of deposition of the same, 1,300 to 1,500 years. Cubic feet in the whole cone, 16,116,408. Time of deposit of the same, 3,965 to 4,576 years. Adding the three hundred years which have elapsed since the deposit ceased, the present age of the lower cone would be from four thousand two hundred and sixty-five to four thousand eight hundred and seventy-six years. The whole cone is, therefore, at a *maximum*, only four thousand five hundred years old. The whole calculation would be still further changed if the gravel was arrested earlier than two hundred or three hundred years ago, or if the Roman coin found was dropped a couple of centuries later than has been assumed, or if, three thousand years ago, the torrent of the Tinière flowed with a bolder current than it did in the Middle Ages.

MM. de Ferry and Arcelin have made some calculations of the age of relics found in the deposits of the river Saône. From their *data* they obtain these results:—

| | M. Arcelin's Calculation. | M. de Ferry's Calculation. |
|---|---|---|
| Celtic Iron Age.......... | 1,800 to 2,700 years. | ........ |
| Bronze " .......... | 2,700 to 3,000 " | 3,000 years. |
| Neolithic " .......... | 3,600 to 6,700 " | 4,000 or 5,000 years. |
| Palæolithic " .......... | 6,700 to 8,000 " | 9,000 or 10,000 " |

We are not informed as to the faithfulness of these calculations, but they are corroborative of the corrected calculations of the Tinière, and present a striking contrast to the hundreds of thousands and millions of years loosely demanded by many archæologists.

## The Recent Date of the Glacial Age.

Chapter xxxiii is devoted to the proof derived from the shores of Lake Michigan, that no enormous period has elapsed since the Glacial Drift of that region was deposited. The investigation sonth is subject are from the "Transactions of the Chicago Academy of Sciences," and were conducted by Professor Andrews. Professor Dawson, of Montreal, remarks of this investigation, that he knows of no calculation of this sort made with equal care either in this country or in Europe.

Lakes Michigan and Huron are hydrographically one sheet of water, being at the same level, and connected by a strait several miles in width. Lake Michigan is three hundred and fifty miles in length, and eighty-five miles in width. Its outlet is at the strait at the north end, the southern extremity being a *cul-de-sac.* Its waves are continually in motion, and rapidly erode the drift clay of its shores. The material washed down by the waves is sorted by the same agency into clay and sand. The clay, floating about, settles whenever it reaches deep water, where the wave-action is too slight to keep it longer suspended; while the sand is carried by certain currents (mapped in the article) along shore southward, and deposited in beaches and dunes on the low sloping plain around the south end of the lake. The beaches thus formed have mapped out on the surrounding country every successive level occupied by the waters, and show by their relative size the length of time during which each one was deposited; while the same periods farther north are indicated by the ancient bluffs from the erosion of which the sands of the beaches were derived. It is by the combined study of the erosion and of the beaches that the total post-glacial time can be deduced.

The elements of the calculation are the following: 1. The average rate of erosion. 2. The width of the subaqueous plateau formed by the erosion since the lake stood at its present level. 3. The amount and direction of the sand movement. 4. The amount of sand in the several beaches.

The lake lies in a basin of bowlder drift, and has existed ever since the close of the Drift Period. Without entering into the dispute between the advocates of the glacier and of the iceberg theories, it appears that in that region a submergence beneath the sea occurred either just at the close of the drift or else continued from the drift itself. This is shown by the fact that the bowlder drift contains a large amount of salt, and its waters are far more saline than either the lake above, or the artesian waters of the rock beneath, and also by the aqueous character of a thin stratum of orange-colored loam covering all the drift hills and valleys. These waters at the close of the period retired abruptly southward, pausing nowhere between the highlands of Wisconsin and the Ohio River long enough to throw up any beach outside of the lake basins. When we reflect that a single storm on the sea will sometimes throw up a beach which no time can obliterate, we see that this retirement which left no beach-lines must have been rapid, and that it marked in a precise and definite manner the close of the Drift Period. The basins of the lakes were left, of course, like huge cups full of water, whose waves from that hour began to erode their shores, and to map out their history on their slopes.

The waters of Lake Michigan have stood at three different levels, which are marked in the north by three bluffs cut at different heights on the shores; and in the region around the southern end of the lake, where the vast amounts of sand brought by the currents shields the shores from wash, the three shore-lines are accurately mapped out by sand beaches, which are on the same level as the bluffs with which they were severally contemporaneous.

## Age of the Lower Beach.

The shores of Lake Michigan are nowhere stationary for long periods. The tearing down of the clay bluffs in the north, and the piling up of sand in the south under the tremendous dashing of the waves, goes on with an energy which is astonishing.

In the north, therefore, the shores are continually receding, and the waters encroaching on the land. The waves of the lake cease to have any erosive power upon the bottom at the depth of sixty feet, hence, where the shores have been worn back, there is left under water a sort of shelf, or terrace, the surface of which slopes gently outward to the depth of about sixty feet, when the bottom dips more suddenly downward below the depth of wave action. The outer edge of this terrace marks the place where sixty feet of water was when the erosion commenced, and gives a clue for finding the approximate position of the old shore line, now washed away. From a great number of observations, it appears that the total recession of the bluffs from the old shore line along the west coast amounts on the average to 2.72 miles, or fourteen thousand three hundred and sixty-two feet. Along this same coast a great number of observations and measurements show that the annual recession amounts on the average to about 5.28 feet per annum. Dividing the entire recession by this amount, we find the age of the lower terrace is two thousand seven hundred and twenty years. Taking fifty miles of the east coast of Lake Huron, (from Brewster's Mills to Point Clark,) the erosions have been less carefully studied, but still they corroborate in the main the other figures; for, dividing the width of the adjacent subaqueous terrace by the annual amount, we get for its age three thousand eight hundred and fifty-nine years.

Around the head of Lake Michigan the sand beaches take the place of the bluffs, and are necessarily of the same age. Soundings have shown that no sand passes out into deep water, nor does any come ashore from below sixty feet. It is all carried south, along both shores, by the two southward currents, till arrested in the *cul-de-sac*, where the currents meet. It is piled up in beaches, or blown by the winds into lofty dunes, often one hundred and sixty feet high. The lower beach is, of necessity, of the same antiquity as the lower terrace and bluff. This beach line contains about 1,747,570,000 cubic yards of sand, and, as before shown, is from twenty-seven hundred to thirty-eight hundred years of age. Above this beach, however, are two other lines of beaches and dunes, which represent the age of the upper bluffs, and

lake came to have any effective power upon the bottom at the

contain about 1,659,881,000 cubic yards of sand. It is obvious that we have here the elements of a proportion, and that as the amount of sand in the lower beach is to the total amount of sand, so is the time of accretion of the lower beach to the time of accretion of all the beaches, that is, the whole time from now back to the Drift Period. Carrying out the calculation, Dr. Andrews finds the time indicated to be between five thousand two hundred and ninety years, and seven thousand four hundred and ninety-one years.

The advantages of the shores of the Great Lakes for these estimates is, that they afford opportunities for numbers of independent calculations more or less complete, which can confirm or correct each other. Professor Andrews has introduced two or three such, showing the utter impossibility of allowing any such time as 100,000 years, so often claimed for the Post-glacial Period.

It is remarkable that the deposits on the shores of Lake Michigan show the same sequence of events as in Belgium, namely:—

1. Bowlder Drift. 2. First low-water period, (Palæolithic time,) mastodon and mammoth. 3. Great inundation, (lœss.) 4. Modern, or second low-water period. Thus far there are no relics of men found around Lake Michigan in the deposits of the first low-water period, which corresponds to the Palæolithic age of Europe. The mud of the great inundation, however, is clearly traceable, and covers over great quantities of vegetation and prostrate timber.

## The Antiquity of Man in America.

In chapter xxxvi Mr. Southall takes up this subject with the following facts and testimonies: For the Red Indians no great antiquity is claimed by any one. Captain Dupaix, in his *Antiquités Mexicaines*, fancies that the ruined cities of Central America were antediluvian, but on what evidence does not appear. The Aztecs had a definite history, with dates of their arrival in Mexico, and founded their new capital A. D. 1326, beginning it first on piles in the lake, making it in fact a pile village. (Prescott's "Conquest of Mexico.")

The Toltecs entered the valley earlier, and had dates reaching back to A. D. 387. The dates in ancient Peruvian history

are less trustworthy than those found in Mexico. The earliest ones only reach to the twelfth century after Christ. The ancient Mexican histories state that their predecessors in the valley, namely, the Toltecs, came from "Old Tlapalan," an empire situated at a great distance to the north-east, where they were skilled in working stone and metals. They state that the journey was long, and that they settled at two intermediate points before finally arriving in the valley of Mexico. They were driven out of "Old Tlapalan," they state, after a struggle of thirteen years, by a combination of barbarous tribes called Chicmecs. "Old Tlapalan" was inland country, but on their migration they halted several years in a land near the sea. The close resemblance in the religion and civilization of the Mound Builders to that found by Cortes in the valley of Mexico, together with the direction and distance of the migration, leads to a probable conjecture that "Old Tlapalan" was the Mound Builders' country. The documentary dates of the native history fix this migration at about A. D. 700.

The old native chronicler, Ixtlilxochitl, "the best authority," says Prescott, "for the traditions of his country," reports that the new Toltec empire, after flourishing in the valley of Mexico, broke up again about the tenth century after Christ, and the fragments of the nation settled in Guatemala, Tehuantepec, and Central America generally. This corresponds to the location of the ruined cities before mentioned.

## The Mound Builders.

In the region apparently called by these native histories "Old Tlapalan," that is, in the valleys of the Mississippi and of the great lakes, and in places lapping over upon the Atlantic slope, flourished the Mound Builders. They habitually buried their dead in mounds of earth. They constructed also mounds for worship, and probably kept up perpetual fires on their summits, like the Aztecs. In fact the Aztec temples were only mounds more developed, and cased in stone or adobe. Dr. Frank Richardson has found in the great mounds opposite St. Louis numerous burnt fragments of human bones, showing that the ancient city which worshiped there kept up the Aztec rites of frequent human sacrifice, and of feasting on the victims.

The Mound Builders were agriculturists, and lived in large settlements. They worked the copper veins of Lake Superior, but generally shaped the metal by hammering, and rarely by melting. Yet bronze chisels have been found, showing that the copper was sometimes melted and alloyed with tin. They had woven cloth, and probably lived in communal houses built of wood, and often elevated on large mounds, but at other times surrounded by a parapet of earth.

Mr. Squier, after investigating the mounds of New York, and comparing them probably with Central American remains, and studying them in connection with the habits and history of the Iroquois, (the Five Nations,) was brought unexpectedly to the conclusion that the New York mounds "were erected by the Iroquois, or their western neighbors, and do not possess any great antiquity."

If this is true, the Iroquois are a remnant of the true Mound Builders. It is commonly said that the modern Indians have no traditions of the mounds. This is not true. The Indians of Michigan, in some instances at least, had accounts of their occupation, and in one instance of a fortification mound being constructed for an emergency only two generations before by the tribe that had the tradition. In the South, the Natchez Indians were apparently living the Mound Builder's life when visited by La Salle in 1681. They also sacrificed human victims to the Sun, and used adobe walls, like the Mexicans. Bartram states that in his day the Choctaws built mounds over the bones of their dead; and Tomochichi pointed out a large conical mound in which he said the Yamacraw chief was interred, who many years before had entertained a great white man with a red beard, who entered the Savannah River in a large vessel. Mr. Charles C. Jones, in his "Antiquities of the Southern Indians," found in the bottom of a mound twenty feet in diameter and seven feet high an old-fashioned sword, (stated in the Smithsonian publications to be iron,) with an oak hilt. This shows evident communication with Europeans. It is agreed on all hands that no enormous antiquity can be assigned to the Mound Builders.

The aborigines of former days seem to have had communication with Asia. In Tennessee a bronze idol is figured, which, by good judges, is pronounced of Asiatic workmanship. At

twenty feet depth, in a shell-mound on the Pacific coast, a number of skeletons were found, one of which was a body wrapped in a long piece of red silk, which was prevented from decay by a coating of asphaltum.

We have already referred to the untrustworthy character of Dr. Koch's testimony, which renders it necessary to throw his statements entirely out of the account. Mr. Southall also effectually disposes of Dr. Dowler's Red Indian; and Col. Whittlesey's ancient Ohio Hearths, though doubtless honestly reported, are merely in river deposits, and subject to the same uncertainties of antiquity that pertain to the deposits of the Nile and the Mississippi.

### The Natchez Pelvis.

Some notoriety has been given to a human pelvis found, along with bones of the mastodon, and megalonyx lying loose in a ravine near Natchez. The bluffs bordering the ravine are lœss. The trouble about this specimen is that the Indian graves at the tops of these bluffs are continually caving down, and mingling their relics with objects at the bottom. This class of specimens is notoriously uncertain, and no experienced scientist attaches any significance to them.

### Skull from Calaveras County, California.

Some years ago two men took a finely developed Indian skull from a cave in the side of the valley, and placed it in a mining shaft, intending to have it fall into the hands of Professor Whitney as a practical joke. It was successful. A workman took out the skull and afterward gave it to the professor, who was so satisfied with the evidence of its authenticity that he neglected to have the shaft pumped out (it was full of water at the time of his visit) to examine the ground, and see whether the cave-stalagmite adhering to the skull could be accounted for on the supposition of its original lodgment in the gravel of the pit. He was effectually deceived, and believed the skull to be of Pliocene Age. A well-known and thoroughly reliable clergyman in California is brother to one of the men who placed the skull in the shaft, and testifies to the fact of the whole thing being a joke.

### Other California Relics.

Although this specimen was not genuine, other human relics have been found, it is said, in the "pay dirt," or gravel, at the depth of one or two hundred feet below the top of Table Mountain. The mass of the "mountain" above the relics is the product of one or more prodigious volcanic eruptions, which filled up the original ravines and water-courses with lava, ashes, etc., so that the subsequent courses of the streams were in entirely new routes, and the old channels became gold mines under the hill, in the excavation of which the relics were found.

The cutting of deep new ravines in the lava and ashes since that day must have taken a considerable period, but there is nothing to show whether it was very long or otherwise. No measure of such action in such material exists by which we could determine, and, if the rainfall there was formerly greater than now, as many investigators think, the time might be very moderate. The volcanic deposit above the relics proves nothing. Existing volcanoes have ejected thicker masses than that in a single eruption. The minor proof of antiquity is this. Professor Whitney thinks that so great a volcanic disturbance in California may naturally be thought contemporaneous with the Bowlder Drift disturbances of the east, and hence reckons the volcanic deposit as the California representative of the Drift Period. Now, as the Pliocene Period was the one next preceding the Bowlder Drift, and as these relics are alleged to come from under the volcanic mass, he thinks they belong to the Pliocene Period, which would make them older than the Bowlder Drift, or any relics of man ever found elsewhere.

This whole argument is a begging of the question. Volcanic eruptions occur in all ages; but even if this is assumed, on account of its magnitude, to have a probable connection with disturbances elsewhere, it is as likely to have been at the time of the lœss as at that of the drift. The fauna found with them ought to have corrected the estimate. The bones of the mastadon and *elephas Americana* are found in the same deposit. Now these are not Pliocene animals, but belong to the period after the drift, and along with Palæolithic man. I should say, also, that torrent deposits present the same obstacles to safe

conclusions that other streams do, because they mix relics of all ages together. The ancient California men may possibly have been contemporary with the Palæolithic men of Belgium.

A fisherman's line-sinker, made of polished syenite, was found by workmen while sinking a well in San Joaquin. The work men alleged that it came from the same quaternary gravel thirty feet down. If so, it may be Palæolithic in spite of its beautiful polish and finish. The authenticity of its location is not proved, however. No scientific man saw it exhumed, and every experienced naturalist knows how prone workmen are to confound the relics, which tumble into an excavation from the edge of the earth at the top, with those properly belonging to the bottom. The positiveness of their false opinions in these cases is often very amusing, and not unfrequently imposes on scientific men themselves. It is said similar stone sinkers are still used by the western coast Indians.

The work of Mr. Southall is a timely one. The archæologists have been industrious, and accumulated a large array of facts, which different observers, with a singular blundering eagerness, assume to prove all sorts of contradictory antiquities for the human race, varying from five thousand up to eight millions of years. It is time to examine their work, to sift and compare their discoveries, to blow among the dust and smoke of enthusiastic assumptions, and see exactly what the facts prove. Mr. Southall has done this in a masterly manner. As before stated, he has given the most thorough and honest statement of all the important discoveries on this subject which has ever appeared in the English language, and made it so complete that very few important facts have escaped him. At the same time he has brought to the work a keen, and often original, analysis, which greatly increases the value of the treatise. He has given a very great labor to it, and this is what is needed. Facts, and facts alone, settle such questions, and to them all appeals at last must come.

The final result of the whole discussion is clearly this. Up to the present hour there has not been found a fragment of any human bone, nor a single relic of human workmanship, which can be clearly shown to be over five thousand years of age.

## ART. III.—THE SCIENTIFIC CONFERENCE AT CHAUTAUQUA.

AT the late Sunday-school Assembly at Chautauqua, one of the highest functionaries of our Church declared its creative and controlling spirit, Dr. Vincent, to be the Napoleon of the Sunday-school cause. We are inclined to carry out the figure a step farther, and name him the Danton of the Sunday-school revolution—for in his work he seems to have adopted as his own the motto of the great French revolutionist, "*l'audace! l'audace!! et encore l'audace!!!*" for year after year he seems to increase in boldness and in boldness, and again in boldness, until we are at a loss to know what to expect from him next.

When this generalissimo of his revolution came to us for the first time to unfold his plans for a Scientific Conference at Chautauqua we listened with fear and trembling, and thought within us—this is a bold experiment. But the leader had determined on a forward movement, and only desired of us counsel as to the members of his staff for this aggressive warfare. We advised as best we knew, and could simply wish him Godspeed! And he sped to victory by a judicious choice of workers, and then commanded success to perch upon his banners by deserving it.

The Scientific Conference has ceased to be a doubtful experiment, and has passed into the field of history; and its decided success merits, we think, a chronicler, and as such we propose to enter into no philosophical disquisition as to the conflict between science and religion—with this we have been both saturated and satiated. We prefer to deal with the practical facts brought forward in this new enterprise, and to show how, in our humble judgment, the developments of the wonders revealed by science will lead the popular mind more surely to a firm belief in the existence of a great and good First Cause, and will leave an impression even stronger than the arguments of Bible defenders, and one that will be proof against the attacks of atheistic scientists.

This Scientific Conference fully proves that Christian men have no desire to refuse a hearing to the devotees of science; on the contrary, they are willing to do even more than "beard

the lion in his den;" they bid him come forth and take their platform with all that he has to reveal, that they may use it to demonstrate the goodness, power, and sublime glory of God. "Truth is mighty and will prevail," and no man ought to fear the development of any truth that can clearly be proved to be such; and so long as scientific men will bring us the actual and wonderful facts of science, and will spare us vague theories about matters in which they are as much in the dark as we, and especially will spare us many of their doubtful deductions, we shall willingly listen to them, and accept them as worthy and desirable coadjutors in the noble and praiseworthy effort to understand all that we may of the marvelous attributes of God.

The enigma to be solved was the feasibility and desirability of presenting scientific truths to Christian workers. Can it be done? Is it well to do it? Will they appreciate it and profit by it? We answer these questions in the affirmative, and are sustained, we believe, by the great majority of the persons who enjoyed the rare opportunity of studying scientific truth as it was presented at Chautauqua. And we shall endeavor to strengthen our position by a collateral approach in the first place.

Some years ago the scientific men of England, under the lead of Faraday, undertook to teach popular science to the poor, with the view of elevating and encouraging them to look to nobler things than the many allurements and vices around them. His Christmas lectures to juvenile audiences years ago may be considered as the inauguration of a system which finally grew into a regular preaching of the gospel of science to the poor. Since his death his successor, Professor Tyndall, has regularly continued these Christmas lectures. And the famous Manchester lectures to the workingmen have now grown into a fixed institution. The object was simply to teach the elements of science in plain and popular language, and to prove the truth of the many curious assertions by actual experiments. The system has become a decided success, and the working poor of England now enjoy great advantages in the study of applied science, though it may be imparted by some men who in a higher sphere have acquired no great credit for their frivolous and disrespectful treatment of the influence of a higher

Being in the affairs of man and the control of the world. These men have doubtless unwittingly taught many sublime and holy truths, that have been better appreciated by their lowly hearers than by themselves.

The success of these lectures has led scientific men to renounce the erroneous notion that has too long prevailed among them as to the value of such efforts. What the French call the *vulgarization* of knowledge is now becoming popular among them, and they are beginning to enjoy the pleasure of addressing unlettered and unwashed audiences, many of which seem to vie in intelligence with their better dressed and housed competitors, and to absorb, to their great profit, the sublime truths imparted to them. And we are pleased to say that the same experiment has been tried now for a few winters with very marked success in our own country by one of the Chautauqua workers in the Scientific Conference, Professor S. A. Lattimore, of the University of Rochester.

This gentleman conceived some years ago the idea of establishing in that city a course of free lectures for the workingmen with their wives and children, to present to them the wonders of science in plain and intelligible language, demonstrated by many of the beautiful experiments at his command with the apparatus used in his class lectures. This idea of giving the workingmen college lectures, so to say, was received at first with much distrust. Will these people come? And will it do them any good? Suffice it to say that they have been continued for several years in Rochester, have been extended by urgent request to Buffalo, and just now Detroit is endeavoring to secure the assistance of the same distinguished and philanthropic Christian gentleman for a course of his lectures in that city under the auspices of the Young Men's Christian Association. And he writes to us in a private letter, in reply to a request for his impressions regarding the work, as follows:—

"All I know is the little I have learned during the last few years in my humble efforts to do something for the working people of this city and Buffalo in the way of lectures on popular science. I began with no encouragement, but only discouragement, from my friends. The unexpected success at first might fairly have been attributed to the novelty of the

enterprise, and the fact that tickets were given away to any workingman free of cost, and no tickets were sold. But as the novelty wore off the interest seemed to increase, and I have always been surprised at the intelligent appearance and the wrapt attention of these great audiences. I have never seen any thing so inspiring and helpful to an extempore speaker. I have always insisted on a few conditions, such as these: All the workingmen (with wives and children, say over fourteen) to be admitted without distinction. Tickets to be free of cost, and other classes not admitted. Many workingmen object to receiving a free ticket, fearing they are accepting a charity. Sunday clothes are not necessary."

Now we know that these lectures have been a grand success, and that many of the manufacturers and merchants of the cities named have found it a great pleasure to contribute to the necessary labor and expense attending them—not in paying the lecturer, for he would accept nothing but the pleasure afforded him in doing a good deed to the poor and lowly, but in defraying bills for lecture halls, tickets, announcements, etc. Year after year these lectures have become more and more popular, and the workingmen now look for their annual pleasure with as great eagerness as the most inveterate popular lecture-goers.

Now it seems but one step to transfer such work from the platforms of great cities to the tabernacle of the tented grove. But who other than the "audacious doctor" would have thought of so doing, and would have boldly ventured to introduce scientific lectures as a part of the proceedings of a Sunday-school assembly? We reply, no other than Dr. Vincent, and to him belongs the credit of whatever success may have been reaped in this peculiar endeavor. It seems to have been his opinion that people need to know something about science before they can intelligently consider whether it conflicts with religion or not. The plan, therefore, as finally developed in his mind, was to give Christians at large, and Sunday-school workers in particular, an opportunity which but few of them could otherwise enjoy, of listening to a group of very distinguished men discuss a series of scientific questions, and present a set of lectures demonstrated by the finest and most interesting apparatus in the country. Dr. Doremus, of New York

city, came with the treasures of two very rich laboratories at his command, bringing no less than three tons of apparatus and material. And Professor Lattimore also brought from Rochester a rich selection of his choicest apparatus. To give their delicate experiments in the forest taxed the ingenuity of both of them to the utmost, and nothing but the most generous aid to each other as brothers in the cause of popularizing science could have brought them through successfully. The parts that were *seen*—the experiments—rather than what was *heard*, were the impressive parts. These experimental illustrations were simply magnificent, and in many cases could not be appreciated by the mass of the hearers; they were worthy of an audience of professional scientists. But, nevertheless, an impression was made that in the opinion of the lecturers themselves was worth all the outlay of money and brains that it cost. It was a great venture and a great success; and though much of such teaching must pass over the heads of a popular audience, it at least teaches them all to look *up*, and still up, to nature's God. Many expressed themselves more thrillingly impressed with the marvelous sermons delivered by the scientists than with those from the theologians.

With this simple presentation as a sort of defense, or logical "*raison d'être*," we proceed to a statement of the course of study in the Scientific Conference, in which we propose to be objective rather than subjective, holding, as far as in us lies, the mirror up to nature that she may tell us what was done by science in its effort to be for the time being the practical handmaid of religion.

This Scientific Conference was to last three days, and the proceedings were logically inaugurated by a general discourse on the "Circle of the Sciences," by Rev. Dr. Buckley. The speaker, after a general introduction, drew an outline map of the world of science, with the avowed object of throwing the gates ajar and pointing out the paths by which we may enter. He treated of the difficulties that stand in the way of the popularization — the "*vulgarization*" — of science under three heads: first, the use of the technical terms and the necessity of that use; second, of the necessary subdivision of science into different fields; and, finally, he gave a very exhaustive schedule of all the sciences, and their evolution or logical co-relation to

each other, closing with the following beautiful tribute to science as the Christian's *vade mecum* and defense:—

The value, then, of scientific knowledge to the teacher is immense, whether in the common schools or the Sabbath-schools. It enlarges his vision, trains his powers, prevents monotony, furnishes abundant material for illustration, and gives stimulus to all his communications. To the minister it is still more important. All that it does for the teacher it does for the minister. And more. It is almost a certain protection of his style from degenerating into mere cant, and it enriches it in every respect. It may, indeed, be pedantically exhibited on every occasion as on the wrong occasion. It may be substituted for the Gospel of the Son of God, and modes of reasoning which are not suited to the presentation of the Gospel may be ignored. But this is true of ancient literature. The abuses of scientific knowledge and processes can never be urged against its use. It would at least save some eloquent and spiritually minded men from exciting contempt by their ignorance. As he who, preaching from the text, "The Lord God is a sun," declared that if it were not for the sun we should be obliged to content ourselves with the "pale and insufficient light of the moon;" or as a quite noted and graduated man who recently published a sermon in which he based certain calculations on the supposed distance of the moon from the earth, making an error of such magnitude in the assured distance as to place him beneath duty.

But some timid soul may say, Is there not peril here? Nay, a devout man walks by faith. A man who dares not pray may be prevented from beginning to pray by skeptic persons' jests as he may by riches or honor. But a devout man may follow the facts of science every-where, and find in them all amazing illustrations and confirmations of the wisdom and power and upright hints of the goodness of the personal and merciful God whom he adores. But if he be not religious he can find materials enough to feed his skepticism, and to fatten it into unbelief.

Those, indeed, who would make the Bible a book of natural science and interpret its incidental allusions in harmony with successive phases of scientific research, thus making it an intellectual chameleon, have undertaken an impossible task; for the spiritual truths which they were designed to convey are draped in the thoughts, language, and supposed knowledge of the ages in which they are given. Job xxviii contains the praise of science, and distinguishes the sphere of religion.

Dr. Buckley's lecture proved a very fitting and acceptable introduction to the exercises. Though abstruse in substance, it was witty and wise, learned and still popular, and eminently adapted by its rare commingling of pleasantry, even with an imposing array of Greek and Latin terms, to attract the atten-

tion of his hearers to his logical analysis and comprehensive display of scientific knowledge, not very common in theological scholars.

Chancellor Haven, of Syracuse University, then followed with a lecture on the "Relation of Material Science to Mind and Spirit." After alluding to various philosophical theories of past ages, including those of Plato and Aristotle, he comes down through Bacon and Fichte to Darwin, who, he says,—

tells us that every thing is developed or comes by a process of evolution, but he fails to tell us how the material arose out of the evolution, or why the evolution began, or what carries it on; and these all alike hover around these infinite mysteries of Nature and Mind. . . . Now, if man is a lie by accident or by creation, then the whole universe is a lie; but, nevertheless, if a lie, it is true to him, for truth is what a man sees; etymologically, truth is what a man thinks, "what a man troweth when he troweth right." Now here you see one connection of science with religion. Science is nothing; science is a mere vagary; science is a kaleidoscope; science is a mere collection of terms, unless there be truth; and all scientific men claim that the profoundest principles are "Love the truth; seek the truth; abide by the truth. Amen." But that is not science—that is religion. We believe that God is truth, and we believe that when man is right, man is truth; consequently, man's honest, clear, sharp, well-defined, accurate views of the universal science are truth.

The doctor then treated of the eternity of matter in all its changes, and found God in it—"God is light." There is in vegetation a mysterious power, and the development, from the highest class of vegetables to the lowest class of animals, teaches us a significant lesson; and there is no objection to development if thereby is meant creation, for development requires a developer. And with this train of reasoning the speaker arrived at the following eloquent and significant conclusion:—

I say, then, to the scientific men, go on with your work; you are building better than you know, unless you catch the idea of religion and faith with your science, as most scientific men do. Why are modern men of science the noblest poets that utter our language, whether in measured terms or otherwise? Tyndall himself and Darwin are better metaphysical men than they think. Men such as Dawson and Winchell, and other men of this kind, show the real vital connection between philosophy and religion. They show the different departments of the great universe of truth, and that the unfolding of the lower prepares the way for the higher, and when the higher comes the lower is not annihilated

but still remains. Here is the crystal imbedded in the rock; so by its fruits, by the little fibers and threads that go out from it, it anticipates the coming vegetable, as Agassiz has so wonderfully shown; and then the vegetable, when it reaches perfection, pretypifies the coming animal, and the animal in its instincts pretypifies the coming understanding and reason of the man, and the understanding and the reason prepare the way for and pretypifies the coming faith—power—the soul-sight. Look upward as well as downward, aspire as well as grovel. The original scientific work, the laboratory work, the kitchen work, has something of the primal curse upon it. It covers the brow with sweat, it begets no high enthusiasm; but when one of those scientific men, catching the spirit of faith and religion, begins to create or tell how the Creator creates, then his eyes sparkle and his voice takes on ring and rhythm, and the multitude listen, and these scientific men gather their strength, and their eloquence, and their influence from the great primal religious truths which are the pillars of the universe. God has built the universe around spiritual truth. God is a spirit, and this material universe is but the clothing, but the instruments, but the machinery of his spirit, and we are but rethinking the thoughts of God when we study science.

The boldest move made during this Scientific Conference was the presentation of practical lectures, illustrated by delicate and expensive apparatus, in an extensive course of the most curious and instructive experiments, and for this purpose the services of the most capable and interesting scientific lecturer in the country had been obtained, namely, R. Ogden Doremus, M.D., LL.D., Professor of Chemistry at the Bellevue Hospital Medical College of New York city. Dr. Doremus was fitly introduced as a high-priest of science, whose name is every-where received with unbounded applause, and his first lecture was on "Heat: Its Sources and Effects." It was a very venturesome and doubtful experiment to undertake to perform in the open forest many of the delicate tests that often fail when surrounded by all the appliances and safeguards of the carefully constructed lecture-room, and the scientists themselves were prepared to submit to some mortifying failures. But these were few and far between, owing, in the first place, to the careful provision that had been made in the supply of instruments and chemical tests, but more especially to the fact that Drs. Doremus and Lattimore, up to that period strangers to each other, and, to a certain extent, rivals on the Chautauqua platform, joined hands as brothers, and, with coats off and sleeves

rolled up, aided each other so heartily and effectively in preparing the apparatus and performing the experiments, that admiring Chautauquans, looking on in surprise, were led to exclaim, "See what religion can do in harmonizing the antagonisms of science!"

This lecture gave unbounded satisfaction, and was a rare treat to many who never had had, and never would elsewhere have, the opportunity of witnessing extensive and delicate experiments illustrative of "heat" in all its various forces and phases. It was a rare sight to many to witness the freezing of mercury and the burning of charcoal in a glass tube at the same time. And nothing could be more wonderful than the illustration showing the formation of the earth from a fluid substance, as well as the solar system and the entire planetary world. In his beautiful experiments, so happily performed and popularly explained, many of the auditors saw so much of the wonders of nature that they were led to exclaim, "Glory to God!" at the culminating marvels of these scientific sermons. Dr. Doremus was ably seconded by his son, who has enjoyed the greatest advantages and the most extensive scientific culture that this country and Europe can afford, and who is ever at his father's side ready to hold up the latter's hands in the performance of their delicate and difficult work, to illustrate which they brought from their home laboratory about three tons of apparatus and a large supply of chemicals in solid and liquid and gaseous form; among the latter, in liquid form, five hundred gallons of laughing-gas and one gallon of liquefied carbonic acid, which, of course, expanded into vast proportions when permitted to assume the gaseous form.

Among the interesting exercises of each day was a "*scientific conversazione*," held at the close of the afternoon lecture, with a view of giving to all scientific scholars and amateurs present an opportunity to exchange views in regard to the particular points presented, or to present any other views of scientific matters that might legitimately pertain to the subject. The special topic of the first *conversazione* was, "The Importance of Science to the Religious Thinker." During the discussion the following positions were maintained: Science, when properly understood, is a true commentary on religion. There is a harmony between the spiritual and the natural. The relig-

ious teacher ought to have a fund of scientific knowledge that he may be able to meet the honest inquiries of Christians and the objections of skeptics. It is not pleasant to hear the assumption that there exists any antagonism between science and religion, for a full proportion--aye, a very large proportion—of scientific men are Christians. Nature is the most instructive illustrator of the truths of revelation. Science is truth systematized, and as such should be regarded as a revelation from God—divine utterance, as much as the written word. If not the infinity, the incomprehensible vastness of God may be seen in the universe around us. And this harmony between geology and revelation may be found in geological deductions of the first chapter of Genesis. In the general subject revelation is the true guide, illustrated by the sciences, for in some instances science greatly enlarges our views of the Scripture record.

Dr. Vincent presented the following summary of the points raised in the *conversazione*. The Christian teacher should study science:—

1. Because true Christianity has always fostered and developed science.

2. Because science is a revelation of the acts, character, and greatness of God.

3. Because science furnishes innumerable illustrations of spiritual truth.

4. Because science furnishes arguments against the conclusions of science falsely so-called.

5. Because scientific studies furnish arguments to satisfy the honest doubts of the young.

6. Because scientific studies promote individual power and a higher range of involuntary thinking.

7. Because it imparts a tone of reality to our habits of thinking and style of expression.

8. Because it creates a taste for a higher style of literature on the part of old and young.

9. Because it is valuable in revealing the works and word of God.

The evening of the first day was devoted to a lecture on "The Physical Forces," by Professor S. A. Lattimore, Ph. D., LL.D., of the University of Rochester, one of the most devoted

and instructive scientific lecturers within the pale of our own Church. His large experience in the matter of popularizing science for the workingmen, alluded to in the introduction to this article, made him a most fitting man to appear on the platform of Chautauqua to popularize science as such to the Christian masses in general and Sunday-school workers in particular. The lecture was given at night, to afford the professor the opportunity of illustrating his teachings by means of the lime light and a stereopticon. He made the physical forces of nature his willing servants, and bade them come forth from their hidden resources and substantiate his assertions as to their power. The beautiful and brilliant illustrations employed in the course of this lecture were received with applause and delight, and the whole effort was pronounced a perfect success, notwithstanding the great difficulty of arranging apparatus and performing such experiments in the open air.

Rev. E. F. Burr, D.D., opened the services of the second scientific day with a lecture on "Celestial Magnitudes." Dr. Burr is now pastor of the First Congregational Church in Lynn, Mass. He is a distinguished lecturer on the scientific evidences of Christianity at Amherst College; and as author he is widely known by his "*Ecce Cœlum*," in which he so beautifully illustrates the truth that "The heavens declare the glory of God, and the firmament showeth his handiwork." In his "*Pater Mundi*" he has made a strong plea for the truth of Christianity as seen in admitted or self-evident facts; and then he has given us the "Doctrine of Evolution," "*Ad Fidem*," etc., and if he has a weakness, it is a penchant for Latin titles to his books; but this we readily forgive him in view of their contents. His lecture on "Celestial Magnitudes" gave him a fine opportunity, in ornate and poetic style, to treat of the sublimest truths of creation, and creep "from nature up to nature's God." We could gladly ascend each round of the ladder with him as he starts with the nebulæ, rises to the clusters of stars, and witnesses the glory of the Creator in the very midst of those remote wonders of the sky; we would with him follow the comets in their flight, study the planets and their moons, and listen to the mysteries of the solar system; but time bids us simply stop at and give his climax and concluding words:—

This mere cluster of stars in which we have our home, grand as it is, gives us something grander in the Author of such a system as that. I see the very apex of being; I see the loftiest summit to which thought can climb; I see a Being of whom the milky way is but a shadow, the sun itself is but his shadow. Having these views, my hearers, I do not accord completely with the gentleman who addressed you yesterday morning. He was not disposed to admit theology into the grand circle of the sciences. I think he did not define science rightly. What is science? The true definition of science is the one given in the afternoon of yesterday. It is systematized knowledge; and have we no systematized knowledge of God? Certainly we have; and if we have, then I say that this is the grandest of all science. All the other sciences ought to revolve about this, and if this center of gravity be removed they necessarily fly into disorganization, and are worth nothing at all; and so I am very glad indeed of this scheme of services in which, as I understand the pivotal idea, the center of gravity, is theology—religion; and it is proposed to make chemistry and all the other members of the circle of sciences revolve about it. God speed you to the fulfillment of this very laudable scheme!

Professor Alexander Winchell, LL.D., whom it would be a superfluous compliment to introduce to readers of the "Quarterly," took up the train of thought of the preceding speaker, as a fitting introduction to his own discourse on "Words in the Rocks," by commencing in these terms:—

Mr. President, Ladies, and Gentlemen: Now that we have been led in thought to those magnificent intervals of space in which exist the planets and the stars and the nebulæ, all in the presence of Deity, and all ruled from the throne of the universe, let us inquire how human thought has been enabled to ascend to such lofty and sublime heights. Theology is a science which consists of the grand conclusions of all the sciences. The other sciences are but door-ways to the science of theology. Theology avails itself of them all; it outlines all truth and recognizes all truth as God's truth, and all the activities which manifest themselves in the world around us and the worlds above us as modes of activity of the one supreme power and intelligence. Man has not arisen in a leap to the contemplation of these lofty themes. Man begins with the earth, his home. He studies the pebble, and the rock, and the atmosphere that bathes his skin, and he finds here the alphabet of a system of learning which elevates his thought and imagination by degrees to the heavens, and the heaven of heavens.

Now we have had a glimpse of the magnificent altitudes to which science has exalted human thought; let us come back to study for a brief interval the alphabet which science has had to con before it had mastered these sublime lessons. And I feel that I have a claim upon your patience in view of the grand conclusions to which

we have just listened, for when you have learned that such are the ultimate conclusions of dry science, you certainly will bear with me in bringing your thoughts for a brief time to the facts which constitute the alphabet of this grand system of learning.

The learned geologist then went on to prove how emphatically he had read sermons in the stones, and found stories in the running brooks. He took his hearers on a tour in the immediate vicinity of Chautauqua, and unfolded to them the mysteries of the cliffs at Panama, not far distant, and read to them in the bowlders and pebbles a history far more ancient than that of man himself. He proved that rocks have a language, and traced their words with consummate skill, making the whole earth seem like a divine word to the man who reads it in a Christian and not in a cynical or skeptical spirit, and concluded as follows:—

If I had time, and if it were my appointed theme, I could show you more clearly still that the life-time of the system of worlds, or of the universe of suns, is but a finite span in boundless eternity; that there is no series of events in progress that is not destined to come to a natural and necessary conclusion, unless an outside Power intervenes to perpetuate and renew and restore some past condition of things again. So, finally, there is no self-supporting existence in all the realm of matter about us. The worlds and systems of worlds are passing through their several histories with their destinies as plainly inscribed on the pages of nature as is the limit of a man's life-time; and by and by this earth must cease to exist, not only as a habitable place for man, but as an abode suitable to any form of recognized existence—a changed, worn-out, senescent body, like the moon hanging uninhabited and uninhabitable in the heavens. And so do we find every thing within the material universe in a changing condition; and it must cease to act and move and be what it is, unless some power independent of matter, and higher than nature, shall be outstretched to renew the cycle of changes; and this is the revelation of God.

In the afternoon Professor Lattimore again stepped before an appreciative and applauding audience to treat of "The Wonders of the Sun." He first told of the Ptolemaic theory of our solar system, which made the earth the center, around which all revolve, and graphically delineated the long course of history which finally opened up to men's minds the wonderful truths of the theory of Copernicus, according to which the sun is the great center of them all. The long and groping

struggle of astronomers to get at and get out the great truth that would settle so many intricate problems in astronomy was related with great beauty while interviewing the story of Galileo, Kepler, and Tycho Brahe. Then came the maledictions and persecutions from the papal throne against those who revealed the truth; but the latter was too powerful to be obscured by pope or cardinal, and soon burst forth to a world that, in its turn, was too tardy in accepting it. For a long time the mechanical powers of the sun, so to speak, were the only ones that men dared to investigate, but at last they became curious about its real nature, and longed to know what the great luminary is made of. Thirty years ago this seemed a bold and silly question; but Dr. Doremus would now settle it to their satisfaction by means of the solar spectrum, which enables scientists to analyze the sun into its chemical constituents. Then came the marvelous data of solar forces in raising water, and supplying heat and light that had been bottled up for ages. Think of "bottled sunlight!" But this it is that gives to the coal its force, and after having lain for long ages concealed in the tissues of plants, comes forth to expand the water into steam and lend it the force that propels the locomotive and drives the machinery of countless manufactories of the industrial world. And we will reach the climax of the "Wonders of the Sun" in the lecturer's own words, leading him up to the God that created it:—

I say it was no extravaganza. A lump of coal may be considered as solidified sunlight. The power it is capable of giving you is not manufactured in it; it is not generated by its combustion; it is only evolved from it, as a spring may long be held down and yet when released exert its power, but you know perfectly well that some man first compressed that spring. So of all the forces we use for economic purposes, they may be traced directly back to the sun itself. These beautiful green leaves are woven by the golden fingers of the sun's rays; every atom is placed here through the agency of actinic force; every movement of these leaves by the wind is due to the sun acting on the atmosphere. The lash of these waves upon the shore all whisper to us in the language of that voice that has its utterance in yonder glorious orb. These are the views, ladies and gentlemen—not as the ancient views were, but the views of science demonstrative, and demonstrable science, that are opening before us, that show us in this new and wonderful light this beautiful universe of God. If, therefore, that is the great fountain of life and of light, how beautiful was the

poetic fancy of the ancient fire-worshipers who, in their ignorance, nevertheless recognized the great truth when they called themselves the children of the sun, when they worshiped his rising beams, and indeed the glorious light as the chosen emblem of God himself. These are thoughts, I think, that should find a lodgment in our hearts as well as in our minds; and as we look up to the glorious orb above, when as we think of his magnitude, as we think of his distance, and yet of his intimate nearness, as we think of our utter dependence day by day upon its light, we may find in this a still more glorious symbol than we have ever seen before of the vastness, the distance, and yet the nearness of Him who is the life of life.

And again, after the labors of this day, assembled another large audience to engage in a *conversazione* as to "The Best Means of Diffusing Scientific Knowledge among the Masses." We give the prominent thoughts that were brought forward: The God of nature and of revelation being the same, all theology that is true and all real science must be in perfect harmony. Truth was writ. Science should be examined in the light of religion, and religion in the light of science. Familiarity with both will enable us to see more clearly their harmony and the beauty of each. . . . All science should be stripped of its abstruseness and technicalities and brought down into the language of the common people. . . . Scientific subjects should, in a religious way, more fully engage the attention of the pulpit. . . . We should organize scientific clubs, institute scientific readings, and introduce more fully scientific works into our higher schools. . . . Special attention should be given to those sciences which lie nearest to Christianity. The religious element in man's nature is recognized by such philosophers as Tyndall, Ewald, and others, and really is the basis of Christianity. Man's religious nature is, then, a scientific principle, and as such it should be fully developed. If it were made to take its proper place in the broad field of science many a problem would be solved in both science and religion, and the harmony of both more clearly seen. . . . Public lectures, such as have been delivered here, should be published and scattered freely throughout the country.

In the evening of this day Dr. Doremus again took the stand to treat of "Heat Converted into Light." His subject was largely illustrated with experiments of the most interesting and valuable character. The Davy Safety Lamp was shown and

explained, metals and chemicals were burned, conductors and non-conductors of heat were explained, many interesting experiments were performed with phosphorus in combustion, the Gulf Stream was treated of, and the rise of balloons from heated air. And, finally, a beautiful allusion was made, in closing, to the great source of heat and light, in the following terms:—

With regard to the sun, philosophers have attempted to determine somewhat the amount of heat received from it, and how, and have constructed instruments to measure it. Careful experiments have been made by great physicists, and it is claimed we know approximately how much heat we receive from that brilliant orb, and attempts have been made to express it by the amount of coal which would be consumed in making a like amount of heat, or the amount of ice that would be melted by it.

It is the great Architect that builds up the great forest; it is the great Chemist that distills those acids and those sweets in the flowers of the world; it is the great Artist that paints the green tints of summer, and causes nature to put on the pantomime garb of autumn, like the hectic flush in the cheek of the consumptive.

It was once thought that these stellar hosts were like many friends, merely to give a glimmering light, but no warmth of heart; but it is claimed now that if each should be expressed numerically as we receive it from the sun, by the number of one hundredths, the number eighty would express the heat received from these stellar masses. Without their warmth plant life, animal life, human life, would be impossible upon this sphere. In the words of the poet Young:—

"One sun by day, ten thousand suns by night,
That lead us upward to the Deity;
How glorious in magnificence and might."

But we have another great source of heat, and that is within our own globe. Yonder chart faintly expresses to us how we are incrusted with a series of layers, and how we receive warmth from within. Our earth is not cold at heart; it is a throbbing, pulsating organ within, which at times bursts forth, causing the rock-ribs to quake and man to tremble.

The Scientific Conference was appointed to last three days, and the morning exercises of the third and last day were opened by Rev. A. A. Hodge, Professor of Systematic Theology in the Western Theological Seminary, Alleghany, Pa. His subject was "The Relation of Bible Miracles to Modern Science," which he thus introduced:—

I wish to say, in commencing, that science itself never has assumed an attitude antagonistic to religion; that men of science have not—and that only a few men, not properly the exponents of science, who have advanced the philosophical speculation, have—declared, have proved not that science was antagonistic to religion, but that that philosophy was antagonistic. I think the most important thing now for us to do is to define what science is, and limit it in its scope. There is just as much difference between science and philosophy as there is between science and religion. Science has been defined as knowledge well grounded and well ordered. If knowledge be not well grounded it cannot constitute science, and if knowledge is not well ordered it cannot constitute science. Now, obviously, science does not include the whole mass of human knowledge. There is a necessary sphere of philosophy which is fundamental to science. It has never been pretended that there is one single property or matter, or a single law of nature ever discovered that was necessarily inconsistent with the idea of a supernatural power. Science justifies the conclusion that there is no case of spontaneous cause in external nature; that all phenomena are to be traced and adequately explained by invariable and self-executing laws; that every physical phenomenon that has been hitherto explained is subject to the operation of this law. The inference is that every phenomenon can be ultimately traced to an explanation by such law. When men in past ages have attributed these things to voluntary action they were mistaken. The inference is that the domain of the supernatural—that is, the operation of voluntary causes—will be proven backward, and if there be a supernatural, it is not only unknown and unproven, but from the very limits of our faculties it is unknowable and not to be proved. We say the supernatural is impossible and therefore unhistorical. In all the great works on the subject you will find the argument is a constructive one, based upon this assumption: the supernatural is impossible, therefore the supernatural is unhistorical, and, therefore, the supernatural element of all these writings which claim to contain a supernatural revelation is to be eliminated from them, and the residuum is to be explained by natural causes.

With this introduction the speaker passed on to the definition of a miracle, speaking of it as something not impossible, but rather as highly probable, and then treating of its relation to human testimony. The word miracle is the most unfortunate one that could be found in the language to express the thought, for it conveys the idea of the wonderful and the marvelous, and, therefore, leads the unthinking and untutored to regard all miracles as such events, whereas God violated no laws in the performance of miracles—he simply interpolated a new cause; and this new condition is the Divine overcoming

the merely natural. Having finished his defense of the logical truth of miracles, he thus paid his respects, in closing, to some of the skeptical scientists of the day:—

I believe the great German physicists are right in the fundamental philosophy at the bottom of the theory of Darwin. I do not assume that the theory of evolution is true, but I mean Darwinism as held by Darwin and his disciples.

The confession that Professor Tyndall is bound to make is, that he sees in matter the promise and potency of every quality of life. In doing so he should have us believe, instead of degrading life down to matter, he would raise matter up to life. He seeks to explain the phenomenon of the mechanical parts, and he begins with the molecule. Each atom is capable in the lowest analysis only of mechanical actions, and these generate force. Heat is a mode of motion, and is simply an expression of mechanical force. So you rise up through all this physical force, and all claim to be equivalent and capable to be transformed one into the other, and then mechanical to vital force, and then vital to mental force. What does this mean? It means when you explain all the physical world by molecular motion that it is mechanical in its very scope and nature, and cannot go beyond it. And then as light and heat and electricity explain life, and life explains thought, then heat is thought, and feeling but a molecular motion at the last. If a man is capable of thinking this, then I acknowledge that for such a man for all time the supernatural is impossible, and so is all religion, and all hope in God, and all hope of immortality. If the soul has power of originating action, and power of discerning immutable truths and coming face to face with infinity; if it has power of moral determination, then I say the whole ground of this mechanical, materialistic objection is swept from under their feet now and forever.

Rev. L. T. Townsend, D.D., of the Boston Theological Seminary, then took the stand to discourse on "The Latest Results of Scientific Investigations, and the Bearings of the Bible Idea of Heaven." Dr. Townsend is well known to our own Church and beyond its pale as the author of "Credo," "Sword and Garment," "God-man," and other works of great interest to the Christian scholar.

His lecture was rather the apex and fitting conclusion to the series of admirable addresses pertaining to the relations between science and religion, and the whole drift of his argument was an endeavor to demonstrate that there is no antagonism between the two; they are all parts of one great truth, chapters of one great volume, and only seem antagonistic

because our eyes are too dim to see all the connecting lines and fill up all the chasms.

Darwin worked twenty years in the discovery of facts upon which to base his development theory; but his facts, so far as they are facts, and not theories, furnish data upon which to build religious as well as physical facts. To Darwin, therefore, as a gatherer of facts, the metaphysician and the theologian are under heavy obligations.

Herbert Spencer employed a still greater number of years in collecting facts to support his theory of the normal and the abnormal; but his facts have their bearing not only upon the theories of social conduct, but also upon all our views of moral and religious life and character. To him, therefore, as a fact gatherer, the naturalist and the religionist are likewise under no trifling indebtedness. To other men no less eminent in England, France, Germany, and America, we are all under profound obligations for their untiring and unwavering search and research; and we may add that it is only when these men become self-opinionist, when they acknowledge nothing beyond the range of their own observations—just as, when the man delving in the earth denies that there are stars, or when the star-gazer denies that there are earth caverns, or when the physicist denies the facts of the metaphysician, or when together they deny the facts of physical life and experience—that we are forced to stand aloof somewhat. Especially is this the case when these investigators, men of science, who are apt to forget that they are not scientific universalists but only specialists, confining their observations and experiments within the limits of their favorite pursuits, deduce those conclusions which they take to apply to the universe at large. But while their facts are invaluable, their conclusions, or rather the application of their conclusions, may be utterly erroneous. It must, therefore, also be evident that the man who stands aloof, and on a plane above all observations and experimenters, and yet friendly to all, and receiving the facts of all, is the only man of all who is qualified to make universal deductions, who holds the entire volume in his hand, instead of a volume or page; he is a universal scientist. When he considers these matters in the school of all arts and sciences, and draws these conclusions from the accumulation of facts furnished by the scientists of every school, he becomes the philosopher of philosophers, he is the prince of philosophers; and when this philosopher seeks to apply such deductions to the human race for its guidance and elevation, then he becomes the prince of philanthropists also. And it is on this ground that the philosophers and scientists of the day stand universally above the skeptic and the disbeliever. That is to say, when, for instance, Darwin insists on remaining with the earth-digger, his conclusions were applied to earth-works and to comparative physiology, but not necessarily to the within and the beyond. He will see development and order according to physical law, but will not see,

cannot see, God and the human soul. When Herbert Spencer allows himself to see nothing but animal man, his conclusions will apply to man and society, but not necessarily to God and the invisible. Now, if these eminent scientists would add to their present accumulation of facts the facts gleaned by other observers and experimenters, the facts, for instance, of religious experience and Christian consciousness, they would modify their conclusion and become princes of science and philosophy.

From this introduction we may truly say that Dr. Townsend evolved an address of singular beauty and thrilling power. It was a splendid defense of Bible truth, and with a master hand laid bare the limping fallacies and gaping arguments of those who would hound on science to question, sneer at, and attack Bible truths. It certainly gave unbounded satisfaction to many that were groping for light in the confusing labyrinth that skeptical scientists had prepared for them, and raised many an ardent Christian's soul from a state of fear and anxiety to a condition of perfect confidence that all is right and safe in the hands of God, whose works and words are destined to outlive and overwhelm the sneers and doubts of those who, knowing but *little* of this great scheme of creation, assume to know *all*, and put limits to God's own power. We would gladly quote more of the lecturer's own words were there time and space, but yield to the warning that we must now sum up the general results of this unique conference, and give an epitome of some of the most patent convictions that it seemed to make on the mind of those who took part in or listened to the proceedings.

In the first place we utter the convictions of all, perhaps, and certainly the loudly uttered assertions of many, that the programme was too full and the matter overdone. It was simply impossible for any one to listen to all the exercises with profit; the physical and the mental powers break down under such a continuous strain; it was like cramming for college examinations, and the moment one exercise was over it was not so much digested as crowded out to make room for a new occupant. And it is not a valid reply to this complaint that one need only take what he wants and leave the rest. Most of the visitors desired to have the whole, but found the strain too great for their capacities. One of the most efficient workers in the conference gives it as his opinion that it would have

been much better every way had the scientific lectures been distributed through the whole time of the assembly rather than crammed into three days. And we coincide in his views, for these reasons, among others: the attendance on these lectures was very excellent when we consider that they occurred during the opening days. But they were, or ought to have been, mainly for the great body of Sunday-school workers, many of whom could not be present so long before the assembly proper commenced, and who, therefore, missed much that would have been new, interesting, and valuable to them. Had the scientific and the religious features of the assembly been blended there would have been more logical harmony in the effort to unite and harmonize the two.

It is quite certain, we think, that the idea of a scientific course of investigation in connection with Sunday-school study worked its way into popularity, and that its influence will be widely felt and not forgotten by Christian workers. The time has come when the liberty of thought and investigation granted to men in religious matters leaves them free to find their pleasures and their profit in studying the higher and more abstruse sciences, if abstruse is a proper term in these days of "vulgarization" of science, by means of practical experiments and plain talks quite comprehensible to the uninitiated. These need some one to point out the way and describe to them the regions yet unexplored. The bold attacks of a few leading scientists of the world on the prominent positions of the Christian religion have led too many to believe that this feeling is quite general among scientific men. Now it is well to have some very effective means of curing this error, for it is not true. All through the course of history nearly all the leaders in scientific investigation have been Christian men. Now and then only some noted scientist has gained an unenviable reputation by boldness rather than by a display of scientific acumen, and the opposition that he has thus evolved has induced him to go still farther in his dangerous path, because it is so gratifying to his vanity to see his name in every journal and hear it pronounced by many lips.

But there is a host of noble names in the fore front of scientific investigation for ages whose voices all spoke praise to the Deity. If there are now Tyndalls and Huxleys, and Spencers

and Darwins, have there not been Newtons, and Galileos, and Davys, and hosts of others of firm religious faith? And were there not on the grounds of Chautauqua some of the most noted scientific men of our land, all using their knowledge and their power to show their belief in God and illustrate the beauty and harmony of his works? The very presence of these men, and the confidence with which they grappled with the augury, filled many a Christian breast with courage and secret satisfaction that God's works and words are still defended by the wisest and noblest of his children. And the crowds that gathered around the scientists and with thoughtful face and eager eye watched their every movement and listened to every word, emphatically answered the question as to the desirability and success of such teachings, and repaid the anxious heart that was to bear all the contingencies of failure.

But the Conference of Science was a success, and was voted so by the hearty thanks of the closing assembly to the man and men who made it so, and by the devoutly-sung doxology, "Praise God, from whom all blessings flow," to Him who gave the incense from the planting of the germ. And no sooner had the benediction of the great Teacher been invoked on the work of the past than the word went forth, "What of the future?" And the reply came, "It shall be an improvement of the past." The groves of Chautauqua shall be like those of ancient Greece, rich in the teachings of the wisest men of the land. The leaders in scientific thought shall again come here, when the year rolls around and brings to us a return of this pleasant season, to mingle their scientific knowledge and love of God with the accents of those who proclaim and teach his word as revealed through his prophets to his children. And then the very rocks and stones shall continue to testify of his marvelous works in making this earth a habitation for the children of men, and a probationary school to prepare them for the better land.

## ART. IV.—CATHOLICISM AND PROTESTANTISM AS PATRONS OF CHRISTIAN ART.

THE pernicious effects of the Reformation of the sixteenth century have been a favorite subject for comment by the Catholic historians, and been deeply deplored even by some of the Church of England. The assertion is reiterated that this great intellectual and religious convulsion was the fruitful cause of the spirit of modern rationalism, which sets aside a traditional faith and boldly challenges every thing which is urged upon its acceptance. Romanism holds Protestantism directly responsible for destroying the unity of the Church, and for shivering it into a multitude of unseemly fragments. It also charges that Protestantism was greatly wanting in æsthetic susceptibility—indeed, that it was essentially iconoclastic in spirit; that it caused a fearful destruction of works of art in the times immediately following the great schism, and that it ushered in a period of fearful art decadence. To examine the truth of these charges in so far as they concern art susceptibility and art inspiration, it will be necessary first to glance at the history of sacred art from the thirteenth century, that the condition of the public taste and the tendencies of art at the beginning of the sixteenth century may be understood.

The dawn of the revival is usually traced from the thirteenth century. The influences that had been powerful in developing that marvel of Christian art—gothic architecture—were multiplying in numbers and intensity. Before the close of this century chivalry and tournaments had been introduced even into Sweden. In Spain literature and science had awakened to a new life. The English Parliament had already been instituted. The Latins had conquered and sacked Constantinople. The weary despotism of ten centuries was yielding. Men were beginning to think and act as individuals. The occupation of Constantinople had re-established the intercourse between the East and West, and several Byzantine painters had emigrated to Germany and Italy. These were employed in the decoration of churches, chapels, and convents, and they naturally continued that traditional style that had ruled in the Orient for more than seven centuries. Few who have not

made these art-works a special study are aware how meager in treatment, how rigid in form, how repulsive in expression, and how limited in range, are the works of this period. At Pisa and Sienna these Byzantine artists had established schools, but none of their pupils yet ventured further than to copy and reproduce what was already at hand.

Nicholas Pisano (1231) first broke away from this bondage, marked out new paths, and attempted a new treatment. Feeling this inspiration, and touched with a measure of that warmth that had begun to thaw the frigidity of the centuries, Cimabue threw over his celebrated Madonna the radiance of hope, and gave to the divine Infant an expression of benignant invitation. The terrible severity that had caused the worshiper to tremble in the presence of Christ and the saints was now relaxed. "It was Cimabue's greatest glory, however, that he was the master of Giotto." The pupil carried the study of form and coloring far beyond his master's teachings. Nature had been the first instructor of this great genius while as a shepherd-boy he tended his father's flocks in the quiet valley of Vespignano. His poetical nature had, doubtless, been greatly stimulated by the companionship and writings of those immortal men—Coryphæi of their own, and towering in every age, Petrarch and Dante. His characteristic independence of thought, his exceptional freedom from the superstitions of his day, and his broad common sense, led him to adopt the best means to realize his ideals. Thus he not only greatly modified and improved the old, but did that characteristic work of true genius—gave to the world new art creations. Cimabue and Giotto were the fair dawn of that mid-day splendor of art that burst upon the world three centuries later in the matchless works of Da Vinci, Raphael, and Michael Angelo.

From the extant works of these artists it is evident that the hard, tyrannical dogmatism of the Byzantine school was then broken. In sacred art the thought had passed from a *theological* to a *religious* type. During the following century the imitators of Giotto, while yet restrained by the prevailing opinions in theology, reveal in their mode of treating religious subjects an increasing freedom. While Mariolatry is well-nigh supreme, and the Virgin is the central figure, yet the treatment now is more chaste and spiritual. The aim of the

artist is now the representation of *spiritual* beauty. The portrait of this period has been declared to be "an abounding religiousness struggling between a subjection to the traditions of the Church and the leadings of its own conscious powers." Notwithstanding the imperfection of drawing, the harshness of outline, and the strong tendencies to exaggeration, the religious artists of the fourteenth and the early part of the fifteenth centuries display a fervency of feeling, an unfeigned humility, an earnestness of soul, and a genuine reverence for the forms of the Church, that render their works a deserving study to every lover of the spiritual.

From the early revival to the first quarter of the fifteenth century art had been almost exclusively employed upon religious subjects. Take, for example, the life of John the Baptist, wrought out in 1330 by Andrea Pisano on the bronze doors of the Baptistry of St. John at Florence. The treatment is pure and simple, and intensely Christian. Likewise Ghiberti, in the next century, on the other two doors of the same baptistry, has represented the scenes from the Old Testament and from the life of Christ in a manner full of chasteness and spirit. Yet in Ghiberti's work there are clear indications of a growing naturalism.

During the fifteenth century two opposite tendencies are observed: One proposed attainment of beauty as an end; it interrogates nature, studies the effect of light and shade, and uses all possible appliances to secure this result. The other values physical beauty not as an end but as a means. With the latter school physical beauty is only desirable as it reveals spiritual loveliness. The feelings of these schools must have been very different as they attempted a subject of sacred art. One would seek a model in nature. If a Madonna is to be portrayed, the voluptuous beauty of a favorite is transferred to the canvas. Mere surface qualities are the result. No genuine religiousness pervades this school. The name only is preserved; yet even this is too often a glaring offense, a solemn mockery. The other school, called not inappropriately the Mystical, is best represented by that wonderful monk, Fra Angelico, in whose character true modesty, genuine sanctity, and matchless genius, so beautifully blended. With him art was a kind of religion. To paint a sacred subject was an act

of devoted piety. His biographer tells us with long-continued fasting and earnest prayer he prepared himself for his work—with what a feeling of conscious inspiration he executed it. Baptized, as he believed, with the Holy Ghost, his soul illuminated by celestial wisdom, his imagination kindled by a live coal from off the altar of sacrifice, Angelico expressed in his paintings a beauty, a spiritual loveliness, a depth of religious feeling, an ecstasy of hope and joy, and a heavenly sweetness, that have never been equaled. As we study the "Singing Angels" and the various other figures in his inimitable "Coronation of the Virgin," we feel assured that these are his own spiritual creations—entirely above mere copies—so varied, and yet so like in earnestness and purity, that they must be regarded as the products of his own deep religious contemplation. The expressions of the enthusiastic traveler, Holtzman, after he had studied his works at Florence, are just and true: "Here in Florence he seems to me like a faithful gardener, who understands how to transplant with tenderest care the beauty, blooming in Paradise, all fresh with life and health, into the soil of this poor earth. What pure reflection of divine rapture falls upon these faces! Here in the created is the echo of the Creator."

Bold investigators had already questioned the assumed prerogatives of the Church. Jerome of Prague and Huss had spoken and suffered; their ashes had proved good seed, and had fallen on receptive soil. The spirit of daring adventure had thrust men out into all lands; mind was stimulated for higher and still bolder flights. Art shared this impulse. It, too, was already loosing itself from the trammels of the Church. Invention was now rife. Already was the love of the antique greatly strengthened. The taste for the classical was reviving. Characters from sacred and profane history were now grouped together in the same painting. Perugino now associated in the same fresco, at Perugia, Moses, David, Isaiah, Daniel, John the Baptist, with Pythagoras, Socrates, Pericles, and Fabius Maximus. By the middle of the fifteenth century, Art, that had originally been a profession in the interest of the Church, was becoming rapidly secularized. But the scathing invectives and matchless eloquence of Savonarola were powerless to arrest the insetting tide of æsthetic and religious degeneracy. For a brief season

only did the sentiments of this great reformer impress the public heart. In vain did he utter his stern protest against the increasing superficiality and irreligiousness of art. His words of warning should sound in the ears of every age: "Only in a *formal* sense can beauty be represented as symmetry and harmony; in its vital essence it is the reflection of the godlike in the creature. Mark that man as he prays, as the divine effulgence illuminates his soul! When such a one returns from prayer, his face beams with the beauty of God, and his expression is that of an angel."

The papal court contributed largely to this degeneracy. No throne was ever disgraced by greater monsters of cruelty and lust than are found among the Borgia. Art, as prostitute as in the age of the Cesars, and artists, now degraded to basest sycophants, attempted the apotheosis of these bloody despots. Think of a Borgia as savior crowning his mistress queen of men and of angels! Little improvement in morals was witnessed under the Medici. Yet the brilliant galaxy of artists of this period has ever since been the marvel of the world. The works of Da Vinci, Angelo, Raphael, (each emphatically his own,) are incomparable. As a portraiture of character, probably Da Vinci's "Last Supper" has never been equaled. The "Christ" of this painting has never been excelled. Michael Angelo's "Prophets and Sibyls," in the Sistine Chapel, and his "Moses," are marvels of grandeur and power. Raphael's "Sistine Madonna," "Transfiguration," "St. Cecilia," etc., are wonderful revelations and interpretations of truth. With the most enthusiastic admirers we gladly recognize Leonardo as "a most profound and original thinker, the greatest mathematician and most ingenious mechanic of his time; architect, chemist, engineer, musician, poet, painter!—the miracle of that age of miracles!" we grant all that has been claimed for Michael Angelo; we indorse the statement that to a rare union of grace and versatility as an artist Raphael added "a bright, generous, genial, gentle spirit, the most attractive manners, and the most winning modesty."

Indeed, the opinion of the half-crazed Fuseli might be accepted as approximate truth:—

Michael Angelo planned for painting what Homer had planned for poetry, namely, the epic part, which, with the utmost simplic-

ity of the whole, should unite magnificence of plan and endless variety of subordinate parts. . . . That character and beauty were admitted only so far as they could be made subservient to grandeur. . . . Hence a beggar rose from his hand the patriarch of poverty, the hump of his dwarf is impressed with dignity; his women are molds of generation, his infants teem with the man, his men are a race of giants. . . . While Michael Angelo had no infancy, Raphael Sangio we see in his cradle, we hear him stammer; but *propriety* rocked the cradle, and *character* formed his lips.

Indeed, no one can deny that, under the hands of Da Vinci, M. Angelo, and Raphael, typical forms reached their highest development, and perfection of *composition* was closely approximated. But that these great artists received their inspiration from the spirit of the Catholic Church of the sixteenth century cannot be honestly pretended. Rather were the influences inspiring these great works absolutely foreign to the principles then recognized by this Church. The character of Michael Angelo was as essentially Protestant as that of Savonarola, whose early friend and admirer he was, and whose fiery discourses were his favorite study. Buonarotti lived in a world of thought totally different from that of the great mass of even the ecclesiastical princes of his day. The garden of Grecian statuary at Florence reveals the chief source of the inspiration of his genius.

So much for painting and sculpture. The study of architecture is equally instructive. From the period just prior to the Reformation, church building in Italy received a wonderful impulse. South of the Alps the Gothic style had never been a favorite; indeed, it was hardly practiced in the Italian peninsula prior to the thirteenth century, and then not in its purest form. The spirit of trust and of aspiring devotion, so well typified by the Gothic architecture, seemed little at home where a spiritual despotism had been so long predominant. Vain dreams of a holy Roman empire had been indulged by temporal princes, but all the essential elements of this absolutism were found in the Roman hierarchy. So that the representative building of the Catholicism of this period—Saint Peter's at Rome—stands as a monument of the idea of Roman imperialism. Its spirit is Roman, not Christian. When Michael Angelo said of its dome, "I will hang up the Pantheon in mid-

air," he insensibly revealed the inspiration of the building. It stands as a monument of genius; but it is a genius inspired with the spirit of pagan antiquity, and not by the spirit of trusting, aspiring Christianity. It stands more as a gratification of selfish ambition than as an offering of humble hearts to the Lord Christ. The very means by which funds for its erection were obtained form the most eloquent commentary on the condition of the Church, and on the spirit of the projectors and patrons of this work. Money from those damnable indulgences, which were peddled throughout Europe as cheap merchandise, went into its walls. Lying to men, robbing God, profaning the holy offices of Christ, periling eternal interests—these contributed its materials. Not a stone laid in this monumental Church that did not imperil an immortal soul. Taine is perhaps too caustic in saying, "The builders of St. Peter's were simply pagans in fear of damnation, and nothing more. All that is sublime in religion, such as tender effusions in the presence of a compassionate Saviour, the fear of conscience before a just Judge, the strong lyric enthusiasm of the Hebrew before an avenging God, the expressiveness of a free Greek genius before natural and joyous beauty—all these sentiments were wanting in them." Yet it is true that the spirit of St. Peter's is not Christian. So with many of the churches of the Jesuits, the most legitimate offspring of Rome. These are usually beautiful, often charming, not infrequently gorgeous in adornings and incomparably rich in furnishings; yet they are usually Roman in spirit, and the life and liberty of the Gospel find in these no congenial representative home.

Contrariwise in Germany and in all the continental lands that embraced the reformed doctrines, ecclesiastical building almost entirely ceased during the last half of the sixteenth century. But the causes of this are far other than a hatred of art, or a spirit of indifference. All reactions are excessive; this one of the Reformation was most violent. The struggle was for life. All merely artistic or æsthetic questions were now swallowed up in the pressing necessities of the desperate contest. Then followed the desolating thirty years' war, from whose awful ruin Germany can never recover. Remembering that a degree of leisure and a surplus of wealth are the almost indispensable conditions of extensive art patronage and cultivation,

we should not be surprised at the fewness of imposing ecclesiastical structures which arose in northern Europe. Nevertheless, Protestantism has not infrequently been more careful to preserve the medieval beauty and simplicity and the purity of architectural style than the Catholic Church itself. Let the visitor to the city of Nürnberg compare the Church of St. Lawrence with that of Notre Dame. The former, which was founded by a pious artistic feeling truly original and charming, has been preserved unchanged, as the Reformation found it; while the latter, which has been given over to Catholic worship, has been largely modernized and ornamented in such tawdry and mannered style as to offend and disgust. Likewise, when we compare the most noted modern church of Catholic lands (St. Paul's in Ostia, at Rome) with the completion of the Cologne Cathedral by Protestant gifts, and largely by the aid of Protestant princes, we are loth to believe that the spirit of Protestantism can be hostile to architectural beauty. The interior of the immensely costly St. Paul's in Ostia professes to be an imitation of the early Christian basilica. While this is immense and simple, yet it is cold in effect, and its exterior, in tower and façade, is a conglomeration of varied styles jumbled together in such inextricable confusion as to remind the visitor of the crazy freaks of a drunken man. On the contrary, the Cologne Cathedral is being finished in the same purity and beauty of style in which it was conceived five hundred years ago. (See Hase, *Protestantische Polemik*, p. 601.)

When we examine the history of the Phonetic arts—music, poetry, and oratory—we find that the record of Protestantism is especially honorable; indeed, she has here achieved very marked triumphs. Brendel (*Geschichte der Musik*, Band I, sec. 8) has remarked that while music was carefully cultivated among the Greeks, the results attained were comparatively meager. This came from no lack of talent, but rather because music found there no truly congenial soil. Music is eminently the art of the emotions. As such it expresses the innermost feelings of the soul. But this inner world could not be moved by the cold and cheerless system of heathenism; it could first be reached and stirred by the warmer and more genial influence of Christianity. Just as far, then, as the distinctive spirit of Christianity is preserved in any system will it fulfill the con-

ditions of the production and patronage of a superior sacred music; contrariwise, in so far as there is a return to the spirit of heathenism by any nominally Christian Church, to that extent will the conditions of high musical creation be wanting. That the Romish Church imbibed much of this spirit was pointed out by Zuinglius in his controversy with the hierarchy when he charged that it was a heathenish corruption of pure Christianity. And many able writers on Christian doctrine have boldly reiterated this change. (De Valenti, Neander, Hase, etc.) The music used in the Church service prior to the middle of the sixteenth century was mostly indifferent, and poorly adapted to the sacredness of worship. The rude beginnings of the Oratorio, in the attempts of St. Philip Neri to draw away the crowd from the influence of the Roman theater, are most instructive. The spirit of Romanism was revealed in seizing upon whatever was striking and dramatic to arrest the attention of the populace. Secular melodies had been freely accepted by this Church, and were the suggestion of the music for the most sacred festivals. The names of masses were sometimes derived from the initial words of these secular songs that were accustomed to be used in most indecent relations. "The Armed Man," "the Jolly Red Nose," "Kiss me, dear," as names of sacred music suggest their origin. So wide-spread had become this degeneracy that the Council of Trent deemed it important to give the subject a thorough and protracted discussion. Yet the suggestions made during its twenty-second sitting were too little heeded. Even in our time, some of the musical performances even of St. Peter's and the Sistine Chapel provoked the remark of Felix Mendelssohn, that to him their singing sounded like the efforts of a lot of men who are maliciously squabbling to drown each other by their brawling.

In this connection is suggested the name of Palestrina, the prince of Italian composers of sacred music, the pride of Catholicism. But it must be remarked that Palestrina is as distinctly Protestant in the spirit of his music as was Michael Angelo in his art creations. Palestrina was the pupil of Goudimel, who set to music the Psalms of Clement Marot, and afterward suffered martyrdom as a Huguenot on St. Bartholomew's day. Moreover, Palestrina's wonderful service to music was only one result of the strong reactionary influence of Protestantism upon

the Catholic Church in reforming its morals and its forms of worship. Goudimel's music has continued prominent in the worship of the Reformed Church to the present day, and the long line of able writers of sacred music, as Tallis, Hans Walter, Rumpf, Schütz, Bach, Handel, Hiller, Bennett, Rinck, Mason, and others, illustrates the liberal cultivation and patronage of sacred music on the part of Protestant Christianity. Equal musical genius is found in the Catholic Church. Hayden, Mozart, and Beethoven were all in this communion. Yet not one of these incomparable masters is influenced to any considerable extent by the spirit of the Romish Church. Hayden was outwardly a Catholic, adhering to the forms of antiquity; inwardly and in his works he lives and moves in a totally different world. Mozart leaps all the barriers of Church authority, and in his methods contradicts many of the fundamental principles of his communion; while with Beethoven this lack of harmony of profession and life is most manifest and outspoken. With all these musical Coryphæi is the spirit of the Church of the mediæval centuries entirely without authority. Both in secular and sacred music they entirely break away from all these restraints, and created their immortal works in accordance with that peculiar and darling principal of Protestantism—the unrestrained freedom of individual genius.*

The comparative examination of the poetry and oratory of these two branches of Christendom constitutes an interesting and instructive study, but the limits of this paper will allow us to glance only at the sacred lyrics of the two communions. The history of hymnology, since the sixteenth century, will show the great superiority in number, in earnest devotion, glowing fervor, and deep spiritual insight of the hymns of the lands which accepted the Reformation. In the Lutheran Church alone are found more than 80,000 of these hymns. It is difficult to estimate the wealth of spiritual treasure bequeathed to the Church by the long line of Protestant writers of sacred lyrics. Luther, almost the prince of them all, Paul Fleming, Schirmer, Zinzendorf, the Wesleys, Watts, Toplady, Lavater, Novalis, Arndt, Knapp, and a host of others, have comforted repentant souls, have stimulated religious life, and have lifted trusting hearts toward heaven on

* See Brendel, *Geschichte der Musik.*

the wings of rapturous praise. It has been the especial bequest of Protestantism to the Church of believers to give to the congregation sacred lyric wedded to sacred music, and to realize the exhortation of the psalmist: "Let all the people praise Thee."

Nor is the statement (so freqnently reiterated) that the Romish service is more æsthetic than that of Protestantism, the result of the careful study of the central principles of the two systems. We hear much of the baldness of the Protestant service, of the lack of artistic accompaniment, and much is said by tourists to the old world of the grandeur of the Catholic ritual. We believe that this view is radically erroneous. It comes from confounding semi-barbaric pomp with the genuinely and intrinsically beautiful and sublime. Years ago Hengstenberg wrote:—

> The opinion that the Romish worship is more poetic than the Protestant has widely obtained, and even now controls many weak natures. Yes, if poetry consists in mere mechanical forms and surface ornamentation for delighting the sensuous nature, then this opinion might be just. But poetry is soul, which speaks to soul again; and the simple singing the hymns of a Luther, or Paul Gerhard, out of the heart of a living communion, is more poetical than all the sensual gratification of the eye and ear afforded by the most pompous Catholic ceremony.*

It is somewhat remarkable that a Protestant of an entirely different school, in an estimate of the relative effect of Romish and Protestant ritual, entirely agrees in spirit with this remark of the high Lutheran, Hengstenberg.†

2. During the latter half of the sixteenth century Christian art rapidly declined, and at the close of this century it had reached a stage of great degeneracy. Not only the number of superior *works*, but also of superior *artists*, had greatly diminished. Grüneisen has well said: "When a great genius departs this life he may and must impress his own powers, unconquered by death, on his surviving works; but very rarely does he bequeath these powers to his followers."‡ The excellence of Raphael and his contemporaries being well-nigh absolute, a decadence might be expected. But we have indicated

* Hengstenberg, in *Ev. Zeitung.*

† See E. E. Hale in *Ch. Union*, August 13, 1873.

‡ *De Protestantisme*, p. 4.

that the prime cause of the decline in pure spirituality in art lay far back of the Reformation; indeed, it was the legitimate fruit of that degeneracy which was the occasion of rousing the spirit of protest in the bosom of the Church, and of leading the Reformers to assume an attitude of opposition and independence. The circumstances attending the beginnings of Protestantism were confessedly very unfavorable to the encouragement of the fine arts. Attention was absorbed in the solution of other and more pressing questions. Violent agitation is generally unpropitious to art encouragement. A degree of leisure and accumulated wealth are the usual conditions of æsthetic culture and art patronage. For one hundred and fifty years after the beginning of the great Reformation these conditions were almost totally wanting to Northern Europe. Human history scarcely presents a period of more profound and universal agitation. The fierce conflicts of temporal princes on the battle-field were surpassed by the struggles of intellectual and theological athletes. The picture presented is not that of the overpowering mastery of one sovereign, or of one party, and the consequent accumulations of the wealth of subject provinces in the capital of the conqueror. We witness no grand triumphal processions, no wars of permanent settlement, no final solution of religious problems; but continental Europe presented, down to the peace of Westphalia, a picture of evenly-balanced, destructive, and exhaustive warfare. However this question of adverse influences may be answered by different schools of history, all thoughtful persons must feel a common regret at the wanton destruction of rarest works of art during these years of convulsion. The fiercest spirit of iconoclasm seemed rampant. The French Huguenots burned indiscriminately the altars and statues, wherever found. During three days of popular frenzy the inhabitants of Brabante and Flanders laid waste more than four hundred churches. The same spirit involved nearly all Belgium in the most calamitous loss of sacred relics, and prevailed very widely throughout Scotland, Switzerland, Bohemia, and some parts o Germany.

It is a noteworthy fact that with the mad zeal which mani fested itself in this indiscriminate ruin the leaders of the Re formed Churches had no sympathy. This destruction wa

largely the work of the lawless rabble under the leadership of frenzied fanatics. Even John Knox earnestly exerted himself to check this spirit in Scotland, and in the Netherlands no prominent leader of the Protestant party was guilty of this vandalism.

In Zürich still stands the church in which Zuinglius preached a purer faith. In the interior the visitor finds no trace of ornamentation, not a statue, or picture, or any such thing; but the walls are as plain and white, and the seats as simple, as in the Moravian church at Herrnhut. The unthinking traveler is ready to conclude that here, surely, are the footprints of the stern reformer, who is wanting in all æsthetic sensibility, and whose warrior hand would sweep away without one soul-twinge even the masterpieces of art. Yet we find him in the retirement of home relieving his severer studies and his racked brain by the practice of music, changing from harp to flute, and giving his buoyant nature free vent in light fantastic strains. We hear his cheerful, and even mirthful, conversations with bosom friends; at times we note even an exuberance of joy. Zuinglius was no harsh, fanatical hater of sacred art; his was no stolid soul, insensible to æsthetic charms. He was only an honest Christian, zealous for the true welfare of the people and for the glory of God. Turning from his private life to his own utterances, made under the most solemn and trying circumstances, we are further confirmed in this opinion. Hear him:—

> No one is so foolish as to believe that statues and paintings ought to be destroyed, if the people manifest for them no reverence. Only those images ought to be removed that cause piety to stumble, or that threaten our faith in God. Of this class are such as bear the human countenance, which are placed in front of altars or churches, even though they have not been reckoned among things devoted to God. because age itself renders an image sacred. In like manner we do not think that those figures that are inserted for the purpose of ornamenting the windows should be disturbed, provided they represent nothing base, because no one is in danger of worshiping these. . . . We will not speak at all of feelings and preferences in this matter; *for none have greater admiration for paintings, statues, and portraits than we; but whatever thus offends piety ought not to be tolerated, but should be destroyed by the firm authority of the magistrates.*

Calvin, a man of more culture, and, in some respects, of sterner type than Zuinglius, has recorded similar opinions of art. He writes:—

Nor yet am I affected with that degree of superstition as to suppose that no images at all ought to be tolerated. But inasmuch as painting and sculpture are God's gifts, I only demand that the use of each shall be pure and legitimate. For why should that which God has conferred upon us for his glory and our own welfare be not only degraded by absurd use, but even turned to our own ruin? It follows, therefore, that only those things ought to be sculptured and painted which are designed to appeal to the eye. The majesty of God, which so far transcends the power of vision, should not be marred by unworthy images. To this class [of legitimate subjects] belong historic personages and events; to some extent, also, images and representations of forms that have no regard to historic truthfulness. The former class have a certain value for purposes of teaching and admonition; what the latter class can impart, aside from pleasurable amusement, I do not see. Yet it is certain that the images that have been set up in the churches belong for the most part to this latter class. Hence it is just to conclude that these have been placed there not with judgment and discretion, but through a vain and thoughtless spirit. I decline to point out how defective, and, for the most part, indelicate are these portrayals, how without restraint the painters and sculptors here wanton: I only say that even if no vice inheres in these works, they are nevertheless valueless for purposes of edification and instruction.

Calvin here expresses an opinion more extreme than would have been accepted by Zuinglius; nevertheless, he appears to be more appreciative of art than his friends or his enemies are wont to suppose. We are not interested to criticize the æsthetic propriety of the opinions expressed in these quotations; we believe that they find sympathy with a very considerable class of tourists as they come into the presence of some of the nude and shameless paintings and statues of European galleries. This one thing is certainly clear, namely: that the object of Calvin's hostility is not art *per se* but rather its prostitution to base and unworthy ends.

Beza, the companion of Calvin, one of the most noted religious poets of his age, discourses in very similar spirit, and makes like careful discriminations, thus vindicating the Reformation from the charge of hostility to art. He says:—

We recognize that painting and sculpture have great utility in civil affairs; of this there can be no question whatever. . . . We

do not condemn, but, on the contrary, approve, these arts, and aver that they ought to be cultivated because useful to the State. But while we do not deny the utility of art, either pictured or sculptured, by which events in sacred history may be represented, we do not readily admit them to places consecrated to worship, since we think it especially unsafe to place sculptured images in the churches. This is not because we suppose this is unlawful or impious *per se*, but on account of the mournful appearance presented by congregations in Romish churches; which sad spectacle seems to date its origin from the use of images and pictures.

All are familiar with the love which Luther cherished for art. Less thorough in breaking away from the Romish ritual than his fellows, he inclined to retain in the forms of service much that the Reformed Church regarded dangerous to the edification and purity of worship. He that could find relief from the vexatious and overwhelming burdens of life in the production of poetry and music, often had his great soul tried by the rude, unfeeling iconoclasts of his day. He says:—

I am by no means of the opinion that the Gospel teaches that all art should be destroyed and should disappear, as some fanatics hold; but I would gladly see all the fine arts, especially music, pressed into the service of Him who has created and given them to us.

He sternly rebuked Carlstadt for his false notions of reform:—

Since the evil disposition in Carlstadt is so stubborn, I can less than ever yield to his obstinacy and insult. I will first speak of images under the law of Moses; next according to the spirit of the Gospel. I affirm that, according to the law of Moses, no other image than that of God was interdicted. But a crucifix or the image of a saint is not forbidden to us.

Again he writes:—

I have seen and heard the iconoclasts themselves read out of my German Bible; I also know that they have this Bible in their possession. Now there are many pictures in these books of God, of angels, of men, and of beasts; especially in the Apocalypse of John, and in the books of Moses and Joshua. So that we earnestly request them to permit us to do what they themselves practice, namely: that we may paint such pictures on the walls for their better remembrance and understanding, since they are as harmless when on walls as when in books. It is better to paint on the walls representations of the creation of the world, the building of the ark by Noah, and other events in sacred history than some shameless profane subject. Indeed, God willing, I

would persuade the noble and the wealthy that it would be a Christian work to paint the scenes of the entire Bible on the walls of houses, within and without, before the eyes of every one If it is not only not sinful but blessed to bear the image of Christ in the heart, why should it be regarded a sin to bear it in the eye. Surely the heart is of more consequence than the eyes, and it should be less defiled by sin; since in the heart is the proper residence and dwelling-place of God.

So much for the opinions of the chief reformers. They all go to show that with these earnest men there is a real appreciation of the beautiful—indeed, a true love of art. The whole force of their protest is directed against the shameful prostitution of sacred art to vulgar and unworthy ends, and against supplanting, by the adoration of images, the pure thoughts of God and Christ from the soul of the worshiper. The seeds of degeneracy had long before been sown. These men were struggling to cast into the oven the baneful harvest. The Reformation, so far from being the *cause* of the decadence of sacred art, was a protest against that spirit which was destroying the very capacity for high art—a spirit that had already produced a wide-spread moral degeneracy; had brought corruption into high places; had quenched the ardor of piety; had insinuated itself into the religious houses of every order; and had thoroughly relaxed the sinews of monastic discipline. It is believed that a like vindication of the reformers and the Reformation would appear on a careful comparison of the religious art of the lands that embraced the Reformed doctrines with that of nations that were little influenced by its spirit. This would form a suggestive chapter in the history of sacred art. It must suffice here to mention such men as Albert Dürer, in his latest works, Hans Holbein, and Lucas Cranach, as compared with Titian and Correggio; or later, Van Dyck and others, as contrasted with the brothers Carracci. Who can hesitate to accord to the north the greater depth, earnestness, religious fervor, and spirituality?

3. Some diversities of Catholicism and Protestantism, which would affect, to a degree, the respective attitudes of these confessions toward religious art, and determine how far the two systems furnish the necessary conditions of art stimulus and encouragement, need next to be examined. It is not the purpose of this paper to enter the field of religious polemics;

but it seems necessary to glance at the nature of these diversities in order to see clearly their effect not on questions of theology, Church life, ethics, etc., only, but also on questions of an æsthetic character. It should be distinctly understood that Catholicism and Protestantism have vastly more than merely formal or surface differences. They are radical and fundamental; they affect the foundations of faith and life. Möhler, one of the profoundest Catholic dogmatic writers of the present century, has most justly said: "The great rupture of the sixteenth century took its departure from the innermost and deepest profound of human history, since it had reference to the mode and means by which fallen man must come into fellowship with Christ and become partaker of the fruits of redemption." Indeed, it can be truly affirmed that no more distinct are the great oceanic currents that run side by side for a thousand miles without once commingling, than are these two tides of theologic thought. From the fundamental differences of opinion respecting the nature of the original, unfallen man, and the effects of transgression upon this nature, would also arise very diverse systems of soteriology. Catholic anthropology holds that the unfallen man was righteous by virtue of a supernatural working of divine grace upon him, and not by virtue of the action of the natural powers of the human soul. A true, life-giving knowledge was, therefore, in itself impossible; but a power must be superadded to raise this finite to a saving relationship to the infinite Creator. Luther says: The pure nature of man, proceeding from the word of power of the Creator, possessed absolutely *in itself* all the necessary capabilities for pleasing God. Specially the religious capabilities of the original man flourished under the favor of God by virtue of their own increated fullness of power. Catholicism says: The fallen man has experienced a *weakening* (*in deterius commutatum fuisse*) of his natural powers for good. Evangelical Protestantism says: By the loss of original righteousness the fallen man has experienced a *total depravity* of his spiritual nature, whereby he has become alienated from God and inclined to evil. This diversity of opinion respecting the nature of the unfallen man and the nature and effects of sin would occasion corresponding divergencies with respect to the ground and nature of justification, the nature and efficacy

of the sacraments, the whole theory of worship, and the nature, constitution, duties, and prerogatives of the Church. Without stopping here to compare these systems, we only remark that there appears in the Catholic theology more of superficiality; in that of Evangelical Protestantism more thorough radicalism. The original man of Catholicism was holy by virtue of an *added* power, (*dona supernaturalia;*) that of Protestantism was holy by *nature*, (*vere naturalem.*) The fallen man of Catholicism has lost only the *added* power; that of Protestantism lies in hopeless ruin.* The restored man of Catholicism can do something and merit something by this doing; that of Protestantism knows no possible merit of works. The trinne God is equally the sole object of true worship in both these systems. Yet, while the Catholic worshiper finds Christ not the only Mediator, but invokes and adores the virgin and the saints, the Protestant worshiper sees in Christ Jesus the *one* Mediator between God and man. While the Catholic worshiper is looking outward toward the virgin, and saints, and images, and relics, and shrines, and works of supererogation, and the cleansing fires of purgatory for means of salvation, the Protestant worshiper turns his thought inward to discover the attitude of the will, and to note and cherish a growing faith in the Son of God, and in the Holy Spirit, who is the promised sanctifier.

4. Another most important difference of these systems has reference to the grounds of authority and the right of private judgment; in other words, it respects the great question of freedom of thought and action.

As ground of authority in religious questions Catholicism says: Scripture, tradition, and the Church. "Tradition" has too often been the shibboleth of Rome. Its practice has been too much like that of Pharisaism in the Saviour's day—hiding the spirit and letter of the law under the traditions of men. Protestantism cries: "The Bible the word of God; this is the sole ground of authority, the source of religious enlightenment." Catholicism is ever looking to the past, and trying to press modern thought into the molds of bygone centuries. The genius of Protestantism does not propose to study the ancient Church and its pristine glory only, but to push forward the cause

* See Winer, *Comparative Symbolik*, ch. iv, v.

of God with all the appliances which the unfolding history of the race has placed at her command. Catholicism, like heathen art in its decrepitude from the time of Mark Aurelius, turns its weary eyes backward to find its golden age. Protestantism, like the earliest Christian art, is full of hope, and joy, and promise—projecting the grandest triumph of its Christ on the sky of the future. Theoretically Romanism binds the consciences of men, individual and collective, by the will of one man, and cries, "Here alone is the oracle of God; here immolate your personality; passive obedience is a means of salvation." Protestantism proposes to bring the individual soul into the conscious presence of the King Eternal, and says, "Here pay your *active, willing* obedience." Romanism has too often brought outward compulsion upon human mind as upon inert matter, to drive it hither and thither at pleasure. It has too often anathematized; it has hurled thunderbolts to frighten men to outward submission; it has abridged liberty; it has maimed, and shackled, and palsied the soul. Protestantism, like the Bible, and the God of its Bible, has come with reason, persuasion, and entreaty. It has come with threatening and with promise, with invitation and denunciation. It proffers illumination, guidance, and powerful incentive to lead the soul godward; but "it exhorts to an uncompelled, undamaged service of the man to God."* The wall of protection which the Almighty has thrown around every man's personality, and within whose sacred precincts he himself does not come unbidden, Romanism seeks to break down; Protestantism respects and guards. Romanism, like Jesuitism, its most powerful ally, treats man individual too much as a thing, a tool, a corpse, to be acted upon by external force, to be urged hither and thither at the will of another. Protestantism recognizes man individual as a spiritual force; he belongs to the realm of *powers*. Romanism dictates, excommunicates, and forces its dogmas upon its votaries. Protestantism proposes systems, expresses opinions, urges arguments, and gives a reason for the hope within it. It is not now claimed that the invariable *practices* of these rival systems are here described. That there have been instances of generous toleration within the Romish communion a L'Hopital and Lord Baltimore

* Isaac Taylor: "Loyola and Jesuitism."

abundantly witness; that bitterest intolerance has at times disgraced Protestantism, the Servetus affair must ever attest. Both communions have been at times unrelenting persecutors; both have invoked the aid of the civil power to suppress heresy; both have piled and lighted fagots to consume the unrecanting offender. Universal history utters its solemn warning against the danger of intrusting irresponsible power to *any party whatsoever*. Yet the conclusions of a writer who cannot be accused of concealing the short-comings of Evangelical Protestantism are forced upon us. "It can surely be no exaggeration to say that the Church of Rome has inflicted a greater amount of unmerited suffering than any other religion that has ever existed among mankind."* It is equally certain that in the indulgence of the spirit of persecution Protestantism has appeared more offensive than her rival, because it was in glaring contradiction to one of her dearest fundamental principles; while the violent suppression of heresy is not inconsistent with the teachings of the approved standards of the Catholic Church. Indeed, Romanism has manifested this spirit in a thousand ways, by cramping thought, by stifling investigation, and by putting shackles upon genius. The study of the literary policy of Rome, as found in her damnatory indexes and in the decisions of the Council of Trent, compels the conviction that the spirit of this Church toward literature and art is in the last extreme arbitrary and repressing.†

The application of these principles to our discussion is simple and manifest. All agree that freedom is the indispensable condition of art development and progress. Religious art, especially, languishes in the absence of liberty. The fixedness of type, and the centuries of stagnation while art was under the ecclesiastical control of the East, is an instructive example of this truth. We have already mentioned that this authority bound religious art in fetters for nearly a thousand years. This does not imply that the artist is not to consult tradition. To him, as well as to the religionist, is tradition invaluable, since by this means there is noted an historic progress and development. For this very reason, however, must the artist equally with the religionist and the scientist, the individual as well as the

* Leckey: "History of Rationalism," vol. ii, p. 46.

† See Mendham: "The Literary Policy of the Church of Rome Exhibited."

Church, remain unshackled by tradition. "To ascribe to tradition, or to any, even a classical rule, an absolutely binding value, would be as senseless as to prevent a tree from further growth because it *had hitherto been vigorous.* On the contrary, because growth is the very law of the tree, it must continue to grow if it would not wither and rot." * Just so because artists *have* created art forms, must they continue to create them under the largest freedom if they would avoid falling into a stiff, cold, and fatal mannerism. We do not mean by freedom any wild, unrestrained, or arbitrary exercise of power; this is *license*, not liberty. In political and social life liberty does not mean lawlessness; but living in accordance with the laws of our nature, modified only by the necessary limitations of society. So the artist must ever work under law in order to the exercise of his highest freedom, but this law cannot be imposed from without; it must be an impulse springing from his own native and distinct individualism. This law must not be to him an external, written canon, which he feels bound to observe, but a part of his own untrammeled, undamaged self. Since art, then, is an essentially organic process in the development of human civilization, it must have a freedom of adjustment to the shifting circumstances; and there only can it be a factor and true index of civilization where, unrestrained by external authority, it can embody in its works the changing spirit of the centuries. This is the peculiar doctrine of Protestantism; and by so much does this form of Christianity promote and stimulate the highest art culture.

5. In the examination of the opinion that Protestantism has been lacking in æsthetic susceptibility and has been indifferent to the patronage and encouragement of religious art, it has been seen that at the beginning of the sixteenth century there was in the bosom of the Catholic Church a fearful moral degeneracy which tended to destroy all capacity for high art; that the wonderful revival in art which was then witnessed was not due to the fostering spirit of the Romish Church, but depended on influences foreign to this Church; that the comparative sparseness of art works, especially architectural monuments, in Northern Europe was not owing to an indifference to, or hatred of, art, but to extreme poverty, to

* See Horwicz, *Æsthetik*, p. 210.

wasting wars, and to the seething agitation of more absorbing questions; that the leading Reformers, so far from being rudely iconoclastic, were themselves warm lovers of art, and were only striving to save the worshiper from temptation to idolatry; that in some respects, as in architecture, sacred lyric, and sacred music, Protestantism has demonstrated an equal, if not superior, creative power; that while both systems stand almost equally closely related by history and practice to the encouragement of Christian art, their diverse views of anthropology and soteriology have caused them to assume different attitudes—Catholicism inclining more to the real and the objective, Protestantism to the ideal and the subjective; and, finally, that Protestantism, by its declaration and defense of the doctrine of individual responsibility and individual freedom, has thus recognized the only true conditions of a high and progressive Christian art.

## Art. V.—MOHAMMEDANISM AND THE NEGRO RACE.*

The following article was originally written by its author for the "Methodist Quarterly Review," but was intercepted in England, published in "Frazer's Magazine," and then sent in a copy of the Magazine to us for republication. We had a right to object to the discourtesy of thus reducing us to a second-hand position. But as Professor Blyden was himself innocent of this discourtesy, and his article furnishes matter which our readers would unquestionably desire to have before them, we present it in our pages. We may here add that Mr. Blyden's articles formerly published in our Quarterly have attracted attention by the richness of their scholarship and their grace of style. One of the notes appended to this article indicates the fact that he claims a purity of Negro blood, and insists that the word Negro, which he proudly claims to be legitimate, honorable, and needing no euphemistic substitute, is entitled to an initial capital N. We fully agree with W. H. Seward, that "no man is fit to be President who spells [or pronounces] Negro with two g's."—Ed. Meth. Quar. Review.

To students of general literature in Europe and the United States, until within the last few years, the Orientals most celebrated in religion or politics, in literature or learning, were known only by name. The Oriental world, to the student

* The author of this article, a Negro of the purest African blood, is Mr. Edward W. Blyden, Principal of the Presbyterian High School, Liberia, West Africa.—*Ed. Fraser's Mag.*

aiming at practical achievements, presented a field of so little promise that he scarcely ever ventured beyond a distant survey of what seemed to him a boundless and impracticable area. But, thanks to the exigencies of commerce, to philanthropic zeal, and to the scientific impulse, the East is daily getting to be "nearer seen and better known," not only in its outward life, but in those special aspects which, in religion and government, in war and policy, differentiate Eastern from Western races. It has been recently stated by a distinguished authority that "the intimate acquaintance with the languages, thoughts, history, and monuments of Eastern nations is no longer a luxury, but a necessity." And the visit, within the last ten years, of Oriental rulers to Europe—the Sultan of Turkey, the Khedive of Egypt, the Shah of Persia, and the Seyyid of Zanzibar—has stimulated in the popular mind a livelier curiosity as to the character, condition, and influence of Mohammedan countries.

Drawn away from the beaten track of Roman and Greek antiquity by considerations for the most part of a material nature, and wandering into paths which heretofore were trodden only by such enthusiastic pioneers as Sir William Jones, the Western student finds rewards far rarer and richer than he had anticipated. And even those who have not the opportunity of familiarizing themselves with Oriental languages find enough in translations—inadequate and unsatisfactory as they often are—to inspire them with a desire not only to increase their acquaintance with Eastern subjects, but to impart the knowledge they glean to others.

To the latter class belongs Mr. R. Bosworth Smith, the author of the work before us.* He informs us at the outset that "the only qualification he would venture to claim for himself," as a writer on Islam, "is that of a sympathetic interest in his subject," his work having been "derived in the main from the study of books in the European languages."

Mr. Bosworth Smith, who is a graduate of one of the English universities of only twelve years' standing, and, therefore,

* "Mohammed and Mohammedanism."—Lectures delivered at the Royal Institution of Great Britain in February and March, 1874. By R. Bosworth Smith, M.A., Assistant Master in Harrow School, late Fellow of Trinity College, Oxford. London: Smith, Elder, & Co.

we gather, a comparatively young man, may be regarded as one of the earliest collateral results of that increased activity in Oriental research which Dr. Birch has told us "marks the advance of civilization." And if he does stand upon the shoulders of Caussin de Perceval, Sprenger, Muir, and Deutsch, he may, without immodesty, claim to be taller than they; for we are very much mistaken if his book does not form an important starting point on the road to a more tolerant—if not sympathetic—view among popular readers of the chief religion of the Oriental world. The works of the writers just mentioned were designedly not popular, but written by scholars for scholars, maintaining or opposing theories for the most part of merely literary or historical significance. Mr. Bosworth Smith has brought to his work not only a thorough appreciation of the literary and historical questions involved, but an earnest respect "for the deeper problems of the human soul," cherishing the sound and fruitful conviction, which he strives to impart to his readers, "that Mohammedans may learn much from Christians, and yet remain Mohammedans; that Christians have something at least to learn from Mohammedans, which will make them not less but more Christian than they were before."

Mr. Bosworth Smith pursues the discussion of this important subject, which, as a labor of love, he entered upon with a degree of earnestness, perspicuity, catholicity, and force of reasoning that renders his work not only most instructive, but highly interesting as an indication of the tendency and direction of cultivated thought in England. He has entered into the spirit of Islam in a manner which, but for the antecedent labors of Lane, Sprenger, Deutsch, and Weil, would be astounding in a Western scholar and an Englishman.

Dean Stanley's lecture on the same subject, though marked by the breadth of view, generous impartiality, and geniality of spirit which so honorably distinguish all the writings of that scholarly and Christian divine, is fragmentary—necessarily limited in its range by the nature and scope of the work. To

acknowledged or not, must be felt throughout the literary world. Such works as those of Maracci, Prideaux, and White, are hereafter impossible in polemico-religious literature. No cultivated man, however inquisitorial his temperament, will ever, in the future, be tempted—or at least yield to the temptation — to subject any religious system to the Procrustean ordeal.

And, so far as Islam is concerned, scholars are arising within its ranks imbued with Western learning, and taking the part not only of defenders of their faith, but of interpreters between the Eastern and Western world. It has recently occasioned some surprise and comment that a Mohammedan writer should have written an able work in the English tongue, "challenging European and Christian thinkers on their own ground."* Since the appearance of Syed Ahmed's essays, another work has appeared in the English language, written by a young Mohammedan, in which he has briefly, temperately, and ably discussed the various subjects in relation to which Islam is usually assailed.†

But it is not only in recent days, as the writer in the "British Quarterly Review" would seem to imply, that Mohammedans have availed themselves of the power of the pen in defense of their faith. There have always been, and there are now, able controversialists among them altogether unknown to Western fame. The celebrated work of Dr. Pfander, the Mizan-al-Hakk, attacking the Mohammedan system, has been reviewed in the Arabic language by a Mohammedan scholar, Rahmat Allah, in a learned and incisive reply, in which he reveals a marvelous acquaintance with European literature. We have heard of no attempt at a rejoinder to the work of Rahmat Allah. We saw a copy of this book in the hands of a West African Mohammedan at Sierra Leone, who was reading and commenting upon it to a number of his co-religionists.

We are glad to notice that Mr. Bosworth Smith's book has been republished in the United States, and that the able article

* "British Quarterly Review" for January, 1872, in a Review of "A Series of Essays on the Life of Mohammed," etc. By Syed Ahmed Khan Bahador, C.S.I. Vol. I. London: Trübner & Co. 1870.

† "Critical Examination of the Life and Teachings of Mohammed." By Syed Ameer Ali Moulvi, M.A., LL.B., of the Inner Temple, Barrister-at-Law, etc. London: Williams & Norgate. 1873.

of Deutsch on Islam has been reproduced in the same volume as an appendix. They are fit companions—*par nobile fratrum.* The traveler, contemplating a visit to Mohammedan countries, or the theologian wishing to get a clear view of a religious system which is shaping the destiny of millions of the race, may now carry in his pocket a complete compendium of Mohammedan literature. If we except the very remarkable article on the "Historical Statements in the Koran," written in 1832 by the then stripling reviewer, Mr. J. Addison Alexander, of Princeton, and the able "Review of the Koran," by Professor Draper, of the New York University, in his "History of the Intellectual Development of Europe," American scholarship has as yet, as far as we are aware, produced nothing of importance in this branch of literature.

The portion of the interesting work now before us, which we propose more particularly to notice, is that part of the first lecture which refers to the character and influence of Islam in Western and Central Africa. Dean Stanley says:—

> It cannot be forgotten that Mohammedanism is the only higher religion which has hitherto made progress in the vast continent of Africa. Whatever may be the future fortunes of African Christianity, there can be no doubt that they will be long affected by its relations with the most fanatical and the most proselytizing portion of the Mussulman world in its Negro converts.*

If this view be correct, then the Christian world cannot be indifferent to the discussion of a subject so full of importance affecting one branch of the philanthropic interests into which the Christian Church, more than ever before, is now pouring its most eager life.†

Three streams of influence have always penetrated into Negroland: one from Egypt through Nubia to Bornou and Hausa; another from Abyssinia to Yoruba and Ashantee; the third from the Barbary States across the Desert to Timbuctoo. By the first two Egypt and Arabia exchanged their produc-

* "Eastern Church," p. 259.

† Mr. Monier Williams, the Boden Professor of Sanscrit at Oxford, has recently expressed the opinion, in a paper read at the Conference on Foreign Missions held at the Cannon-street Hotel in London, (June 22, 1875.) that, unless a fresh and powerful impulse is given to Christian missionary effort, Mohammedanism will speedily overrun the whole African continent.

tions for the raw materials of Soudan. By the third the ports of the Mediterranean, through the Great Desert, having Timbuctoo as a center, became outlets for the wealth of Nigritia. Even in the days of Herodotus there appears to have been intercourse between the region of the Tsad and the Mediterranean, and the valuable products collected at various centers by the itinerant traffic, which still flourishes in the interior, shared by numerous caravans, found their way by means of Phenician ships to different countries of Europe and the Levant.

Central Africa has never been cut off commercially from European and Asiatic intercourse. But it was not until the ninth century of the Christian era that any knowledge of the true God began to penetrate into Negroland. To Akbah, a distinguished Moslem general, belongs the credit or discredit of having subdued North Africa to Islam. He marched from Damascus at the head of ten thousand enthusiastic followers, and in a short time spread his conquests along the shores of North Africa, advancing to the very verge of the Atlantic, whose billows alone checked his westward career.* But the energy which could not proceed westward turned northward and southward. In its southern progress it crossed the formidable wastes of the Sahara, penetrated into Soudan, and established the center of its influence at Timbuctoo. In less than a century from that time several large Nigritian tribes had yielded to the influence of Islam; and it shaped so rapidly the ideas, the manners, and the history of those tribes, that when in the Middle Ages Ibn Batoutah, an Arab traveler, visited those regions, he found that Islam had taken firm root among several powerful peoples, had mastered their life and habits, and dominated their whole social and religious policy. Among the praiseworthy qualities which attracted his attention as a result of their conversion, he mentions their devotion to the study of the Koran, and relates the following illustrative incidents, which we give in the French version now before us:—

Ils ont un grand zèle pour apprendre par cœur le sublime Coran. Dans le cas où leurs enfants font preuve de négligence à cet égard, ils leur mettent des entraves aux pieds et ne les leur ôtent pas qu'ils ne le sachent réciter de mémoire. Le jour de la fête, étant entré chez le juge, et ayant vu ses enfants enchainés, je lui dis:

* Gibbon's "Decline and Fall," etc., chap. li.

"Est ce que tu ne les mettras pas en liberté?" Il repondit: "Je ne le ferai que lorsqu'ils sauront par cœur le Coran." Un autre jour, je passai devant un jeune nègre, beau de figure, revêtu d'habits superbes, et portant aux pieds une lourde chaîne. Je dis à la personne qui m'accompagnait: "Qu'a fait ce garçon? Est-ce qu'il a assassiné quelqu'un?" Le jeune nègre entendit mon propos et se mit à rire. On me dit: "Il a été enchaîné uniquement pour le forcer à apprendre le Coran de mémoire." *

Mohammedanism in Africa counts in its ranks the most energetic and enterprising tribes. It claims as adherents the only people who have any form of civil polity or bond of social organization. It has built and occupies the largest cities in the heart of the continent. Its laws regulate the most powerful kingdoms—Futah, Masina, Haüsa, Bornou, Waday, Darfur, Kordofan, Senaar, etc. It produces and controls the most valuable commerce between Africa and foreign countries; it is daily gathering converts from the ranks of paganism; and it commands respect among all Africans wherever it is known, even where the people have not submitted to the sway of the Koran.

No one can travel any distance in the interior of West Africa without being struck by the different aspects of society in different localities, according as the population is pagan or Mohammedan. Not only is there a difference in the methods of government, but in the general regulations of society, and even in the amusements of the people. The love of noisy terpsichorean performances, so noticeable in pagan communities, disappears as the people come under the influence of Mohammedanism. It is not a fact that "when the sun goes down all Africa dances;" but it might be a fact if it were not for the influence of Islam. Those who would once have sought pleasure in the excitement of the tom-tom, now repair five times a day to the mosque, where they spend a quarter of an hour each time in devotional exercises. After the labors of the day they assemble in groups near the mosque to hear the Koran recited, or the Traditions or some other book read. In traversing the region of country between Sierra Leone and Futah Jallo in 1873, we passed through populous pagan towns, but the transition from these to Mohammedan districts was

* *Voyages d'Ibn Batoutah*, texte et traduction. Par Defremery et Sanguinetti, Paris, 1858, vol. iv, pp. 422, 423.

striking. When we left a pagan and entered a Mohammedan community, we at once noticed that we had entered a moral atmosphere widely separated from, and loftier far than, the one we had left. We discovered that the character, feelings, and conditions of the people were profoundly altered and improved.

It is evident that, whatever may be said of the Koran, as long as it is in advance of the Shamanism or Fetichism of the African tribes who accept it—and no one will doubt that Islam as a creed is an enormous advance not only on all idolatries, but on all systems of purely human origin—those tribes must advance beyond their primitive condition.

The Koran is, in its measure, an important educator. It exerts among a primitive people a wonderful influence. It has furnished to the adherents of its teachings in Africa a ground of union which has contributed vastly to their progress. Hausas, Foulahs, Mandingoes, Soosoos, Akus, can all read the same books and mingle in worship together, and there is to all one common authority and one ultimate umpirage. They are united by a common religious sentiment, by a common antagonism to paganism. Not only the sentiments, but the language, the words of the sacred book are held in the greatest reverence and esteem. And even where the ideas are not fully understood, the words seem to possess for them a nameless beauty and music, a subtle and indefinable charm, incomprehensible to those acquainted only with European languages. It is easy for those not acquainted with the language in which the Koran was written, and, therefore, judging altogether as outsiders, to indulge in depreciation of its merits.* Such critics lose sight of the fact that the Koran is a poetical composition, and a poetical composition of the earliest and most primitive kind, and that therefore its ideas and the language in which they are conveyed cannot well be separated. The genuine poet not only creates the conception, but the word which is its vehicle. The word becomes the inseparable drapery of the idea. Hence the highest poetry cannot be translated.

* The case cited by Dr. Mühleisen Arnold, in his work on Islam, of an Arab philosopher and unbeliever in Mohammed, who lived in the eighth century, depreciating the literary merits of the Koran, is no more in point as an argument against the book, it appears to us, than if a Mohammedan controversialist were to quote from Voltaire or Tom Paine against the Bible.

We see this in the numerous versions by which it has been sought in every age to reach the sense of the poetical portions of the Bible. No words yet furnished by Greek, Roman, or Teutonic literature have been fully adequate to bring out the subtle beauties of the Semitic original. Among Mohammedans written or printed translations of the Koran are discouraged. The Chinese, Hindoos, Persians, Turks, Mandingoes, Foulahs, etc., who have embraced Islam, speak in their "own tongues wherein they were born," but read the Koran in Arabic.

Mr. Bosworth Smith was right to commence his preparations for the valuable work he has written by a careful study of the Koran. But it is to be regretted that he had not access to the force and beauty of the original, which neither Sale, Kasimirsky, Lane, nor Rodwell have been able—though they labored hard to do so—to retain in their excellent translations. A distinguished Oriental scholar and critic says:—

> There can be no doubt that to understand thoroughly this wonderful book, the aid of those learned men, Arabs and others, who have devoted themselves to the careful study of it, is not only desirable, but necessary. . . . The subject is of sufficient importance to men of research to render it advisable that it should be examined from all points of view, for by no other means can we hope to obtain as clear an insight into the origin of Islam as by a careful study of the book which contain sits fundamental principles.*

To the outside world, easily swayed by superficial impressions, and carried away by matters of mere dramatic interest, there may be nothing attractive in the progress of Islam in Africa, because, as far as known to Western readers, the history of African Mohammedanism is deficient in great characters and in remarkable episodes. There has been, it is supposed, no controlling mind developed which has moved great masses of men. But the words of Horace are applicable here:—

> Omnes illacrimabiles
> Urgentur, ignotique longa
> Nocte, carent quia vate sacro.

It is not, however, that no bard has written, but they have had very few readers in Christian countries. To those acquainted with the interior of Africa—to the Mohammedan world of North

* W. Nassau Lees, in the preface to his edition of the "Commentary of Zamakhshari."

Africa and Arabia—it is well known that numerous characters have arisen in Africa—Negro Moslems—who have exerted no little influence in the military, political, and ecclesiastical affairs of Islam, not only in Africa but in the lands of their teachers. In the biographies of Ibn Khallikan are frequent notices of distinguished Negro Mohammedans. Koelle, in his *Polyglotta Africana*, gives a graphic account of the proceedings of the great Fodie, whose zeal, enthusiasm, and bravery spread Islam over a large portion of Nigritia.

One of the most remarkable characters who have influenced the history of the region of country between Timbuctoo and the West Coast was a native of Futah Toro, known as the Sheikh Omaru Al-Hajj. He is said to have been a Waleen,* a man of extraordinary endowments, of commanding presence, and great personal influence. He was educated by the Sheikh Tijani, a Moslem missionary from Arabia. Having spent several years under the instruction of this distinguished teacher, visiting Mecca in the meanwhile, he became profoundly learned in the Arabic language. After the death of his master he went twice to Mecca on pilgrimage. On his return to his country the second time, he undertook a series of proselytizing expeditions against the powerful pagan tribes on the east and south-east of Futah Toro. He conquered several powerful chiefs, and reduced their people to the faith of Islam. He banished paganism from Sego, and purified the practices of several Mohammedan districts which had become imbued with heathenish notions. He thus restored Jenne, and Hamd-Allahi, and was on his way to Timbuctoo, about ten years ago, when, through the treachery of the Arabs of that region, he was circumvented and killed at a town in Masina. One of his sons is now king of Sego, another rules over Hamd-Allahi, two of the largest cities in Central Africa.

Al-Hajj Omaru wrote many Arabic works in prose and poetry. His poems are recited and sung in every Mohammedan town and village, from Futah-town, in Sierra Leone, to Kano. His

* This word is used by the Mohammedans of Negroland in a peculiar sense. It means one called of God, and endowed with special gifts to exercise authority in ecclesiastical and sometimes political matters, inferior in official rank, according to their estimation, only to a prophet. Such men have, from time to time, arisen among African Mohammedans, and have carried out important reforms in Church and State.

memory is held in the greatest respect by all native students, and they attribute to him many extraordinary deeds, and see in his successful enterprises, literary and military, proofs of divine guidance.*

We have heard of numerous instances of these "half military, half religious geniuses," as Mr. Bosworth Smith calls them, "which Islam always seems capable of producing."

To the Mohammedans of Negro-land, far away from the complex civilization of European life, with its multifarious interests, the struggle for the ascendency of Islam is the one great object which should engage the attention of a rational being. It is a struggle between light and darkness, between knowledge and ignorance, between good and evil. The traditional enthusiasm of their faith makes them utterly indifferent to the sufferings of any who stand in the way of the dissemination of the truth, and patient of any evils they may have to endure in order to insure the triumph of their cause. "Paradise is under the shadow of swords," is one of their stimulating proverbs.

There is one passage in Mr. Bosworth Smith's book of which we do not think that the author, who it seems has not himself been in Africa, understood the full import, but which the Christian world, it appears to us, would do well to ponder. It is as follows:—

Christian travelers, with every wish to think otherwise, have remarked that the Negro,† who accepts Mohammedanism, acquires at once a sense of the dignity of human nature not commonly found even among those who have been brought to accept Christianity.‡

Having enjoyed exceptional advantages for observation and comparison in the United States, the West Indies, South Amer-

* Report on the Expedition to Timbo made to the Governor of Sierra Leone, 1873. See also the "African Sketch-Book," by Winwood Reade, vol. i, p. 317.

† Mr. Bosworth Smith writes this word with a small *n;* but we do not see why, if it is used to designate one of the great families of man, it should not be entitled to the same distinction as such words as Indian, Hindoo, Chinaman, etc. Why give more dignity to the specific than to the general? Why write Ashantee, Congo, Mandingo, with capitals, and Negro, the generic appellation, with a small *n?* Is not this in deference to the sort of prejudice against which Mr. Smith himself protests?

‡ Lecture i, p. 32.

ica, Egypt, Syria, West and Central Africa,* we are compelled, however reluctantly, to indorse the statement made by Mr. Smith. And we are not surprised at his seizing hold in his researches of this most important fact and giving it such prominence—a prominence it richly deserves—in the discussion. Wherever the Negro is found in Christian lands, his leading trait is not docility, as has been often alleged, but servility. He is slow and unprogressive. Individuals here and there may be found of extraordinary intelligence, enterprise, and energy, but there is no Christian community of Negroes anywhere which is self-reliant and independent. Haïti and Liberia, so-called Negro Republics, are merely struggling for existence, and hold their own by the tolerance of the civilized powers.† On the other hand, there are numerous Negro Mohammedan communities and states in Africa which are self-reliant, productive, independent, and dominant, supporting, without the countenance or patronage of the parent country, Arabia, whence they derived them, their political, literary, and ecclesiastical institutions. In Sierra Leone, the Mohammedans, without any aid from government—imperial or local—or any contributions from Mecca or Constantinople, erect their mosques, keep up their religious services, conduct their schools, and contribute to the support of missionaries from Arabia, Morocco, or Futah, when they visit them. The same compliment cannot be paid to the Negro Christians of that settlement. The most enlightened native Christians there look forward with serious apprehension—and, perhaps, not without good grounds—to the time when, if ever, the instructions and influence from London will be withheld. An able paper on the "Condition and Wants of Liberia," by an intelligent and candid Liberian, has the following:—

We want, as a people, the spirit of liberality. We have learned to depend upon foreign institutions to support our Churches. This should not be so. If, indeed, we have not enough of the Christian religion to induce us to contribute liberally to the cause of the

* The writer, of pure African extraction, was born in the West Indies, but received his educational training in Liberia, West Africa, where he has lived for twenty-five years.

† The "Official Journal," dated May 1, 1875, contained intelligence of a conspiracy which had just been suppressed, and a presidential decree banishing forty of the conspirators.

Gospel; if we have not enough zeal for the cause of Christ to make us willing to sacrifice time and money for its good, etc., we had as well give up Churches and religion. . . . I have known some persons to change a two cent piece so as to get one cent for the Church. Alas for such religion! alas for the Churches thus supported!*

In the recent Ashantee war the most trustworthy Negro troops were the Haussas, who are rigid Mohammedans. The West India Christian Negro troops were not relied on to the same extent.

Now, what has produced this difference in the effects of the two systems upon the Negro race? In reply, we remark generally that the difference must be attributed to the difference in the conditions under which the systems came to those of the Negro race who embraced the one or the other. Mohammedanism found its Negro converts at home in a state of freedom and independence of the teachers who brought it to them. When it was offered to them they were at liberty to choose for themselves. The Arab missionaries, whom we have met in the interior, go about without "purse or scrip," and disseminate their religion by quietly teaching the Koran. The native missionaries—Mandingoes and Foulahs—unite with the propagation of their faith active trading. Wherever they go they produce the impression that they are not preachers only, but traders; but, on the other hand, that they are not traders merely, but preachers. And in this way, silently and almost unobtrusively, they are causing princes to become obedient disciples and zealous propagators of Islam. Their converts, as a general thing, become Moslems from choice and conviction, and bring all the manliness of their former condition to the maintenance and support of their new creed.

When the religion was first introduced it found the people possessing all the elements and enjoying all the privileges of an untrammeled manhood. They received it as giving them additional power to exert an influence in the world. It sent them forth as the guides and instructors of their less favored neighbors, and endowed them with the self-respect which men feel who acknowledge no superior. While it brought them a

* The Annual Address delivered before the City Council and Citizens of Monrovia, July 27, 1874, by Jehu T. Dimery.

great deal that was absolutely new, and inspired them with spiritual feelings to which they had before been utter strangers, it strengthened and hastened certain tendencies to independence and self-reliance which were already at work. Their local institutions were not destroyed by the Arab influence introduced. They only assumed new forms, and adapted themselves to the new teachings. In all thriving Mohammedan communities, in West and Central Africa, it may be noticed that the Arab superstructure has been superimposed on a permanent indigenous substructure; so that what really took place, when the Arab met the Negro in his own home, was a healthy amalgamation, and not an absorption or an undue repression.

The Oriental aspect of Islam has become largely modified in Negroland, not, as is too generally supposed, by a degrading compromise with the pagan superstitions, but by shaping many of its traditional customs to suit the milder and more conciliatory disposition of the Negro. As long as Timbuctoo, which was but a continuation of Morocco, retained its ascendency, Islam kept up its strictly Arabian aspect; but since the seat of literary activity and ecclesiastical influence has been transferred to Kuka, and since Kano has become the commercial center—two purely Negro cities grown up under Moslem influence—and since the religion has taken root among the large indigenous communities near the source of the Niger, it has been largely affected by the geographical and racial influences to which it has been exposed. The absence of political pressure has permitted native peculiarities to manifest themselves, and to take an effective part in the work of assimilating the new elements.

Christianity, on the other hand, came to the Negro as a slave, or at least as a subject race in a foreign land. Along with the Christian teaching, he and his children received lessons of their utter and permanent inferiority and subordination to their instructors, to whom they stood in the relation of chattels. Christianity took them fresh from the barbarism of ages, and forced them to embrace its tenets. The religion of Jesus was embraced by them as the only source of consolation in their deep disasters. In their abject miseries, keen anguish, and hopeless suffering, they seized upon it as promising a country where, after the unexampled sorrows of this life, "the wicked

cease from troubling, and the weary are at rest." It found them down-trodden, oppressed, scorned; it soothed their sufferings, subdued their hearts, and pointed them, in its exhaustless sympathy, to the "Man of Sorrows, and acquainted with grief." In their condition of outcasts and pariahs, it directed their aspirations to a heavenly and eternal citizenship; it put new songs in their mouths—those melodies inimitable to the rest of the world—which, from the lips of emancipated slaves, have recently charmed the ears and captivated the hearts of royalty and nobles in Europe by a tenderness, a sweetness, an earnestness, and a solemnity born of adversity in the house of bondage. A popular London preacher says:—

> The Negro is more really musical than the Englishman. . . . Singing very often merrily with the tears wet upon his ebony cheek, no record of his joy or sorrow passed unaccompanied by a cry of melody, or a wail of plaintive and harmonious melancholy. If we could divest ourselves of prejudice, the songs that float down the Ohio River are one in feeling and character with the songs of the Hebrew captives by the waters of Babylon. We find in them the same tale of bereavement and separation, the same irreparable sorrow, the same wild tenderness and passionate sweetness, like music in the night.*

These are great and precious advantages; but, nevertheless, owing to the physical, mental, and social pressure under which the Africans received these influences of Christianity, their development was necessarily partial and one-sided, cramped and abnormal. All tendencies to independent individuality were repressed and destroyed. Their ideas and aspirations could be expressed only in conformity with the views and tastes of those who held rule over them. All avenues to intellectual improvement were closed against them, and they were doomed to perpetual ignorance.

Mohammedanism and learning to the Moslem Negro were coeval. No sooner was he converted than he was taught to read, and the importance of knowledge was impressed upon him. The Christian Negro came in contact with mental and physical proscription and the religion of Christ contemporaneously. If the Mohammedan Negro had at any time to choose between the Koran and the sword, when he chose the former he was allowed to wield the latter as the equal of any

* Rev. H. R. Haweis in "Music and Morals," p. 500. London, 1874.

other Moslem; but no amount of allegiance to the Gospel relieved the Christian Negro from the degradation of wearing the chain which he received with it, or rescued him from the political and, in a measure, ecclesiastical proscription which he still undergoes in all the countries of his exile.* Everywhere in Christian lands he plays, at the present moment, the part of the slave, ape, or puppet. Only a few here and there rise above the general degradation, and these become targets to their unappreciative brethren—

Apparent rari nantes in gurgite vasto.

Is it any wonder, then, that "Christian travelers, with every wish to think otherwise," in commenting upon the diffference between Christian and Mohammedan Negroes, with respect to true manliness, must do so to the disadvantage of the former?

Another reason for the superior manliness and *amour propre* of Negro Mohammedans may be found in the fact that, unlike their Christian brethren, they have not been trained under the depressing influence of Aryan art. Deutsch says:—

> The Shemites from some strange idiosyncrasy, perpetuated by religious ordinances, abhorred, all of them, at certain stages, the making visible pictures of things they revered, loved, or worshiped.†

The Second Commandment, with Mussulmans as with Jews, is construed literally into the prohibition of all representations of living creatures of all kinds; not merely in sacred places, but every-where.‡ Josephus tells us that the Jews would not even suffer the image of the emperor, which was represented on the eagles of the soldiers.§ The early Christian Fathers believed that painting and sculpture were forbidden by the Scriptures, and that they were therefore wicked arts. Among the Mohammedans of Negroland it is considered a sin to make even the rudest representation of any living thing on the ground or on the side of a house. We shall never forget the disgust with which a Mandingo from Kankan, who was for the first time visiting the seaboard at Monrovia, turned from a marble figure

* For an interesting discussion on this subject from the pen of a Negro, see Tanner's "Apology for African Methodism" in the United States.

† "Literary Remains," p. 161.

‡ "Mischat ul-Masabih," vol. ii, p. 368. § "Antiquities, xviii–iii, 1, etc.

in the cemetery, through which we were showing him, exclaiming, *Amâl Shaitân! amâl Shâitan!*—the work of Satan.*

No one can deny the great esthetic and moral advantages which have accrued to the Caucasian race from Christian art, through all its stages of development, from the Good Shepherd of the Catacombs to the Transfiguration of Raphael, from rough mosaics to the inexpressible delicacy and beauty of Giotto and Fra Angelico.† But to the Negro all these exquisite representations exhibited only the physical characteristics of a foreign race; and, while they tended to quicken the tastes and refine the sensibilities of that race, they had only a depressing influence upon the Negro, who felt that he had neither part nor lot, so far as his physical character was concerned, in those splendid representations. A strict adherence to the letter of the second commandment would have been no drawback to the Negro. To him the painting and sculpture of Europe, as instruments of education, have been worse than failures. They have really raised barriers in the way of his normal development. They have set before him models for imitation; and his very effort to conform to the canons of taste thus practically suggested, has impaired, if not destroyed, his self-respect, and made him the weakling and creeper which he appears in Christian lands. It was our lot not long since to hear an illiterate Negro in a prayer-meeting in New York entreat the Deity to extend his "lily white hands" and bless the waiting congregation. Another,‡ with no greater amount of culture, preaching from 1 John iii, 2, "We shall be like him," etc., etc., exclaimed, "Brethren, imagine a beautiful white man with blue eyes, rosy cheeks, and flaxen hair, and we shall be like him." The conceptions of these worshipers were what they had gathered from plastic and pictorial representations, as well as from the characteristics of the dominant race around them. The Mohammedan Negro, who is not familiar with such representations, sees God in the great men of his own country. The saying is attributed to an

* See Koran, v. 92.

† See a paper on the Roman Catacombs, etc., read by Dean Stanley before the Royal Institution, May 29, 1874.

‡ The putting forward of thoroughly illiterate men to expound the Scriptures among Negro Christians has been another great drawback to their proper development.

ancient philosopher,* that if horses, oxen, and lions could paint they would certainly make gods in their own image:—

> If oxen or lions had hands, and could work in man's fashion,
> And trace out with chisel and brush their conception of Godhead,
> Then would horses depict gods like horses, and oxen like oxen,
> Each kind the divine with its own form and nature endowing.

This is no doubt true, and the Negro who grew up normally would certainly not be inferior to lions, horses, and oxen. The Christian Negro, abnormal in his development, pictures God and all beings great in moral and intellectual qualities with the physical characteristics of Europeans, and deems it an honor if he can approximate by a mixture of his blood, however irregularly achieved, in outward appearance, at least, to the ideal thus forced upon him of the physical accompaniments of all excellence. In this way he loses that "sense of the dignity of human nature" observable in his Mohammedan brother.

A third very important influence which has retarded the development of the Christian Negro may be found in the social and literary pressure which he has undergone. It is not too much to say that the popular literature of the Christian world, since the discovery of America, or at least for the last two hundred years, has been anti-Negro. The Mohammedan Negro has felt nothing of the withering power of caste. There is nothing in his color or race to debar him from the highest privileges, social or political, to which any other Moslem can attain. The slave who becomes a Mohammedan is free.† Mohammedan history abounds with examples of distinguished Negroes. The eloquent Adzân, or Call-to Prayer, which to this day summons at the same hours millions of the human race to their devotions, was first uttered by a Negro, Bilâl by name, whom Mohammed, in obedience to a dream, appointed the first Muezzin or Crier.‡ And it has been remarked that even Alexander the Great is in Asia an unknown personage by the side of this honored Negro. Mr. Muir notices the inflexible constancy of Bilâl to the faith of Islam under the severest trials.§ Ibn Khallikan mentions a celebrated Negro khalif,

* Xenophanes of Colophon, (six centuries, B. C.)
† Ockley's "History of the Saracens," sixth edition, London, 1871, p. 14.
‡ Muir's "Life of Mohammed," vol. iii, p. 54.
§ Ibid. vol. ii, p. 129.

who reigned at Bagdad in the ninth century.* He describes him as a man of great merit, and a perfect scholar. None of the sons of khalifs spoke with greater propriety and elegance, or composed verses with greater ability. The following lines were addressed to him by a contemporary poet:—

Blackness of skin cannot degrade an ingenious mind, or lessen the worth of the scholar or the wit. Let blackness claim the color of your body; I claim as mine your fair and candid soul.

The poet Abu Ishak Assabi, who lived in the tenth century, had a black slave named Yumna, to whom he was greatly attached, and on whom he made some remarkable verses which are much quoted by Moslems. Notice the following:—

The dark-skinned Yumna said to one whose color equals the whiteness of the eye, "Why should your face boast its white complexion? Do you think that by so clear a tint it gains additional merit? Were a mole of my color on that face it would adorn it; but one of your color on my cheek would disfigure me."

Here is another:—

Black misbecomes you not; by it you are increased in beauty: black is the only color princes wear. Were you not mine, I should purchase you with all my wealth. Did I not possess you, I should give my life to obtain you.†

Ibn Muslimeh, an enthusiastic lover, exclaims, "If a mole be set in an ugly cheek it endows it with beauty and grace; how then should the heart-stricken be blamed for looking upon his mistress as a mole all over? ‡

Mr. Gifford Palgrave, whose travels in Eastern countries have no doubt diminished the sensitiveness of his Western prejudices, concludes his brilliant "Essays on Eastern Questions" with a poem composed by a Negress in memory of her celebrated semi-Arab son, who had perished in one of his daring adventures.

Now, it must be evident that Negroes trained under the influence of such a social and literary atmosphere must have a deeper self-respect and higher views of the dignity of human nature than those trained under the blighting influence of

* "Biographies of Ibn Khallikan," translated by Baron de Slane, vol. i, p. 18.
† Ibn Khallikan, vol. i, p. 32.
‡ Chenery's Translation of the "Assemblies of Hariri," vol. i, p. 345.

caste, and under the guidance of a literature in which it has been the fashion for more than two hundred years to caricature the African, to ridicule his personal peculiarities, and to impress him with a sense of perpetual and hopeless inferiority. Christian literature has nothing to show on behalf of the Negro comparable to Mohammedan literature; and there is nothing in Mohammedan literature corresponding to the Negro—or "nigger," as even a liberal clergyman like Mr. Haweis will call him *—of Christian caricaturists. A distinguished American scholar and thinker has noticed this. He says:—

The black man in literature is either a weakling or caricature. The comic side of him alone comes into view. The single sonnet of Wordsworth upon the chieftain Toussaint, and the "sparkles dire of fierce, vindictive song" from the American Whittier, are almost the only literary allusions to the sublime and tragic elements in the Negro's nature and condition; certainly the only allusions that, without any abatement and introduction of ludicrous traits, ally him *solely* with human

. . . Exultations, agonies,
And love, and man's unconquerable mind.†

No one will charge the Negro Mohammedans with giving ground for the notion, put forward recently from a very distinguished source, that the African entertains "a superstitious awe and dread of the white man." Ibn Batoutah, cited above, though a Mohammedan, experienced no greater respect among the Moslems of Negroland on account of his color than a Negro in the same position would have received. He complains of the cool and haughty bearing of a certain Negro prince toward himself and a number of European or Arab traders who appeared in the royal presence. "It was then," he says, "that I regretted having entered the country of the Negroes on account of their bad education, and the little regard they have for white men." And what was the evidence of this "bad education and little regard for white men?" The chief chose to speak to them through a third party, "although they were

* "Music and Morals," p. 550.

† Professor W. G. T. Shedd, in an Address delivered before the Massachusetts Colonization Society, Boston, May 27, 1857. The remarkable address of Wendell Phillips on Toussaint L'Overture must not be forgotten. Mr. Phillips is the only American orator who has had the temerity to lavish flowers of a brilliant rhetoric in adorning the memory of a Negro.

very near him." "This was done," observes the sensitive traveler, "solely on account of his contempt" for them. Réné Caillié, the French traveler, who made the journey from West Africa to Morocco, *via* Timbuctoo, was compelled to travel in strict disguise as a poor Moslem. His sojourn in Timbuctoo was of only fourteen days; and, as he was in constant danger of being discovered, he could neither move about freely nor note down all that he wished. Even Barth was obliged, for a short time, to adopt the character of a Moslem. Of course these things occurred before the days of Sir Garnet Wolseley, who, in a grave official document, thought it necessary to reassure his troops in the following terms:—

> It must never be forgotten by our soldiers that Providence has implanted in the heart of every native of Africa a superstitious awe and dread of the white man that prevents the Negro from daring to meet us face to face in combat.*

But Sir Garnet also deemed it important to bring to bear against these awe-struck Negroes armed with cheap flint muskets all the appliances of modern warfare, and no doubt bore in mind the Roman poet's advice—*Ne crede colori.* As *a ruse de guerre*—a military expedient—the statement served its purpose, and is one among the many evidences of Sir Garnet's skill and readiness in not only availing himself of advantageous elements in the situation, but of creating them if they do not exist. In this case he adroitly played upon the "superstition" of white men:—

> An dolus an virtus, quis in hoste requirat?

A cool and discriminating critic at home, however, at the close of the war assured us that, "without arms of precision, guns and rockets, and English skill and discipline, no invader could have made his way to Coomassie."

Had Sir Garnet, even before his practical experience, read the history of the great Civil War in America, he would have found in the thrilling records of many a desperate encounter, in which the Negro proved himself no mean antagonist when he met the white man "face to face in combat," materials for imposing a check upon that exuberance of imagination which

* Notes issued for use of the troops by order of Sir Garnet Wolseley, dated Cape Coast Castle, December 20, 1873.

tempted him to the sweeping assertion that the Negro in Christian lands, and all along the coast where he has been under the training of the white man, exhibits a cringing and servile spirit; but this, as we have endeavored to show, is the natural result of that habit of mind which it was the interest of his masters to impress upon him. Sir Garnet's dogma is only one of the innumerable lessons which the Negro is constantly made to imbibe, even at times from his religious guides and teachers,* the tendency to which is to blunt his "sense of the dignity of human nature."

Another very important element which has given the Mohammedan Negro the advantage over his Christian brother is, the more complete sympathy which has always existed between him and his foreign teacher. Mr. Bosworth Smith says:—

> The Mussulman missionaries exhibit a forbearance, a sympathy, and a respect for native customs and prejudices, and even for their more harmless beliefs, which is no doubt one reason of their success, and which our own missionaries and schoolmasters would do well to imitate.—Page 34.

Long prior to the rise of Islam, as we have seen above, the Arab merchant had been in communication with the interior of Africa, and had opened the way for the Arab missionary. When, therefore, the Moslem missionary came as the propagator of a higher religion than any that had been known, he did not enter the country as a stranger. The political and social institutions of the Arabs had already been tried and found suitable to the wants and tastes of the Negro tribes; indeed, the two peoples, if not of cognate origin, have by protracted intercommunication, and by the similarity of the physical influences which have for ages operated upon them, become similar in tastes; and it was not difficult for the Arabs to conform to a great extent to the social and domestic customs of the Africans. The Moslem missionary often brought to the aid of his preaching the influence of social and domestic relationships—an influence which in all efforts to convert a people is not to be entirely

* See an article on the "Negro" in the "Church Missionary Intelligencer" for August, 1873. The special correspondent of the "Daily News" at Cape Coast, under date of Oct. 2, 1873, speaks of the native chiefs as follows: "There is nothing that seems to signify power about their dignity; and knowing, as we did, that it has been our policy on the Coast for years to deprive these chiefs of all real influence, their very solemnity of manner left on me an impression of the theatrical."

ignored. "The conversion of the Russian nation," we are told by Dean Stanley, "was effected, not by the preaching of the Byzantine clergy, but by the marriage of a Byzantine princess." * So the Arab missionaries often entered into the bonds of wedlock with the daughters of Negroland; † and by their teaching, by their intelligence, by their intermarriages with the natives, by the trade and generosity of their merchants, they enlisted so many interests and such deep sympathies, that they rapidly took abiding root in the country. Some of the brightest names in the annals not only of Islamitic but of pre-Islamitic literature, are those of the descendants of Arabs and Africans. One of the authors of the "*Muallakat*," for instance, was half Arab and half Negro.

The sympathy, therefore, between the Arab missionary and the African is more complete than that between the European and the Negro. With every wish, no doubt, to the contrary, the European seldom or never gets over the feeling of distance, if not of repulsion, which he experiences on first seeing the Negro. ‡ While he joyfully admits the Negro to be his brother, having the same nature in all its essential attributes, still, owing to the diversity in type and color, he naturally concludes that the inferiority which to him appears on the surface must extend deeper than the skin, and affect the soul. Therefore, very often in spite of himself, he stands off from his African convert, even when, under his training, he has made considerable advance in civilization and the arts. And especially is this the case in West Africa, where, living among large masses of his countrymen, the African Christian, who, from the pressure of circumstances has been forced into European customs,

* "Eastern Church," p. 34.

† Mr. Palgrave tells us that intermarriages between Arabs and Negroes have been at no period rare or abnormal; to such admixtures, indeed, the East owes not a few of her best celebrities.—*Essays on Eastern Questions*, p. 337.

‡ Bishop Heber, in one of his letters written on his first arrival in India, says: "There is, indeed, something in a Negro which requires long habit to reconcile the eye to him, but for this the features and hair, far more than the color, are responsible.—*Life of Heber*, by Taylor, second edition, p. 147. And what this distinguished prelate experienced and so candidly avowed, must be experienced in a still greater degree by minds of less caliber and less culture than his. "The more ignorant the whites are," says Dr. Charles Hodge, of Princeton, New Jersey, "the more violent and unreasonable are their prejudices on this subject."—*Hodge's Essays and Reviews*, p. 519.

presents very often to the foreign observer, in contrast with his native brethren, an artificial and absurd appearance. And the missionary, looking from a comfortable social distance, surveys the Europeanized native, sometimes with pity, sometimes with dismay, seldom with thorough sympathy. He

> "Back recoils, he knows not why
> Even at the sound himself has made."

Or like the stream in Racine, at the sight of the monster it had washed to the shore:—

> Le flot qui l'apportat recule épouvanté. *

The African convert, under such practical teaching, looking upon his instructor as superior to himself—or at least *apart* from himself, not only in spiritual and temporal knowledge, but in every other respect—acquires a very low opinion of himself, learns to depreciate and deprecate his own personal characteristics, and loses that "sense of the dignity of human nature" which observant travelers have noticed in the Mohammedan Negro.

The Arab missionary, on the other hand, often of the very complexion of his hearer, does not "require any long habit to reconcile the eye to him." He takes up his abode in Negroland often for life, and, mingling his blood with that of the inhabitants, succeeds, in the most natural manner, in ingrafting Mohammedan religion and learning upon the ignorance and simplicity of the people. Innocent of the scientific attainments of the day, and with no other apparatus than his portable bed and dingy manuscripts, he may be inferior to the theological and classical scholar just from college in Europe or America, but he has the advantage of speaking to the people in a sympathetic and perfectly intelligible language.

We will conclude with one more extract from Mr. Bosworth Smith:—

> That Mohammedanism may, when mutual misunderstandings are removed, be elevated, chastened, purified by Christian influences and a Christian spirit, and that evils such as the slave-trade, which are really foreign to its nature, can be put down by the heroic efforts of Christian philanthropists, I do not doubt; and I can, therefore, look forward, if with something of anxiety, with

* Racine: "*Phèdre*," Acte V, Scène 6.

still more of hope, to what seems the destiny of Africa, that Paganism and Devil-worship will die out, and that the main part of the continent, if it cannot become Christian, will become, what is next best to it, Mohammedan.—P. 40.

West Africa has been in contact with Christianity for three hundred years, and not one single tribe, *as a tribe*, has become Christian. Nor has any influential chief yet adopted the religion brought by the European missionary. From Gambia to Gaboon, the native rulers, in constant intercourse with Christians, and in the vicinity of Christian settlements, still conduct their government according to the customs of their fathers, where those customs have not been altered or modified by Mohammedan influence. The Alkali of Port Loko, and the chief of Bullom, under the shadow of Sierra Leone, are *quasi* Mohammedan. The native chiefs of Cape Coast and Lagos are pagans.* So in the territory ruled by Liberia the native chiefs in the four counties—Mesurado, Bassa, Sinou, and Cape Palmas—are pagans. There is not a single spot along the whole coast, except, perhaps, the little island of Corisco, where Christianity has taken any hold among large numbers of the indigenous tribes.

But we do not believe that these tribes are hopelessly inaccessible to the influence of the religion of the Gospel. We believe that "when mutual misunderstandings are removed;" when the race is better understood; when the effort at indiscriminate Europeanizing ceases; when the missionary keeps before his mind—if he knows, or learns if he does not know—that "the idiosyncrasy of a people is a sacred gift, given, for some Divine purpose, to be sacredly cherished and patiently unfolded;"† there will be nothing to prevent Christianity from spreading among the pagan tribes, and from eventually uprooting the imperfect Mohammedanism which so extensively prevails. In the meantime, we ought not to grudge the Africans the glimpses of truth which they catch from the Koran; for "a knowledge of a part is better than ignorance of the whole."‡

* See Governor Pope Hennessy's Blue Book Report. Papers relating to her Majesty's Colonial Possessions. Part II, 1873, 2d division.

† Compare the views of Stopford Brooke in Sermons on "Christ in Modern Life," p. 58.

‡ Abu-l-Fida.

A singular anxiety seems to prevail in certain quarters to disparage and depress the character of Mohammedan influence, especially in Africa, by endeavoring to show that wherever it prevails it erects an insurmountable barrier to our further progress—that it produces a far greater than Chinese immobility. We are surprised that a writer, apparently so well informed as the author of the article on Mohammed, in the *Birtish Quarterly Review* for January, 1872, should have put forward the following:—

Islam is a reform which has stifled all other reforms. It is a reform which has chained down every nation which has accepted it at a certain stage of moral and political growth.

In keeping with this is a remarkable statement of Mr. Freeman's in his "History and Conquest of the Saracens," a work described by a recent subtle and eloquent writer as "more equitable and conscientious than Gibbon's!" Mr. Freeman says that Mohammedanism has "consecrated despotism; it has consecrated polygamy; it has consecrated slavery;" and Dean Church, to whom we are indebted for the quotation, not only indorses it, but adds, "it has done this directly, in virtue of its being a religion, a religious reform." *

A Mohammedan writer, taking the same superficial view of the effects of Christianity, and with the same love for epigrammatic terseness, might say, "Christianity has consecrated drunkenness; it has consecrated Negro slavery; it has consecrated war;" and he might gather ample materials for sustaining his position from the history of Christianity during the last three hundred years, especially in the Western hemisphere. When we see so many evils known to be antagonistic to the Christian religion still, after eighteen hundred years, prevalent in Christian lands, why should Mahommedanism be so assailed because, during twelve hundred years of its existence, it has not extirpated from the countries in which it prevails all social evils? Must we not suppose, that as with other creeds, so with Islam, its theology is capable of being made subservient to worldly interests? May we not believe that many of the evils in lands under its sway are due, not to its teachings, but

* Lectures on the "Influences of Christianity," etc. By R. W. Church, M.A., Dean of St. Paul's, p. 8.

to human passions? "As late as the fifteenth century," we are told by Mr. Maclear, "the Church in Europe was engaged in eradicating the remains of Sclavonic heathenism, and protesting against a rude Fetishism and serpent worship." *

It is to be regretted that statements such as those referred to above continue to be made by men whose character, position, and literary ability make them the guides of thousands. They tend to perpetuate in the Christian Church the feeling of distrust in any effort to evangelize the Mohammedan—to keep alive the suspicion that "the successes of the Mohammedan missionary condemn beforehand the labors of the Christian missionary to be in vain"—feelings with a closer acquaintance with the facts—we speak especially for Africa—does not justify. We are satisfied, however, that with the light which, increasing every day, is now being thrown upon the religion of Mohammed, writings based more upon the opinions and theories of the Middle Ages—as Mr. Bosworth Smith has so well shown—than upon the demonstrated facts of to-day, are almost sure, in proportion to the growth of a more accurate knowledge and a more thoroughly discriminating and literary appreciation of Islam, to be riddled out into oblivion as inappropriate platitudes and barren superfluities.†

We entertain the deliberate conviction—gathered not from reading at home, but from travels among the people—that, whatever it may be in other lands, in Africa the work of Islam is preliminary and preparatory. Just as Ishmael came before Isaac in the history of the great Semitic families, so here the descendant of Ishmael has come before the illustrious descendants of Isaac. The African Mohammedans, as far as we have observed, are tolerant and accessible, anxious for light and improvement from any quarter. They are willing to have Christian schools in their towns, to have the Christian Scriptures circulated among them, and to share with Christians the work of reclaiming the pagans. ‡

* "Apostles of Mediæval Europe," p. 32.

† See an able discussion of this subject in Syed Ameer Ali's "Life and Teachings of Mohammed," chap. xv.

‡ Bishop Crowther, in his report for 1874, says: "I have not met with a stern opposer of Christianity, as far as I had conversation with Mohammedans up the Niger.... The reception of an Arabic Bible, which was presented to the Emir of Nupe from the Church Missionary Society, with a childlike glee, in the presence of his court-

In view, then, of the work which Islam has already accomplished for Africa and the Negro race, and the work which it may yet accomplish, we may express the belief of Möhler, quoted by the *Guardian*, (Nov. 4, 1874,) that "one day the true laborers may find (in Africa) a harvest ready for their reaping, and the Gospel speed thither on its way rejoicing, and Mohamed prove a servant of Christ." Till then, all earnest Christians may consistently join in the prayer of Abraham, adopted in the liturgy of the Moravian Church: "O, that Ishmael may live before Thee!" EDWARD W. BLYDEN.

## ART. VI.—THE NEBULAR HYPOTHESIS AND MODERN GENESIS.*

SINCE the speculations of the evolutionists have been advanced with such boldness and plausibility, the nebular hypothesis has assumed an importance which it did not possess in the time of Herschell and Laplace. It is, in fact, the first link in the development theory by which it is attempted to bind together all nature in a rigid system of materialism, forever excluding the interposition of mind and the idea of a divine cosmos. Final cause is pronounced a chimera, and the first great cause is remanded to the sphere of the unknown.

The heavens no longer declare the "glory of God," but the transcendent genius of Newton and Laplace. The responsive cry of the angels in the vision of Isaiah, "Holy, holy, holy, is the Lord of hosts: the whole earth is full of his glory," is

iers, was a proof that this people desire to hear and search after the truth. Another copy was sent through him to Alihu, the king of Ilorin, who is also an Arabic scholar. . . . In all our religious conversations with these Mohammedans we never met with an obstinate disputer, or a bigoted denial of what we read or said to them."—"*Monthly Reporter*" *of Church Missionary Society, February*, 1875.

* *Mécanique Céleste* and *Systeme du Monde*. Laplace.——The Modern Genesis. Rev. W. B. Slaughter. Methodist Book Concern.——Poisson's Mechanics.——Climate and Time. Professor Croll.——Correlation and Conservation of Force. Youmans.——Lectures on Some Recent Advances in Physical Science. Professor Tait.——Sketches of Creation and Geology of the Stars. Winchell.——Schellen's Spectrum Analysis.——Smithsonian Contribution to Knowledge, vol. xviii. Stockwell.——American Journal of Science, 1860, 1874, vol. ix.——Natural Science Review, 1875.——Popular Science Monthly.——Proctor's Lectures in America.

drowned by the vociferous chorus of the scientific world celebrating the *wonderful* observations of Darwin, the *hasty* generalizations of Huxley, and the hazy speculations of Spencer. In his "System of the World," Laplace, or at least his translator, writes the word "Geometer" with a capital "G;" while "nature," as the grand source of all things, is spelled with a small "n." In the same irreverent spirit the great Geometer responded to Napoleon, who asked him how he could write such a work as *Mécanique Céleste* without a recognition of God, "Monsieur, I have no need of such a hypothesis."

It is not improbable that the nebular hypothesis suggested to Herbert Spencer his wonderful definition of evolution. "It is," says he, "a change from an indefinite incoherent homogeneity into a definite coherent heterogeneity through continuous differentiation and integration." The principles on which the marvelous transformations are accomplished, are the "instability of the homogeneous," the "multiplication of effects," and the "integration of correspondences." According to the nebular hypothesis, we have first an extended cloud-mass, incoherent, indefinite, and homogeneous, out of which the cosmos is to be evolved by the multiplication of effects and the integration of correspondences. The earlier theorists assumed the existence of rotary motion, while modern speculation attempts to account for this motion on the principle of the "inherent gravitative force of matter." Motion being initiated in the nebula, it will be accelerated on account of the particles drawing nearer to its center by condensation resulting from cooling, on the same principle that the uncompensated balance-wheel of a watch will vibrate faster in winter than in summer. As this motion increases the particles of matter at all latitudes press from both hemispheres toward the equator, forming an oblate spheroid. When the centrifugal force, or tendency to fly off, becomes greater than the centripetal force, or the attraction toward the center of the mass, a ring is separated at the equator, and eventually broken into fragments. This is what Spencer calls "differentiation." These fragments, obeying the law of gravity, unite in most cases to form a planet or satellite. This is "integration." The outer part of the ring having a greater motion than the inner part, the differentiated body will revolve about an axis. This body passes through the same

stages of development as the original mass, hence the satellites. This process is not carried on *ad infinitum*, resulting in tribes, households, and families, in the planetary realm, because, after a while, the affection of the parent becomes stronger than the prodigal tendencies of the child. Thus out of a single homogeneous mass we have the heterogeneous solar system, with its sun as the residuum of the original nebula, together with the planets, the asteroids, and satellites.

*The Origin of the Nebular Hypothesis.*—Laplace, a celebrated French astronomer and mathematician, already mentioned, advanced this theory of planetary genesis in its definite form, though the speculative views of Lambert and Kant led them to the adoption of a nebular hypothesis, and the idea of a perpetual development in the regions of space. Sir William Herschell embraced similar views in relation to the existence of a self-luminous substance, of a highly attenuated nature, distributed through the celestial regions. But he made no attempt to extend his hypothesis to a cosmogony of our solar system. If, therefore, this hypothesis is restricted to the view which professes to explain the genesis of our solar system, it is only analogically related to the loftier speculations of Herschell in regard to the processes of star-formation going on in the stellar spaces.

With a modesty becoming true philosophy, which distinguishes speculation from scientific facts, Laplace suggested his hypothesis, "which," he says, "I present with that diffidence which ought always to attach to whatever is not the result of observation and computation." In harmony with this spirit he did not give this theory place in the body of his system of philosophy, but added it in the form of a note in his "System of the World"—a work comprising the *results* of celestial mechanics and adapted to the popular mind. That he never regarded this theory as any thing more than a plausible supposition, unsupported by mathematical reasoning, is manifest from the following phraseology: "If the *conjectures*, which I have proposed on the origin of the planetary system, have any foundation," etc Among the principles of his philosophy may be found a very different theory of planetary motions. He says, in accounting for planetary motions, "Thus to explain the double motion of rotation and translation of the earth,

it is sufficient to suppose that at the beginning it received an impulse of which the direction was at a small distance from its center of gravity."

What were the chief considerations which recommended this hypothesis to the mind of Laplace, and what is its relation to the facts of science at the present time? He says:—

> We have the five following phenomena to assist us in investigating the cause of the primitive motions of the planetary system: (1.) The motions of the planets in the same direction, and very nearly in the same plane; (2.) The motions of the satellites in the same direction as the motions of the planets; (3.) The motions of rotation of these different bodies, and also of the sun in the same direction as the motion of projection, and in planes very little inclined to each other; (4.) The small eccentricity of the orbits of the planets and satellites; (5.) Finally, the *great eccentricity* of the orbits of the comets, their *inclinations* being at the same time entirely *indeterminate.*

Among all the different phases in which this theory is presented by modern scientists, we have been unable to discover a single instance in which the last phenomenon mentioned above has come under consideration. The nearest approach to a recognition of the important bearing of the cometary system on the nebular hypothesis is made by Le Conte in an article on this subject in the "Popular Science Monthly." He observes: "That they (the first four phenomena) are not consequences of the law of gravitation, is evident from the fact that comets *transgress* every one of these laws which could be applied to them."

*The Cometary System.*—In view of the important relation of cometary orbits to the nebular hypothesis, as set forth by its illustrious author, it is certainly remarkable that the author of the "Modern Genesis" should use the following language: "One other class of objects demands our attention. The comets revolve around the sun, and must be recognized as erratic members of the cosmical system, and our inquiry is incomplete if it do not ask, How did they originate? How were they cast off from the cosmical sphere?" To these questions the nebular hypothesis replies: "The comets *do not* belong to the solar system," neither were they derived from it, but are foreigners, wandering through space from sun to sun, and occasionally becoming fellow-citizens of the solar family.

After "a somewhat careful study of the subject for thirty

years," Mr. Slaughter should not have chosen the phenomenon regarded by Laplace as the chief support of his hypothesis, as one of his grounds of objection to that hypothesis.

In view of the importance of this point, and the fact that it is generally overlooked by writers on this subject, let us try to understand the bearing of cometary motions on the nebular hypothesis. We shall seek the interpretation of Laplace himself. He remarks:—

> Another phenomenon of the solar system equally remarkable is the small eccentricities of the orbits of the planets and satellites, while those of the comets are *very large;* and we find that the mean inclination of the orbits of all the observed comets approach near 90 degrees. The orbits of this system present no *intermediate shades* between great and small eccentricities. *Chance* alone could not have given a form nearly circular to the orbits of all the planets.

The great work of Laplace had been to reduce all the phenomena of the heavens to the single principle of gravitation. He is now trying to account for the genesis of the solar system by the operation of the "primordial laws of nature." As a natural philosopher dealing with second causes only, he felt bound to admit no other consideration. The comets, having been drawn in by solar influence, appear from all points of space, and with every degree of velocity, giving rise to the greatest diversity in their orbits. But, on the contrary, the planets have *uniformities* in their orbital motions inconsistent with the hypothesis of chance. Newton had proved that the law of gravitation allows bodies to move in orbits of every degree of eccentricity, from a circle to a hyperbola. Laplace had demonstrated "that the planetary ellipses always have been, and always will be, nearly circular; from whence it follows that no planet has ever been a comet—at least, *if we only take into account the mutual action of the bodies of the planetary system.*" He holds that the same cause which rendered the planetary orbits nearly circular must also have influenced the great eccentricities of the orbits of the comets and their motion in every direction, which would be the case if the bodies had been "projected at *random.*"

In order that effects so diverse might be attributed to the same cause, Laplace considered the conditions of its operation very dissimilar. The comets, having been projected at random

from the spaces beyond, possess great *diversities* in their elements. Since the planets possess "marvelous uniformities" in their elements, they must have been evolved from a revolving nebula. Since the orbits of the planetary and cometary system present no "intermediate shades between great and small eccentricities," he was prevented from adopting an hypothesis applicable to both classes of bodies. He concedes the possibility of cometary orbits becoming planetary orbits under influences *other than* "the mutual action of the bodies of the system." A resisting medium might change a "parabolic or hyperbolic cometary orbit into an ellipse." The same cause would eventually change an elongated ellipse into one of small eccentricity. If it can be shown that later discoveries have filled up the "intermediate shades" of planetary and cometary orbits, wanting in the time of Laplace, the hypothesis will be deprived of its chief support; for in the system of Laplace the hypothesis rests not so much on the "*marvelous uniformities*" observed by later theorists, as on the *dis*-uniformities of the solar system. Within a few years this gap between the *circular orbits* of the planets and *very eccentric* orbits of the comets has been filled up by the discovery of 159 planets and planetoids, besides many comets.

The following table will present to the eye the gradation by which planetary orbits pass into cometary orbits, thus proving that the genesis of all the bodies of the system should have a *single hypothesis.* We give the average of the elements of the planets, asteroids, and comets, placing the planetoid of greatest eccentricity next to the comet of smallest eccentricity:—

| | Eccentricity. | Inclination. Degrees. | Direction of Motion. |
|---|---|---|---|
| The average for seven primary planets.............. | 0.0602 | $1\frac{1}{3}$ | direct. |
| The eccentricity and inclination of 21 of the earliest asteroids (average)............................ | 0.1637 | $8\frac{3}{4}$ | direct. |
| The eccentricity and inclination of Mercury.......... | 0.2056 | 7 | direct. |
| " " of Polyhymnia...................... | 0.3397 | .. | direct. |
| " " of Aethra........................ | 0.3819 | .. | direct. |
| " " of second comet, 1867............. | 0.5075 | .. | direct. |
| " " and inclination of Fay's comet...... | 0.5560 | $11\frac{1}{3}$ | direct. |
| The average of twelve comets, whose aphelia are nearly equal to Jupiter's mean distance.................. | 0.7446 | $11\frac{1}{4}$ | direct. |
| The average of the comets whose orbits extend to orbit of Saturn.......................................... | 0.7567 | .. | direct. |
| Those whose perchelia extend to the orbit of the planet Uranus........................................ | 0.9005 | .. | direct. |
| The average of six comets whose orbits extend to the orbit of Neptune:........................ | 0.9508 | 49 | one retrograde. |

Of twenty-one comets, whose mean distance exceeds the limits of the solar system, the eccentricity approaches unity, and their orbits are very eccentric. With this shading off of the characteristics of planetary orbits into those of the comets, it is impossible to say which orbits belong to the planetary system, and which to the cometary; which bodies were evolved from a central nebula, and which were drawn in from the celestial spaces.

Are the phenomena which are made the basis of the nebular hypothesis explicable according to the "theory of accretion," which seems to be the only alternative *physical* theory of the genesis of the solar system? We apply Laplace's hypothesis of the cometary system to the motions of *all the bodies* of the solar system, not because it is specially superior to his hypothesis to account for the motions of the planetary system, or is more in harmony with the teachings of natural theology, but in order to show how far we are, after all, from a correct theory of the universe. Directing our attention to the cause which Laplace admits is sufficient to transform a parabolic or hyperbolic orbit into an ellipse, we shall indicate the effect of this cause on the motions of all celestial bodies. Poisson, in his Mechanics, demonstrates the effect produced on the orbit of a celestial body, by a "resistance supposed, as in the motion of projectiles in the air, to be proportional to the square of the velocity." In addition to diminishing the mean distance, and accelerating the velocity, it is apparent from his formula that the effect of the resisting medium is much greater in aphelion when the motion is slower, than it is in perihelion. Consequently the aphelion distanced iminishes more rapidly, and the orbit becomes less eccentric. For instance the comet of 1843, whose aphelion distance is 112 times the mean distance of the earth, has a motion 400,000,000 times greater in perihelion than in aphelion. This position agrees with a conclusion, in *Mécanique Céleste*, in the case of orbits of small eccentricity. "Therefore, at the same time that the planet approaches toward the sun by the effect of the resistance of the medium, the *orbit will become more circular*."

The problem by which the stability of the solar system is established seems clearly to indicate that one of the indispensable conditions of stable equilibrium, is that all the bodies

shall revolve in the *same direction.* If a body should come into the system in the opposite direction from the prevailing motions, the perturbations would eventually bring it into collision with some heavier body, by which it would be absorbed and borne along in the common direction. This, perhaps, accounts for the fact that so few of the known elliptical comets have a retrograde motion. The planet Jupiter exerts a controlling influence in the solar system, especially over the inclinations of the orbits of all other bodies. His action has a tendency to bring all other orbits to coincide with his own. The influence of Jupiter, and the major planets generally, over the cometary orbits, is seen in the fact that the aphelion of the comets whose orbits are included within the limits of the solar system very nearly coincide with the orbits of the larger planets. There are twelve comets whose mean aphelion distance is 5.6, the mean distance of Jupiter being 5.2, and his aphelion being 5.5 times the mean distance of the earth from the sun. There are two comets and a meteor ring whose mean aphelion distance is 19.62, the mean distance of Uranus being 19.18. There are six comets whose mean aphelion is 34.03, the mean distance of Neptune being 29.77. These coincidences clearly prove a physical connection between the planets and comets. With this position agrees the observation of Laplace: "The attraction of the planets ought to change several cometary orbits into ellipses."

It may also be shown that the rotary motion of the planets, in consequence of a resisting medium, should be in the direction of the orbital motion, and in a plane nearly coincident with that of the orbit. The solar attraction on a body, with free vapors or liquids on its surface, converts it into an ellipsoidal figure with the longer axis directed to the sun. But in consequence of the greater attraction on the particles nearest the sun, the bulge will be slightly greater within the orbit than on the opposite side of the body. The center of gravity through which the axis passes will be farther from the particles on the side toward the sun than from those on the opposite side. Consequently the resistance will be greater at that point, causing it to move in a direction opposite to that of the motion of projection, and the whole body to rotate in the direction of the orbital motion, which is the case of the planets and satellites.

It may be objected, that the luminiferous ether, notwithstanding its supposed effect on the motion of Encke's comet, is too hypothetical to be made the basis of a bolder hypothesis. Admitting this to be so, observation has demonstrated the existence of an abundance of cosmical matter distributed throughout space, which must present a real resistance to all bodies moving against it. This matter becomes manifest as it is encountered by the earth, in its motion through space, in shooting stars, fire-balls, and aerolites. This matter is not uniformly diffused, but seems to cluster about certain points, or fall into rings, which, in some cases, have a close connection with cometary orbits. These shooting stars may be the remains of cometary disintegration resulting from the powerful action of the sun on the comets, in their perihelion passage. Seven principal streams of meteors have been detected and very well located, through which the earth passes at certain seasons of the year. Besides these, Schiaparelli, and others, have located the "radients," or points of emanation, of more than fifty sparsely strewn meteor-systems encountered by the earth in its annual revolution. No doubt the comets and all other bodies meet with cosmical matter, which is "diffused profusely throughout the universe," according to the observation of Laplace. In the course of ages this diffused matter must present a sensible resistance to the motion of bodies through the universe.

Professor Newton, of Yale College, estimates the number of shooting stars encountered by the earth during each year at about 400,000,000. Calculations based on their apparent magnitude, as viewed from different points of the earth's surface, give them a diameter ranging from 80 to 120 feet. Supposing their density to be the same as hydrogen, the lightest known substance, the earth during the past 100,000,000 years has encountered and absorbed into itself a mass of matter equal to $\frac{1}{12134}$ of its own mass. Such an amount of resistance would be sufficient to change the earth's orbit from an extreme oval into its present shape.

This is essentially the "theory of accretion," advocated by Proctor and some other astronomers. We have seen no attempt to bring this theory into harmony with the phenomena of the solar system. Mr. Proctor attempts to account for the

distribution of planetary masses on this hypothesis. The nebular hypothesis has never succeeded in its attempt to account for the anomalous collocation of the planets. According to the view of Proctor: "The solar system had its origin in the gathering together of matter toward a great center of aggregation.' The nebulous masses would be thrown into the great center. There would be one center of aggregation. That center would grow continually in size and power—gradually drawing in more and more matter to it. How, then, does the secondary aggregation take its origin? I suppose that would arise not in one direction only, but some in one, some in another, with a superabundance in one direction; great subordinate masses would be formed, perhaps, not continuing separate for any length of time."

*The Satellites and "Kirkwood's Analogies."*—"One of the most remarkable phenomena of the Solar System," observes Laplace, "is the rigorous equality which is observed to subsist between the angular *motions of rotation* and *revolution* of each satellite. It is infinity to unity that this is not the effect of hazard." He attempts to account for this phenomenon in the case of the moon on the assumption that, being originally in a state of vapor, it would assume the form of an elongated spheroid. The terrestrial attraction ought at length, by making the two motions of the satellite to approach each other, to cause their difference to fall within the limits at which their rigorous equality commences to establish itself." According to the modern theory of energy, the same result is secured by the action of free fluids on the surface of a *solid* body. It is maintained that tidal friction will eventually bring the rotary motion of the earth into an equality with its annual motion.

The motions of the first three satellites of Jupiter present a phenomenon still more extraordinary than the preceding, one which consists in this, that the mean longitude of the first, minus three times that of the second, plus twice that of the third, is constantly equal to two right angles. Laplace claims that these motions were brought within certain limits, when the mutual attraction of the three satellites was sufficient to "render this relation accurately true," by the resistance presented by "the less condensible molecules" remaining around the

primary immediately after their formation. If this is the true cause of such a remarkable relation, the resistance presented by an etherial medium, or cosmical matter, will account for it equally well. Mr. Kirkwood, of Indiana, has recently discovered the same relation between certain asteroids, thus showing that the cause is more general than that given by Laplace.

In the year 1850 Mr. Kirkwood, whom Proctor calls the "modern Kepler," discovered a certain relation between the rotary and orbital motions of the planets, which was hailed as a powerful support of a waning hypothesis. This relation is called 'Kirkwood's Analogy,' and is thus expressed: The square of the number of rotations made during one revolution, divided by the cube of the diameter of the sphere of equal attraction, is a *constant* quantity for all the members of the solar system. When the discovery was communicated to the Academy of Science it was discussed *pro* and *con.* Prof. Walker remarked: "We may, therefore, conclude that, whether 'Kirkwood's Analogy' is or is not the expression of a physical law, it is at least that of a physical fact in the mechanism of the universe." If we accept either the theory of a luminiferous ether or tidal friction, or both, this relation cannot be permanent, since the orbital and rotary motion, supposed to be related by this analogy, are affected by forces which are wholly independent of each other. While a resisting medium accelerates orbital motion, tidal friction retards rotary motion. But the failure of the analogy in its application to the satellites is fatal to it, as a general principle. Prof. Walker remarked: "In the secondary systems the day and month are the same. This fact has remained hitherto unexplained." "In this case we may conclude that the rotary motion had exceeded the orbital motion immediately after the breaking of the ring, and only arrived at a state of equality by the loss of *caloric* from radiation." Contraction, consequent on radiation, has a tendency to *accelerate* rotation instead of retarding it. The development of the theory of energy since the discovery of the analogy entirely changes the bearing of this subject on the nebular hypothesis.

*The Spectra of the Nebulæ.*—After the resolution of many of the nebulæ by Lord Ross's great telescope, it was assumed, in opposition to Herschell's speculations, that all nebulæ might

be resolved by increased telescopic power. But the spectroscope, supplementing the work of the telescope, has revealed the fact that of the sixty nebulæ, whose light is sufficient to give reliability to the results of examination, twenty are found to be in a gaseous condition. Thus, what was lost to the nebular hypothesis by the telescope of Lord Ross, was supposed to be regained by the spectroscope of Huggens. These nebulæ may be divided into two classes. "All planetary nebulæ," says Huggens, "yield the same spectrum, the bright lines appearing with considerable intensity." The ordinary nebulæ give spectra of two or three bright lines, indicating the existence of masses of luminous gas, of which hydrogen and nitrogen are the chief constituents. If we compare these spectra with those of the gases hydrogen and nitrogen, we shall be able to arrive at some knowledge of their *density*. We have from two to four spectra of each of these gases, according to the degree of density. At a pressure of one-six-hundredth of an atmosphere, we have the three characteristic bright lines of hydrogen, deep-red, greenish-blue, and blue-violet. At the *minimum* pressure there are lines in the green alone. Up to a pressure of about one fourth of an atmosphere the spectrum of hydrogen attains its full brilliancy; but as the pressure increases to about one half of an atmosphere, it gradually loses in intensity without its general character being essentially changed, excepting that its individual lines, as was observed by Plucker, "*begin to widen.*" With a higher pressure the spectrum becomes continuous, and cannot be distinguished from that of star clusters. "Irresolvable nebulæ of high pressure cannot be distinguished by the spectroscope."

With these observations agrees the *theory* of spectrum analysis founded on the vibratory theory of light, as presented by Prof. Tait. "From free particles we get in general a few definite forms of vibration, corresponding each to a fine line in the spectrum, except in so far as this is modified by the relative velocities of the particles with regard to one another. When there are collisions, but not very numerous, we get slight modifications. So these lines broaden out on both sides. The effect of increased pressure and temperature is to make all the bands of the spectrum broader and broader; and finally, when we compress sufficiently to reduce the gas to what is

perceptibly a solid, or at all events an incandescent liquid, the bands have so spread out that they meet one another, and you have got, in fact, a practically continuous spectrum."

Hence we see that the spectroscope is capable of telling us still more regarding the nature of the light analyzed by it, than the nebulous condition of the matter from which it emanates. It is just here that the evidence it gives is unfavorable to the hypothesis of Laplace. The density of a gas produces an effect upon the spectrum, and is measured by the *breadth of the lines* composing it. Now the nebular hypothesis requires, as a necessary corollary—and it has accordingly always been admitted as such—that nebulæ of every degree of condensation should be found in the heavens, and the *variation* of the *brilliancy* of these bodies has therefore been pointed to as evidence of variation of density. The width of spectral lines, however, provides us with much more certain, reliable, and delicate test.

Mr. Plummer, in an article in the "Natural Science Review," says: "From the observations of Huggens, it would appear that the bright lines in the nebular spectra present no appreciable thickness in all those cases in which it has been possible to use a very narrow slit. The lines have invariably been found to be exceedingly fine, and hence we are furnished with distinct proof that the gases so examined are not only of *nearly equal* density, but that they exist in a very low state of tension. *This fact is fatal to the nebular theory.*" In the spectra of the nebulæ we have only a double line of nitrogen and the second line of hydrogen. The question why the characteristic bright lines of terrestrial hydrogen and nitrogen are not visible in the spectra of nebulæ has long occupied the attention of Huggens. Schellen remarks: "The only reliable conclusions reached by these spectroscopic investigations are: the temperature of the nebulæ is *lower* than that of the *sun*, and that their density is *remarkably small*, being in a highly rarefied condition."

These nebulæ, instead of lying beyond the stellar system, may even belong to the solar system, and be in some way connected with the comets. Assuming their distance to be half that of the nearest fixed star, and that they are moving at right angles to the line of vision, it would require about 250 years

to pass over one second of an arc, and their parallax would be less than two seconds. Such a motion could not be detected since the time these bodies were catalogued. This view seems very probable, especially in the case of extensive nebulæ, since the enormous magnitude which must be attributed to such a mass as the great nebula, Orion, is unfavorable to the assumption of an extra stellar position.

But a still more fatal objection to the assumption that nebulæ are the first stages of system-development would appear to be, that the gases which have been identified in the nebulæ do not seem to be, in themselves, adequate to form a system such as our own, unless by the addition of foreign matter. The addition of cometary matter would not give rise to the complex condition of the terrestrial elements, since the spectra of comets reveal little else than carbon.

All things considered, it may be doubted whether the nebular hypothesis has made any substantial advancement since it was set forth by Laplace, as a mere "conjecture," three quarters of a century ago. In view of this fact, it is remarkable that Dr. Winchell should make the following comparison, equaled only by that recently made by Professor Huxley. The former observes: "We said this account of planetary genesis (nebular hypothesis) was but an hypothesis. So was the doctrine of universal gravitation a hundred years ago. The latter says: "And the doctrine of evolution at the present time rests upon *exactly as secure* a foundation as the Copernican theory of the motions of the heavenly bodies."

Nearly two centuries ago the "*Principia*" appeared, in which its immortal author establishes the truth of the law of gravitation on the firm basis of induction and deduction. More than a hundred years have passed away since this theory was found to be in perfect accord with *all* the phenomena of celestial motions. The accuracy with which predictions are made relative to celestial motions, is a standing demonstration of the correctness of the theory of Newton. Newton was led to the general fact by a series of inductions, and from this principle he descended again to explain the heavenly motions. "This great man," says Laplace, "would justly have merited the reproach of re-establishing the occult qualities, if he had

been content to ascribe to universal attraction the celestial and terrestrial phenomena, without demonstrating the *connection* of his principle with these phenomena. This analytical connection of particular with general facts is what constitutes a theory," as distinguished from a mere hypothesis.

The nebular hypothesis rests on neither induction nor deduction, but has been evolved from the cloudy imagination of the theorist, and is about as attenuated as the original world-stuff. Professor Winchell placed before the gaze of Mr. Slaughter his "stupendous object lesson, which, like *curdled fire-mist*, engirts the sun." The pupil exclaims, "Curdled fire-mist that engirts the sun! Curdled nonsense. It is little less than charlatan dogmatism introduced into the domain of science." We should feel like sharing in this indignant outburst were it not that we have great respect for the memory of Herschell, who was the first to employ the word "Curdled" in this connection. It is certainly a remarkable phenomenon that a mere speculation, a "conjecture" of a great mathematician, should, in later times, be accepted as a scientific verity, without having passed the ordeal of every hypothesis before it is entitled to be installed as a true theory. Science should either support the nebular hypothesis by a greater array of facts and arguments, or else remand it to the category of mere plausible conjectures, which have outlived their day. This opposition to "science, falsely so called," on the part of the theologian, may possibly be pardonable in view of the following opinion entertained by Dr. Winchell concerning those who are not entitled to speak by "authority" on this subject: "Occasionally we hear a dissenting voice, but it proceeds almost always from persons who, whatever their eminence in theology or letters, have little authority in matters of scientific opinion."

*The Hypothetical Nebula in its relation to Molecular Science and Geology.*—It is assumed in this hypothesis that the matter of the system existed originally at such a temperature as to be in a condition of vapor of great tenuity stretching across limits wider than the orbit of the remotest planet. This assumption seems utterly at variance with some well ascertained facts of "molecular science." The fundamental principle of this science, deduced from the observed laws of gases, is also found to be in harmony with the general phenomena of matter in its gaseous state.

The application of this principle in accordance with mechanical laws has led to some remarkable results. Under standard conditions of pressure and temperature at the earth's surface, the molecules of hydrogen have a motion among themselves of an average velocity of about 6,000 feet per second. Oxygen has a motion of 1,800 feet per second. The molecules of air vibrate at the rate of 1,400 feet per second.

Professor Cook observes: "That molecules of a body like the planets are in constant motion. In a gas this motion is supposed to take place in straight lines, the molecules hurrying to and fro encountering each other. The molecules, or atoms, if unconfined, would move off indefinitely into space." We can easily calculate the *density* of a nebula consisting of the matter of the solar system, and filling the orbit of Neptune. "It would require several cubic miles of such matter to weigh a single grain." We can also determine the *pressure* exerted by gravity at the surface of such a nebula. Having the pressure and density referred to the standard of hydrogen, we can ascertain, by the formula of Maxwell, the motion of hydrogen particles. At the temperature of freezing, this motion of the hydrogen atoms is about 9,000 feet per second. We can also calculate the velocity with which a body or particle must be projected from the surface of the nebula so as to pass off into space, beyond the control of gravity. A projection causing a velocity of about one tenth of a mile per second would forever separate a particle from the mass. Hence we see that not only hydrogen, but the heavier molecules, would be dissipated into space, and the continuity of the mass would be impossible.

On the assumption of the original nebular condition of the matter ot the solar system, Sir William Thompson has demonstrated by a threefold argument that about ten millions of years is the limit that can be allowed from a physical point of view for all the changes that have taken place on the earth's surface, since vegetable life of the lowest known form was capable of existing thereon. His argument is based on the internal heat of the earth as showing the time of *consolidation*, on the tidal retardation of the earth's rotation, in its relation to the time when the earth solidified, as indicated by the amount of oblateness, and on the time, which the sun's temperature could supply the earth with heat. The gravitation the-

ory of the sun's heat, as held by Helmholtz, gives about twenty millions of years for the original nebula to condense to the dimensions of the sun. Mr. Crall, after making the most favorable assumption possible relative to the specific heat of the nebula produced by the coming together of two equal masses, having a large velocity of projection, from the stellar spaces, can only give us seventy millions of years. But both he and Thompson, as if to accommodate their geological friends, substantially agree that: "The general conclusion to which we are led, from *physical* considerations, regarding the age of the sun's heat, is, that the entire geological history of our globe must be compassed within less than one hundred millions of years." The problem is still further complicated by the experiments of Bischoff upon cooling basalt. He shows "that for our globe to cool down from 2,000 degrees to 200 degrees centigrade, would require three hundred and fifty millions of years.

But there are geological phenomena, material and vital, which point to a much longer period than that given by Thompson and Crall. The amount of denudation and stratification, as well as the slow modifications, of animal types, require, according to the geologist and palæontologist, from fifty millions to five hundred millions of years. Darwin demands three hundred millions. Lyall was content if he could have two hundred and forty millions. Huxley seems to point to the round number of a thousand millions of years in which to arise from protoplasm to man. Here is a clear conflict between the naturalist and philosopher. Either the geologist must be compelled to surrender some hundreds of millions of time, or the physicist must give up the nebular theory as the foundation of the condensation hypothesis of the sun's heat and the earth's present temperature. The geologist will probably carry the day, and the nebular hypothesis will have to give way to some other speculation relative to the origin of the solar system.

*The Origin of Rotary Motion.*—Laplace in his speculations assumes the existence of the rotary motion of the nebula as an unexplained fact. Helmholtz remarks, that there was "a motion of rotation originally slow, the existence of which must be *assumed.*" The more modern speculators endeavor to account

for this motion on the principle of gravitative force. Spencer holds that the irregular "flocculi," or flakes of condensed matter, moving in a rarer medium, and passing to one side of the center of gravity on account of their irregular shape, impart a rotary motion to the mass. Why they have a tendency to pass on one side of the center of gravity rather than on the other, we are not told. Mr. Slaughter holds that this theory violates the law of motion, "that action and reaction are equal."

Winchell, in his "Sketches of Creation," has presented his view of this subject as follows: "The attractive influences of Sirius, Capella, Vega, and all the other fixed stars, were felt. The cosmical vapor which might otherwise have been perfectly spherical became *distorted* in its form. The position of the center of gravity was changed." If Mr. Slaughter, in his "Modern Genesis," had acquainted himself with the views of the author of the "Geology of the Stars," he could not have fallen into the error of using the following language: "There is no force contemplated as acting on the cosmical mass *from beyond* itself to give it rotary motion. But the contraction would be in the direction of the center."

Le Conte rejects Winchell's theory, and advances one of his own liable to precisely the same objections. He holds that "the nebular mass is formed of discrete masses which, by their collision, engender rotary motion." On the contrary, the collision of the last one of the "discrete" bodies of our isolated system would produce complete equilibrium. We can reply to Le Conte in the language which he uses to demolish the condensation theory. "How can we," says he, "reconcile a generation of rotation in the whole mass, in consequence of cooling and condensation, with the fundamental principles of the equality of action and reaction?" His own theory violates this law.

Let us examine Winchell's theory more at length. In reply to a note of the writer setting forth the atheistical tendencies of his position, he says: "I state that without the exertion of force *ab extra* no rotation would ensue." The effect of the attraction of the stars on the nebula would be to convert it into an ellipsoid, with its longest axis in the direction of the most powerful influence. While it is true that the particles in the course

of condensation will not move toward the center of gravity, but on a line normal to the surface, there is no reason why the particles similarly situated should not press equally on opposite sides of the axes, and thus produce equilibrium. The effect of the attraction on the shape of the nebula was similar to that exerted on the moon. Laplace observes: "We may conceive that the moon in a state of *vapor* assumed, in consequence of the powerful attraction of the earth, the form of an elongated spheroid, of which the greater axis would be constantly directed toward the earth."

Granting, however, that motion may be initiated about the shortest axis on account of prevailing impulses in some one direction, still the effect of tidal friction would be to instantly *check* this motion. These *ab extra* bodies which distort or bulge the nebula in the direction of the most powerful attraction, would not be less effectual in creating a tide in case the nebula began to revolve. Such an effect seems to be recognized by Laplace in his reasoning on the cause of the libration of the moon. "The terrestrial attraction acting while the moon is in a state of fluidity ought to make the two motions of the satellite to approach each other." That is, the external force which distorts the body has power to retard or check its rotary motion. The tidal wave must have acted just as surely on the original nebula "as a brake," as it once did in arresting the rotation of the moon, or as it does now on the earth. According to the views of Winchell we have the same cause, the action of exterior bodies, virtually giving rise to motion at one stage of the development of matter and destroying it at another stage. Such diverse effects should not be attributed to the same cause.

From the above considerations it is extremely doubtful, in the first place, whether an attenuated nebular mass filling the orbit of Neptune could exist in harmony with the conclusions of molecular science. In the second place it is equally doubtful whether gravitative force could initiate rotary motion without violating one of the plainest principles of philosophy. Finally, if such a rotation were commenced, tidal friction would doubtless at once destroy it.

*Ring Formations and Equilibrium of Revolving Spheroids.*—In our further investigations of this subject we shall have special

reference to "The Modern Genesis," by Rev. W. B. Slaughter, a work to which reference has already been made. This book is an attempted refutation of the nebular hypothesis, chiefly on the ground that the phenomena of the solar system are not in harmony with the mechanical principles on which the hypothesis is based. The avowed purpose of the author is "to examine the nebular theory in its *present phases.*" The phase, however, presented by Dr. Winchell in one of the "Half-hour Recreations of Popular Science," entitled "The Geology of the Stars," is the one which claims the chief attention of Mr. Slaughter. As Mr. Winchell, and other nebular theorists, accept both the principles and conclusions of Laplace, presenting few "new phases" of this subject, we shall examine the "Modern Genesis" in the light of celestial mechanics and the nebular hypothesis.

There is not wanting evidence that Mr. Slaughter not only failed to grasp some of the most important principles of natural philosophy lying at the foundation of this subject, but that he neglected to study the nebular hypothesis as sketched by the master-hand of its author. He observes that "the peripheral ring was detached by the centrifugal force, but *how* the ring was changed into a planetary mass the advocates of the theory do not try to show." On the contrary, Laplace gives the entire *modus operandi* of this change. He remarks: "Almost always each ring of vapor ought to be divided into several masses—Saturn's rings being an exception. If one of them was sufficiently powerful to unite successively by its attractions all the others about its center, the ring of vapors would be changed into one sole spheroidal mass."

On the question of revolving spheroids Mr. Slaughter remarks: "But the *equation* of the gravitation and centrifugal forces will always be such that there cannot be such a thing as the casting off any portion of the mass."

In the absence of definite information given by Mr. Slaughter as to this important equation, let us present some of the most important results reached by profound mathematical analysis. In celestial mechanics it is demonstrated that the shortest period of rotation of a homogeneous fluid in *equilibrio* of the same density as the earth is 0.1009 of a day, or about one tenth, and this limit varies reciprocally as the square root of the density.

When the motion of rotation increases in rapidity, the fluid mass becoming more flattened at the poles, its period of rotation becomes less, and ultimately falls within the limits of equilibrium. This paradox is easily understood if we bear in mind that a particle at any degree of latitude has less rotary motion than a particle on the equator. As it reaches the equator it will act as a brake on the rotation. "After a great many oscillations, the fluid, (or gas,) in consequence of the friction and resistances which it experiences, fixes itself in a state of equilibrium."

It is extremely doubtful if the rotary motion, as the result of secular cooling and contraction, could ever exceed these limits of equilibrium. Is the formation of a ring possible at this limit? It has been proved that in the spheroid of equilibrium the equatorial diameter is about two and seven tenths (2.7197) times the polar diameter. It might be supposed that this limit is that in which the fluid would begin to fly off because of its too rapid rotary motion. Such is not the case, since this "could only happen when the whole action at the equator is nothing, or when the centrifugal force becomes equal to the attraction of the spheroid. In the case of the limit of equilibrium, the gravity at the equator is still about one half that of the pole." The advocate of the nebular theory ought to prove that the tendency to acceleration of the motion resulting from cooling and consequent contraction, is greater than the tendency to retardation resulting from friction among the molecules while the mass is in a state of unstable equilibrium.

*Actual Velocities.*—In discussing the subject of actual velocities Mr. Slaughter makes two assumptions, neither of which is accepted by the advocates of the nebular hypothesis. The first one is, "The periodic times may be said to be the same from age to age." From this assumption he makes the inference, that "we are justified in the declaration that the present orbital period of each planet must indicate what the original period of the cosmical mass was at the time the planetary mass was detached." This assumption is invalidated by the hypothesis of a resisting medium which presses the planets and comets toward the sun, and consequently accelerates their motions "from age to age."

A single outburst of Dr. Winchell's "enthusiasm" in his "Sketches" should have been sufficient to set his reviewer right on this question. Mr. Slaughter thus describes this enthusiasm: "Nothing can exceed the enthusiasm of Winchell, unless it be the inconceivably high temperature of the original world-stuff. Nothing can compare with the grandeur of his periods, unless it be the original grand rotation itself." This glowing rhetoric is illustrated by the following passages from the "Sketches of Creation:" "Hark! from the highways of the comets come tidings of *friction* in the machinery of the heavens. The filmy wanderer encounters *resistance* in his long journey to the confines of the solar system. He plows his way through a resisting medium. He falls toward the sun and his orbit is diminished. Not only are the cloud-like comets slowly approaching the sun in spiral curves, *but every revolving planet.*" It is passing strange that Mr. Slaughter never heard this "music of the spheres," which breaks on the ear of scientific speculation. While, however, his philosophy is bad, the conclusion to be drawn is not invalidated, since the motions of the planets were slower at their origin than they are now.

He applies his *dictum* to the motions of Neptune and Mercury in order to show that nebulæ filling their respective orbits would be but slightly spheroidal on account of a rotary motion, corresponding with the present orbital motions of those bodies reaching "the conclusion that the ascertained rate of the supposed cosmical rotation is totally inadequate to produce a very *considerable oblateness* of the cosmical sphere." In coming to this conclusion why did not Mr. Slaughter give us the result of the rotation of a mass, not of the density of water, but of the actual density of the matter of the solar system, filling the planetary orbits? And why, in the second place, did he compare this homogeneous nebula with the solid mass of the earth, which is not homogeneous, instead of giving the oblateness produced, on the supposition of homogeneity? As the case stands, his conclusion is little better than a rough guess.

He asks a question in connection with Neptune which he should have answered himself for his readers: "Will you show us that a rotation at the rate of one eleventh of a second per hour is sufficient to produce even a great degree of oblateness in such a body as the original cosmical mass is supposed to

have been?" We can answer this question definitely by the application of the rule given by Laplace, as found on pages 146 and 147 of this Review. We can readily ascertain the time of revolution beyond which equilibrium ceases to be possible. Having computed the density of the nebula filling the orbit of Neptune, we are furnished with the time of revolution, which is about 274 years in the case of Neptune, producing an oblateness such that the equatorial diameter will be about two and seven tenths times the polar axis. But Neptune revolves in his orbit in 164 years. Hence the oblateness will be further increased unless checked by the friction of the molecules, as previously observed. To a similar question, whether Mercury, under the same conditions as those of Neptune, "would exhibit any perceptible oblateness?" we reply: Should the mass revolve in 112 days, it would assume the shape of a spheroid of equilibrium whose equatorial diameter would be two and seven tenths times the polar diameter. But since the period of Mercury is 88 days, the oblateness will be still greater.

*The Relation of Orbital and Rotary Motion.*—Mr. Slaughter asks the question, "What must be the ratio of the axial to the orbital rotation of any given planet?" As the rotary motion of a planet results from the *difference* of the motions of the *outer* and *inner* particles of the ring, after its fragments have coalesced, we should expect the outer planet to have the slowest rotation, while the motions of the other planets would regularly increase as we approach the sun. Such, however, is not the case. The conclusion resting on the fact that there is no ratio between the two planetary motions, depends on the assumption of the "*invariability* of rotary motion." Our remarks on "Kirkwood's Analogy" will apply to this branch of the subject. Mr. Slaughter has not seen fit to call the attention of his readers to the bearing of this "analogy" on this subject. There are two causes affecting the length of the day of all the planets possessing free particles. Condensation accelerates rotary motion; tidal friction retards it. The latter cause is most effectual in checking the motions of the planets nearest the sun, and least effectual on the motions of massive planets.

It may be said that we have laid entirely too much stress

on the theory of "dissipation of energy" as illustrated by tidal friction and resisting medium. Laplace seems to have recognized the influence of molecules among themselves in modifying motions of small intensity. "The fluids which cover this planet have destroyed by their friction and resistance the primitive oscillations of its axis of rotation." Helmholtz observes: "The motion of the tides produces friction; all friction destroys *vis viva*, or living force. We, therefore, come to the unavoidable conclusion that every tide, although with infinite slowness, still with certainty, diminishes the store of mechanical force of the system; and as a consequence of this the rotation of the planets, having fluids on their surface, round their axis must become more slow." Sir William Thompson and Prof. Tait have elaborated this theory more fully than any other philosophers. They say: "Whatever may be the relative importance of tidal friction and of the resisting medium, there can be but one ultimate result for such a system as that of the sun and planets. That result is the falling together of all into one mass, which, although rotating for a time, must in the end come to rest relatively to the surrounding medium. The tendency of retardation is not counterbalanced to more than a slight degree by the tendency to acceleration which results from secular cooling. Allowing for the retardation of the moon's mean motion by tidal friction or reaction, Adams estimates twenty-two seconds as the amount of error by which a perfect clock would get ahead of the earth in a century." It is claimed that there is an error in Laplace's theory of the earth's constancy of rotation, resulting from an inaccuracy in the amount of the moon's secular variation, which later mathematicians have corrected.

In the "geology of the stars," under examination by Mr. Slaughter, the influence of tidal friction in "destroying the *vis viva* and making the rotation continually slower," is distinctly set forth. Why Mr. Slaughter entirely ignores this principle in his discussions we are unable to understand. It would not be proper to hold that he was ignorant of the bearing of this theory on the questions discussed "after a careful study of the subject for more than thirty years."

Assuming the solar system to be an isolated system, not subject to external influences, we can readily show, by the appli-

cation of the principle of the "conservation of areas," fully developed in Celestial Mechanics, that the nebular hypothesis is untenable. This principle is thus expressed: "If we suppose a system of bodies acting on each other in *any manner whatever*, the sum of the products of the mass of each body into the area which the projection of its *radius vector* traces is *proportional* to *the time*." That is, for the same duration at any two epochs, however widely separated, this quantity is *constant*. We can compute the value of this constant from the present masses and motions of the system. If all these masses are viewed as diffused throughout the system as the original hypothetical nebula, possessing the same constant amount of *vis viva*, we can calculate the rate of rotation of the masses successively filling the respective orbits at the time each planet was detached. The rotary motion will be such that the sum of the areas described in a given time by the particles projected upon the plane will be the same as at the present time. Applying the principle to the sun and Mercury, we find that the rotation of the combined mass would be accomplished in about 470 years, or 1800 times the present period of Mercury's revolution. If, therefore, Mercury was detached from the sun, the quantity of motion must have been about 1800 times greater then than it is now.

*The Direction and Perturbations of Planetary Motions.*—The direction of planetary motions is the next subject discussed by Mr. Slaughter. He starts out with the assertion, "that the projectile always moves in a direction at right angles with the axis of rotation;" hence "the planes of the planetary orbits and the plane of the cosmical equator must be *exactly coincident*. We *demand uniformity*." Neither nature nor the nebular theorist has seen fit to comply with this arbitrary demand. Laplace, anticipating the objections which might be urged on the ground of *disuniformities*, gives the following explanation: "But we may suppose that the innumerable varieties which must necessarily exist in the temperature and density of different parts of these great masses ought to produce the *eccentricities* of their orbits and the deviations of their motions from the plane of this equator." In answer to Mr. Slaughter's question, "Will any one aver as a fact that stellar attraction affects the movements of a planet so as to change the plane of its orbit?"

Mr. Winchell would reply by pointing to Sirius, Capella, and Vega, "hanging on the verge of the firmament," exerting "their attractive influences on the solar system in its earliest infancy."

In reducing the planetary orbits to the plane of the solar equator, Mr. Slaughter has made an egregious blunder by *adding in all cases* the inclination of the sun's equator to the ecliptic to the inclinations of the planetary orbits, overlooking the important fact that the respective longitudes of the ascending nodes of the solar equator and planetary orbits must determine whether we shall *add* or *subtract* these quantities. If the ascending nodes of the solar equator and planetary orbit have the same longitude, the inclinations should be subtracted; if they are 180 degrees apart, they should be added. Applying this rule, we make the following very important corrections of Mr. Slaughter's numbers. As the ascending nodes of the solar equator and Mercury's orbit are nearly coincident, we subtract the inclination of the orbit, which is seven degrees, from the inclination of the sun's equator, which gives for the inclination of the two planes to each other one third of a degree instead of fourteen degrees. Approximately this rule gives for Venus four degrees instead of thirteen; for Mars five degrees instead of nine. Since the longitudes of the ascending nodes of the other planets approach to 180 degrees, the error is much smaller.

According to Laplace, the deviation of a planetary equator from the plane of its orbit, and of this plane from the solar equator, may be the result of the same causes. He observes: "If any comets have fallen on the planets, their fall has caused the *planes* of the orbits and of the *equators* to deviate from the plane of the solar equator. It is probable that such encounters have taken place in the immensity of ages which have elapsed since the commencement of the planetary system."

The author of the "Modern Genesis," in dealing with the subject of "direction of planetary motions," has entirely ignored the very important bearing of "planetary perturbations" on this question. Mr. Stockwell has conducted an elaborate and careful investigation, published in the "Smithsonian Contributions to Knowledge," in which he shows the limits of the variations of the planes of the planetary orbits, referred to

what is called, in Celestial Mechanics, "the invariable plane" of the solar system. These changes require vast periods of time to pass through a complete cycle. I have calculated the inclination of this plane and find it to be $6\frac{1}{12}$ degrees. It is an easy matter to refer the planes of the planetary orbits to the plane of the sun's equator, and then determine, from the variations given by Stockwell, how nearly these planes may coincide with the solar equator during the "secular variations" of the planetary elements. I have made this calculation with the following results: The orbit of Mercury may *coincide* with the sun's equator. At the nearest approach of the planes of the orbits to the solar equator the following numbers give the inclination in degrees: Venus $2\frac{5}{12}$, the Earth 3, Mars $\frac{1}{6}$, Jupiter $5\frac{3}{4}$, Saturn $5\frac{1}{12}$, Uranus 5, and Neptune $5\frac{3}{10}$ degrees.

In consequence of perturbations the retrograde motion of the moon's orbit may reduce the angle of its inclination to the earth's orbit from 29 degrees, the figures employed by Mr. Slaughter, to 18 degrees, as may be verified by comparing the moon's greatest declination during the present year with its minimum nine years ago, as given in the Nautical Almanac. The precession of the equinoxes of all the planets is also dependent on the same cause, and produces great variations of the angles made by the solar and planetary equators. The extent of variations resulting from this cause is about 12 degrees, or twice the inclination of the solar equator to the ecliptic. Hence, any valid objection to the nebular hypothesis based on the variation of the orbits or equators from the solar equator, must be subject to the above limitations. The conclusions of the "Modern Genesis" resting on such variable data are not very reliable. The *uniformities* of the ideal Jovian system, less subject to perturbing influences, in which the orbital planes of the satellites coincide with that of Jupiter's equator, should have admonished Mr. Slaughter of the weakness of his positions.

There are many other positions of the "Modern Genesis" open to attack on philosophical and astronomical grounds, but space will not allow of their examination. The chapter on "Relative Densities" is specially at fault, both as to principles and reasoning. As a presentation of superficial objections the work may have a place; but will fail to have much, if any, weight with scientific minds.

*The Stable Equilibrium of the Solar System.*—There are phenomena connected with the solar system inexplicable either by the nebular hypothesis or the "theory of accretion.' Granting that the "marvelons uniformities" may be reasonably accounted for by either of these views of planetary genesis, still there are certain "dispositions of matter in the planetary system," pointed out by Chalmers, or "an adjustment of bodies with their properties in respect to space" indicated by M'Cosh, which have never been traced to the action of the "primordial laws of nature," but which seem to have been "fixed at the original setting up of the machine" by a power transcending these laws. Newton explains these uniformities thus: "This admirable arrangement can only be the work of an intelligent and most powerful being." The writer of the article on "Nebularism," in "Appleton's Encyclopedia," admits that "It does not explain the *distribution* of the *masses* of the solar system." Proctor says: "A gradually contracting nebulous mass could scarcely, in my opinion, have produced a system in which the masses are at first view so irregularly scattered as in the solar system." Proctor's explanation of the fact is equally unsatisfactory.

If the perpetuity of the solar system was the object sought by the Author of nature, Laplace admits that such an end is admirably secured by its actual arrangement. That is no other system governed by existing laws, could more clearly manifest intelligence, as far as we know. In the solution of the problem of the stability of the solar system, the uniformities seem to be an indispensable condition of the reliability of the result. Even in the phenomenon of "precession," depending on the spheroidal form of the planets, there is some indication that rotary and orbital motion must be in the same direction in order to insure stability.

Assuming that the ultimate aim of the planetary system was to furnish a fit theater for the display of *vital* phenomena, we see the importance of its stability, and of those changes which result from perturbations and on which the vicissitudes of climate depend, being confined within the narrowest limits possible. Although the earth's eccentricity varies only between narrow limits, yet, as Mr. Crall has shown in his work entitled "Climate and Time," this slight change, in its rela-

tion to other influences, is sufficient to produce a glacial epoch alternating from one hemisphere to the other, thus giving the widest possible range to the distribution of species, as affected by climate, without utterly annihilating them.

There are some remarkable relations between the motions of the planetary orbits, pointed out by Mr. Stockwell, which serve to reduce the effects of perturbations to a *minimum* quantity. These relations seem to depend on the relative positions and magnitudes of the planets. Whether they have ever resulted from gravitation has not been demonstrated. In many respects these relations are analogous to those observed in the orbits of Jupiter's satellites, and which are the result of the remarkable commensurability of their motions, noticed on a previous page. Laplace succeeded in tracing this relation of Jupiter's satellites to the action of gravitation only on the assumption that such a relation was *very nearly* established at the commencement of their motion. Very likely the relation about to be mentioned depends on a primitive "collocation" of the major planets, such as to indicate Divine interposition. The relation seems to answer the purpose of a balance-wheel in the system. The perihelion of each planet has a motion in space caused by the attraction of all the other planets. This motion is exceedingly slow, and in some cases very irregular. Mr. Stockwell succeeded in proving that the motions of the perihelia of Jupiter and Uranus, referred to the "invariable plane," are equal to each other, being between three and four seconds of an arc, and performing a revolution around the heavens in 384,730 years, and continuing, on an average, 180 degrees apart. The same fact is observed in the motions of the first three satellites of Jupiter. Saturn's orbit, lying between those of Jupiter and Uranus, performs a revolution in one sixth of this time, while Neptune requires six times as long.

By virtue of this singular relation the orbit of Saturn is affected only by the *difference* of the perturbations by Jupiter and Uranus; whereas if the mean places of the perihelia of these two planets were the *same*, instead of differing by 180 degrees, the orbit of Saturn would be affected by the *sum* of these disturbing forces. But notwithstanding this favoring condition, the elements of Saturn's orbit would be subject to very great perturbation from the superior action of Jupiter,

were it not for the comparatively rapid motion of its perihelion, "its equilibrium being maintained by *the very act of perturbation*. The mean disturbing influence of Uranus on the eccentricity of Jupiter's orbit is identically equal to nothing by reason of the relation which exists always between the perihelia of their orbits." The mean motion of Jupiter's node on the invariable plane is exactly equal to that of Saturn, and the mean longitude of these nodes differs by exactly 180 degrees. By reason of the rapid motion of these nodes the secular changes of the inclination of the orbit of Uranus pass through a complete cycle of values in the period of 56,300 years. The corresponding cycle of perturbations in the eccentricity of Saturn's orbit is 69,140 years. "It is the rapid motion of the orbit, with *respect* to the *forces*, in the one case, and the rapid motion of the forces, with *respect to the orbit*, in the other, that gives *permanence* of *form* and *position* to the orbits of Saturand Uranus."

The spheroidal form of the earth and planets which Laplace and others urge as one of the consequences of the nebular theory has an important bearing on the *extent* of variation of equator and ecliptic. The actual limits are $2\frac{1}{3}$ degrees, only slightly affecting the seasons, which depend on this angle. If the earth were not spheroidal, but spherical, the inclination of the ecliptic to the equinoxial would vary to the extent of $12\frac{4}{13}$ degrees. While the earth's orbit vibrates through several degrees, the attraction on the protuberant matter of the equator draws it down toward the plane of the orbit.

Mr. Stockwell, reflecting on the phenomena of the solar system, connected with its stability, makes the following observation: "A system of bodies moving in very eccentric orbits is one of manifest instability; and if it can also be shown that a system of bodies moving in circular orbits is one of unstable equilibrium, it would seem that between the two supposed conditions a system might exist which should possess a greater degree of stability than either. The idea is thus suggested of the existence of a system of bodies in which the masses of the different bodies are *so adjusted to their mean distances* as to insure to the system a *greater degree of permanence* than would be possible by *any other distribution of masses.*"

The grand progressive scheme of life, as revealed by geology,

requiring vast ages for its development, clearly points to the perpetuity of the solar system as an indispensable requisite. This *adjustment* of the physical system—in view of the many perturbing influences which threaten its existence—to the system of life, incapable of enduring great vicissitudes, must be regarded as a striking proof of a Divine Intelligence in creation and preservation.

Laplace criticises Newton for indulging in speculations which connected the Almighty with the solar system, while he himself framed an hypothesis virtually excluding him from the realm of nature. The Christian philosopher will do well to imitate the devout spirit of Newton, the great discoverer of the law of gravitation, rather than the irreverent spirit of Laplace, its greatest expounder.

---

## ART. VII.—SYNOPSIS OF THE QUARTERLIES AND OTHERS OF THE HIGHER PERIODICALS.

### *American Quarterly Reviews.*

BAPTIST QUARTERLY, October, 1876. (Philadelphia.)—1. The Literary Elements in Theology. 2. Horatio Balch Hackett. 3. The Future of Catholic Nations. 4. Education among the Baptists of this Country during the Last One Hundred Years. 5. Progress of a Century. 6. Modern Evolution Theories.

BIBLIOTHECA SACRA, October, 1876. (Andover.)—The Madonna Di San Sisto. 2. The Synthetic or Cosmic Philosophy. 3. Recent Works Bearing on the Relation of Science to Religion. 4. The Immortality of the Human Soul. 5. An Exposition of the Original Text of Genesis i and ii. 6. The Idea of God in the Soul of Man. 7. Dale on the Atonement.

CHRISTIAN QUARTERLY, October, 1876. (Cincinnati.)—1. Baptism and Christian Union—the Real Question. 2. Animal Life. 3. Faith in the Unseen. 4. Materialism. 5. The Work Assigned to Faith. 6. Baptism for Remission of Sin is Justification by Faith. 7. Behold the Man. 8. Foreign Missions.

NEW ENGLANDER, October, 1876. (New Haven.)—1. The Influence of the Crusades upon European Literature. 2. The Belfast Address in another Light. 3. The Last Century of Congregationalism; or, the Influence in Church and State of the Faith and Polity of the Pilgrim Fathers. 4. The New Theology. 5. Mr. Lettsom's Version of the Middle German Epic. 6. *Logos and Cosmos:* Nature as Related to Language. 7. Necessary Truths and the Principle of Identity. 8. On some of the Relations between Islam and Christianity. 9. Muller's Rig Veda and Commentary.

NEW ENGLAND HISTORICAL AND GENEALOGICAL REGISTER, October, 1876. (Boston.)—1. Memoir of Charles W. Moore, Esq 2. The Field Family of New Jersey. 3. Notes on American History. Nos. IX–XII. 4. The Garrison Family of Massachusetts. 5. Gleanings. No. 69. Capt. John Ayres. No. 70. Farrars and Brewers of Essex County, Mass. 6. Deaths in Stratham, N. H., from 1741. 7. Extracts from the Diary of the late Hon. William D. Williamson. 8. Ab-

stracts of the Earliest Wills in Suffolk County, Mass. 9. The Second Foot Company of Newbury, 1711. 10. Memoranda from the Rev. William Cooper's Interleaved Almanacs. 11. Record of the Boston Committee of Correspondence, Inspection, and Safety. 12. Samuel Allen of Windsor, Conn., and his Descendants. 13. Baptisms in Dover, N. H., 1717–66. 14. Abstracts of the Earliest Wills in Middlesex County, Mass. 15. Passengers and Vessels to America. 16. Ancestry of Admiral Porter.

North American Review, October, 1876. (Boston.)—1. The Southern Question. 2. Whisky Ring. 3. Von Holt's History of the United States. 4. An Episode in Municipal Government. 5. The "Independents" in the Canvass.

Presbyterian Quarterly and Princeton Review, October, 1876. (New York.) 1. American Methodism in 1876. 2. The Indian Question. 3. Our Indian Policy Further Considered. 4. Organization of the Fundamental Principles of Social Science. 5. The Organic Unity of the Church. 6. The Great Awakening of 1740. 7. The Revivals of the Century. 8. Recent German Works on Apologetics. 9. Philosophy and Science in Germany. 10. Current Notes.

Quarterly Review of the Evangelical Lutheran Church, October, 1876. (Gettysburg.)—1. Of Confession. 2. An Hour with the Fathers. 3. The Theological Seminary of the General Synod. 4. Protestantism and Catholicism in their Influence upon the Liberty and Welfare of Nations. 5. Our Home Mission Work in Cities. 6. Additional Remarks on the Ministerium.

Universalist Quarterly, October, 1876. (Boston.)—1. Beauty in Common Life. 2. Egyptian Book of the Dead. 3. The Avesta. 4. Immer's Hermeneutics of the New Testament. 5. Luther and Schleiermacher as Preachers. 6. Tyndall and Martineau; or, the Debatable Ground between Materialism and Religion. 7. The Polity of the Universalist Church.

American Catholic Quarterly Review, October, 1876. (Philadelphia.)—1. The Church and the People. 2. What the Church and the People Have Done for the Science of Geography. 3. The Past and the Present Indissolubly United in Religion. 4. A Plan for the Proposed Catholic University. 5. The Nine Days' Queen. 6. Who is to Blame for the Little Big Horn Disaster? 7. How Shall we Meet the Scientific Heresies of the Day?

We have received the first four numbers of this stately Quarterly, and looked over its pages with gratification. In our country, where the Protestant principle of the right of private judgment prevails, it is desirable to hear the highest and best utterances of those who deny that right. No little ability of thought and grace of style appear in its pages. Besides fine literary articles, there are able defenses of our common Christianity, skillful argumentations in behalf of Roman peculiarities, and, we may add, sharp aggression upon Protestant communions, among which Methodism comes in for a very explicit share.

The Roman communion, like its elder and more authentic sisters, the Syriac and the Greek Churches, erred not so much by the corruption of primitive doctrines as by spurious additions to them. The Reformation of the sixteenth century was an attempt, very honest and to a great degree successful, to fling off the later and spurious, and fall back upon the primi-

tive and pure. It aimed to discard the modern and retain the ancient. Hence Protestantism is more ancient and primitive than Romanism. The primitive truth contained in Romanism, and in the written canon preserved by the Roman as well as by the other Churches, is essential Protestantism.

Among these Roman novelties, most pre-eminent in spuriousness and pregnant with danger, is the ascription to the Bishop of a single city of a supremacy over all other Bishops, culminating in a final ascription to the same prelate of the attribute of "infallibility"! The city selected as the theocratic city was the old Pagan Rome! This strange anomaly really arising from the fact that Rome was the politically imperial city, was theologically based upon the late and fanciful myth that St. Peter was once a Bishop there; and under pretense that the attributes of Peter descend along the whole descending line of Roman Bishops, we honest American Christians are called upon to abdicate our own reason and conscience, and accept the pronouncements of the present Roman Bishop in their stead. This is a decidedly tall demand. It calls for a very tall pile of resistless reasons authenticating itself. But the reasons are not impressive. Most well read and thoughtful Protestants recognize upon their very face ample warrant for prompt rejection, excusing us from wasting time in any extended examination.

Old Hugh Broughton remarks that Rome is not a favorite locality in biblical estimation. In the Apocalypse it is uniformly Babylon, an antitheocratic city, doomed to destruction. The great red dragon of Paganism has his native home in Rome. And Gibbon somewhere gives us a splendid passage picturing the fact that the stupendous pagan political empire of Rome was succeeded by a spiritual empire of deeper despotism, longer duration, and wider extent. And on the very surface of the Apocalypse we have the same fact pictured to the most transient eye. The great red Roman dragon of seven heads and ten horns is succeeded by the Roman beast with seven heads and ten horns. How far the scrutiny of details would verify the first impressions we will not now inquire. We only say that the first impressions are profoundly suggestive.

But the greatest practical Roman error, that which opens the deepest and broadest chasm between her and Catholic Christendom, is her claim to punish doctrinal dissent with physical

inflictions. Roman Catholicism is thus a standing vocal menace against the religious freedom of the world. We quoted a few years ago, from the "Catholic World," the assertion of the right of the Church to punish physically those who were "criminal in the order of ideas;" in other words, to kill us if we refuse to be Romanists. And lately, a leading French Catholic said to the Protestants, "You are bound by your principles to tolerate us, we are not bound by our principles to tolerate you." What is the proper reply to such a statement? Our reply would be, We are bound to tolerate you as Romanists in the exercise of your own religion, but we are not obliged to tolerate you as menacers of our rights to the exercise of our religion. In the last character you are secular enemies, to be guarded against, defeated, and punished. If they reply, *But this claim to not tolerate you is part of our religion;* then we must answer, *So much the worse, for then no Protestant principle requires us to tolerate even a religion that menaces our religious freedom.* Prudentially, the tolerance should be maintained so far as safety allows; but in dealing with a religious communion bound by irrepealable pledges never to tolerate where there is power to inflict, we can never forget what the law of self-preservation requires.

Roman Catholicism, so far as it is Catholic, is doubtless Christian: so far as it is Roman, it is deeply pagan.

SOUTHERN REVIEW, October, 1876. (Baltimore.)—1. Christian Theology. 2. Mind and Matter. 3. Caroline Herschel. 4. The Theistic Conception of the World. 5. Robert Emmet. 6. Capital Punishment. 7. Louisa, Queen of Prussia. 8. The Heart of the Continent. 9. The Teachings of our Lord in Regard to a Future Life.

Dr. Bledsoe accepts the work of the Joint Commission at Cape May in the following frank and whole-souled style:—

In our humble opinion the Joint Commission which recently met at Cape May to adjust the difficulties between the two Methodist Episcopal Churches of this country have done a great and good work. Indeed, we have always been in favor of "an era of *good feeling*" between the two Churches, provided it were, at the same time, an era of *just principles;* and such an era we now have reason to believe has been inaugurated by the action of said Commission. As to the books by Myers and Fuller, which we intended to dissect and discuss in this number of our Review, they may now fight out their own battle in their own way. We have buried the hatchet. We are more than satisfied with the work of the

Joint Commission. God grant it may prove a permanent blessing to both Churches, and to the people of America!

Dr. Summers notices the work of the same Commission in the following bitter and accusatory way:—

The plan of fraternity is intended to be a finality, so far as the points agreed upon are concerned. We expect to keep it in good faith, as we did the Plan of Separation. But we are not sure that the Northern General Conference so intended, or, if it did, that its successor in 1880 will be bound by it. We are reminded of 1844 and 1848.

We fear the good doctor will die of that fatal "Plan of Separation," and that he will die with the fictitious phrase mouttering upon his lips. Dear doctor, there never was any "Plan of Separation." The document, untruly so-called, was also repealed by our General Conference of 1848, for the reason, fully assigned and formally evidenced, that the Church South had repeatedly violated it. Dr. S. very well knows that our Church earnestly denies having committed any such breach of faith as he here charges, and his reiterating such a charge at this point is an unfraternity which endangers his right of objecting, as he so often does, that utterances on the part of northern editors are unfraternal. We should like to see the editor of the Nashville and of our Northern shake hands as the two representative Bourbons of their respective Churches.

## *English Reviews.*

BRITISH QUARTERLY REVIEW, October 1, 1876. (London.)—1. Secular Changes of Climate. 2. Dean Hook on the English Reformation. 3. The American Centennial. 4. Disestablishment and Disendowment. 5. American Ecclesiastical Law. 6. The Turks in Europe. 7. Daniel Deronda.

LONDON QUARTERLY REVIEW, October, 1876. (London.)—1. The Microscope and its Revelations. 2. The Holy Spirit in the Epistle to the Ephesians. 3. The Problem of Human Existence. 4. Philosophy in Ancient India. 5. Wordsworth's Prose Works. 6. Retribution. 7. America in the Centennial Year.

LONDON QUARTERLY REVIEW, October, 1876. (New York: Leonard Scott Publishing Company, 41 Barclay-street.)—1. Strawberry Hill. 2. The Arctic Regions and the Eskimo. 3. London Alms and London Pauperism. 4. The Papal Monarchy. 5. The Suez Canal an International Highway. 6. Pictorial Illustrations of Shakspeare. 7. The Turkish Empire. 8. The Life of the Prince Consort. 9. The Eastern Question and the Government.

WESTMINSTER REVIEW, October, 1876. (New York: Leonard Scott Publishing Company.)—1. Indian Affairs: Recent Legislation. 2. William Godwin. 3. Political Economy as a Safeguard of Democracy. 4. Lord Althorp and the First Reform Act. 5. Shakspeare's Young Men. 6. Political Development and Party Government.

EDINBURGH REVIEW, October, 1876. (New York: Leonard Scott Publishing Company.)—1. Bancroft's Native Races of North America. 2. Secret Correspondence on Marie Antoinette. 3. The Declaration of Paris. 4. Sir Philip Sidney. 5. Dr. Smith's Dictionary of Christian Antiquities. 6. Daniel Deronda. 7. Morality without Metaphysic. 8. Depreciation of Silver. 9. Bosnia and Bulgaria.

In a notice of a book on Byron, by Mr. Minto, the "Westminster" has the following startling hint touching Mrs. Stowe's publication in regard to that part:—

It was perhaps necessary that he should make but scant allusion to Byron's daughter Allegra, the story of whose brief life is so intertwined with that of one still living; and he is perhaps right in dismissing with all but silent contempt the scandal bruited by a "celebrated living authoress who was slightly acquainted with Lady Byron." We warn Mr. Minto, however, that he may find it necessary to revert to these unsavory matters, as there are those in London who profess to speak with authority, and murmur the scandal still.—P. 285.

The following critique on Stanley's "Jewish Church" (noticed in our Book-table) is suggestive of both the position and ability of Stanley:—

It would not be easy to find among the books of this year one which presents us with more delightful reading than the third volume of Dean Stanley's "Lectures on the Jewish Church," occupied with the period from the Captivity to the Christian Era. Whether we agree or disagree, it is impossible not to be fascinated by Dean Stanley's picturesque style, by his extraordinary wealth of illustration, by the power with which, without effort, he shows likeness as well as unlikeness in the struggles and difficulties of old days to those of our time, by his large-hearted sympathy. We do not, indeed, look in Dr. Stanley for the careful striving after accuracy which distinguishes such writers as Ewald or Kuenen. We distrust at times his brilliant generalizations, and the conclusions which he draws from picturesque phrases in prophet or psalm; but both for the scholar who uses this book as a rapid survey of that which he has already gained by slow, laborious work, or for the general reader who desires that the result of other men's reading should be put clearly and broadly before them, the book is invaluable. For the first time, and in the compass of less than two hundred pages, the Jewish history from Judas Maccabeus to the dawn of Christianity is presented to us in a manner entirely free from confusion and difficulty; while the earlier part of the history, and the manner in which the thoughts of other creeds filtered into and mingled with the Jewish faith, are placed before us with keen insight and careful research. In a book so valuable we do not like to hint at defects; but in one point we find the same fault that runs through the whole of

Dr. Stanley's works, and renders them unsatisfactory to those who desire to know the stand-point of the teacher from whom they learn so much. Whenever Dr. Stanley speaks of the miraculous he gives an uncertain sound. He indulges in poetic phrases which, whether meant to do so or not, disguises his real opinions, and we rise from the perusal of the book totally unable to say whether the writer intends us to believe in miracles, or to regard them as entirely the creation of a later time. This is especially the case in the present volume in regard to the account of Belshazzar's feast. The relation is animated, brilliant, even impassioned; but we are wholly at a loss to know whether Dr. Stanley believes that the writing on the wall, if it were really there, was formed by the hand of man or by the divine hand. When will our liberal divines say what people look for on this point? Instead of ambiguous utterances, we look for plain statements, as plain as are Dean Stanley's assertions that he does not hold, with the High-Church party, that the Christian minister is descended from the Jewish priesthood and their "mechanical, bullock-slaying, fumigating ministrations." With the style in which the "Lectures" are written we have one fault, and only one, to find. The dean, like Lord Macaulay, is too allusive. His books are no mere magazine articles, which would die with the month or the year in which they are produced, but should be permanent when the mere *brochures* of the day are forgotten, and the allusions of the day are known no more. He should not, therefore, speak of the Book of Judith and its imaginary invasion in these terms: "It is a romance intended to inspire the Israelite maidens with a sense of their duty in case of a new foreign invasion; even as in our own days an imaginary battle in the hills of Surrey was intended to delineate in the possible future the needs of England under like circumstances."

We trust that the "Lectures on the Jewish Church" will be read when the "Battle of Dorking" has, as must be the case in spite of its brilliancy, wholly passed out of mind; and though such references give vivacity to the style, they cannot but in some measure detract from the value of the permanent volume. But enough of fault-finding. The book is, on the whole, thoroughly worthy of its author's reputation; and if he will only speak his opinions, whatever they may be, distinctly and plainly about the miraculous, we trust that he will carry his labors into the yet more difficult and dangerous ground on the borders of which he has halted.—Pp. 243, 244.

British and Foreign Evangelical Review, October, 1876. (London.)—1. Schleiermacher Interpreted by Himself and the Men of his School. 2. The Apologetic Function of the Church in the Present Time. 3. Romanism in the United States. 4. On the Translation of Galatians iii, 20, and Hebrews ix, 16, 17. 5. The Ecclesiastical History of Ireland. 6. The Scientific Doctrine of Continuity.

The Third Article is one of several discussions of the character of the United States which have appeared in different British reviews drawn forth by our centennial, characterized

generally by great accuracy of statement, and universally by great fairness of spirit. The writer treats his subject with the more accuracy from the fact of a two years' residence in the country not long ago.

We were struck with a passage, written by a Calvinist, probably a minister, in a theological journal, noticing the New York NATION. The spirit of favorable anticipation with which such a man names the NATION contrasts suggestively with the bitter and malignant meanness with which the NATION has treated men of his class. We quote his words to show how he (as we also for a while) too favorably mistook the character of that paper:—

> The "New York Nation," which is conducted by Mr. Edwin Godkin, an Irishman, has been trying, with some success, to put down the system of mean and malignant depreciation by which the newspapers are generally polluted and disgraced, by showing the example of a dignified but effective journalism, which proscribes all base advantages, and adjusts quarrels by the laws of honor and chivalry.

The NATION did at the first speak in its political editorials with so stern an ethic in regard to public men, even of its own professed party, that, in spite of its persistent semi-infidelity, (if the *semi* is not surplusage,) we did, for some time, consult its columns as a politico-ethical oracle, and inclined to form severe opinions of any man it condemned. But the oracle has proved an imposture. For the last few months it has become the unflinching apologist of political knaveries. It has disclosed so genuine an affinity with public dishonesties that we assign it a permanent place in the ranks of what Horace Greeley once so piquantly and truly dubbed the "Satanic Press." Of Protestant evangelical Christianity it has generally spoken only to sneer; of the Protestant evangelical ministry it has very uniformly spoken only to insult. We can call to mind a few instances. Years ago it maintained that ministers were unfit to be educators by reason of that moral effeminacy by which women and clergymen are classed together. More lately it warned the ministry not to express any public opinion as to the innocence or guilt of Henry Ward Beecher, inasmuch as their habits of mind disqualified them for right judgment of the force of evidence; that quality, we suppose, being the

high prerogative of newspaper paragraphists like Mr. Godkin. Still more lately, in several pages of twaddle, it advises the ministry not to publicly discuss the subject of evolution, for here, too, their studies disqualify them for logical discussion. We have only to say that the American Protestant ministry has within its limits as learned and able a body of thinkers as any existent profession, whether legal, medical, or editorial. When the editor of the NATION undertakes, time after time, to teach that profession its manifold incompetencies, he only shows himself a very conceited addle-head. Any minister who is imbecile enough to go to the NATION for counsel in his duties deserves the insult he is sure to encounter.

CONTEMPORARY REVIEW. Eleventh Year. Strahan & Co., Paternoster Row. London.

Dr. Rigg's article in this number furnishing a history of the position of John Wesley in regard to the Church of England and to Church government in general, exhibits full ability and mastery of the subject. It fully sustains the true Wesleyanism of the present position of English Methodism. He demonstrates the conclusion that "Wesley not only pointed but paved the way to all that has since been done, and that the utmost divergence of Methodism from the Church of England at this day is but the prolongation of a line the beginning of which was traced by Wesley's own hand." And he concludes with the following significant paragraph:—

> It is manifestly now too late to think of the reabsorption of Methodism into the Church of England, for English Methodism is not only itself now a large and consolidated communion, but it has been the fruitful mother of many other communions—of the Methodist Episcopal Church of the United States, by far the largest Protestant Church in America, (perhaps in the world,) and of Colonial Methodist Churches and Mission Churches almost without end—not to mention the seceding Methodist Churches in both hemispheres. With such a family of Churches derived from itself, that parent stock of Methodism, which claims direct descent from John Wesley, and which has hitherto walked more strictly in his counsels than any of the offshoot Churches, is never likely to consent to merge its own identity or annul its historical position.—P. 681.

Dr. Rigg makes the following noteworthy statement in regard to our own episcopacy:—

In his independent organization of American Methodism, he [Wesley] embodied in general his own ideal of an independent Methodist Church.—P. 673.

In full view of this concession we have some surprise to express at Dr. Rigg's published utterances from our late General Conference, hostile, to a partisan degree, against our episcopacy.

## *German Reviews.*

THEOLOGISCHE STUDIEN UND KRITIKEN. (Theological Essays and Reviews.) 1877. First Number. *Essays:* 1. RIEHM, The Idea of Atonement in the Old Testament. 1. KÖSTLIN, State, Law, and Church in Evangelical Ethics. *Thought and Remarks:* KLEINERT, Remarks on Isaiah xx–xxii and 2 Kings xviii–xx. *Reviews:* 1. LANGE. History of Materialism, reviewed by SCHMID. 2. SIEGFRIED. The Task of the History of Old Testament Exegesis at the present time, reviewed by RIEHM.

Professor Julius Köstlin, now one of the editors of the *Studien und Kritiken*, has established, by a number of able works, especially his biography of Martin Luther, (see Methodist Quarterly Review, 1876, p. 760,) the reputation of being one of the foremost theologians of Protestant Germany. He begins in this number a series of articles on the rights and duties of secular governments, especially with regard to the religious and moral interest of mankind. It is time, he thinks, for Protestant theology to subject the prevailing theories of the essence, boundaries, and estimation of the State to a new examination; for on the answer given to these questions will depend the solution of the old problem of the relation between State and Church, and the modern problem of the relation of both State and Church to the great social questions of the day. In the first article the passages of the Bible relating to State authorities, the opinions of Luther and the other reformers of the sixteenth century, and the views of modern Protestant writers on ethics are stated. Among the writers whose views are stated at length are Wuttke, (*Sittenlehre*, 3d edit., by L. Schulze.) Stahl. (*Philosophie des Rechts*, and *Staats und Rechtslehre.*) Mühler, late Prussian minister of ecclesiastical affairs, (*Grundlinien einer Philosophie der Staats und Rechtslehre nach evangelischen Principien.* 1873.) Rothe, (*Theologische Ethik*, 2d edit.,) Schleiermacher, Alexander Vinet, Beck, (*Kirche und Staat.*) Vilmar, (*Theologische Moral*, 1871,) Harless, (*Staat und Kirche,*) Oettingen, (*Christliche Sittenlehre.*)

## Art. VIII.—FOREIGN RELIGIOUS INTELLIGENCE.

### THE ROMAN CATHOLIC CHURCH IN EUROPE.

From a comparative work on the States of Europe by one of the best living statisticians, Professor Brachelli, (*Die Staaten Europas*, 3d edit., Brünn, 1876,) which is now in the course of publication, we extract the following statistical summary of the Roman Catholics in Europe:—

"The supreme ecclesiastical power in the Roman Catholic Church is exercised by its head, the pope, in Rome, who is assisted by the college of cardinals. The pope enjoys the position and all the honors of a sovereign, and, in accordance with an ordinance of 1059, is chosen for life by the college of cardinals among its own members by a two-thirds majority of the electoral votes. The election takes place on the eleventh day after the decease of a pope, in the Vatican palace, in the so-called conclave, a wholly secluded place, which the cardinals are not allowed to leave until the new pope is chosen. The candidate for the papal see must be at least fifty-five years old, and not have any bodily defect of importance; otherwise the cardinals are only bound by an oath to make a choice according to the best of their knowledge. This includes the duty not to elect the candidate which the Catholic governments of Austria, France, Spain, and Naples, according to the vote of exclusion belonging to them, may designate as not acceptable. The pope-elect assumes a new name, is proclaimed to the people, is accustomed, in accordance with tradition, to confirm certain laws, and receives the consecration, the pallium, and the tiara from the bishop of Ostia, as dean of the college of cardinals. The pope has the title of 'Holiness,' or 'Holy Father.' He possesses a numerous court, and confers four orders of knights: 1. The order of Christ, which was founded in Portugal, recognized by the pope in 1320, and is conferred upon persons of the highest rank; 2. The order of St. Gregory the Great, which was founded in 1831, and has four classes; 3. The order of Pius, for all religious denominations, founded in 1847, and containing three classes; 4. The order of St. Sylvester, which was established in 1871, and comprises three classes. The order of the Holy Sepulchre, which was founded in 1099, and in 1868 divided into three classes, is conferred in the name of the pope by the Latin patriarchs of Jerusalem; and the ecclesiastical order of the Knights of St. John of Jerusalem, which was founded in 1118, is likewise under the auspices of the papal chair. The relation of the pope to the kingdom of Italy has been regulated by the law of May 13, 1871. According to it the person of the pope is sacred and inviolable; the Italian government renders to him sovereign honors, and guarantees to him an annuity of 3,225,000 lire, and the enjoyment, free from taxes, of the Vatican and Lateran palaces and the villa of Castel Gondolfo, which places are not subject to the jurisdiction of the State,

and endowed with the rights of immunity, as well as those rooms which are temporarily occupied by the pope, or in which a conclave or a council are held. The pope shall not be impeded in the full exercise of his ecclesiastical functions. In the same way the free intercourse of the Holy See with the Episcopate and the entire Catholic world is guaranteed. The embassadors of the pope, and those of foreign powers accredited near him, enjoy the privilege of the law of nations.

The cardinals constitute, under the presidency of the pope, the sacred college, in which important affairs of the Roman Catholic world are discussed. The college of cardinals is divided into three classes: The cardinal-bishops, (6,) the cardinal-priests, (50,) and the cardinal deacons, (14.) The first and third classes have their permanent residence in Rome; to the second class belong a number of cardinals, who in other cities occupy the position of archbishops or bishops. The oldest cardinal-bishop is the cardinal-dean, with various honorary rights. The cardinal-chamberlain makes the necessary preparations for the conclave, and governs with the heads of the three classes of the college during the vacancy of the papal chair. The cardinals are appointed by the pope, have the rank of princes of sovereign houses, and bear the title 'Eminence.'"

Under the pope the ecclesiastical power is exercised by archbishops and bishops. The archbishops are also, as metropolitans, placed over one or several episcopal dioceses, which, in union with the archbishop's diocese, constitute an ecclesiastical province. In this respect the archbishops rank the suffragan-bishops. Some bishops are exempt from the metropolitan jurisdiction of archbishops, and are immediately subordinate to the pope. The vicars-apostolic and prefects-apostolic, who depend immediately upon the pope, as well as the abbots and prelates, (*nullius dioecescos*,) also enjoy episcopal jurisdiction. The archbishops may hold provincial councils, and the bishops diocesan synods, in accordance with the Church laws. The former, which are presided over by the metropolitan, and composed of bishops, prelates, and other clergymen of high rank, have a concurrent power in questions of ecclesiastical legislation; while the latter, consisting of the provosts, parish priests, and heads of monasteries, appear solely as clerical assemblies of the diocese with advisory powers. The ecclesiastical authorities of the Roman Catholic Church of Europe were, in 1876, composed as follows:—

| Countries. | Archbishops. | Bishops. Suffragan. | Bishops. Exempt. |
|---|---|---|---|
| Austro-Hungarian Monarchy | 14 | 47 | .. |
| Germany | 5 | 14 | 6 |
| Great Britain and Ireland | 5 | 37 | 1 |
| France | 17 | 67 | .. |
| Italy | 19 | 143 | 69 |
| Russia | 1 | 8 | .. |
| Sweden and Norway | .. | .. | .. |
| Denmark | .. | .. | .. |
| Netherlands | 1 | 4 | .. |
| Luxembourg | .. | .. | 1 |
| Belgium | 1 | 5 | .. |
| Switzerland | .. | .. | [illegible] |
| Spain | 9 | 45 | .. |
| Portugal | 8 | 16 | .. |
| Greece | 2 | 4 | .. |
| Turkey | 4 | 4 | 1 |
| Total | 81 | 399 | 82 |

Of vicars-apostolic there are: 3 in Germany, 1 in Austria, 4 in Great Britain and Ireland, 1 in Sweden and Norway, 2 in Roumania, 4 in Turkey—total, 15. Of prefects-apostolic: Germany, Sweden and Norway, Denmark, and Switzerland, each have 1; and of abbots (*nullius dioceseos*) Austria has 1, Italy 11, Switzerland 2, and Monaco 1.

The secular and regular clergy in the several countries numbered, in 1876, the following:—

| Countries. | Secular Clergy. | Monks and Members of Religious Congregations. | Nuns. |
|---|---|---|---|
| Austro-Hungarian Monarchy | 24,400 | 9,398 | 7,673 |
| Germany | 18,300 | 1,933 | 16,666 |
| Great Britain and Ireland | 5,000 | .... | .... |
| France | 43,000 | 17,776 | 90,343 |
| Italy | 100,000 | .... | .... |
| Russia | 6,000 | .... | .... |
| Netherlands | 2,060 | 815 | 137 |
| Luxembourg | 850 | .... | .... |
| Belgium | 5,000 | 2,991 | 15,205 |
| Switzerland | 2,000 | 550 | 1,880 |
| Spain | 40,000 | 719 | 12,990 |
| Portugal | 10,000 | .... | 1,500 |
| Total | 256,110 | .... | .... |

If these figures are compared with the Roman Catholic population, it will be found that the proportion of priest to population is as follows:—

| Countries. | No. Inhab'ts for every Priest. | Countries. | No. Inhab'ts for every Priest. |
|---|---|---|---|
| Italy | 267 | France | 823 |
| Spain | 419 | Belgium | 1,050 |
| Portugal | 436 | Austro-Hungarian Monarchy | 1,144 |
| Switzerland | 540 | Russia | 1,200 |
| Luxembourg | 571 | Great Britain and Ireland | 1,820 |
| Netherlands | 630 | | |
| German Empire | 812 | Total | 9,262 |

The following is the proportion of monks and nuns to the Catholic population:—

| Countries. | No. Rom. Cath. for every Monk. | No. Rom. Cath. for every Nun. | Countries. | No. Rom. Cath. for every Monk. | No. Rom. Cath. for every Nun. |
|---|---|---|---|---|---|
| Netherlands | 1,530 | .... | German Empire | 7,600 | 900 |
| Belgium | 1,630 | 325 | Spain | 21,760 | 1,200 |
| France | 1,970 | 390 | Portugal | .... | 2,900 |
| Switzerland | 2,000 | 590 | | | |
| Austro-Hung. Monarchy | 2,970 | 5,637 | Total | 39,460 | 11,942 |

In Italy all monasteries and ecclesiastical congregations were abolished by royal decree of July 7, 1866. The monasteries of male orders and congregations were suppressed in Portugal in 1834, and in Spain in 1841. In the latter country, however, the orders and congregations devoted to foreign missions, education, and the nursing of the sick, were exempted from the prohibition. In Sweden and Norway the establishment of monasteries is not permitted by law. In Switzerland the Federal Constitution forbids the reception of Jesuits, and of any congregations affiliated to them in any part of the confederation; also the estab-

lishment of any new, and the re-establishment of abolished, monasteries. Germany, by an imperial law of July 4, 1872, excluded the Jesuits; and Prussia, by a law of May 31, 1875, all ecclesiastical congregations except those which devote themselves to the nursing of the sick. In Hesse, a law of April 23, 1875, provided that new establishments of religious orders shall not be admitted into the grand duchy, and that those now existing, except female orders devoting themselves to education, shall not be permitted to admit new members. Only congregations which occupy themselves with nursing the sick are not included in the provisions of the law. In the kingdom of Saxony there are only two monasteries of Cistercian nuns, and the establishment of new monasteries is prohibited for all time. In the kingdom of Wurtemberg and the grand duchy of Baden, the establishment of any new monastery requires a special authorization by the government.

### The Greek Oriental Church.

In the Greek Oriental Church, which also calls itself the Orthodox, and in Russia and Turkey the Greek Catholic, the constitution is different in the several States. In Russia its head is the emperor, under whom the highest ecclesiastical power is exercised by the Holy Synod, the members of which, both clerical and lay, are appointed by the emperor. The bishop of Montenegro receives his consecration from the Russian Synod. In Turkey the ecclesiastical power is vested in the Ecumenical patriarch of Constantinople and the Holy Synod. The latter consists of the four metropolitans who carry the patriarchal seal, and of from six to eight other metropolitans who are called by the patriarch; but all the Greek bishops who are present in Constantinople can take part in its deliberations. The national Churches of Roumania, Servia, and Bulgaria are dependent upon the patriarch of Constantinople in doctrinal matters, but are otherwise independent. In each of these three countries the ecclesiastical power is in the hands of a Synod, which in Servia consists of the bishops, and in Roumania and Bulgaria of the bishops and archbishops. In Greece the Church is ruled by a permanent "Holy Synod," and in the Austro-Hungarian monarchy by an "Episcopal Synod," the monarch in both countries having the chief superintendence. The "Holy Synod" of Greece consists of five members, who are either bishops or other high ecclesiastical dignitaries; the Synod of Austria is exclusively formed by metropolitans and bishops. In the Austro-Hungarian monarchy there are three different ecclesiastical provinces: one in Austria proper, with a metropolitan at Czernovitz, in the Bukovina; and two in the lands of the Hungarian crown, of which one, with a metropolitan at Carlovitz, is for the Servian, and the other, with a metropolitan at Hermannstadt, is for the Roumanian nationality. The bishops of each province form a Synod, under the presidency of a metropolitan. All the bishops of the monarchy, moreover, unite in a General Synod, in which the metropolitan of Carlovitz is the presiding officer. The latter bears the title of a patriarch, and in ecclesiastical affairs all

the bishops of the empire are subordinate to him. In each of the three provinces Church Congresses are occasionally held, consisting of the bishops and representatives of the clergy and laity. In the administration of his diocese every metropolitan, archbishop, and bishop is assisted by a consistory. The statistics of this Church, in 1876 were as follows:—

| Countries. | Metrop's & Archb'ps. | Bishops. | Secular Priests. | Monks. | Nuns. |
|---|---|---|---|---|---|
| Austria proper | 1 | 2 | 863 | .... | .... |
| Hungary | 2 | 8 | 3,100 | 200 | .... |
| Russia (inclusive of Asiatic provinces) | 16 | 32 | 50,758 | 10,862 | 14,707 |
| Greece | 16 | 15 | 4,661 | 1,830 | 150 |
| Roumania | 2 | 6 | 9,702 | 4,762 | 4,076 |
| Servia | 1 | 3 | 712 | 122 | .... |
| Turkey | 49 | 51 | .... | .... | .... |
| Montenegro | .. | 1 | .... | .... | .... |
| Total | 87 | 118 | .... | .... | .... |

The proportion of the secular clergy and monks and nuns to the total population is as follows:—

| Countries. | No. of Inhabitants for every Secular Priest. | Monk. | Nun. |
|---|---|---|---|
| Austro-Hungarian Monarchy | 884 | 10,900 | .... |
| Russia | 1,060 | 5,000 | 3,700 |
| Greece | 350 | 900 | 10,000 |
| Roumania | 420 | 857 | 1,003 |
| Servia | 1,900 | 1,1000 | .... |
| Total | 4,614 | 28,657 | 14,703 |

## Art. IX.—FOREIGN LITERARY INTELLIGENCE.

The revised and enlarged edition of Herzog's "Theological Cyclopedia," the first number of which has just been issued, will be welcomed throughout the Protestant world. (*Real-Encyclopedie für Protestantische Theologie und Kirche.* Leipsic, 1876.) This work, the first edition of which was begun in 1853 and finished in 1863 with the eighteenth volume, (exclusive of several supplementary volumes published afterward,) gave to Protestant Theology its first worthy representative in the literature of Cyclopedias. While in nearly all departments of scientific theology the Protestant Churches have run ahead of Roman Catholicism in the province of comprehensive theological Cyclopedias, Catholic Germany was already in the field when the work of Herzog was begun, having produced two works, Aschbach's *Allgemeines Kirchenlexicon*, (1846–1850, 4 vols.,) and Wetzer's and Welte's *Kirchenlexicon*, (1846–1860, 12 vols.,) which, in spite of the biased stand-point from which they are written, contain a number of articles of recognized value. As Protestant Germany contains an infinitely larger number of eminent scholars than Catholic Germany, it was to be expected that this work of Professor Herzog would exceed in scien-

tific value its Catholic predecessors and rivals. That this expectation has been fully realized, even very few Catholics will at present dispute. Herzog's Cyclopedia has forever secured a high and honorable position in theological literature, and in the literature of special dictionaries. Works of this kind are invariably of greater importance and value for their own than for foreign countries. They cannot be expected to treat the affairs of foreign countries with the same fullness, nor even with the same accuracy, as those of their native land. Herzog's work forms no exception to this rule. Many of the articles relating to foreign countries are disproportionately meager, and America in particular occupies so little space that the German work is not only altogether insufficient to supply the wants of American Protestants, but, even from a German stand-point, it seems to us, a country like the United States, which has a larger Protestant population than any other country of the globe, should have received a more prominent attention. It was to be expected that an attempt made in this country to translate Herzog's work would fail, not only because the war interrupted the publication, but still more, because no sufficient provision had been made to supply the utter insufficiency of its American department. The Cyclopedia of Drs. M'Clintock and Strong, which, while carefully using the excellent articles in Herzog, Aschbach, Wetzer and Welte, aimed at an equal fullness in its American department as the German work possesses in its German department, was, therefore, a real want of American literature, and it is creditable to the Protestant Churches of the United States that they have produced the second great Protestant Cyclopedia. Protestant France has waited until 1876 before a work of similar comprehensiveness (Lichtenberger's *Encyclopédie de Theologie*) was begun; (see "Methodist Quarterly Review," Oct., 1876;) and England has up to this time not been heard from, though it has produced a number of smaller compends. Although we cannot bestow our approval upon the American department of Herzog's Cyclopedia, we cannot too warmly recommend its general excellences. The world-wide fame of German theology, which draws, in increasing numbers, theological students from the United States, England, Holland, France, and all other countries, to the German universities, has been honestly earned and is fully deserved. No one has ever looked into the foremost theological publications of Germany, be it in the original or in translations, without giving a ready and thankful recognition of the profound and unparalleled scholarship by which they have been produced. Herzog's Cyclopedia is one of the masterworks, perhaps the greatest, of German theology. It is, really, a vast theological library in itself, containing the important results of the ripest scholarship in all departments of theology. The new edition will be edited by Professor Herzog and Professor Plitt, both professors at the University of Erlangen. It will comprise fifteen volumes of eight hundred pages each, and is to be completed in about eight years. The list of contributors embraces among others the theologians Dillman, Dorner, Ebrard, Gass, Harnack, Jacobi, Kahnis, Keim, Köstlin, Lechler, Lutt-

hardt, Julius Müller, Piper, Reuss, Ritschl, Schweizer, Thiersch, Tholuck, Zöckler of Germany, Bersier and Pressensé of France, Oosterzee of Holland, Schaff of the United States, the jurists Hermann, (president of the Supreme Ecclesiastical Council in Berlin,) Friedberg, Hinschius, Dove, Mejer, and Wasserschleben; the Egyptologist Lepsius; the Orientalist Spiegel. The first number contains a number of articles which have been thoroughly revised by their authors or by other scholars, (some of them had appeared in the first supplementary volume, or the nineteenth volume of the whole work,) as *Alpha and Omega*, by F. Piper; *Abbadie*, by C. Schmidt; *Abendmahlsfeier*, (celebration of the Lord's Supper,) by Stähelin; *Abgaben Kirchliche*, (Church Rates,) by Mejer. Some articles have been entirely rewritten by other authors, and substituted for the articles of the first edition, as *Abendmahl*, (Lord's Supper,) by Burger and Herzog; *Aberglaube*, (Superstition,) by R. Hofman; *Abessininische Kirche*, (Abyssinian Church,) by Lüttke. It cannot, of course, be expected that all articles in a work like this should be of equal excellence. Thus, in the article on the *Abyssinian Church*, the history of the Protestant and Roman Catholic missions is too meager, and the ample literature on Abyssinia, which was called forth by the English-Abyssinian war, should have been noticed more fully; for as Volz, in an interesting essay (which we think deserved itself a mention in the article of the Cyclopedia) on *Die Christliche Kirche Aethiopiens*, in the *Studien und Kritiken*, 1869, (see a synopsis of this article in the "Methodist Quarterly Review," 1869,) showed, it contained a considerable amount of new information on the Abyssinian Church. But imperfections like this are the merest trifles in comparison with the general thoroughness which characterizes all the articles of this number, and which leave no doubt that the new edition of Herzog's Cyclopedia will be an entirely new work, and so rich in new matter that even all the owners of the old first edition will be anxious to obtain also the new one. To the theological seminaries of our country, in particular, the new edition of Herzog's Cyclopedia cannot be too strongly recommended; their library will be incomplete without it.

## Art. X.—QUARTERLY BOOK-TABLE.

### *Religion, Theology, and Biblical Literature.*

*Lectures on the History of the Jewish Church.* By ARTHUR PENRHYN STANLEY, D.D., Dean of Westminster, Corresponding Member of the Institute of France. Third Series. From the Captivity to the Christian Era. With two Maps. 8vo., pp. 519. New York: Scribner, Armstrong, & Co. Price, $4.

This third series of Stanley's magnificent survey of Hebrew history extends from the Babylonian era to the advent of Christ. It commences with a brilliant survey of the power and downfall of

Babylon, depicting that downfall as a great epoch in history, the demise of Shemitic supremacy, and the first ascendency of the Aryan or Japhetic race under the Persian Cyrus. The return of the Jews to their native land, the days of the later prophets, the close of the Persian period, and the influence of Persia and Zoroaster on the doctrines of later Judaism, are traced through an obscure period with a luminous hand. Alexander the Great, one of the truly greatest intellects of history, closes the Persian and inaugurates the Grecian Period. Of the Grecian race and period, as Alexander is the greatest secular leader, so Socrates is shown to be the greatest spiritual phenomenon. The gradual infusion of Grecism into Judaism, especially in their confluence at Alexandria, produced the Greco-Jewish books of the Apocrypha, and resulted in the Greek translation of the Old Testament called the Septuagint. Then arose the Maccabees, and the illustrious Jewish age of the Asmonean family, bringing us to the epoch when John the Baptizer announced the Advent. Upon this entire period between the Return and the Advent, over which the learned Prideaux shed his accurate but tedious erudition, Stanley pours the light of modern study, given in a style of gorgeous splendor, fascinating the reader's attention, and leaving vivid pictorials upon the memory.

The two traits that deeply mark Stanley's work are the broad *comprehensionism* by which he gathers into one Church all the good of all climes and ages as the true elect, and the strong *negativism* with which he seeks to reduce all supernaturalism to a minimum or a nihil. With his *comprehensionism* we can largely sympathize. From our old Hollandic Arminian ancestry, through Wesley and Fletcher, down to Pressensé and Cocker, we are able to hold that myriads in all lands are saved by a universal atonement to them historically unknown. We are open to all the most cheering lessons of the new comparative theology. And so far is this new and pleasing view from diminishing our missionary zeal, it rather cheers our missionary in his work, and endows him with a new skill in kindly meeting all there is good in heathendom, and revealing unto it a still more excellent way.

Far less do we sympathize with Stanley's negativism. He sets slight value on the opening chapters of Genesis, emphasizing the fact that no allusion is made thereto in all the subsequent Hebrew canon. He easily discards traditions of authorship, and subjects the sacred books to the freest criticism. Zechariah and Isaiah both he cuts in two, and assigns one part to some unknown author. The

book of Daniel was written in Palestine forsooth in the age of the Maccabees. And now if you suppose that by these appalling surrenders the very foundations are all destroyed, he delights to show what a priceless and indestructible residue remains. The part is better than the whole. For let criticism have all its say, and tumble about the documents as it pleases, you have but to compare the Jewish records with any other literature of antiquity to see that they are impregnated with a strange divinity. The people stands alone a deeply inspired race. That people, through its legislators, prophets, and psalmists, was the front leader of humanity into the empyrean regions of spiritual truths; truths which, easily conceding to criticism and science all they claim, remain indestructible. And, then, centrally, but not alone, Hebraism is the prophetic antecedent of the divine Prophet of our and all faith.

Having rejected the creational and Adamic myths of Genesis, Stanley rather rejoices in Darwinism. He is pleased with the conception that man has acquired possession of the noblest faculties and divinest truths by long aeons of development. Those intuitive truths of God, holiness, retribution, and especially of *immortality*, the race has been enabled to grasp by successive growths. With advancing time these priceless gems of divine truth will shine to the eye of the soul with a clearer luster and a surer reality. And it is not by Judaism alone, but by Zoroastrianism, and Buddhism, and Hellenism, that contributions to this divine treasury have been made. If there is an intenser spiritualism, a loftier solemnity, a deeper inspiration in Hebraism, still there is one truth, that of *immortality*, that Hebraism but faintly uttered before the captivity had schooled her in the eastern lores, to which the Grecian Socrates gave the most distinct pronunciation. And, then, in a most beautiful chapter on Socrates, he shows how wonderfully the wonderful philosopher illustrates the prophets of Israel, yet even in his highest phases is their inferior. And from all the ages and races the rays converge upon One whom all the wise of every race are growing to acknowledge as the Prophet and teacher of all.

For the richness of the hues flung on sacred history we recommend to all our thoughtful ministers the reading of Stanley, checked by safer authorities, such as Keil's Introduction and Pusey on Daniel.

*Exodus;* or, the Second Book of Moses. By PETER LANGE, D.D., Professor of Theology in the University of Bonn. Translated by CHARLES M. MEAD, Ph.D., Professor of the Hebrew Language and Literature in the Theological Seminary, Andover, Mass. 12mo., pp. 141. New York: Scribner, Armstrong, & Co.

*Leviticus;* or, the Third Book of Moses. By FREDERIC GARDENER, D.D., Professor of the Literature and Interpretation of the Old Testament in the Berkeley Divinity School, Middletown, Conn. In which is incorporated a Translation of the greater part of the German Commentary on Leviticus. By PETER LANGE, D.D., Professor of Theology in the University of Bonn. 12mo., pp. 206. New York: Scribner, Armstrong, & Co.

It will be noted that both Exodus and Leviticus are issued from the exegetical hand of Dr. Lange himself. There is a general Introduction by him unfolding what Dr. Schaff calls "an original and ingenious view of the organic unity and trilogy of the Three Middle Books of the Pentateuch and their typical import." The work done by the American annotators, as usual, is not the least valuable part of the volume. We again heartily congratulate our biblical brethren on the advance toward completion of a work so honorably uniting the biblical scholarship of Germany and America.

## *Philosophy, Metaphysics, and General Science.*

*The History of Creation;* or, The Development of the Earth and its Inhabitants by the Action of Natural Causes. A Popular Exposition of the Doctrine of Evolution in General, and that of Darwin, Gœthe, and La Marck in particular. From the German of ERNST HAECKEL, Professor in the University of Jena. The Translation Revised by Professor E. RAY LANKESTER, M.A., F.R.S., Fellow of Exeter College, Oxford. Two Volumes, pp. 408, 374.

Atheism plus Darwinism equal Brutalism; the beastliest philosophy that ever nightmared the human soul. We have never, indeed, said that Darwinism was necessarily Atheism, as Spencerism is; we have even endeavored to show that the Darwinian need not reject Moses. But Professor Haeckel, taking the nebular theory for his cosmogony,* and Darwinism for his biology, educes all existence from the primitive essence of unconscious matter, and thus brings out Atheism of the most pronounced kind. To the primary Dualism of God and nature, mind and matter, he opposes the "*Monism*" of essential matter alone; and he writes this eloquent, frank, and learned book to demonstrate that this one Primitive is alone needed for the entire problem of the universe. The rule of a just, benevolent intelligence, or of any intelligence at all, over the world, immortality, free-will, responsibility, essential soul, are

* It is to be noted that Haeckel admits that he cannot account for the commencement of rotary motion required in the nebular theory.

all rejected as the infantile conceptions of the world's non-age. By necessary laws primitive matter has developed into a great synthesis of things rising into a tall pyramid, of which, by conditions favorable to him, man, the *ex-ape*, is the *apex*.

To Haeckel's solution through Darwinism of the problem of nature we decline to concede the very first starting-point. Two things he assumes as his great premises, namely: Heredity, by which like begets like; and Adaptation, by which exact likeness is varied to the demands of surrounding conditions. Heredity preserves the uniformity and permanence of species so far as they exist, and Adaptation secures their unlimited variation in time and space; so that, given but a single animal organism to start with, all the ranks of living nature can be accounted for. Now, to an Atheist, or Monistic denier of antecedent overruling mind, no concession can be made of Heredity or Adaptation. Both are intellective terms, terms that implicitly affirm material substances, overruled by anterior and superior mind.

Were the universe a vast mass of orderless chaos, an indiscriminate slag, it would afford no proof of an overruling mind. We agree with Chalmers, that the proof for a God arises not so much from the existence, as from the "collocations," the orderly arrangements of matter. The moment this slag shapes into symmetrical plans—plans not consisting of geometrical shapes, but plans whose parts correspond on an intellective selective principle—we have phenomena that presuppose selective mind and will. And this distinction between the geometrical and the selective is here very important. Matter might be supposed by its own necessities to tumble unconsciously and undirectedly, like crystals, into geometrical form, though we do not concede that crystals do so. But an organism like a human body, with parts combined upon a plan to execute obvious purposes and ends, can be only mind-shaped. The correspondent parts are not *necessarily* resultant, but are selected and located on an alternative and volitional principle. This presupposition of intellective plan increases when there is added a subserviency of plan to utilitarian results; further increases with the increased amount of plans, complexities, and utilitarian results; and illimitably increases when an immense system is contemplated, over which any great all-pervading Purpose is seen as grasping into subordination to itself an infinite number of subordinate purposes. Now Heredity implies a symmetrical contingently shaped organism produced regularly by a preceding similar organism, and such organisms are mind-molded objects. If we judge things, as we must,

by their properties, this organism presents three phases: *first*, a substance which by its properties appears to be materialistic; *second*, a correspondence of parts, or a selective plan, which is volitional; and, *third*, a subordination of the materialistic to the intellectively volitional, by which it is constructed and overruled. An Atheist has no right, therefore, to assume Heredity as a premise to account for any results whatever. He has no right to any such intellective volitional terms as plan, organism, type, laws, and such like, for these are all intellective and volitional terms, implying that matter is preceded, shaped, and overruled by mind.

The doctrine of an evolution of created things in gradual historic series, unified as one great whole, has always been maintained since thought has begun to contemplate the subject, The Bible contains an outline of an evolution. Pope's "Essay on Man" contains a complete system of mundane evolution. John Wesley was an evolutionist. The problem of human and brute immortality Wesley solved by conceding immortality to brutes. "Wesley," says Dr. Stevens, "believed that there was a regular gradation of creation from the animalcule to the archangel; 'an opinion,' says Southey, 'confirmed by science as far as our physiological knowledge extends.' He also thought it probable that each class in the series advances, and will forever advance, men taking the rank of angels, and *brutes the rank of men*, and eternal progress and felicity be thus the lot of all saved beings."—*History of Methodism*, vol. ii, p. 422. Here is an evolution more complete than Darwinism presents; including apparent Darwinism itself in the words we italicise. Theistic Darwinism is apparently not very anti-Wesleyan. But generally the evolutionism of past times embraces all life in a great unit, produced by successive creations in accordance with a law subjective to the divine mind, objective in the created unit.

Professor Haeckel's work is not only a "history," it is a romance, an epic. His mastery of the science enables him to collect and group an immense number of facts in form favorable to his theory. And so convinced is he of the inductively certain truth of the theory as a whole, that he skillfully and abundantly fills all inconvenient blanks with hypothetical facts, facts made to order. That is, his view of the whole system is so clear that he can tell you with fair probability what the missing facts are. The omitted link is conclusively indicated by the very nature of the hiatus. He believes that man is not so properly descended from monkeys as from an earlier genetic point, from which the monkey

branch and man branch diverge. He indicates the very geographical spot where man began to emerge from brute. It is now submerged by sea, lying beneath the waters between the promontory of India and the shores of Africa. This is the scientific Paradise. And he gives us a splendid map on which are traced the lines of humanizing descent, starting from the primitive point and diverging over all the continents and islands of the earth. His whole work flows forth in a strain of rich and variegated eloquence. The translation is a model of lucidity.

Haeckel spreads out in description and picture the wonderful fact in Embryology, that the human *fœtus* in the womb passes successively through the forms of fish, reptile, and quadruped before fully forming into the final man. We have every one of us in our unborn state gone through these metamorphoses. And this, with all Darwinists, he claims as proof that the human race is generatively descended and derived through these successive gradational races. It certainly is a wonderful parallelism. But it seems to be only illustration; it is no proof. There is no logical or causative relation discernible between the two lines of succession. The embryo, in its successive transformation, is an image or picture of the evolutional transformation through which the external animal world passes. One shows no causation of the other, and the embryonic series only illustrates the fact that there is an order of creation. But be it specially here noted, it does not illustrate *a generative order.* The succeeding stage of the *fœtus* is not *born* of the preceding stage. It fails, therefore, in the very vital point of illustrating the *generative* descent of later animal species from earlier. The embryonic stages are produced simply by changes of the relative positions of the molecules, but these changes do not embrace the process of sexual concurrence, parturition, and birth. If I take a mass of putty and manipulate it through exactly the same changes of form, I have precisely imaged the embryonic image of external evolutionary animal developments, and the successive stages are most surely not genetically connected. The successive changes of shape, that is, the successive changes of molecular position, are produced by the interposition of the formative forces proceeding from the hands. The process is an admirable image of and comment on the Mosaic text of the creative order of succession. It illustrates the divine fact that man is a microcosm, a miniature of the macrocosm, summing up all his created predecessors in himself, and rising in himself above them all. If there had been so many successive births in the

womb of successive *fœtuses*, it would have been an illustration of Darwinism. But being only a formal *succession*, so far as it is proof it establishes a formative, but not generative, succession.

But whatever the external *form* of a human *fœtus*, it never was at any stage a real fish, or tortoise, or dog. From the first seminal element to the birth it was a man and nothing else. That is, there resided in the human seminal essence at the first the formative power, superior to and overmastering all its forms, which did not reside in that of the lower animals, and which was human first and last, and sure to produce a man. Prof. Haeckel can snuffle at that immaterial superior formative power as much as he pleases; true reason recognizes its existence as a supreme fact, for which his philosophy does not account.

But the theory of a mind-formed, mind-ruled world is stigmatized by Haeckel as *anthropomorphism*. This is a popular taunt with thinkers of his class. Spencer, with a clumsy jest which proves that sarcasm is not one of the gifts of his most serious nature, calls it "the carpenter theory of creation." And Tyndall objects to Clerk-Maxwell's calling matter a "manufactured article," as derogatory to the Infinite. It is a curious conscience that shows such sensitiveness to a supposed insult to a supposedly non-existent entity! It is a still more curious notion of dignity that rejects the *anthropomorphic*, and substitutes therefor a *mechanomorphic* theory, as if unintelligent mechanism were more dignified than intellective man. It increases the dignity immensely, forsooth, to strike from a creative or formative agency the attribute of intelligence and reduce it to idiocy! If ours is an anthromorphic, theirs is a *moro-morphic*, a *fool-formed* theory. If instead of in effect calling God here a "carpenter" we substitute *architect*, a term essentially identical, yet incidentally more esthetically dignified, Spencer's sarcasm loses all its point; for both poetry and oratory have ever delighted to call God the "architect of creation." And why should a genius so radical and essentially democratic as Spencer's appeal to the low conventional contempt of "a carpenter," as if there was not something truly divine in the humblest act of mind shaping matter to intelligential form and benevolent use? How infinitely superior to this unseemly snobbishness is that most divine conception of our Christian religion which narrates that the Son of God was putatively a "carpenter's son" and himself a "carpenter!" What a flash of unexpected grandeur does that fact let down upon our most humble lowliness, revealing to our view the sublime truth that man, in the legitimate

use of his noble faculties, is, in spite of homely conventionalities both in nature and act the image of God! God is anthromorphic because man as productive mind is theomorphic. But it is false that our theory is anthropomorphic any more than theirs. For if an intelligential origin is anthropomorphic because *man possesses the attribute of intelligence*, it follows that their own mechanical or force *origin* is anthropomorphic, for surely *man possesses the attribute of force.* Newton, it is said, no matter whether truly or not, constructed his theory of universal gravitation from seeing the fall of an apple; and so gravitation is *appleomorphism!* His problem was to account for the motions of the astronomic system, and of all the systems of the universe; and he found the solution in the apple moving to the earth. That appleomorphic solution he extended to immensity. With us the problem is to account for the apparently intelligential forms and combinations that make up the universal system. We find it in *nous, intellect;* that intellect revealed to us most clearly in our own finite mind; just as Newton found attraction in the moving apple. And just as Newton extended his appleomorphism into explaining the gravitation ruling all existing things throughout immensity, just so we as legitimately extend our anthromorphism into an explanation of the intelligent forming and ruling all existing things. Most surely if we cannot be allowed to explain the infinite by finite instances, all extended reasoning is at an end. But what right have these men to maintain that there is no intellect but human intellect? Or, still more, what right have they to charge us, who do not limit intellect to humanity, with holding an anthropomorphic theory, because we hold the intelligential theory? We hold that *intelligence*, in its own nature, irrespective of any finite *intelligent*, solves creation. Ours is not specially the *anthromorphic*, but the *intelligenceo-morphic* theory. We hold, and none can disprove, that intelligence belongs to higher natures than man. Intelligence is in itself not only anthropomorphic, but it may be angelo-morphic, archangelo-morphic, nay, theomorphic. The Force philosophers of the present day find Force exemplified in special finite instances, and they generalize it to infinity. The Intelligence philosophers find intelligence exemplified in given finite instances, and they generalize it in the same way into infinity. And as the Intelligence philosophers recognize this universal Force presented by their brother philosophers, so they also recognize that said Force does operate according to intelligential methods, produces intelligential shapes and movements, and appears to act under the guidance and control of Intelli-

gence. They generalize, then, most legitimately, that this universal identity of Intelligence-ruled Force is God. It is God unlimited, so far as we know, in Power and Wisdom; God omnipotent and omniscient. And inasmuch as this limitless Force of our brother philosophers is not prevented by its infinity from acting in the most minute quantities, and producing the most minute effects, so God omnipotent is under no difficulty, and no disqualification, arising from his great dignity, in manufacturing an atom, or carpentering a world. God omnipotent finds no difficulty in creating a hair. All the metaphysics about the impossibility of the finite being produced or moved or modified by the Infinite is infinite humbug.

As to the moral attributes of God, Haeckel is trenchant and destructive. Life through all its ranks is hate, war, and destruction; and all living species can say with Job's messengers, "I have alone escaped to tell thee." Over a pessimism like this does there reign, he asks, a benevolent God? It is, indeed, terrible; and Haeckel deems the negative conclusion self-evident. But a few hundred pages further on, near the close of his last volume, he relents. Some misgivings seem to arise that his theory is too hateful for human acceptance, and he feels it necessary to irradiate it with a few optimistic hues, very relieving to its horrors, and quite contradictory to his logic. In this exterminating struggle for life, he graciously assures us, lies the assurance of human progress. Ever and ever *it is the fittest who survive;* and therein lies a future of human elevation in which, relieved from all fear of God, the race will be interminably great and glorious. Happy atheistic millennium! But, alas! we reply, neither he nor we will be there to see. With our ancestral snails, toads, and apes, we shall have tumbled into that abyss of nothingness from which no future recollection will ever recall our image, and even the denizens of that millennium will be perpetually tumbling in after us. But that optimism is the very argument which, with far more force, the theologians use to defend the goodness of God, who permits evil, indeed, but only because from the permission of evil he can educe a transcendent good; a higher good, on the whole, than if the evil were not permitted. It is our theology which proclaims not only an advancing progress and an earthly millennium, but points to glory and eternal life as the crowning evidence of divine goodness in the history of the world. For our race our theology argues a vast amount of existing earthly happiness, for otherwise death would not be terrible. We all consent and desire to live

because we enjoy; and when faith, hope, and love animate us, our hearts exult aboundingly in contemplation of that goodness of God against which Atheism blasphemes. To the Atheist the world is rightly pessimistic, and God is truly a terrible God. What wonder that he who hates God should realize that God abhors him? Pessimism and Atheism are twin brothers.

---

*Lessons from Nature as Manifested in Mind and Matter.* By ST. GEORGE MIVART, Ph.D., F.R.S., Professor at Kensington and Lecturer in St. Mary's Hospital. 12mo., pp. 462. New York: D. Appleton & Co. 1876.

In reply to certain taunts from the scientists that he was writing under a theological bias, Dr. Mivart informs us that he was really educated in scientific rationalism, but took refuge from its repulsive doctrines in the Roman faith. His "Genesis of Species" gave the first check to Darwinism, and laid down some important doctrines which have not since been invalidated. We specify particularly the following points:—

1. Though evolutionary development be true, yet the changes from one species to another are not always by slow degrees, but by sudden, great, and even revolutionary transformations.

2. The new forms are not accidental, but are evolved by an inherent rational formative potency.

3. Man being first formed by an intellective transformation and the infusion of a high rational soul, was truly *created;* derivatively *created*, indeed, yet still *created* in strict accordance with the Mosaic history.

4. That this view is neither novel nor heretical, but is essentially an old doctrine maintained by many of the ablest old divines of the Catholic Church. Those eminent doctors did not, indeed, teach the full doctrine of universal evolution, but of a "derivative creation" of which evolution is only an expansion. The full doctrine of evolution is, therefore, consistent with the most ultra Catholic orthodoxy, and, therefore, *à fortiori*, is allowable in ordinary Christians.

The old doctrine of Augustine, Thomas Aquinas, and Suarez was, that organisms are often endowed with a productive or creative potency from which new species are evolved. Thus parasites are somehow produced from the organism on which they depend. If Adam was created pure and perfect, how did lice come into existence, except as evolved from the degenerate human body? And so, said the fathers, there spring insects and worms from putrefaction—that is, in fact, by spontaneous gener-

ation; for spontaneous generation, though now rejected as heresy by both theology and science, was once orthodox with both. But these views, according to Mivart, established as orthodox the doctrine of "derivative creation;" and evolution is simply derivative creation universally extended.

Many of the fathers, including Augustine, denied the literality of the Mosaic days. They held that the whole mundane system was created at once; and that the six days were not a succession in time, but an order of thought. This was held by a large series of the Church doctors, from Augustine to the present day, long before geology raised any objections to the literal interpretation.

To Mivart's doctrine of the "derivative creation" of man by formal transformation from a lower animal and infusion of a higher soul, Mr. Huxley replies as follows:—

> If man existed as an animal before he was provided with a rational soul, he must, in accordance with the elementary requirements of the philosophy in which Mr. Mivart delights, have possessed a distinct sensitive and vegetable soul or souls. Hence, when the "breath of life" was breathed into the man-like animal's nostrils, he must have already been a living and feeling creature.—P. 442.

To this Mivart gives the following reply:—

> This doctrine was that the human fœtus is at first animated by a vegetative soul, then by a sentient soul, and only afterwards, at some period before birth, with a rational soul. Not that two souls ever coexist, for the appearance of one coincides with the disappearance of its predecessor—the sentient soul including in it all the powers of the vegetative soul, and the rational soul all those of the two others. The doctrine of distinct souls, which Professor Huxley attributes to me as a fatal consequence of my hypothesis, is simply the doctrine of St. Thomas himself. He says (quæst. lxxvi, art. 3, ad. 3:) "Dicendum quod prius embryo habet animam quæ est sensitiva tantum, qua ablata advenit perfectior anima quæ est simul sensitiva et intellectiva ut infra plenius ostendetur." Also (quæst. cxviii, art. 2, ad. 2:) "Dicendum est quod anima præexistit in embryone, a principio quidem nutritiva postmodum autem sensitiva et tandem intellectiva."—P. 443.

The last sentence we translate as follows: We should say that there exists in the embryo a soul, which at first is merely vegetative, afterward sensitive, and finally intellective.

This doctrine of ascending souls bears a curious anticipative relation to the discoveries by modern embryology of the ascending transition of form through which the fœtus passes up to man. The vegetative soul first appears in the evolution of and from the ovum; the animal soul evolves the fœtus through the animal forms; the rational soul is complete with the completion of the human form. Yet the lower soul is not destroyed, but is immerged into the higher, so that all three are identified in the highest.

This vegetative soul is rightly so called as reigning not only

over the animal, but also over the vegetable world. It supplies the growing and formative energy. It is the "plastic power" of Cudworth. It implies no sensibility in the subject, and is to be explained only as the divine omnipotence working under the form of finite causations and successions.

The animal soul, the soul of all brute life, consists in the energy of the five senses, with the circumscribed power of conception, comparison, and inference, among sensible objects.

The rational soul consists in the power of supersensible intuition, beholding truths not made up of sensible impressions, but transcending the level of sensible objects; such truths as infinity, God, holiness, and Ego.

In man these three are three and one.

Professor Huxley, with his usual dashing chivalry, pounced upon Mivart's "Genesis of Species," and even bravely dipped into Suarez, and claimed to show that that author did not teach Evolution. But, as often, his chivalry proved to be Quixotery. Our author shows that he understands neither Suarez nor Mivart. The writings of Mivart are highly lauded in the Catholic world. They are presented and accepted as *a*, if not *the*, full reconciliation between Genesis and science. They show how a one Adam may have been created in full consistency with Evolution; how, in full possession of a rational soul and the endowment of the blessed Spirit, man may have been created in pure and paradisaic conditions; how the fall of man may be still a historic truth; and how, unless archæological facts contradict, the Hebrew chronology may be held as valid. The views of Augustine, held by him exegetically and without knowledge of geological difficulties, if adopted, entirely vacate all difficulty in the Mosaic cosmogony. Those who wish to appreciate Mivart fully must read both the "Genesis of Species" and this volume.

---

*Phonetic and Stenographic Short Hand:* A Scientific System of Sound and Sight Writing. By Rev. THOMAS MITCHELL. 16mo., pp. 108. New York: J. W. Pratt. 1876.

Mr. Mitchell's system is based upon what he calls the incorporation of vowels with consonants. He has six consonantal alphabets, the first of which consists of consonants simple followed by no vowel; the five others embrace, severally, consonants followed by five vowel elements; so that in writing the consonant you also write the vowel. This is an ingenious invention; but it must be decided by the practical writer how far it is on trial a practical success.

## *History, Biography, and Topography.*

*The Great Republic; from the Discovery of America to the Centennial. July, 1876.* The History of the Great Republic considered from a Christian Stand-point. Revised. By JESSE T. PECK, D.D., LL.D., one of the Bishops of the Methodist Episcopal Church. With thirty-four Steel Portraits. 8vo., pp. 704. New York: Nelson & Phillips. Cincinnati: Hitchcock & Walden. 1876.

This new and beautiful edition, revised and improved by its author, furnishes a lucid and eloquent view of our national history from our earliest origin to the present time. It is written in the true spirit of piety and patriotism—of loyalty to the government founded by Washington and his compeers, loyalty to the principles of freedom promulgated in our Declaration of Independence, and loyalty to God, who is recognized as guiding our historic pathway. It is a work worthy to be placed as both a school and an ecclesiastical class-book in our courses of study.

Honor to whom honor is due. We believe it is Dr. J. T. Peck who first publicly suggested an Ecumenical Union of Methodism. He drew out a plan some years ago which will be found monumentally on record in a former volume of our "Quarterly Review."

## *Politics, Law, and General Morals.*

*Apthorp's Standard Map of Florida*, constructed from the latest United States Surveys and from other Official and Local Sources, by WILLIAM APTHORP, late Chief Clerk of the United States Surveyor General's Office. 1877. Scale, 15 miles to the Inch.

This is the latest, largest, and most accurate Map of Florida extant. It is more accurate both from its access to the most thorough surveys, and from its exhibiting the newly risen towns and initiated railroads. We have received it from Col. J. B. Oliver, who has established in this city a paper entitled the "Florida New Yorker." This paper furnishes to the inquiring Northerner who is attracted toward the "Land of Flowers" answers to the great variety of questions he is interested in asking.

By united concession of the leading men of both political parties the Presidential election in Florida was perfectly peaceful and free. It was not until the special interest of the country n Florida's vote drew Northern politicians down there that any disturbance took place. Meanwhile, in disproof of any danger there to Northern men of any shade of opinion, we may note that Florida is proud

of being the residence of Harriet Beecher Stowe; and deep in the interior is the town of Beecher, where Charles of the "Beecher family" luxuriates in his own orange groves fearless of molestation.

---

## *Literature and Fiction.*

*King Saul.* A Tragedy. By BYRON A. BROOKS. 12mo., pp. 144. New York: Nelson & Phillips. Cincinnati: Hitchcock & Walden. 1876.

Mr. Brooks has attempted in this drama, with no little poetical success, to reproduce one of the most impressive passages of Hebrew history. He holds that he describes "a period," and we might add a race, which was "much nearer the spirit-world than the present, so that the supernatural was natural." The solemn spirit of that age and race, under pressure of the supremacy of the present Jehovah, was strikingly analogous to the spirit of stern overruling fate that reigns in the Grecian drama, and is well represented in the present "tragedy." The character of the seer, Samuel, of the young and aspiring David, of the lofty, yet fated Saul, are delineated with life. The successive scenes are well selected, move with stirring rapidity, and are vividly drawn. The interview of Saul with the sorceress of Endor tasks the writer's powers, and it is here that his poetic ability most decisively appears, in the mastery of so difficult a problem.

The great biblical era awakened by the International Lessons has called out, even in our hebdomadal periodicals, many a commentator; why should it not inspire at any rate one poet? We recommend Mr. Brooks's "Tragedy" to all readers in biblical literature, being assured that, as a poet, he quite equals any of the commentators created by the International epoch that we have read—which is saying nothing depreciatory of them.

---

## *Periodicals.*

*Southern Methodist Press on Negro "Intimidation."*

Our brethren of the Southern Methodist press deny that there is any "intimidation," any attempt at disfranchisement of the Southern negro. The accuracy of this denial is to be tested by verified history and statistics; but what we now wish to discuss

and to place before them is, what we think of negro suffrage, and of the purpose attributed to the Southern whites by responsible thinkers of reducing the Southern negro to disfranchised serfdom.

Universal suffrage, unqualified by any conditions of property or character, we believe to be the great danger of our country. Hence, when the negro population of the South was enfranchised, we believed that such danger was encountered, if not a great wrong done. The greatness of that wrong is now under exhibition in the canvasses for presidential electors in the States of Louisiana, South Carolina, and Florida. When our Southern brethren exclaim, "We are over-laughed with a mass of unintelligent voters; we are being deluged with an uncivilization; we are a 'prostrate State,' calling for mercy," we appreciate and deeply sympathize with their case.

But let us turn the table. We are here in New York overslaughed with as terrible a mass of enfranchised ignorance and depravity as any State in the South. We would gladly swap our Northern Irishry for the Southern Negrodom. We would gladly say, for the city of New York, to the city of Charleston, "Take our Irishmen and give us your Negroes." For the State of New York we would make the same offer to South Carolina. Here in the combined cities of New York and Brooklyn the Tilden majority was over seventy thousand, overruling the rest of the State, which would have given an overwhelming majority for Hayes; would have given him the thirty-five electoral votes of New York; electing him at a stroke. Reverse twenty thousand ignorant, foreign, papistical Irish votes in these cities, and Tilden would not have had the ghost of a chance. It would then be, "As go these votes, so goes New York State, and so goes the nation." Here let us unite our hearts, brethren of the South and North, and say this is a terrible danger and wrong.

What renders this wrong more galling to us of the North is, the knowledge that this arbitrative vote is directed by a foreign power, with no interest in the real good of the country. The Democratic party of our State is governed by the Irishry, the Irishry by the priest, and the priest by the pope; and when the State is governed by the Democracy, it is, in an unknown degree, governed by a foreign power, directing the vote not for the country's interest, but for that foreign interest. More than one entire half of the Democratic State Convention of our "Empire State" was Irish Catholics. And to this foreign vote, as opposed to the so-called "Republican party," must be added the organized "liquor inter-

est," which holds that party as a temperance party. And thus at the present moment it is popery and whisky, Rome and rum, which overslaughs the temperate, intelligent native population of the great State of New York.

Now if that native population should unitedly arm itself, if under guise of "rifle companies" they should quietly become a military power, they could conquer and disfranchise the unintelligent vote. And so to a Democratic friend who was boasting that there would be in the coming election "a solid South," we replied, "If we should shoot down Irishmen as facilely as the southerners can shoot down 'niggers' we could have a solid North." But that we are not likely ever to do. We have another remedy more becoming Republicans and Christians. Our purpose is not to fight it, nor violently disfranchise it, but to educate it. Our remedy is not "rifle companies," but schools and churches and temperance societies. Our method is to overcome evil with good. The grandson of the Irish papist is very probably to be a good native American Protestant. Time and patience in well doing, with God's blessing resting on such a process, will, we have the faith to believe, bring us right.

We may be answered by our Southern brethren that the existence of unqualified suffrage is our own fault; that the South never desired it, and the North alone is responsible for it. But that is a great historical mistake. It was, as we showed years ago, the South that forced unqualified suffrage on the North. It was the "Democratic party," of which Horace Greeley said "its brain and body is in the South, and its tail in the North," which created the unqualified suffrage under which we labor. In our earlier history it was from Southern "Democratic" statesmen, not from the Northern or "Federalist" statesmen, that the broadest maxims of "equal rights" and "universal suffrage" came. Those maxims, as they understood it, were, however, not to be applied to the Southern slaves, but only to the Northern undercrust. And it was the union of the Southern slaveholder with our Northern subterraneans that secured universal suffrage, and ruled both sections with "Democracy." We well remember when, in this great State of New York, qualified suffrage was the rule, and it was safe and right. But under the leadership of Martin Van Buren, the "Northern man with Southern principles," aided by the backing of the Southern oligarchic "Democracy," the votes of the unintelligent were purchased by enfranchisement. For this unkind favor from the South, the North has repaid the South with an

equal favor. As the South enfranchised the Irishry, the North has enfranchised Negrodom. Yet, in behalf of the North, we must call to memory one fact. The Republican party did hesitate to enfranchise the negroes. It offered to the South that *if the representation of the States in the Federal Government could be proportioned to the number of votes*, the voting qualification should be left to the decision of each State itself. That was fair. If a State diminishes the number of its voters, it should thereby reduce its amount of representation in the national unity. That proposition the South rejected. The policy of the violent men in the South seems to be to disfranchise by violence the unintelligent vote, retain the power in a *caste*, and yet claim a full representation in the Unity. That is a restoration of the old oligarchy. It is a wrong pregnant with future strife. It only substitutes serfdom for slavery; it points to a new sectional contest, with unknown yet fearful results.

Let us renounce this policy of violent disfranchisement. Drop the "shot gun" and take up the spelling-book. Do not fear that the educated negro will unduly aspire to social equality before possessing those qualities that render sociality inoffensive. Any one of our Southern brethren can tolerate a negro to wait upon his table; it is only when he sits down, even at the other end, that he smells bad. Some of them could, we hope, sit at table unoffended beside that accomplished scholar and elegant writer, Edward W. Blyden, even, perhaps, in spite of the consciousness of being his intellectual inferior. On the other hand, very few or none of us are fanatical enough to look to "miscegenation" as any attainable or desirable end. Meantime the negro is native born, is Protestant, is aspiring to education and civilization, is a patriot ready to vote for the country's good. He cannot be disfranchised permanently by fraud or force. Serfdom for him is no more possible than slavery. Conceding his civil and political rights, sociality is a matter of individual taste which no one is obliged to concede. But can there not be enacted by constitutional amendment a national *intelligence qualification* of suffrage applicable alike to all races and colors?

The South says to the North: *You are trying to rule us through our unintelligence.* The North replies: *You have long ruled us through our unintelligence.* What is the remedy? A union between the intelligence of North and South by which, with oppression to none, intelligence shall maintain its ascendency. We call for a parley. Let the good people of the North and South understand each other. With our native, educated, tem-

perate, Christian, national people, is the power to control if, forgetting sectional fights, they will unite. Back of our present cohort of politicians there is a people that can rule in the interest of advancing civilization if they can only attain unanimity. Let the Churches lead in this path of peace. Let interchange and intercourse, courtesy and kindness, take place. Let this fatal antithesis between North and South—that is, the North and South lying between the Atlantic and the Mississippi—be abolished. Let Mason and Dixon's line be obliterated. Let the platform of a great *Unanimity* of our true PEOPLE be, *suffrage based upon intelligence*, universal education, civil-service reform, temperance, and tolerant Christianity.

Since the above was given to the compositor we have read with pleasure a recommendation in the President's Message for the national adoption of a system of intelligent suffrage.

---

*Haus und Herd.* A German Family Magazine. HENRY LIEBHART, D.D., Editor. 8vo. Cincinnati: Hitchcock & Walden. New York: Nelson & Phillips. 1876.

Dr. Liebhart justly congratulates the Church and himself on the success of his "*Haus und Herd.*" It unites Germany and Methodism, Melanchthon and Wesley, in a highly delightful way. The number of its subscribers, we are informed, has steadily increased, until not only its existence, but its prosperity for the future, seems to be fully insured, and that in the face of a long-continued financial pressure such as this country has hardly ever experienced. We pray success and increase for our German Methodism, and fervently hope that it may prove a blessed antidote to German rationalism in the future of our country.

---

## *Pamphlets.*

*Methodist Fraternity.* By ENOCH L. FANCHER. 12mo., pp. 19. New York: 1876.

In his early manhood it was the task of Judge Fancher, as junior counsel, to make up the case of our Church in its suit with the Church South. Probably no man living has followed the mutual relations of the two Churches with a more judicial eye. Never specially identified with aggressive antislavery men, yet realizing the evil of slavery, he has looked at both the ecclesiastical and political contest with the calmness and clearness of a

trained jurist. He was wisely selected as a member of the adjustive Commission, and his views here expressed, called forth by the eccentric action of the Central New York Conference, are a very conclusive refutation of the unhistorical statements and fallacious reasoning on which that action was based.

We are unaware of any action of our General Conference through its whole history by which it impugned the legitimacy of the Church South as a Church. On the contrary, the very proposal of fraternity presupposed the legitimacy of the body with whom it was proposed. Our Conference and our Church has repeatedly impugned the *righteousness* of the course pursued by the Church South. Her support of slavery and her withdrawal in behalf of slavery we ever have and do still condemn. But if unrighteousness always destroys the *legitimacy* of a Church, we fear that hardly a legitimate Church could be found extant. Our General Conference in 1844 conceded that the South might withdraw without ecclesiastical "blame." The Central New York Conference in our view, therefore, took issue not merely with the Commission, but with the General Conference through its whole history. The terms expressed by the Commission, we may add, contradict nothing which our Quarterly has ever maintained. On the contrary, we heartily indorse every clause and every word of its report as being perfectly in accordance with all we have said and thought. We have never uttered a syllable, or thought an idea, that denied the Churchdom of *any* now existing regular Methodist Church organization.

We have differed, however, with Judge Fancher as to the use of the term "secession." As he carefully defines the term, limiting it to an illegitimatizing sense, we have, indeed, never applied it to the action of any branch of Methodism. But the term "secession," it must be remembered, is a *vox media*, an intermediate term, susceptible, that is, of a good or bad meaning. Southern statesmen have claimed that politically "secession" was right. The Free Church of Scotland professedly "seceded" from the State Church. Older still, there is a Scotch sect of professed "Seceders," of which the scientist Faraday was an eminent member. An unjust or unlawful secession is a bad thing, but a rightful secession is a good thing. A few years since Dr. James Porter said in our Quarterly that if Bishop Andrew had not been inhibited from Episcopal functions while holding slaves the New England Conferences would have *seceded*. Thereupon some of our Southern editorial brethren flared up. So after all these charges of

secession against the South, they exclaimed, it is confessed that these treacherous Yankees would have "seceded!" Dr. Porter would have readily and truly replied that his condemnation of Southerners was not that they *seceded*, but that they seceded for wicked cause. New England secession, in his view, would have been in the cause of right, namely, justice and freedom; Southern secession was in the cause of wrong, namely, injustice and slavery. And so some years ago Dr. D. A. Whedon maintained in our Quarterly, rightly and conclusively, that the Southern withdrawal was a secession; a secession, that is, in distinction from the idea of a division of the Church by the General Conference into two co-ordinate but independent Churches, as claimed by Judge Taney's court; and, also, in distinction from the idea that the General Conference authorized the withdrawal of the Southern members in the Plan of the Committee of Nine; an idea lately reiterated by Dr. Myers, but not reiterated either by the Southern delegates to our General Conference, or by the Cape May Commission. It was, also, at issue with the inaccurate statement of the Southern Bishops when they boldly said at St. Louis, "We separated from you in no sense in which you did not separate from us." The separation, withdrawal, or "secession" was done *by them*, and on their own responsibility, only with a "Plan" that *after* it was so done by them, wrongly or rightly, we would not ever pass a certain line if they did not. The Plan had no effect or efficient existence until after the revolutionary secession was executed. In that secession they left the regular old organism; left to it its regular series of General Conferences, its old historic name, the archives and records of its history, and formed altogether a new organism commencing a new series. This, as men, citizens, ministers, Christians, they had "a right" to do, whether they rightly exercised that right or not. We are, then, different "branches of Methodism;" but our own old historic branch shoots up straight from the tap-root, through central trunk, to summit; while all the other "branches" glance off in a more or less graceful slant from this same primal center. All the branches are legitimate; one only is central, primordial, parental. It is an historical fact, that can be neither obliterated nor blurred, that every Methodist body on the American continent has *branched* off from that primal trunk, being either a branch or a branch of a branch.

## *Miscellaneous.*

*Journal of the General Conference of the Methodist Episcopal Church.* Held in Baltimore, Md., May 1-31, 1876. Edited by the Rev. GEO. W. WOODRUFF, D.D., Secretary of the Conference. 12mo., pp. 663. New York: Nelson & Phillips. Cincinnati: Hitchcock & Walden. 1876.

We have only room to announce this noble volume, and to say that, in our opinion, both the General Conference and the Editor, Dr. Woodruff, have well performed their work.

*The Expositor.* Edited by the Rev. SAMUEL COX. November. Contents: 1. The Book of Job. (The first Colloquy—Eliphas to Job.) By the Editor. 2. The Sixteenth Psalm. By the Rev. Professor M. ROBERTSON SMITH, M.A. 3. The Epistles of St. Peter. (The Second Epistle.) By the Rev. J. RAWSON LUMBY, B.D. 4. Dr. Pulsford on Ephesians. London: Hodder & Stoughton, 27 and 31 Paternoster Row.

This is a monthly Commentary on Scripture, to which contributions are made from some of the best biblical scholars of England. Annotations are prosecuted through a series of numbers on a single book. Besides the above-named writers, we notice in a previous volume the names of the late Bishop Thirlwall, Canon Farrar, the Dean of Canterbury, Dr. H. R. Reynolds, Prof. Plumtre, Dr. Oswald Dykes, and Rev. J. Hammond. Price per number one shilling sterling.

*The Life of Marie Antoinette, Queen of France.* By CHARLES DUKE YONGE, Regius Professor of Modern History and English Literature in Queen's College, Belfast, author of "The History of the British Navy," etc. 12mo., pp. 473. New York: Harper & Brothers. 1876.

The French queen, whose destiny it was to stand as one of the historical characters in whom mankind takes a permanent interest, is here portrayed from abundant materials by a friendly hand. One wishes to believe the favorable colorings true to fact. The character of La Fayette is presented in a more adverse light than usual.

*The Orient and its People.* By Mrs. J. L. HAUSER, Seven Years a Missionary in Northern India. 12mo., pp. 335. Milwaukee: J. L. Hauser & Co.

This little volume is a series of pen pictures drawn from life, and expressed in popular and attractive style. The book is about equally divided between India and China. It is a fine contribution to our missionary literature.

*Vanquished Victors;* or, Sketches of Distinguished Men who overcame the Obstacles in their Way to Fame, but failed to gain the Self-mastery which is the Greatest and Grandest of all Conquests. By DANIEL WISE, D.D., author of "Uncrowned Kings," "Story of a Wonderful Life," etc. 16mo., pp. 295. Cincinnati: Hitchcock & Walden. New York: Nelson & Phillips. 1876.

A series of brief portraitures of remarkable men.

*Christian Nurture.* By HORACE BUSHNELL. 12mo., pp. 407. New York: Scribner, Armstrong, & Co. 1876.

*Sermons on Christ and His Salvation.* By HORACE BUSHNELL. 12mo., pp. 456. New York: Scribner, Armstrong, & Co. 1877.

*Sermons for the New Life.* By HORACE BUSHNELL. Revised edition. 12mo., pp. 456. New York: Scribner, Armstrong, & Co. 1876.

We are gratified to notice that Scribner, Armstrong, & Co. are issuing a fine new edition in series of Dr. Bushnell's works. Christian thinkers will find in them ample starting-points for thought.

*The Student's Classical Dictionary of Biography, Mythology, and Geography.* Abridged from the larger Dictionary. By WILLIAM SMITH, D.C.L., LL.D., With Illustrations. 12mo., pp. 438. New York: Harper & Brothers. 1877.

This is a highly scholarly and densely compressed manual, admirably adapted to the "student's" use. The abundance of illustrations, true to archæology, forms a valuable characteristic of the volume.

*The Methodist Almanac for the Year of our Lord* 1877. Being the 101st Year of the American Independence and the 111th of American Methodism. 12mo., pp. 60. Edited by W. H. De Puy, D.D. New York: Nelson & Phillips. Cincinnati: Hitchcock & Walden.

*Rachel Weeping for her Children.* By Rev. N. VANSANT, of the Newark Conference. With an Introduction, by Rev. C. N. SIMS, D.D. 16mo., pp. 150. New York: Nelson & Phillips. Cincinnati: Hitchcock & Walden. 1876.

A beautiful gift for parents weeping for departed children.

*Fleda and the Voice.* With other Stories. By MARY A. LATHBURY, ("Aunt May.") Illustrated by the Author. Quarto, pp. 69. New York: Nelson & Phillips. Cincinnati: Hitchcock & Walden.

A highly illustrated and beautifully written holiday gift for the young folks.

*History of the Reformation in Europe in the Time of Calvin.* By Rev. J. H. MERLE D'AUBIGNE, D.D. Translated by WILLIAM L. R. CATES. Vol. VII: Geneva, Denmark, Sweden, Norway, Hungary, Poland, Bohemia, the Netherlands. 12mo., pp. 576. New York: Robert Carter & Brothers. 1877.

*The Rime of the Ancient Mariner.* By SAMUEL TAYLOR COLERIDGE. Illustrated by GUSTAVE DORE. Folio. New York: Harper & Brothers. 1876.

A unique and very splendid gift book.

*The Footsteps of St. Peter.* Being the Life and Times of the Apostle. By J. R. MACDUFF, D.D., author of "The Footsteps of St. Paul," "Memoirs of Gennesaret," "Morning and Night-watches," etc., etc. 12mo., pp. 632. New York: Robert Carter & Brothers. 1877.

*My Old Letters.* By HORATIUS BONAR, D.D. 12mo., pp. 352. New York: Robert Carter & Brothers. 1877.

*Expository Lectures on the Books of Holy Scripture.* Third Series: Romans, Revelation. By Rev. DONALD FRASER, D.D. 12mo., pp. 306. New York: Robert Carter & Brothers. 1873.

*The Judgment of Jerusalem Predicted in Scripture, Fulfilled in History.* By Rev. WILLIAM PATTON, D.D., New Haven. 12mo., pp. 231. New York: Robert Carter & Brothers. 1877.

*Rays from the Sun of Righteousness.* By Rev. RICHARD NEWTON, D.D., author of "The Jewel Case," "The Wonder Case," etc. 12mo., pp. 341. New York: Robert Carter & Brothers. 1876.

*The True Man, and other Practical Sermons.* By Rev. SAMUEL S. MITCHELL, D.D. 12mo., pp. 236. New York: Robert Carter & Brothers. 1877.

*The Uncommercial Traveler, Hard Times, and the Mystery of Edwin Drood.* By CHARLES DICKENS. With forty-five Illustrations. 8vo., pp. 328. New York: Harper & Brothers. 1876.

*Hay Fever;* or, Summer Catarrh: Its Nature and Treatment. Including the early form, or "Rose Cold;" the latter form, or "Autumnal Catarrh;" and a middle, or "July Cold," hitherto undescribed. Based on Original Researches and Observations, and containing Statistics and Details of several hundred cases. By GEO. M. BEARD, A.M., M.D. 12mo., pp. 266. New York: Harper & Brothers.

*Oliver of the Mill.* A Tale. By MARIA LOUISA CHARLESWORTH, author of "Ministering Children," etc. 12mo. New York: Robert Carter & Brothers. 1877.

*The Lesson Compend for* 1877. By Rev. JESSE LYMAN HURLBUT, A.M. 12mo., pp. 137. New York: Nelson & Phillips. Cincinnati: Hitchcock & Walden.

*The Development Hypothesis:* Is It Sufficient? By JAMES M'COSH, D.D., LL.D., President of Princeton College. 12mo., pp. 104. New York: Robert Carter & Brothers, 530 Broadway. 1876.

*Gems and Pearls for Parents and Children.* By Rev. E. DAVIES. 12mo., pp. 154. For sale by the Rev. E. Davies, Reading, Mass.; J. P. Magee, 36 Bromfield-st., J. H. Earle, Hawley-st., Boston; J. S. Inskip, 921 Arch-st., Philadelphia; and booksellers generally.

*Practical Cooking and Dinner-Giving.* A Treatise, containing Practical Instructions in Cooking, in the Combination and Serving of Dishes, and in the Fashionable Modes of Entertaining at Breakfast and Dinner. By Mrs. MARY F. HENDERSON. Illustrated. 12mo., pp. 364. New York: Harper & Brothers. 1876.

*The Other Gipsy.* By JOSEPHINE POLLARD. 16mo., pp. 162. New York: Nelson & Phillips. Cincinnati: Hitchcock & Walden. 1876.

*Mister Horn and his Friends;* or, Givers and Giving. By MARK GUY PEARSE, Author of "Daniel Quorm," "Sermons for Children," etc. 16mo. New York: Nelson & Phillips. Cincinnati: Hitchcock & Walden. 1876.

*The Berean Question Book.* International Series, for 1877. New York: Nelson & Phillips. Cincinnati: Hitchcock & Walden. 1877.

*Through the Eye to the Heart;* or, Eye-Teaching in the Sunday-School. By Rev. W. F. CRAFTS. 12mo. New York: Nelson & Phillips. Cincinnati: Hitchcock & Walden. 1876.

*Old Tales Retold from Grecian History.* By AUGUSTA LARNED. 12mo. New York: Nelson & Phillips. Cincinnati: Hitchcock & Walden. 1877.

# METHODIST QUARTERLY REVIEW.

APRIL, 1877.


## Art. I.—LORD MACAULAY.

*The Life and Letters of Lord Macaulay.* By his Nephew, George Otto Trevelyan, M. P. In two volumes. New York: Harper & Brothers.

Take him "all in all," Lord Macaulay is one of the best examples—we are inclined to say, the best example—of the "literary life" recorded in the history of English literature. As critic, historian, even as poet, orator, and "conversationist," (for he was characteristically "literary" in all,) he may be taken as a type, a very impersonation, of that "elect" life. His political career was long and active enough to render him historical, and pre-eminent above nine tenths of the British statesmen of his day. But his literary life was not incidental to his parliamentary and official life. The latter was but exceptional to the former—a salutary alternative, a wholesome alterative, as medical men would say. Like Addison, whom, above all English writers, save Milton, he most admired, but least imitated in other respects, he was a good example of Coleridge's theory of the literary life—that it should always be associated with some more practical or secular pursuit, which may afford not only a less precarious subsistence, but also the intellectual invigoration that comes of habitual contact with the world. Addison had hardly begun, under the auspices of Dryden, to write fugitive pieces for the public, when he became a party and a pensioned politician. His travels on the Continent, during which he wrote his once famous Epistle to Lord Halifax, and

began his treatise on Medals, his Cato, and the Narrative of his Travels in Italy, were undertaken, at the expense of the Government, as a preparation for its diplomatic service. Nearly all his life he was in Parliament, or in office, in either England or Ireland. The first of his immortal "Essays" were sent from Ireland to Steele, for the Tattler. He was in the Cabinet, as Secretary of State, when he was compelled to retire, by the malady which not long after ended his days; and he died at Holland House, the center of the higher social and intellectual world of London. Addison died comparatively young, aged not forty-eight years; he had ten or eleven years less of life than Macaulay. Had he been permitted to work, in the rich maturity of his powers, through those ten years, he might have achieved as much as Macaulay, and given as crowning a proof of the compatibility of an active public career with the highest style of intellectual culture and literary productiveness.

Walter Scott, Robert Southey, Samuel Johnson, or any other modern Englishman exclusively devoted to literature, can hardly dispute the palm with Macaulay, notwithstanding his active political life. As a poet he was their equal, not excepting Scott. The "Lays of Ancient Rome" have passages of as genuine poetry as can be found in the "Lay of the Last Minstrel," or any other of Scott's metrical productions. As a critic he was incomparably their superior. His linguistic attainments, to say nothing of his rare critical acumen, might have enabled him to compete with Johnson, even, as a lexicographer. Few men have been more capable of reproducing the scheme (repeated by Richardson) of Johnson's great dictionary—the exemplification of the use of words by citations from authors. His powers as an historian were far above those of Johnson as a critical biographer, and may well be compared with those of Scott as a histori-novelist. In the versatility, as well as the accuracy, of his knowledge in languages, ancient and modern, in literature of all ages and nearly all nations, in history, in political, and even theological, science, he immeasurably surpassed them. We cannot, indeed, recall another Englishman who so completely represents the literary life—though, of course, scores can be named who have shown more special genius.

It were much to be wished that the example of such men as Bacon, Clarendon, Bolingbroke, Addison, Fox, Burke, Jeffrey, Brougham, Mackintosh, Macaulay, Gladstone, Disraeli, Lubbock, Grote, Bulwer, Derby, Kinglake, and hosts of others in English political life, could be imitated by our own public men. If some of our statesmen have, like Franklin, Jefferson, the younger Adams, Everett and Sumner, carried into public life some devotion to letters or philosophy, few, if any of them, have ever yielded any direct results of such culture after they have once entered the political arena. American politics are an engulfing abyss, fathomless and shoreless. Bancroft, Motley, Bryant, Irving, Hawthorne, and a few others, have kept up their literary aims, with a partial devotion to political or official life; but we have yet to produce a single example of high statesmanship wedded to high and productive literary culture. Gibbon records that he found his experience in a camp of British militia a help to the composition of his great History, and that his intellect was never more vigorous, nor his style more facile, than "in the winter hurry of society and Parliament." His services as Commissioner of Trade and Plantations, and the exhilarating debates of the House, relieved his mind of the fatigue of study, and healthfully stimulated his faculties to resume, the next day, their wonted task. Macaulay's biographer says that "the routine of the Pay-office, and the obligations of the Treasury Bench in the House of Commons, were of benefit to him while he was engaged upon Monmouth's invasion and the Revolution of 1688." His vivid and virile style; the athletic manner, at once graceful and powerful, with which he attacks every difficulty of his subject; his liberal and wholesome temper; his universal humanity, without a tinge of pharisaism or cant—the whole individuality of the man, in fine, spontaneously breaking out on every page, and bearing his reader irresistibly along with him, must be attributed largely to the fact that he was no literary recluse, but a man of affairs, a man of society, "a man of the world," in the best sense of the phrase. There is no figure of more manly bearing in the whole lists of English authorship since the day of Raleigh. His every step is strong and forward, down to the last few years, in which, by the splendid success of the early volumes of his History, he became absorbed in the com-

position of the remainder, retired mostly from public life, declined dinner invitations and society generally, became mortally sick, and began to record in his journals new and startling experiences of low spirits, irresolution in work, and most of those more or less disabling weaknesses of heart and head which, though common enough in the ordinary, exclusive life of literary men, were seldom or never known to him before.

It would be an interesting task to trace, if possible, in his writings and memoirs, the conditions of his vigorous and manifold intellectual life. We attempt this task, not without foreseeing, however, that the limits and necessarily cursory manner of a review article must render it only an attempt.

He built on a good natural basis—the *mens sana in corpore sano.* We need hardly affirm that he possessed that ambiguous something called *genius.* If extraordinary native powers, or special aptitudes of mind, are meant by the word, he certainly had it to a rare degree, for in historical painting, in biographic portraiture, in dramatic effects, he has seldom been equaled. If Buffon's definition of genius is correct, we may still more decidedly claim it for him. The great naturalist, who ranks among his countryman as a literary model as well as a "scientist," defined it to be a habitude of patience in intellectual work. "I trace," he said, in the not ungenial egotism of his old age, "a first sketch, and in doing this I do what a hundred writers in Europe can do. I copy it, and obtain a result which but twenty writers can obtain. I re-copy a second and a third time, and achieve at last what Buffon alone can do." Macaulay has, at least, a "genius" for work; and is not this the most normal and most effective genius for our "work-day planet?" Before his health failed he went to his daily task with the zest with which an epicure goes to a banquet. His biographer says that "he would do nothing against the grain;" but with his healthy and versatile nature nothing (save mathematics and metaphysics) was against the grain. He followed, in this respect, Goethe's theory of education and intellectual life, as taught in "Wilhelm Meister," that the training and work of a man should be in the line of his natural aptitudes, his natural proclivities, these being the instincts of his natural capabilities. Like all healthy minds, he loved labor for its own sake as well as for its sure results. "The pleasure of

writing," he said, "pays itself." He lived in books more than in politics, or in society, or in any thing else. It may be doubted whether any man of his day read more, or more indiscriminately. He devoured books, good, bad, or indifferent. His friend, Sydney Smith, said, "Macaulay not only overflows with knowledge; he stands in the slop." Bad or indifferent books were, at least, of negative advantage to him; they warned him against their own faults. In his usual walks through the streets of London, he wended his way among the crowd, poring over a volume. His research for his writings was tireless, and the minutest or obscurest data, in obsolete periodicals, pamphlets, street ballads, caricatures, seldom eluded his keen glance. He never recoiled from the lowest drudgery of composition. He reconstructed chapters, recast paragraphs, added or erased sentences, for the slightest improvements. In finishing either his manuscript or his "proof," he was fastidious even to the smallest matter of punctuation. He equaled Buffon in labor on his style, and his manuscript pages (an example of which may be seen in the British Museum) were a maze of interlineations, erasures, and blotches. He knew, by experience, the value of Johnson's rule, not to pause in the heat of composition for any verbal matters whatever, but to reserve these for correction when the inspiration of his subject should be exhausted. His usual daily task was, after his first rough draft, to cover six foolscap pages, filling in the outlines, and then to correct and complete them with elaborate care, condensing the six manuscript into two of his printed pages.

Mr. Trevelyan says that "the *secret* of his process lay in this, that to extraordinary fluency and facility he united patient, minute, and persistent diligence." He "never allowed a sentence to pass muster till it was as good as he could make it."

It was in this laborious manner that he acquired his transcendent style—a style so elegant, and yet so impetuous and swift, that it always reminds us of one of its finest examples, in one of the finest passages of his "Lays:"—

"Now, by our sire Quirinus,
It was a goodly sight
To see the thirty standards
Swept down the tide of flight."

"That is the way of doing business," exclaimed Wilson, (of Blackwood,) though his critical as well as political antagonist —"a cut-and-thrust style; Scott's style when his blood was up, and the first words came like a vanguard impatient for battle." It was Scott's style only when his blood was up, but it was, more or less, Macaulay's habitual style, for his blood was always up when his subject allowed it to be so. His style was like a full-blooded steed on the race-course, fleet, direct, and of simple but splendid proportions. A society of English workmen sent him a vote of thanks for having written a history of their country which they could understand; and yet what English scholar does not read him with enthusiasm for his style, in spite of its occasional obvious defects? Doubtless what we may call his intellectual temperament had something to do with it, for, to cite Buffon again, "the style is the man," or, as he more pertinently has it, "*de l'homme;*" but it was labor, we repeat, that made it the most vigorous and perfect, perhaps, in our literature. It is a dangerous style for imitators, as he himself said; more so than even Johnson's pompous Latinism. He had early to combat its tendency to rhetorical excess. Some of the finest passages of his essays are more or less marred by that tendency. The gorgeous description of Westminster Hall, at the trial of Hastings, shows it. But in spite of it, his healthful temperament and his inexorable self-discipline and labor made him, to both foreign and native readers, the best of English "stylists."

Macaulay was precocious, and his precocity, probably, gave him some eight or ten years' advantage over most students. Intellectual precocity is usually supposed to imply premature decay; but, while some facts favor the supposition, more facts contradict it Most great men have given more or less promise of their greatness in childhood. It is seldom that intellectual greatness is not founded in some original or inborn capability. "The child is father to the man" in this, as in other respects, and human nature is more self-revealing in childhood than in any other period of life. Intellectual precocity, with physical feebleness, may, naturally enough, prematurely break down; but with a sound body it may be an enviable vantage ground. It was so with Macaulay. He was small but robust in stature, with strongly knitted limbs, and broad, rugged features, express-

ive of health and the mental self-command which comes of health. There was little, if any, Gaelic or Celtic blood in him. If not precisely Anglo-Saxon, he was, as both his mental and physical constitution showed, of as good metal; for the Teutonic element was strong in him. His mother was Anglo-Saxon. His father, though a Scotchman, was descended from the old Norwegian invaders who settled in the Western Isles. Carlyle, a genuine Scotchman, discerned at a glance his lineage. "I noticed," he says, "the homely Norse features that you find every-where in the Western Isles, and I thought to myself, 'Well! any one can see that you are an honest, good sort of a fellow, made out of oat-meal.'" One of the feats of his precocious genius was an epic, in his eighth year, on Olaus, the king of Norway, from whom the Scotch clan to which the young writer belonged received its name. Two cantos remain, extracts from which, given by his biographer, show ability astonishing in a child.

Incredible things are told of his early habits and achievements. From his third year he read incessantly, "lying on the rug, before the fire, with his open book on the ground, and a piece of bread and butter in his hand." At other times he would "sit in his nankeen frock, perched upon the table, expounding to the parlor-maid out of a book as big as himself." In his walks with the maid or his mother he would tell innumerable stories out of his own head, using already, as the maid said, "quite printed words." It cannot be doubted that his speech often appeared, as Mr. Trevelyan says, "quite droll." He was carried to the famous Strawberry Hill of Walpole, and ever afterward bore in his head a catalogue of its "Oxford Collection." While there a servant waiting upon the company spilled some hot coffee over his legs. After the kind hostess had done what she could for his relief she inquired how he was feeling. "The little fellow looked up in her face and replied, 'Thank you, madam, the agony is abated.'" He wrote hymns which Hannah More, one of the best friends of the family, pronounced "quite extraordinary for such a baby." Of course, his fond mother, a gentle Quakeress, was delighted with his surprising gifts. She wrote, "My dear Tom continues to show marks of uncommon genius. He gets on wonderfully in all branches of his education, and the extent of his reading, and

of the knowledge he has derived from it, are truly astonishing in a boy not yet eight years old. He is, at the same time, as playful as a kitten. He took into his head to write a Compendium of Universal History about a year ago, and he really contrived to give a tolerably connected view of the leading events from the creation to the present time, filling about a quire of paper. He told me one day that he had been writing a paper which Henry Daly was to translate into Malabar, to persuade the people of Travancore to embrace the Christian religion. On reading it I found it to contain a very clear idea of the leading facts and doctrines of that religion, with some strong arguments for its adoption."

Almost every essay of his shows a minute accuracy of research, of which even his letters and journals abound in examples. He makes particular criticisms and emendations of the original text of his favorite Latin and Greek authors. Besides abundant marginal notes, he pencils, at the end of each drama of the three Greek tragedians, small critical essays, and, judging from the specimens given by Mr. Trevelyan, they show not only good sense and taste, but exact scholarship. He changes his early estimate of Euripides, the representative of the decline of the Attic tragedy, and gives good critical reasons for the change; he places him above Sophocles, the representative of its climax; he exults over the genius of Æschylus, and traces in him the studies of Milton, not without correcting Milton's "sad Electra's poet," by showing that he alluded to the Orestes, not the Electra. Even the dull pages of the Thebaïs of Statius are critically studied, and marked with such observations as "Gray has translated this passage;" "Racine took a hint here;" and "Nobly imitated, and, indeed, far surpassed, by Chaucer." He gives thanks for having been able to "finish" Silius Italicus, (for he "finished" the very fag-ends of Greek and Latin literature,) and remarks that "Pope must have read him before me; in the Temple of Fame and the Essay on Criticism are some touches plainly suggested by Silius." He looks over Coleridge's "Remains," and exclaims:—

What stuff some of his criticisms on style are! Think of his saying that scarcely any English writer before the Revolution used the Saxon genitive, except with a name indicating a living being, as where a personification was intended. About twenty

lines of Shakspeare occurred to me in five minutes. In King John: "Nor let my kingdom's rivers take their course." In Hamlet: "The law's delay." In Romeo and Juliet: "My bosom's lord sits lightly on his throne." In Richard III., strongest of all: "Why, then, All Souls' Day is my body's doom's day."

He dines at Baron Parke's, with Brougham, his malicious enemy, and says:—

He was pleasant, but, as usual, excessively absurd, and exposed himself quite ludicrously on one subject. He maintained that it was doubtful whether the tragic poet was Eurīpides or Eurīpīdes. It was Eurīpīdes in his Ainsworth. There is, he said, no authority either way. I answered by quoting a couple of lines from Aristophanes. I could have overwhelmed him with quotations. "O," said this great scholar, "those are iambics. Iambics are very capricious and irregular, not like hexameters. I kept my countenance, and so did Parke."

Macaulay was seldom, probably never, caught napping, and woe to any pretentious critic who was so found in his presence.

Both the swiftness and the accuracy of his strange acquisitive power were shown in his method of learning a language. He says:—

My way is always to begin with the Bible, which I can read without a dictionary. After a few days passed in this way I am master of all the common particles, the common rules of syntax, and a pretty large vocabulary. Then I fall on some good classical work.

In a few weeks he was reading the classical works as readily as his favorite English books. He proposed to "make himself a good German scholar" on his passage back from India to England, and did so. After reading Luther's New Testament, he plunged into Schiller's Thirty Years' War, and was soon familiar with Goethe, Müller, Tieck, Lessing, and most of the classics of the language. During the years which he spent in India, though he did splendid official work in education and legislation, especially in his "Code," through which he is becoming recognized as the modern legislator of India, he seemed, nevertheless, buried in miscellaneous books. Not even Southey, at Keswick, was more a book-worm, for he could in three hours do more study than most students could do in fifteen. He

went through, critically, nearly the whole course of Greek and Latin authors in serial editions, which Napier, of the Edinburgh Review, had sent out to him, and this besides an incredible amount of French, Italian, Spanish, and English reading. Many of the largest Greek and Latin classics he read over and over again, and meanwhile sent to Napier some of his finest review articles. On his way out to India he kept himself in his state-room, among his books, with the devotion of an old Benedictine monk in his studious cell. He writes:—

Except at meals I hardly exchanged a word with any human being. I never was left so long a time so completely to my own resources, and I am glad to say that I found them quite sufficient to keep me cheerful and employed. During the whole voyage I read with keen and increasing enjoyment. I devoured Greek, Latin, Spanish, Italian, French, and English; folios, quartos, octavos, and duodecimos.

Again he says:—

My power of finding amusement without companions was pretty well tried on my voyage. I read insatiably the Iliad and Odyssey, Virgil, Horace, Cesar's Commentaries, Bacon's de Augmentis, Dante, Petrarch, Ariosto, Tasso, Don Quixote, Gibbon's Rome, Mill's India, all the seventy volumes of Voltaire, Sismondi's History of France, and the seven thick folios of the Biographia Britannica. I found my Greek and Latin in good condition enough.

He proceeds to give striking critical observations on many of these authors, for, rapid as his reading was, it was, nevertheless, by his peculiar faculty of quick apprehension and insight, remarkably thorough.

After being some time in India he writes:—

During the last thirteen months I have read Æschylus twice, Sophocles twice, Euripides once, Pindar twice, Callimachus, Apollonius Rhodius, Quintus, Calaber, Theocritus twice, Herodotus, Thucydides, almost all Xenophon's works, almost all Plato, Aristotle's Politics, and a good deal of his Organon, besides dipping elsewhere in him; the whole of Plutarch's Lives; about half of Lucan, two or three books of Atheneus twice, Plautus twice, Terence twice, Lucretius twice, Catullus, Tibullus, Propertius, Lucan, Statius, Silius Italicus, Livy, Velleius Paterculus, Sallust, Cesar, and, lastly, Cicero. I am now deep in Aristophanes and Lucian.

Mr. Trevelyan says that these works were read critically, as the penciled notes, covering the margins and blank leaves,

show. He read (page 22) as a mental recreation not only the great masters, but, as we have intimated, the minor and least read of Greek and Latin writers—their poorest remnants—annotating them with learned particularity, but dispatching them with his usual speed. At the conclusion of each volume of his own History he read through, as a relaxation, Herodotus, who, next to Thucydides, was his model historian. He would read through the Melpomene in a single sitting. He read through the last five books of the Iliad "at a stretch, on a walk," and with hearty appreciation. He writes:—

> I could not tear myself away. I was forced to turn into a by-path lest the parties of walkers should see me blubbering for imaginary beings, the creations of a ballad-maker, who has been dead two thousand seven hundred years. What is the power and glory of Cæsar and Alexander to that!

He finished Buckle's first ponderous volume in one day—skimming some parts, certainly, but accurately comprehending the whole, and critically estimating it. Elaborate works, in foreign languages, over which most scholars would pore for weeks, he could dispatch in as many days, closing them often with criticisms important and minute enough to elate the pedantry of a plodding German professor.

We may well again lift a warning voice to youthful literary aspirants who would wish to imitate him. "Admirable Crichtons" are fatal models. Macaulay's example would be ruinous to most students who should attempt to copy it. He was an intellectual anomaly, and had it not been for the rare balance of his mental constitution, he would have been an intellectual monster.

Some of our readers are, doubtless, by this time disposed to suspect that we have been dealing in exaggerations. Not at all; and we proceed to notice another of his characteristics, which was as remarkable as those already treated—his precocity, his genius, his working power, his quickness of apprehension and insight—and which, in union with these, was one of the most important conditions of his intellectual growth and literary success: we refer to his remarkable memory.

In his fiftieth year he writes, "My memory I often try, and find it as good as ever." Two years later he says, "I walked in the portico, and learned by heart the noble fourth act of the

Merchant of Venice." There are four hundred lines in the act; he had known one hundred and fifty of them. In two hours he now made himself master of them all, including the prose letter. This was about three years before his death. The only difference in his wonderful memory between his childhood and this period was that in the former "whatsoever he took a fancy to" was involuntarily remembered; now to learn by heart was a voluntary, but never a laborious, act. It was an intellectual recreation. When made a peer he "studied the peerage," and could repeat the entire roll of the House of Lords. When done with the peerage he turned to the calendars of Cambridge and Oxford, and wrote, "I have now the whole of our university *Fasti* by heart; all, I mean, that is worth remembering—an idle thing, but I wished to try whether my memory is as strong as it used to be, and I perceive no decay." Such acquisitive and retentive faculties are absolutely beyond all estimation for a student. They enable him to work miracles. They relieve him of nearly all the drudgery of scholarship.

Another notable characteristic, the result of these rare powers, was his extraordinary versatility. Our remarks thus far have necessarily anticipated this fact. Its proofs are visible in all his works, and throughout his "Life and Letters." We have mentioned his knowledge of languages. He knew their respective literatures well enough to be a professor of any of them in any university of England, France, Germany, Italy, or Spain. He studied the Portuguese to read Camoëns, but found the Lusiad "enough" for him in that tongue. In a casual conversation at a dinner table he could discuss any of their important authors with critical minuteness, discriminating not only the best plays, but the best characters, in Moliere and Corneille, Goethe and Schiller, Alfieri and Goldoni, or in the almost endless lists of Calderon and Lope de Vega. Nearly every one of his essays is a good example of his versatility, an ample *résumé* of the best students' knowledge not only of the character or subject treated, but of its epoch, summarized with a marvelous tact, and colored by an artist's hand. Thackeray wrote:—

Take, at hazard, any three pages of the essays or history, and, glimmering below the stream of the narrative, you, an average

reader, see one, two, three, a half score of allusions to other historic facts, characters, literature, poetry, with which you are acquainted. Your neighbor, who has *his* reading and *his* little stack of literature stowed away in his mind, shall detect more points, allusions, happy touches, indicating not only the prodigious memory and vast learning of this master, but the wonderful industry, the honest, humble, previous toil, of this great scholar. He reads twenty books to write a sentence; he travels a hundred miles to make a line of description.

We can hardly be surprised that, with such versatility and voracity of appetite for books, he became well acquainted with theological as with all other kinds of literature. Few clergymen have excelled him in the knowledge of their own science and its standard authors. He was familiar with the history and doctrines of the numerous sects of his country. He understood well the great "Methodistic movement," a portion of which his own father represented in the "Christian Observer." Methodists have been, naturally enough, partial to him for his estimate of their founder, of whom he said, in his article on Southey, that he was the founder "of a most remarkable moral revolution, and a man whose eloquence and logical acuteness might have made him eminent in literature, whose genius for government was not inferior to that of Richelieu, and who, whatever his errors may have been, devoted all his powers, in defiance of obloquy and derision, to what he sincerely considered as the highest good of his species." He speaks with contempt "of some writers of books called Histories of England, under the reign of George II., in which the rise of Methodism is not mentioned," and says that in a hundred years "such a breed of authors will be extinct." Mr. Trevelyan says "he was never tired of ranging" in works of "religious speculation," and was "widely and profoundly read in ecclesiastical history. . . . His partiality for studies of this nature is proved by the full and elaborate notes with which he has covered the margin of such books as Warburton's 'Julian,' Middleton's 'Free Inquiry,' Middleton's 'Letters to Venn and Waterland,' and all the rest of the crop of polemical treatises which the 'Free Inquiry' produced. . . . It may be safely asserted that in one corner or another of Macaulay's library there is his estimate of every famous or notorious English prelate from the beginning of the sixteenth to the end of the eighteenth century."

We have alluded to his rank as essayist, poet, and historian. No one will dispute his unapproachable pre-eminence as a critical essayist. He was first recognized by the literary world in this character, and the recognition was immediate and general. From his first article, (on "Milton," in the "Edinburgh Review,") written in his twenty-fifth year, he was acknowledged as a new power in the intellectual world. The most exclusive circles of London society opened their doors to welcome him, and from that day to his death he was one of the "lions" of the metropolis. He became the chief dependence of the great Scotch review; it was importunate for his contributions, and he could command his own price for them. Murray declared that it would be worth the copyright of Childe Harold to have Macaulay on the staff of the "Quarterly"—the competitor of the "Edinburgh." Nearly every one of his articles produced a sensation through not only the literary and social, but often through the political, circles of the country. They made Brougham rancorously jealous, and eclipsed Sydney Smith, Mackintosh, and even Jeffrey himself. The latter, unlike Brougham, hailed with a sort of rapture the new ascending star, and deeply mourned the departure of Macaulay from England for India; for the veteran editor never expected to see him again. In the collected republication of his essays Macaulay deprecates criticism on his "Milton," and his other early reviews, especially on their youthful enthusiasm; but the world has demanded no apology for them. They are so replete with knowledge and reason—their rhetoric itself has, with whatever faults, such superb yet genuine qualities—that we would not wish them retouched. We have known grave and cultivated men to burst into tears over his vindication of the blind old Puritan bard, who, abandoned of the world, remained superior to it. He did more for the right appreciation of Milton than any other critic save Addison. In this and other writings he has proved to Englishmen that, while they had in Cromwell the greatest of their sovereigns, and in his Roundhead army the greatest of their soldiers, they had, also, in his secretary the sublimest of their poets, and one of the noblest models of British manhood.

Other, and even more surprising, papers than "Milton" followed, all making an impression never before known in English

periodical literature: in his twenty-seventh year that on Macchiavelli, so comprehensive of his epoch and so decisive of the old problem of his "prince;" in his twenty-eighth year that on Hallam's "Constitutional History," so thorough on the religious questions of the times of Elizabeth and the Commonwealth, and so grandly appreciative of Cromwell; that on Southey's "Colloquies," so able in its discussions of political economy; that on Croker's Johnson, so remarkable for its critical corrections, and its estimates of Boswell and Johnson; that on Bunyan, in which he vindicates the high rank of the "Bedford Tinker" among Englishmen of genius; that on Gladstone's "Church and State," in which he has made out the best argument for religious liberty and for the "voluntary principle," though without propounding—perhaps without intending—the latter; that on Ranke's "Popes," so thoroughly appreciative of the era of the Reformation, and of the comparative policies of Popery and Protestantism; that on Temple, in which the notable "Phalaris" fight between Oxford and Bentley, and Bentley's signal victory, are commemorated; the two articles on Clive and Warren Hastings, so comprehensive of the history and policy of British India, and so dazzling in their rhetoric; the masterly articles on Burleigh, Hampden, and Chatham; those on the Comic Dramatists of the Restoration; on Byron, Walpole's Letters to Sir Horace Mann, Madame d'Arblay's Life and Letters, and Miss Aiken's Life and Writings of Addison, so full of entertaining information and literary gossip and criticism; and the unrivaled essay on Bacon, in which he drew with as much impartiality as ability the character of the great philosopher, and made the best statement of his system ever given by any of his critics. The latter is the largest and most elaborate of his review articles. It was written in India, and sent to the "Edinburgh" with an apology for its "interminable length." He wrote to Napier, Jeffrey's successor in the editorial chair:—

My opinion is formed, not at second hand, like those of nine tenths of the people who talk about Bacon, but after several very attentive perusals of his greatest works, and after a good deal of thought. I never bestowed so much care on any thing I have written. There is not a sentence in the latter half of the article which has not been repeatedly recast. The trouble has been so great a pleasure to me that I have been greatly overpaid.

Napier sent it to Jeffrey for advice on the propriety of dividing it. Jeffrey wrote back:—

What mortal could ever dream of cutting out the least particle of this precious work to make it better fit in your review? It would be worse that paring down the Pitt diamond to fit the old setting of a dowager's ring. Since Bacon himself, I do not know that there has been any thing so fine. The first five or six pages are in a lower tone, but still magnificent, and not to be deprived of a word.

It was inserted entire, filling a hundred and four pages of the review.

These essays excited so much interest in America that they were first published here in a collected form. Copies of the edition were sent over "wholesale," and Macaulay diffidently consented to prepare a new collected edition for the English market, in order to protect Longman, his publisher, from the enterprising American house. Mr. Trevelyan says:—

The world was not slow to welcome, and, having welcomed, was not in a hurry to shelve, a book so unwillingly and unostentatiously presented to its notice. Upwards of a hundred and twenty thousand copies have been sold in the United Kingdom alone by a single publisher. Considerably over a hundred thousand copies of separate essays have been printed in the series known as the "Travelers' Library." More than six thousand copies have, one year with another, been disposed of annually. In the United States, in British India, and the Continent of Europe, these productions, which their author classed as ephemeral, are so greedily read, and so constantly reproduced, that, taking the world as a whole, there is probably never a moment when they are out of the hands of the compositor.

Macaulay's literary reputation became universal by his essays alone. No other man had ever won equal fame by mere review articles. They were a monument seen and read of all cultivated men throughout the Anglo-Saxon world. No one beyond the circle of his immediate friends suspected that he was capable of success in poetry till his "Lays of Rome" appeared. Of course, he cannot be ranked among the great poets any more than Addison, Johnson, Southey, or Scott can be so ranked; but had he lived before Johnson he would certainly have had a place in the "Lives of the Poets," and a place above three fourths of Johnson's characters. But if he cannot be placed among the gods in the *cella* of the temple, he is entitled

at least to a prominent position among the demi-gods who stand in its exterior niches. The rhythmical instinct was inborn with him, and was as early, if not as thoroughly, developed as in Pope. We have already seen it in his childhood, and throughout his youth he could throw off poetry, or, at least, verses, in the sports of his home, impromptu and without end. But there is often a "fatal facility" in versification, seducing the young aspirant from the deeper things of poetry. It came near spoiling Pope himself. The Horatian lesson of delay and labor can never be disregarded with impunity in this highest department of literary art. Macaulay was the last man to disregard it, and his "Lays," therefore, met with immediate success.

Niebuhr had revived the theory that most of the romantic stories which fill the first three or four books of Livy come from lost ballads of the early Romans. Macaulay was no disciple of Niebuhr, and rather discredited him as an historical critic, but he was fully convinced of the truth of this theory. As a mere literary recreation he attempted, in India, to restore some of these long-lost poems, and the "Lays" sprung from the attempt full-winged. His friend, Arnold of Rugby, a disciple of Niebuhr, saw some of them in manuscript, after Macaulay's return to England, and was so struck with them that he wrote to the author "in such terms of eulogy" as to kindle his ambition for a higher literary fame than he had yet attained; he declined the importunities of Napier for new review articles, and gave himself to the correction and completion of his poems. He bestowed the utmost labor upon them, doing what, perhaps, is the hardest, though the most indispensable, task of the poet—abridging and condensing. He ruthlessly cut out scores of lines—at least thirty out of the battle of Regillus alone. The ancient Roman ballads were, most probably, in the Saturnian meter, pure examples of which have been preserved by the grammarians. It was a proof of the poetic instinct of Macaulay, a proof which could not but cheer him, that his own ballads were, without intention, very like the Saturnian meter. Goethe had succeeded, in his "Iphigenia" and Roman elegies, in reproducing the spirit of classic antique poetry; Macaulay, with less poetic genius, reproduced the Latin legends by recreating the Latin ballads—reproduced them in form and substance, as well as in spirit, not merely by his meter and perfect detail of facts

and allusions, but by the affinities of his own robust nature with the old Roman energy and heroism.

He was anxious about the success of his new venture, but, says his biographer, "the little craft, launched without noise, went bravely down the wind of popular favor." We have already seen Blackwood's opinion of it. Wilson had been his relentless political and literary antagonist. He had sarcastically described him as, "twenty years ago, like a burnished fly, in pride of May, bouncing through the open window of Knight's Magazine"—a short-lived periodical, to which he had been a contributor. He now hailed the "Lays" with "a pæan of hearty, unqualified panegyric." He exclaimed:—

What! poetry from Macaulay? Ay, and why not? The House pushes itself to hear him, even though Stanley is the cry? If he be not the first of critics, (spare our blushes,) who is? Name the young poet who could have written the Armada. The young poets all want fire; Macaulay is full of fire. The young poets are somewhat weakly; he is strong. The young poets are rather ignorant; his knowledge is great. The young poets mumble books; he devours them. The young poets dally with their subject; he strikes its heart. The young poets are still their own heroes; he sees but the chiefs he celebrates. The young poets weave dreams with shadows transitory as clouds, without substance; he builds realities lasting as rocks. The young poets steal from all and sundry, and deny their theft; he robs in the face of day. Whom? Homer!

For twenty years editions of the "Lays," averaging two thousand copies a year, have been sold, and by the spring of 1875 upwards of a hundred thousand had been issued. They were received by the public not only as an example of his versatility, but as a work of genuine art.

He had a still loftier ambition, and is to be immortal chiefly as an historian. He was not unconscious of his powers for his historical task. Many of his essays had been splendid historical studies; studies in historical biography, at least. Their success could be taken as a presage of the success of his higher undertaking. He had reason, however, for diffidence. The English historians were pre-eminent. They were at the head of the artistic historians of modern literature; and history has its artistic properties as well as the epic or the drama. The Germans excelled in research, but were heavy by the very masses of their *materiale*, and the plodding drudgery of their work-

manship. The French were mostly dramatists and rhetoricians in historical writing, with an occasional exception, like Guizot, in which the "philosophy of history" excluded most of its artistic qualities. The English, with Gibbon—who, in spite of his great faults, stands imperially supreme over all modern historians—at their head, had shown a special genius for the art. There were many giants, if not many artists, among them —Clarendon, Gibbon, Hume, Robertson, Lingard, Thirlwall, Grote, Arnold, Milman, Hallam, not to speak of Alison, Russell, Stanhope, and a host of others. It required not only ability, but courage to step into the ranks of such men. Among good ordinary writers Macaulay could be certain of pre-eminence, but it might be otherwise among the giants. Swift's Gulliver among the Liliputians found that the emperor was taller by about the breadth of his finger-nail than any of his court, "which was enough to strike awe into the beholders." But it required other proportions for distinction among the Brobdignagians. Hume had written English history as a Jacobite, Lingard as a Roman Catholic; Macaulay wrote it as a Whig, believing (and justly, as we think) that the doctrines of British Whig politics are the fundamental ideas of modern civilization and progress. How he succeeded we need not here say; the whole Anglo-Saxon world has said it. It can hardly be questioned that his History, with whatever faults, has done more to promote Whig principles than any other contemporaneous agency. There was no great reform in English politics in which he was not a representative statesman, down to his last year; his History is, and for indefinite time will be, an oriflamme in front of the onward march of the Anglo-Saxon race. Hume will always be read for his entertaining manner, the ease and felicity of his style, in spite of its Scottisms; Lingard (whose ability Macaulay acknowledged in his article on Temple) will always be valuable for his research, and for his qualification of religious prejudices in English historical literature; Macaulay will always be read, not only for his brilliant style, but for his

impulse, judicial impartiality, wide research, deep thought, picturesque description, and sustained eloquence. Was history ever better written? Guizot praises Macaulay." Of "his immense research," said Buckle, "few people are competent judges. I cannot refrain from expressing my admiration of his unwearied diligence, of the consummate skill with which he has arranged his materials, and the noble love of liberty which animates his work."

Taken as a whole, Macaulay's work is one of the most genuine examples of historical writing in our literature. He did not much esteem Voltaire's unveracious histories; but Voltaire was the founder of modern history as not a mere record of king-craft, diplomacy and war, but a record of national life—of laws, manners, and religions. Macaulay's work is a history of the English people as well as their government, and no other writer has so well described them. We have seen how, at the close of each volume, he renewed himself for the next by reading Herodotus, the "father of history," and the greatest of "story-tellers." He read and reread Thucydides, the father of "philosophic history," and pronounced him "the greatest historian that ever wrote." He was acquainted with every other historical model in ancient or modern literature. But, while availing himself of these, he faithfully maintained the individuality of his own genius, and stands conspicuously alone in historic literature. His relative rank we need not try to determine; that is usually a fallacious attempt, and a right which belongs to posterity alone. But that his history will be a permanent monument to his memory no man can doubt.

He knew the importance of little things, of even petty data in the illustration of the life of a people—the eccentricities of character, the sayings of great men, the personal peculiarities of statesmen and kings, the characteristic anecdote, the habits of the common people; and, like Cromwell before the painter, insisted that every feature, and even the wart on the face, should be given. To him George Fox's leathern breeches, and the veriest antics of his honest fanaticism, were essential indications in the genesis of a new form of religion. He disdained no hint which a street ballad could afford him. Having formed with "consummate skill," as Buckle says, his outlines—the chronological skeleton of the earlier historians, made up

regality, diplomacy and war—he filled it out, giving it body and living blood, by the common facts of the popular life. He feared not the critics, for he knew they would fall before the verdict of the aggregate good sense of the people. He knew that critical pretenders—"his puny detractors," as Buckle again says, "unworthy to loosen his shoe-latchet"—would disparage his facts and call his style irrelevant "fine writing;" but to him no facts indicating the real life of a people were unworthy of history, and nothing worthy of history was unworthy of the best literary art. Some one said to Dr. Johnson that he surpassed all his competitors in writing biography. "Sir," replied the veteran author, "I believe that is true; the dogs don't know how to write trifles with dignity."

As he wrote for the people, though in the highest style of the art, the people gave him a recognition such as no other historian has ever received. "Within three days after the appearance of the book," says Mr. Trevelyan, "its fortune was already secure. It was greeted by an ebullition of national pride and satisfaction." Three competing editions were quickly published in the United States. Our own Harpers wrote him that "no work of any kind has ever so completely taken our whole country by storm." Edward Everett wrote him that "no book has ever had such a sale in the United States, except the Bible, and one or two school-books of universal use." Tauchnitz, in Germany, had sold ten thousand copies (in English) within six months after the third and fourth volumes appeared. Six rival translators were at work, at one and the same time, turning it into German. There have been Polish, Danish, Swedish, Italian, French, Dutch, Spanish, Hungarian, Russian, Bohemian, and even Persian versions. He had said, "I shall not be satisfied unless I produce something which shall for a few days supersede the last fashionable novel on the table of young ladies." His biographer says that "the annual sale of the History has frequently, since 1857, surpassed the sale of the fashionable novel of the current year." "Within a generation of the first appearance of the work, upward of a hundred and forty thousand volumes will have been printed and sold within the United Kingdom alone." Twenty-six thousand five hundred copies were sold in ten weeks. "I should not wonder," wrote Macaulay, "if I made twenty thou-

sand pounds ($100,000) clear this year by literature. His publishers actually deposited in the bank for him a hundred thousand dollars, "as part of what would be due him in December" of that year. "What a sum," he exclaimed, "to be gained by one edition of a book!" At another time he speaks of receiving thirty thousand dollars in a single year. Longman could hardly keep pace, sometimes, with the demand for the work. Twenty-five thousand copies of the third volume were ordered before the day of publication. The stock at the book-binder's was insured for fifty thousand dollars. "The whole weight was fifty-six tons!" "No such edition was ever published of any work of the same bulk."

We cannot spare room enough to speak of him adequately as a statesman and parliamentary orator, for, as we have intimated, he stands pre-eminent above nine tenths of contemporary British statesmen, and would be historical in this character, aside from his literary fame. It is a proof of the generous instincts of his heart that he early broke away from the prejudices of his Tory education; for, curious as the fact may seem, his father, Zachary Macaulay, the philanthropist, the anti-slavery leader, and the editor of the evangelical "Christian Observer," was inclined to Tory politics. Zachary Macaulay was one of the "good men of Clapham," commemorated in Methodist history as the Calvinistic Methodists in the Low Church party of the Establishment, who had arisen under the religious movement conducted by Wesley, Whitefield, and the Countess of Huntingdon. Though leaders in most of the philanthropies of the day, these good men were inclined to Tory politics by their dread of the Jacobinism of the French Revolution, which had considerably infected England. Macaulay while yet at the university emancipated himself from their prejudices, but retained through life their best political ideas. Though he believed, with Buckle, that expediency, or "compromise," must be fundamental in any successful administrative policy, yet he held the boldest theoretical political ethics, and fearlessly avowed his theories and their consequences. The old English common sense dominated in all his speculations, and if he believed that a given public evil should be exterminated root and branch, yet he deemed it a violation of not only political sagacity, but of political ethics, to take to-

day, by assault and the sacrifice of thousands of lives, a fortress which would have to surrender at discretion to-morrow; and that many a good cause famously won might have been better won. In other words, he was a genuine statesman. He came into public life, and remained till his death, an unwavering reformer. He was found at the front in the fight of every great Parliamentary question of his times—the Anti-slavery question, the Reform bill, the India bill, the Franchise bill, the Factory bill, West India Apprenticeship, the Ballot, the Corn Laws, Catholic Emancipation, Jewish Disabilities, Copy-right. He was virtually the author of the Copy-right Law, which now protects British authors and their families—the "charter of his craft"—after the defeats of Talfourd and Lord Mahon in the same good cause. A speech of remarkable logic and lucidity rallied the House to his position with enthusiasm. Peel walked across the floor, and told him that within twenty minutes his views on the question had been entirely altered; and one member after another of the opposition acknowledged a similar change.

He was one of the most eloquent speakers in Parliament, without being precisely an orator. His first public speech was at a London antislavery meeting, in his twenty-fourth year. He was surrounded by the good men of Clapham on the platform, his anxious father among them. The "Edinburgh Review" spoke of the speech as "a display of eloquence so signal for rare and mature excellence that the most practiced orator may well admire how it should have come from one who then for the first time addressed a public assembly." "It was hailed with a whirlwind of cheers," says his biographer. "That was probably the happiest hour of Zachary Macaulay's life." When Wilberforce rose to speak, he said of the father:—

> My friend would doubtless willingly bear with all the base falsehoods, all the vile calumnies, all the detestable artifices, which have been aimed against him to render him the victim and martyr of our cause, for the gratification he has this day enjoyed in hearing one so dear to him plead such a cause in such a manner.

After the first of his Parliamentary "reform" speeches the Speaker of the House sent to him, and "told him that in all his prolonged experience he had never seen the House in such an excitement." Denman, who spoke afterward, "said with

universal acceptance that the orator's words remained tingling in the ears of all who heard them, and would last in their memories as long as they should have memories to employ." Peel remarked that "parts of the speech were as beautiful as any thing I ever heard or read. It reminds one of the old times." "The names of Fox, Burke, and Canning were," says his biographer, "during that evening in every body's mouth." Jeffrey, who heard him later on the same subject, said his speech "was prodigiously applauded, and I think puts him at the head of the great speakers, if not the great debaters, of the House." Mackintosh wrote from the library of the House, "Macaulay and Stanley have made two of the finest speeches ever spoken in Parliament;" he pronounced them "the chiefs of the next, or, rather, of this, generation." Lord Althorp said of one of his speeches, that "it was the best he had ever heard." Graham, Stanley, and Russell made similar remarks, and O'Connell followed him out of the House to "pay him most enthusiastic compliments." The "principal men" on the Whig side "agreed that it was the best ever made since the death of Fox." Of his speech on the India bill one of the speakers said, "I will venture to assert that it has never been exceeded within these walls."

It is the uniform testimony of those who heard him that he owed nothing to the usual artifices of the orator. He had few gestures and little inflection of the voice. "Vehemence of thought, vehemence of language, vehemence of manner, were his chief characteristics," says the "Daily News." It was "fullness of mind, which broke out in many departments, that constituted him a born orator." He "plunged at once into the heart of the matter, and continued his loud, resounding pace from beginning to end, without pause or halt." "Macaulay," says another witness, "was wonderfully telling in the House. Every sentence was perfectly devoured by the listeners."

Cicero says the orator should be a good man, for the popular conviction of his integrity gives sevenfold force to all he says. Macaulay's unquestionable honesty made him mighty. He resigned office in the ministry in order to make, honorably, a speech against a bill of the Government—of his own party; but the cabinet had the good sense not to accept his resignation. He lost his election in Edinburgh rather than yield to a Scotch

religious prejudice; but his constituents became, in time, ashamed of their conduct, and re-elected him with honors, and proudly kept him till the infirmities of his last years compelled him to retire, when they took leave of him with demonstrations of affection and admiration. Sydney Smith said that he was absolutely incorruptible; that no money, no title, ribbon, or coronet, could change him.

Pre-eminent in so many respects, he was almost equally so as a "conversationist." Never in the saloons of Paris, from the days of Rambouillet down to ours, nor in the circles of London, not excepting Johnson's Club, with the "great moralist," and Burke, Reynolds, and Goldsmith around its table, had conversational talent been more a social power than during the life of Macaulay. Coleridge, Charles Lamb, Sydney Smith, Rogers, Mackintosh, Carlyle, Brougham, Milman, Dickens, Thackeray, and many others, were his rivals, but hardly his equals, much less his superiors, in the "table-talk" of the metropolis. If Coleridge, with his interminable monologues, was their oracle in philosophy, Sydney Smith and Charles Lamb their oracles in humor, Macaulay was their supreme oracle in universal knowledge and criticism. Crabb Robinson, whose entertaining autobiography gives, perhaps, our best view of the best London society of this period, alludes to Macaulay's earliest appearance in it, about his twenty-sixth year, and says: "I had a most interesting companion at the table in young Macaulay, one of the most promising of the rising generation I have seen for a long time: very eloquent and cheerful, overflowing with words, and not poor in thought, he seems a correct as well as a full man. He showed a minute knowledge of subjects not introduced by himself. He was a good example of Bacon's well-known remark in all its three particulars: 'Reading maketh a full man, conference a ready man, and writing an exact man.'" Lord Carlisle's Journal gives many a fine picture of Macaulay at the London symposia. "Never," he says on one occasion, "were such torrents of good talk as burst and sputtered over from Macaulay and Hallam." At a breakfast with Macaulay he says: "The conversation ranged the world—art, ancient and modern; the Greek tragedians; characters of the orators. It is a refreshing break in commonplace life. I stayed till past twelve." At another time, "Macaulay rather para-

doxical, as he is apt to be. The greatest wonder about him is the quantity of trash he remembers. He went off at a score with Lord Thurlow's poetry." Again, "Macaulay's flow never ceased once during the four hours, but it is never overbearing." Again, "On being challenged, he repeated the names of the owners of the several carriages that went to Clarissa's funeral." Though never overbearing, in temper, at least, yet in the affluence of his thoughts he was disposed, like Coleridge, to usurp the conversation. Sydney Smith, whom he could usually overwhelm, once remarked to him with mock pathos, "Macaulay, what a loss you will suffer when I die, having never heard me converse." Lord Carlisle describes a scene in which Macaulay, Hallam, and Whewell, discussing, too, a grave ethical question, got so high ("without, however, the slightest loss of temper") that when his lordship left the table "not one sentence could any of them finish." Says Mr. Trevelyan:—

His appearance and bearing in conversation were singularly effective. Sitting bolt upright, his hands resting on the arms of his chair or folded over the handle of his walking-stick, knitting his great eyebrows if the subject was one which had to be thought out as he went along, or brightening from the forehead downward when a burst of humor was coming, his honest glance and massive features suited well with the manly, sagacious sentiments which he set forth in his pleasant, sonorous voice, and in his racy and admirably intelligible language.

But, brilliant as he was in society, his absorption in literature made his library far more attractive to him than any dinner party. He at last had a thorough "distaste for the chance society of a London drawing-room," and almost entirely abandoned it, as he "also relinquished that House of Commons, which the first sentence of his speeches hushed into silence, and the first five minutes filled to overflowing." He consecrated his last years to his History. He became a devotee of the "literary life," of which, as we said in the outset of our article, he is one of the most admirable examples in English literary history, and in which we have endeavored chiefly to consider him. Finally, giving up politics, as well as society, he lived almost exclusively in his library, and the circle of his immediate kindred. He found genuine happiness in this literary consecration, for every virtue, as well as every muse, dwelt with him there. Gibbon said that he would not exchange his enjoyment

of books for the riches of the Indies: Montesquieu declared there was no trouble, no chagrin, he could not get rid of in his library; Lessing said that if the alternatives were offered him, by the Creator, to acquire knowledge immediately by intuition, or in his usual way, by laborious study, he would choose the latter, for study is itself a felicity. Says Mr. Trevelyan:—

Macaulay's way of life would have seemed solitary to others, but it was not to him. While he had a volume in his hands he never could be without a quaint companion to laugh with him or laugh at, a counselor to suggest wise and lofty thoughts, and a friend with whom to share them. When he opened for the tenth or fifteenth time some history, or memoir, or romance, every incident and almost every sentence of which he had by heart, his feeling was precisely that which we experience on meeting an old comrade whom we like all the better because we know the exact lines on which his talk will run.

He wrote from India:—

Books are becoming every thing to me. If I had this moment my choice of life I would bury myself in one of those immense libraries that we saw together at the universities, and never pass a waking hour without a book before me.

He found, as he said, that a "book is the best of anodynes" for hours of suffering. A bibliomaniac is never a pessimist. His strong affections rendered the death of his youngest sister almost a fatal blow to him. When the sad news reached him in India, he wrote:—

That I have not sunk under this blow I owe chiefly to literature. What a blessing it is to love books as I love them; to be able to converse with the dead and live among the unreal.

He wrote still later:—

Literature has saved my life and my reason. Even now I dare not, in the intervals of business, remain alone for a minute without a book in my hand. I am more than half resolved to abandon politics, and give myself wholly to letters.

No man has left us more delightful experiences of the pleasures of literature. In his library he could summon around him the great bards, to chant to him their immortal lays; the great historians, to recite their narratives; the great orators, to exhilarate him with their eloquence; the great novelists, to entertain him with their stories; the great travelers, with whom he could

traverse the world without leaving his fireside, and witness the wonders, without sharing the perils, of their adventures. A good library was to him the best of material provisions for happiness, and a good author the best of companions. In his essay on Bacon he eloquently says:—

These friendships are exposed to no danger from occurrences by which other attachments are weakened or dissolved. Time glides on, fortune is inconstant, tempers are soured, bonds which seemed indissoluble are daily sundered by interest, by emulation, or by caprice; but no such cause can affect the silent converse which we hold with the highest of human intellects. The placid intercourse is disturbed by no jealousies or resentments. These are the old friends who are never seen with new faces, who are the same in wealth and in poverty, in glory and in obscurity. With the dead there is no rivalry; in the dead there is no change. Plato is never sullen, Cervantes is never petulant, Demosthenes never comes unseasonably, Dante never stays too long; no difference of political opinions can ever alienate Cicero, no heresy can excite the horror of Bossuet.

It was befitting that such a man should die in his library. He was found dead, says his biographer, "in his library, seated in his easy chair, and dressed as usual, with his book on the table, still open." He died in his sixtieth year, and was buried in Westminster Abbey, where, amid the monuments of Addison, Johnson, Gray, and Goldsmith, his tomb bears the inscription, "His body is buried in peace, but his name liveth for evermore."

We have endeavored, as we proposed, to trace, in his memoirs and writings, the chief conditions and most salient facts of his manifold intellectual life, without restricting ourselves mechanically to any chronological order. We should not be willing to take leave of him without saying something on his religious character, but his biographer is strangely reticent respecting it, giving hardly an intimation on the subject. We regret this singular defect in a work which we can, nevertheless, commend as one of the most able and most entertaining of recent biographies.

## Art. II.—THE WESTMINSTER REVIEW ON "THE RECENT ORIGIN OF MAN."

The facts which I submitted to the public nearly two years ago in my work entitled "The Recent Origin of Man" have been criticised in various periodicals, especially in England, by writers entertaining mostly a different opinion from my own; and I have watched with some interest—not with anxiety—to see what reply would be made to them. I set out to study this subject of the antiquity of man with little expectation of arriving at a different conclusion from that which had been reached by such great authorities as Sir Charles Lyell, Sir John Lubbock, Mr. Prestwich, Mr. Boyd Dawkins, M. Edouard Lartet, M. de Mortillet, Nilsson, Worsaae, and a host of others in all parts of Europe, and by Professor Agassiz, Professor Cope, Dr. Daniel Wilson, Dr. Foster, etc., in America. I presently began to suspect that they were mistaken, and the continuance of my investigations subsequently strengthened this impression. From that day to this, some five years, during which I have devoted a vast deal of time and labor to the subject, as my knowledge has enlarged, and as the facts have accumulated, I have become more and more clearly convinced that the science of Anthropology and Prehistoric Archæology is an elaborate and baseless delusion, which has led astray many of the most eminent scientific men of the world. The generalizations have been hasty, and the edifice has been hurried to completion without proper attention to the foundation on which it was erected. The Danish archæologists, without due consideration, led the way in these premature conclusions, propounding, upon the special facts applicable only to a very limited district in Europe, their theory of "The Three Ages." In the same manner Sir Charles Lyell, and Mr. Evans, and Sir John Lubbock, and the French archæologists after the visit of the English scientists to the valley of the Somme in 1860, adopted without sufficient consideration the theory of the high level and low level gravels, and the excavation of the valley of the Somme since the deposition of the former by the Somme river, an inconsiderable, sluggish stream, some fifty feet in width.

The argument for the antiquity of man rests upon the theory of three successive, protracted ages, designated the Stone Age, (divided into two periods,) the Bronze Age, and the Iron Age, which ages have their respective relics revealed to us in the Megalithic Monuments of Europe, in the Pile Villages, in the Danish Shell Mounds, in the Peat Deposits, in the Bone Caverns, and in the River Gravels of the river valleys of Europe.

The oldest barrows and cromlechs have been conjectured to be contemporaneous with Menes, the first king of Egypt, who was supposed to have lived about thirty-five hundred or four thousand years before our era. The older lake dwellings or pile villages belonged also to the Second or Polished Stone Age, and were represented to be at least six or seven thousand years old; indeed, Professor Agassiz considered that their antiquity was so high that they "connected humanity with geological phenomena." The lower beds of the peat belonged to the same period. Sir C. Lyell declined to indicate any approximate date for the peat of the Somme valley, but, following M. Boucher de Perthes, he intimated that the growth of these beds, which are more than thirty feet thick in some places, seemed to have been at the rate of three centimetres (one and one fifth inches) in a hundred years. The shell mounds are thought by Sir John Lubbock to belong to the transition period between the Palæolithic and Neolithic Ages. The caves and the river gravel belong to the First Stone, or Palæolithic, Age, and are supposed to be from one to five hundred thousand years old. For we find here rude flints, evidently worked by man, and also (in the caves) beautifully worked implements of horn and bone, and in each case these works of art are in association with the bones of the mammoth, the rhinoceros, the hippopotamus, the reindeer, the cave bear, the great Irish elk, and other extinct animals; and, further, it was represented that the rivers had excavated their valleys since the "high level" gravels were laid down. It was further urged that great changes in the relative level of land and sea had taken place since the days of the mammoth; and it was also pointed out that in the bone caves thick floors of stalagmite had formed over the relic beds, which stalagmite must have required, it was alleged, thousands of years to be deposited.

Sir Charles Lyell and Mr. Evans mention this as one of the proofs of the great antiquity of these relics, and Mr. Alfred Russell Wallace calculates that it took five hundred thousand years for the stalagmitic floors to form in Kent's Cavern; while Mr. Vivian, at the meeting of the British Association in 1871, asserted that it must have taken a million of years for these two floors to form.

These are the points, and I undertook to meet them. In doing so I collected a vast multitude of facts, and swelled my book to six hundred pages, determined to give the evidence in full, at the risk of making my work tedious.

I have published a short piece in England in reply to Mr. Boyd Dawkins, but I have not noticed any criticisms which appeared in this country in any way.

As my book has recently been reviewed, however, in the "Westminster Review," which has a high standing in England, and is reprinted in this country, and as a review has, moreover, recently appeared in *Matériaux pour l'Histoire de l'Homme*, one of the leading anthropological periodicals of France, I desire to say something more formal in reply; and at the same time I may take occasion to notice again, if space permits, the review by Mr. Dawkins, published in "Nature."

I have taken the pains to state the grounds on which the geologists and archæologists rely as the proof of the antiquity of our race, in order to indicate the points which ought to be grappled with in any discussion of this subject.

Now I affirm that all of my English and American critics have failed to handle these points, and have offered no reply to the facts I have adduced under most of these heads.

The "Westminster" reviewer addresses himself chiefly to a criticism of some preliminary remarks I make on Egyptian chronology, and assails the chronology of Usher, and comments on the limited time I allow for the dispersion of mankind, and kindred topics. This is a very interesting subject, but it was touched only incidentally in my book, and I expressly, in my preface, as well as afterwards, cut off all such discussion by granting that the human period may have begun ten thousand years ago. I do not think that it did, but I did not wish to embarrass the subject with questions about the precise biblical chronology. I make some mention, it is

true, of probable dates,. as B. C. 2700 for the beginning of Egyptian history; but I expressly refrain from committing myself explicitly, and in any case it was only a casual allusion in the first chapter, and aside from the main theme I proposed to discuss.

Before entering upon more important topics, I wish to say that the reviewer repeatedly misstates my positions.

1. He makes me say that the human race is only six thousand years old. I do not say so. Six or eight I do not object to.

2. On page 47 (English edition) he says that I regard the palæolithic implements "as pre-glacial or antediluvian." There is not a line to this effect in my book. On the contrary, I argue distinctly and expressly against Mr. Geikie's pre-glacial man.

3. On page 48: "Mr. Southall calls upon us to believe things more astonishing still, when he asserts that in two or three hundred years, at the most, after all mankind, excepting eight persons, according to his belief, had been cut off by the universal deluge, all the great kingdoms of the East had risen to the height of their power, filled with peoples of distinct races, . . . while at the same time people of the same descent had forgotten all this splendor, and were hunting the mammoth in Scotland in naked freedom, oblivious of Memphis and Babylon."

I am here made to believe, without any ground for it whatever, in a universal deluge.

I am made to say, further, that "all the great kingdoms of the East had risen to the height of their power in two or three hundred years, *at the most*," after the flood. I suggest 2400–2200 B. C. for the fourth Egyptian dynasty, (supposed to have been contemporary with the third,) and I remark in italics, on page 18, that "human history commenced about forty-five hundred or five thousand years ago." This, instead of "two or three hundred years, at the most;" for the interval in question, would give eight hundred years, which is abundantly long, as the post-diluvians, of course, inherited, through Noah, the civilization of the antediluvians.

The brief sentence quoted contains a third blunder on the part of the reviewer. He speaks of "hunting the mammoth

in Scotland." Now, the mammoth never was hunted in Scotland, for, as I show in my thirty-second chapter, (and with this Lyell agrees,) palæolithic man never entered Scotland; he was kept out of it by the ice. No palæolithic tools are found in Scotland, Denmark, or Sweden.

4. On page 55 I am represented as stating that the "potter's wheel was unknown until the time of the Romans." I make no such statement; what I say is, that it was not known in northern and western Europe until the Romans introduced it. The potter's wheel was known to the Egyptians and Assyrians and Hebrews, and Dr. Schliemann found various traces of it at Hissarlik.

5. On page 61 I am represented as suggesting that a certain subterranean aqueduct (see page 252 of my book) "was constructed in tertiary times." This would place me in the attitude, in a work written to prove "the recent origin of man," of representing that our ancestors were living, and occupied in works of drainage, or water supply, in the Pliocene Age. A reviewer in a periodical of the character of the "Westminster" ought not to be ignorant of the facts he writes about; it is still more to be expected that he shall not, through carelessness or mental dullness, absurdly distort the plain meaning of the text he is engaged in dissecting.

6. On page 47 the writer remarks that he "believes no chronology places the flood earlier than B. C. 3000," etc. This is remarkable in view of the fact that the Septuagint fixes the date of the flood at about B. C. 3200.

I will now proceed to notice some of the positions taken by the reviewer.

1. On page 45 he expresses the opinion that the Palæolithic Age covered two distinct periods, represented by the rude implements of the river gravels and the presence of the cave bear, and by the much finer work of most of the caves, and the presence of the mammoth. It is M. Lartet's Cave Bear Epoch and Mammoth Epoch. It is only necessary in reply to this to say that this division is rejected by Sir John Lubbock, by Mr. Evans, and by Mr. Dawkins. The latter observes: "The classification will apply, as I have shown in my essay on the pleistocene mammalia, neither to the caves of this country, of Belgium, nor of France, and my views are shared by M. de

Mortillet, after a careful and independent examination of the whole evidence." *

2. The main and capital point which the reviewer urges, however, is this: that if the post-diluvians, as represented in Scripture, set out with a knowledge of the arts of life, and were dispersed over the face of the earth, he does not understand how the palæolithic people of Western Europe "forgot so soon the use of the metals, which must have been known in the ark, and used in building the tower of Babel, as well as the Pyramids." This involves the question of the diversity of type observable among the races of mankind, which diversity appears to have existed from a very early period, and is akin to the other difficulty which has been raised, about the divergence of language and the rapid development of so many different languages among the families of mankind. These questions are barely touched upon in "The Recent Origin of Man," for the reason that the author has in view another class of topics, namely, the discoveries of the relics and traces of man in the river gravel, the bone caves, etc. It would have led him too far away from his subject to have gone deeply into these other questions, which would of themselves require a volume for their elucidation. His work is intended as a reply to the books of such writers as Sir John Lubbock and Sir C. Lyell; and these authors merely give to the points now mentioned a passing consideration; indeed, Lubbock hardly refers to them.

And, waiving any attempt at any explanation of them on natural principles here, it is sufficient, so far as Language is concerned, to say that those who believe in the Bible have an adequate explanation of the diversity of tongues in the statement which is made in connection with the attempt to build the tower of Babel—a statement supported by the Chaldæan records. The diversity of races may have occurred in a similar manner. The descendants of Noah may have been characterized in a few generations by marked diversities of type, of which, indeed, there is some intimation in the biblical narrative. The same divine power which confounded the languages of men may have established, with an eye to a future multiformity in humanity, emphatic differences, physical as well as spiritual, among those who were to be the primeval stocks from

* "Cave-Hunting," p. 352.

which the nations of the earth should proceed. Is this improbable? It is only necessary to mention, in reply, Jacob, the great progenitor of the Jews, and Ishmael, the great progenitor of the Bedouin Arabs. The peculiarities of the latter, at least, were, in express language, embodied and anticipated in the son of Hagar.

Or it may be, as Archdeacon Pratt suggests, that the diversity of type originated *before* the flood; the three sons of Noah may have married wives of dissimilar types.

But how, then, shall we account for the non-employment of the metals by the Stone Age people of Western Europe?

In the first place, we may suppose those tribes inferior to those who settled in Egypt and built the Pyramids, or those who settled in Chaldæa and built the cities on the Euphrates. Why can we not civilize the Indians? Why are the Bedouin Arabs in ceaseless motion? "Who hath made them to differ?" How shall we explain the difference between the Village and the Roving Indians of North America?

In the second place, in the very oldest Chaldæan tombs we find *rude stone axes and knives* along with bronze and iron, the iron being so precious as to be used only for ornaments. The metals were scarce in those days, in the infancy of the race, and just after the earth had been swept by a flood. It is the same in Egypt; stone axes and lance-heads and knives are delineated on the tombs of Beni-Hassan, of the fourth dynasty; and Dr. Pickering tells us, in a paper on the Gliddon mummy case in the Smithsonian Institution, that the stone adze is figured in the third dynasty. Nor is this all: M. Mariette informs us that flint arrow-heads and knives are found in numbers in the later Egyptian tombs, even in the time of the Ptolemaic sovereigns. If, then, a primitive tribe, and that an inferior tribe intellectually, should have wandered from Asia, two thousand or twenty-five hundred years before our era, and should have found itself in the unvisited solitudes of central or western Europe—pushed into the wilderness, perhaps, by their more powerful kinsmen—is it strange that they, too, would make use of flint implements? They had not (the first immigrants) "forgotten" the metals, but where were they to get them? They may have been in the bowels of the earth, but they were not competent, perhaps, to find them, or to mine them, or to work

them. In a few years their children or their grandchildren would have "forgotten" them. Iron was not known in America among the Aztecs or the Peruvians. Iron was not possessed by the Massagetæ, (the powerful Scythian tribe who defeated and slew Cyrus the Great in the fifth century before Christ,) nor, indeed, did they make use of it as late as the time of Strabo. The reviewer cannot understand how the cave-dwellers in the valley of the Izère had "forgotten" the use of the metals. Can he explain how it was that the Ichthyophagi, on the north coast of the Arabian sea, between India and Persia, in the days of Strabo, knew nothing of the metals? The civilization of Southern Arabia, the empire of Persia, the arts of India, and—separated only by the Persian Gulf—the cities of the Chaldæan plain, for four or five thousand years, according to the archæologists, had fenced them in. Can the reviewer explain how it is that in the Isle of Lewis a stone knife was used as late as 1824 to cut out a wedding-dress, or that, but a few years ago, the spade was unknown in modern Greece? Were the Ichthyophagi unrelated to all the civilized races around them? and had they enjoyed no opportunity of seeing "the metals?" Doubtless the primeval tribes that reached Western Europe did not improve in that inhospitable region, although the reviewer would be slow to credit the retrogression of humanity, forgetful alike of the plains of Marathon and the ruins of Iona. Can he explain the presence of the flint and bone implements found in association with wheel-made pottery by the Abbé Moretain and the Duc de Luynes, near Bethlehem, in Judea? or on what principle it is that the Bojos of northern Abyssinia at the present day manufacture and use stone hatchets and flint knives along with hatchets and poniards of iron? From the same region nearly two thousand five hundred years ago the Ethiopian contingent in the army of Xerxes, which invaded Greece, had antelope's horn for the heads of their javelins, and their arrows pointed with sharpened stones. This was from the country of the great Tirhakah, where had flourished from a remote period the Golden Napata, and, later, the Golden Meroe; where we find now, on the banks of the Nile, at Jebel-Berkel, great Pyramids and avenues of Sphinxes leading up to the ruins of the Ammonium; where Osiris was worshiped; and where, at a far later period still, in the first or second century

of our era, the kingdom of the Auxumitæ flourished, whose greatness is attested by the ruins of the modern Axum in Tigré.

Why should the reviewer allow such weight to such a point when we are confronted by the astounding revelations of Dr. Schliemann at Troy and Mycenæ? Does he not know that no iron was found in the relic-beds at Troy, and that up to the surface or historic Greek beds (B. C. 650) *all* the beds contained stone implements, the same stone implements greatly preponderating over the bronze in the fourth and highest layer from the bottom? If bronze and stone (and apparently no iron) were used on the Asiatic coasts of the Ægean from 1500 B. C. continuously down to 650 B. C., is it very incomprehensible that in 2500 B. C. or 2000 B. C. there should be no working in iron and bronze in north-western Europe? If fifty per cent. of the implements at Troy from 1000 B. C. to 700 B. C. were of metal, and fifty per cent. of stone, why may not one hundred per cent. of the implements in the Thames valley have been of stone 2500 B. C.?

This is what I should say in reply to the objection that the post-diluvians of the European bone-caves "could not have forgotten so soon the use of the metals."

3. I undertake to show in my book that the theory of the Three Ages is practically a delusion, and even venture to doubt, except in Ireland and the Baltic region, the existence of a Bronze Age. I show by innumerable examples that these ages run into each at every point; that the Stone not only overlaps the Bronze, but laps *across* the Bronze into the Iron Age; that while one race was in its Iron Age another was in its Stone Age; that in the same country stone would be in use in one district while metal would be in use in another; and that stone implements are found constantly with Roman remains, and even in Saxon and Merovingian graves.

On this the reviewer remarks:—

Mr. Southall occupies pages in proving that which no one denies, namely, that stone, bronze, and iron were used together, and that even to a comparatively recent date. . . . Nevertheless, the broad facts remain, of a time in all countries when iron was unknown, but in most cases bronze was used instead of it. Further back, again, and bronze disappears, polished stone alone being used; one step further still, and implements of a rougher, unpolished type appear.—Page 65.

The reviewer admits (says "no one denies") that stone, bronze, and iron were used together, "and that even to a comparatively recent date." He is compelled to admit this. On the site of Hissarlik, (Troy,) in the four relic-beds superimposed the one on the other, coming up to the Greek bed, which is the fifth and last, bronze implements and stone implements occur together in all the beds, and no iron—the last of the four beds, counting upwards, coming down to the dawn of the Greek period, that is to say, about 650 B. C.

If stone was used in the Troad as late as this, and bronze, what must have been the fact in Britain and Gaul? Bronze swords have been found in the peat of the valley of the Somme, with coins of Caracalla and Maxentius. A large number of bronze tools and weapons were found at the lake station of Unter-Uhldingen, in Switzerland, with implements of iron and the fragments of glass goblets—glass being introduced into this region by the Romans. Bronze implements were found again with Roman relics at the lake-stations of Nidau, Sutz, Little Island, Ile des Lapins, (Lake of Bienne,) and at La Tène, (Lake of Neufchatel.) They were found by M. Boucher de Perthes in the Abbeville peat with Gaulish coins. And the bronze daggers are constantly found in the tumuli and dolmens dating after the Christian era. Bronze (and stone) weapons were found again in the trenches before Alise, where Julius Cæsar besieged and captured the army of Vercingetorix.*

As for the continued use of stone, the Abbé Cochet found, as the usual accompaniment of the urn-interments in the Roman cemeteries opened in Normandy, "pieces of chipped flint, generally formed into the shape of wedges." Stone implements were found with Roman relics in a tumulus at Crubelz, (France,) in a tumulus on Hartshill Common, (England,) in Rolley Low, at Moot Low; at the lake-stations of Unter-Uhldingen, Sipplingen, Nidau, Sutz, Little Island, Ile des Lapins, La Tène, Colombier, Chez les Moines, Concise, Corcelettes, Montellier,

* The same fact was developed by the excavations carried on in 1862 between Trévoux and Riottier, on the plateaux of La Bruyère and Saint Bernard, where Cæsar defeated the Helvetii on the Saone. The Emperor Napoleon III. remarks that there are numerous Gallo-Roman and Celtic sepultures on this spot, which yielded many fragments of arms in flint, ornaments in bronze, iron arrow-heads and fragments of sockets.—*Hist. of Julius Cæsar.* Tran., vol. ii, page 65.

(all in Switzerland;) they were found with Roman objects again at Ash, (in Kent,) at Leicester, at Great Whitcombe, (Gloucestershire,) at Ickleton, (Essex,) at Alchester, (Oxfordshire,) at Eastbourne, at Stoneham, (Suffolk,) in the Isle of Thanet, at Hardham, (Sussex,) all in England. In France, stone implements occurred with Roman relics at La Souterraine, (Creuse,) at Le Chezlounet, (Haute-Loire,) in the necropolis of Varenne-sur-Allier, in the funeral pits of Beaugency, in the cavern of Condere, (Hautes-Cevennes,) in the Gallo-Roman sepultures of Luneray, (Seine-Inférieure,) at Sainte Privat d'Allier, in the Gallo-Roman villa of La Tourette, (Cher,) in a Roman *sacellum* near Conches, (Eure,) in another *sacellum* near the Chateau des Roches, (Sarthe,) in the sarcophagi of Bray, (Oise,) in an ancient iron mine near Guêret, (Creuse.)

Later still, stone weapons have been found with objects of the Saxon period at Stand Low; and in Ireland a stone celt was found with a hoard of Anglo-Saxon coins of the tenth century. In France implements of flint have been found in several instances in Merovingian cemeteries, as at Labruyère and Caranda. At the latter place there are great numbers of graves, and they generally contain implements of flint or some other stone.*

If we pass to the other extremity of Europe it has been recently ascertained by the examination of great numbers of the tumuli or kurgans of Russia that they contain implements of stone, bronze, and iron; and the date of these graves is fixed by the discovery in them of Byzantine and Asiatic coins of the tenth century, and other objects belonging to about the same period. The bronze arrow-heads are especially abundant.

Our object in citing these cases is to make it plain that the reviewer was compelled to admit that "stone, bronze, and iron were used together, *and that even to a comparatively recent date.*" This being admitted, we do not care to argue about the priority or succession of stone, bronze, and iron. Of course, there was a period in Western Europe when the metals were

* Since this was written I have met with the statement in *Matèriaux pour l'Histoire de l'Homme*, in an article by M. G. Soreil on the Cave of Chauvaux, that "we possess a short but authentic and precious monument of old Germanic poesy which proves that in the time of Odoacer (the fifth century) the principal German warriors were still armed with hatchets of stone."—See *livraisons* 9ᵉ *et* 10ᵉ, 1876, page 385, note.

unknown; we state this—it is implied in the Palæolithic Age. But if stone, bronze, and iron are all found in the trenches before Alise, or if the flint implements occur constantly on Roman sites in France and England, and abound in the Merovingian cemetery of Caranda, then it is obvious at once that stone implements are no longer a proof of a high antiquity. If the stone continued to be used in these countries after the Christian era, *the Stone Age* cannot be very far behind. That was our argument. The reviewer does not seem to apprehend the significance of the facts. Again: the archæologists are fond of Mr. Evans' illustration that, "like the three principal colors of the rainbow, these three stages of civilization overlap, intermingle, and shade off the one into the other, and yet their succession, as far as Western Europe is concerned, appears to be equally well defined with that of the prismatic colors." But while the red, yellow, and blue of the rainbow blend into each other at their edges, the red does not *cross* the yellow to mingle with the blue; it does not touch the blue; but we find the flints in use in the Iron Age; it has lapped *across* the bronze. And a lapping of this kind simply means that the distinctions amount to nothing. The metals did not reach Western Europe (except through an occasional trader) until a few centuries before the Christian era; they had not reached the interior districts of Britain before the advent of the Romans. The more advanced tribes (those on certain coasts, for example) used metal implements; those in the interior continued to use stone. There was also a distinction between the rich and the poor. The rich managed to procure metallic weapons; the poor could not always afford to do it.

The American Indians were in constant communication with all parts of the Continent at the time of the Spanish conquest of Mexico: why did they not throw away their stone weapons and use bronze? Why did the Mexicans use stone? Why do some of the Pacific tribes use stone at this day?

Nor need it be supposed that the use of stone implements implies the want of intelligence, or even refinement of feeling. The pottery and the jewelry in the two oldest relic-beds at Hissarlik, as well as at Santorin, are of an advanced type; and if any one will take the trouble to refer to the Appendix to Prescott's "Conquest of Mexico," he will see there a letter of advice from

an Aztec mother to her daughter that is touching and beautiful in the extreme, and full of hints in regard to the latter's deportment in society that would be valuable to a young lady of even the present time in a Christian country. The main thought that I wish to convey, however, is, that this continued use of stone down to and after the Christian era destroys the presumption of antiquity for the Stone Age in Western and Northern Europe. It is only the question of *date* with which I am concerned; the sequence is only a secondary matter.

At the same time (though I cannot go fully into the subject here) I am inclined to the opinion that there was no Bronze Age in Gaul and Britain, and in some other parts of Europe. There was a Bronze Age in Denmark and Southern Sweden; these people were using bronze when the nations of Southern and Central Europe and Gaul were using iron, and their Iron Age does not commence until the third century of the Christian era. There are no evidences of a Bronze Age in the Swiss Lake-Dwellings, if we adopt the definition of such a period given by the archæologists; namely, that it was characterized by the use of bronze for *weapons* and *cutting implements*. Very few bronze weapons have been found at these stations, as may be seen by referring to page 43 of Sir John Lubbock's "Prehistoric Times," where he gives a table of the various objects found at them. At six of the principal bronze stations and "other places" (not specified) four thousand three hundred and forty-six objects of bronze were found, and only four swords, six arrow-heads, sixty-seven celts, forty-seven lance-heads, two daggers, and one hundred and ninety-three knives. This is the Bronze Age in Switzerland. The stone implements are not reported; but we ascertain this item, from another table, at the principal Bronze Age station at the Swiss Lakes—Nidau, (on the Lake of Bienne;) and it appears that the stone axes here amounted to thirty-three, while the bronze axes amounted to only twenty-three—there being in addition three hundred and thirty-five "other objects" of stone—chiefly weapons, of course. Now, Nidau is *par excellence* THE bronze station. And yet, according to Sir John Lubbock's own definition, (see page 3,) he ought to have called it a Stone Age station, for it is evident

hundred stone celts were found, "besides arrow-heads, chisels, stone hammers," etc.

Where is the Bronze Age in Britain? It is not in the caves, for Mr. Boyd Dawkins observes that "up to the present time (1870) all the prehistoric caves discovered in Britain belong either to the Age of Stone or Iron," ("Macmillan's Magazine," December, 1870.) It is not in the lake-stations; few of these have been found in Britain. It is not in the barrows or dolmens; for Sir John Lubbock gives us a tabulated statement (page 142) of the finds from two hundred and fifty of these, and in all these graves he reports of bronze weapons only fifteen daggers, two axes, and one lance-head—no swords, or knives, or arrow-heads. And yet he refers many of these graves to the Bronze Age.

I am not alone in this opinion as to the non-existence of the Bronze Age in some countries. It is the opinion of Mr. Thomas Wright, one of the most eminent archæologists of England, and of the no less eminent Mr. Roach Smith. It is the opinion of the distinguished Egyptologist, M. Chabas, who declares that there was no Age of Stone, or Bronze, or Iron in Egypt—nor, indeed, in Europe. I cannot say that M. Mariette denies the existence of a Bronze Age in Egypt, but he expressly denies that there are any traces of a Stone Age. The great Assyriologist, M. Oppert, insists that there was no Bronze Age and no Iron Age in the East. At the Stockholm Congress of Anthropologists, in 1874, M. Bertrand, one of the editors (I believe) of the *Revue Archéologique*, declared that "not only did the Bronze and Iron Ages overlap one another, but they had positively been contemporaneous—and in Germany (that) the Bronze Age prevailed to the fourth century after Christ." At the same Congress Mr. Leemans declared that there was no distinction between the Age of Bronze and the Age of Stone in Holland. As to England, Mr. John Evans declared at the same Congress that the bronze swords found in that country are invariably provided with handles of a different metal, which would seem to countenance the opinion of Mr. Roach Smith and Mr. Thomas Wright, that these swords are of *Roman* origin. At the Congress, last year, at Budapest, Mr. Evans stated that the "flat" or "knife" hatchets of bronze in England were always found mixed with objects of stone.

The statement of M. Bertrand as to Germany is confirmed by the declaration of M. Virchow, at Budapest, that in Southern Germany the archæologists insist that bronze is not found without iron. (*Matériaux*, 1876, p. 449.)

It is equally true that there was no Bronze Age in Poland or Russia. Dr. Heinrich Wankel, giving an account of the Russian Archæological Congress at Kiew, (1875,) in the *Mittheilungen der anthropologischen Gesellschaft in Wien*, after passing under review the kurgans of Russia, remarks that "the separation of the bronze and iron periods has no justification, certainly, for great districts of Russia." "We know, moreover," he adds, "from the investigations of Professor Pryborovsky in Warsaw, that among the people who lived on the Vistula a bronze period did not exist at all, and that the stone period of these people continued into the iron period, and continued to exist with the same a considerable time." *

One more authority to the same purport will suffice: it is that of M. Lenormant, in his work entitled "*Les Premières Civilizations.*" This eminent Orientalist remarks that—

> The distinction between the age of bronze and the age of iron has been from the first too much exaggerated from an observation of the special facts in the Scandinavian North, and it tends to be effaced. In the greater number of countries the two metals were known at the same time, and it was local circumstances, facilitating rather the working of bronze, which made it at first predominate among certain peoples, while the fabrication of iron was developed in preference among others from an extreme antiquity.

Bronze adzes, saws, chisels, falchions, arrow-heads, etc., occur in numbers in the ruins at Thebes in Egypt. The Egyptians, after the capital was removed from Memphis, continued, during the later Theban Monarchy, to use bronze apparently in preference to iron.

On the other hand, in other parts of Africa, as we are informed by M. Lenormant, bronze does not appear to have been used; but the negroes of Central and Southern Africa appear "to have passed at once from the exclusive use of stone to that of iron." †

This is enough on this point. It is plain to any unpreju-

* *Mittheil. anthrop. Gesells. in Wien*, 1875, s. 29.

† *Matériaux pour l'Hist. de l'Homme*, 1874, 2e *livraison*, p. 82.

diced reader that the theory of the Three Ages, as presented by the archæologists, is incorrect as a scheme of chronology, and almost worthless as a formula of human progress.

4. *The Peat.* Great stress has been laid on the *peat* of the Somme valley. Thirty feet of it (in some places) overlie the implement-bearing gravel beds at Abbeville and Amiens. This alone, we are told, has involved the lapse of a vast period of time, entirely at war with the old chronology. In my book I undertake to show that these deposits do not go back of (say) 1,000 years B. C., and that, in fact, much of it is post-Roman.

There are two arguments for this. One is that made by Dr. Andrews, who observed at Amiens that in the peat deposits the stumps of birch-trees were still standing erect three feet high. On this Dr. Andrews remarks that, as the stumps of trees do not stand long uncovered in the damp air of a swamp without decay, it follows that all which were found standing erect in the peat must have been covered to their present summits before they had time to rot away. But one hundred years is a long life-time for an oak-stump under such circumstances, and every trace of almost every other tree would disappear in fifty years. Birch-stumps are especially perishable. There were also prostrate trunks of oak four feet in diameter, and so sound that they were manufactured into furniture. They must have been covered by the peat in a hundred years, and the birch-stumps in much less time. At three feet in a century, the thirty feet of peat would have formed in a thousand years, instead of the thirty thousand required by M. de Perthes. At one foot in a century, the whole would have formed in three thousand years.

The second argument for the moderate age of the peat was drawn from M. Boucher de Perthes' book, (the *Antiquités celtiques et anté-diluviennes.*) I showed from this work that relics of Roman origin were found in the peat or silt at the lowest depths, and instanced, in addition, from Lyell, the discovery, near Abbeville, at the bottom of the peat, of *a boat laden with Roman bricks.*

I cited also from Ireland and Denmark, England and Scotland and Germany, many other cases to prove that the peat deposits of Europe are ordinarily no older, or little older, than

the beginning of our era. I think the point was established; but the reviewer meets it by suggesting that "rivers are constantly shifting their course more or less rapidly, . . . and it seems to us probable that a laden boat, sinking in the mud of a swollen river which excavated for itself a new channel, would quickly become silted up with sand and mud, and, on the river resuming its normal proportions, it would remain buried below the level of the peat, the superincumbent mass of which might have become pressed down and spread over the spot, undermined by the flood, without having grown there."

This supposes that our Roman boat was caught at Abbeville, before it had time to unload, in a sudden flood of the river; that the river got out of its banks, and excavated a new channel in the adjacent peat; that this peat had been quietly forming there before for thousands of years without interruption; that the boat went to the bottom in the new channel during the flood; that the river then retired, and in some mysterious way the peat then closed over the stranded boat.

If the peat of the Somme valley has been thrown about after this fashion, it has no significance one way or the other; if the Roman relics at the bottom of it are not indicative of the age of the peat, then neither are the relics of the Neolithic Age found there reliable witnesses of the time which has elapsed since the peat began to form; nor is the mere thickness of the peat; for if the floods may have undermined it and upturned it, we can know nothing about its normal thickness whatever, and can base no calculations on it. But we never heard of peat being treated in this way; it would not be going much further to suggest that the whole of it has been washed into the Somme valley.

The reviewer ought to know that peat will not form in muddy water, or over a valley subject to violent floods. Thus, as M. Belgrand says, discussing this very question, there is no peat in the valley of the Marne, which is subject to floods of muddy water.

The reviewer of my book in *Matériaux pour l'Histoire de l'Homme* (8$^e$ *livraison*, 1876) is much more candid on this point than the "Westminster" reviewer. He says:—

According to Mr. Andrews, the peat, which is only produced under very special conditions of abundant vegetable decomposition and humidity and repose, can only be formed in a rather rapid manner. If his conclusions, which seem the fruit of careful observations, were admitted, it would be necessary to reject every hypothesis of the formation of peat on a scale slower than that of two feet in a century. . . . It seems proved that under favorable circumstances the thickest beds of peat have been formed in the course of one or two centuries, even where it can be produced no longer in our day from the absence of the same necessary conditions for its development.

5. *The Stalagmite.* The reviewer (page 78) says that it would be ridiculous to apply the admeasurement of stalagmitic deposit in the Ingleborough Caves to the stalagmite of Kent's Cavern. I cannot see the logic of this. We have been told by Mr. Alfred Russell Wallace that it must have taken five hundred thousand years for the stalagmitic floors in Kent's Cavern to form; and Mr. Vivian, as I have stated, at the British Association in 1871, put it at "more than a million years." In reply, I showed that at the Ingleborough Cave, in Yorkshire, stalagmite is being accumulated at the present moment at the rate of 0.2946 of an inch in a year, which is at the rate of nearly one inch in three years, or about three feet per century. Why may not the process have been equally rapid in Kent's Cavern? It may have been *more rapid.* The rate depends on the supply of carbonic acid, and this may have been much greater formerly, either from subterranean sources, or from the greater accumulation of vegetable matter in the soil.

I mentioned that the stalagmite had been recently observed to be forming at Poole's Hole, near Buxton, at the rate of one inch in four years; that in Martin's Cave, at Gibraltar, a floor eighteen inches thick had formed since the twelfth or thirteenth century; that at San Vignone, in Tuscany, half a foot of solid limestone is formed every year in a conduit-pipe, inclined at an angle of thirty degrees; that at the baths of San Filippo, in the Apennines, the water has been known to deposit a solid mass thirty feet thick in twenty years; that in a lead cave, near Dubuque, Iowa, stalactites three feet long have formed in three years.

And yet the reviewer deems it a sufficient reply to all this

to say that it would be ridiculous to apply the admeasurement in Ingleborough Cave to Kent's Cave.

I will settle the matter by an authority that the reviewer will, perhaps, bow to.

In his work entitled "Cave-Hunting," Mr. W. Boyd Dawkins (who believes in pre-glacial man, and who ranks second to none in the school of Prehistoric Archæology) remarks upon the Ingleborough Cave as follows:—

> It is evident, from this instance of rapid accumulation, that the value of a layer of stalagmite in measuring the antiquity of deposits below it is comparatively little. The layers, for instance, in Kent's Hole, which are generally believed to have demanded a considerable lapse of time, may possibly have been formed at the rate of a quarter of an inch per annum, and the human bones which lie buried under the stalagmite in the cave of Bruniquel, are not for that reason to be taken to be of vast antiquity. It may be fairly concluded that the thickness of layers cannot be used as an argument in support of the remote age of the strata below. At the rate of a quarter of an inch per annum, twenty feet of stalagmite might be formed in one thousand years.*

6. *No Palæolithic Age in Egypt.* Says the Westminster reviewer:—

> Over and over again Mr. Southall affirms that no palæolithic implements have been found in Egypt, and that there is no trace of any thing behind the Pyramids; but Sir John Lubbock produces numerous specimens found by himself in Egypt, scarcely to be distinguished from those found in our caves—found, too, in situations suggestive of the highest antiquity.

Of course, if there is nothing in Egypt behind the Pyramids, or in Chaldæa behind Erech and Calneh and the Tower of Babel, the argument is nearly ended; and that is precisely what I affirm, (allowing a margin of a few centuries—possibly five hundred to one thousand years.)

The reviewer does not understand the subject, and has, moreover, made an important addition to Sir John Lubbock's statement. Sir John Lubbock does not state that he found there implements "in situations suggestive of the highest antiquity." He says that he found them in the Nile Valley on the surface of the ground.

Nor has Sir John Lubbock found any implements of the "Pa-

* "Cave-Hunting," p. 40.

læolithic Age," (as that term is understood in connection with the Somme Valley and Western Europe) in Egypt. All that he found—and that on the surface of the ground—was implements of "palæolithic type," resembling those of the Somme Valley in character. He *did not* find them in the same geological horizon; he *did not* find them in association with the bones of the mammoth and the cave-bear.

I have already stated that implements of palæolithic type have been found in the old Chaldæan tombs. Implements of the same type were found in abundance by Col. J. Lane Fox at Cissbury, which are admitted to belong to the Neolithic Period; and Prof. Charles Rau informs us that such implements "are by no means scarce in North America. . . . and must be classed with the other chipped and ground implements in use among the North American aborigines during historical times." Messrs. Squier and Davis found six hundred flint implements of this type in one of the "sacrificial" mounds of Clark's Work, on the North Fork of Paint Creek, Ross County, Ohio.

The *type*, however, is of no significance; the antiquity of such objects must be judged from the geological position and the associated fauna.

I stated deliberately, and I reiterate the statement, that there are no traces of the Palæolithic Age in Egypt. Not only was there no Palæolithic Age in Egypt and Chaldæa, but there was *no Stone Age of any kind.* There are plenty of stone implements found, belonging to the Neolithic type, but they are found in the tombs and on the surface of the ground, and are delineated on the Egyptian monuments.

The circumstance that some implements of this type have been found in the Nile Valley points to the same conclusion which is suggested by their presence in the Chaldæan tombs; namely, that the palæolithic implements of the West *are of the same date, and originated in the East.*

THE EXTINCT ANIMALS AND THE CHANGES IN PHYSICAL GEOGRAPHY.

I have now noticed the points made by the reviewer. They do not touch the main issue in the case. The difficult facts to account for in this matter are *the association of human relics*

*with the remains of the mammoth, the hippopotamus, the reindeer, etc., in England and France, and in Central Europe;* and, secondly, *the modifications of the crust of the earth which have taken place since the Palæolithic Period.*

The reviewer ought to have grappled with these points. The first of them is, perhaps, the most important. It is pointed out that a new fauna has been introduced into Europe since the Palæolithic Period, and that there has been a change from an arctic to the present mild climate in England and France. Moreover, the imagination is impressed when we are told that since the human period elephants and rhinoceroses and reindeer and lions and hyænas have lived in the Thames and the Somme valleys. It is at once inferred that this must have been ages ago.

I undertook to show, however, that this inference is unwarranted, and that all of these animals survived to a comparatively recent period: that the urus survived in Germany to the sixteenth century; that the aurochs was found in Prussia in the last century, and still survives in the Caucasus; that the reindeer is mentioned as living in Germany by Cæsar and Sallust; by Torfæus as found in Scotland in the twelfth century; as found (its remains) in the Scottish burghs, and in the peat of England, Scotland, and Denmark, and as found in association with implements of polished stone and bronze; that the remains of the great Irish elk are found in Irish crannoges (which have no antiquity) and in the Irish peat in association with implements of iron; in the Irish peat with the tendons still undecayed, and the bones yielding forty per cent. of animal matter; and that Brandt and Agassiz believe it to have survived in Germany to the fourteenth century of our era; that the remains of the cave bear are found in Italy and Denmark in association with neolithic implements—and, indeed, that there is no specific distinction between the cave bear and the common brown bear; that the lion was found in Thessaly as late as the third century before our era, and that the cave lion is now identified with the Asiatic lion; that the cave hyena and the cave horse are now considered also as identical with existing species; that the American mastodon and mammoth have left their bones in the most superficial deposits all over the country; that there is good reason to believe that one of these animals is represented in the

Wisconsin mounds—and, possibly, in the monuments of Central America; that in Siberia entire carcasses of the mammoth and rhinoceros are found completely preserved in the frozen sand; that in America, in Siberia, and in Europe the tusks and bones of these animals still retain a large proportion of animal matter—in Siberia the ivory constituting an important article of commerce.

It appears to me that these facts destroy the presumption of a remote antiquity (one hundred or two hundred thousand years) for the palæolithic fauna. Since I published them I have seen no attempt to answer them. Mr. Boyd Dawkins, who reviewed my book in "Nature," did not refer to them; Mr. Joseph Anderson, who reviewed it in "The Academy," does not refer to them; the "Westminster" reviewer passes them over in silence; and M. Rioult de Neuville makes only a passing allusion in his review in "*Materiaux*." The truth is, there is no answer to be made. The carcasses found in Siberia would alone demonstrate the recent existence of the mammoth. The occurrence of the bones of the mastodon in shallow peat-bogs from the St. Lawrence to the Gulf, and in the shell-marl of small lakes and ponds, is *conclusive* of a recent date. "Almost any swampy bit of ground," says Professor Shaler, in the "American Naturalist," vol. iv, page 162, "in Ohio or Kentucky contains traces of the mammoth and mastodon;" and at Big Lick, Kentucky, he adds, "the remains are so well preserved as to seem not much more ancient than the buffalo bones which are found above them."

If these circumstances were not sufficient to prove the case, all doubt would seem to be removed by the evidence of the existence of the reindeer and the great Irish elk down to historical times, and by the facts mentioned touching the cave lion, cave bear, and cave hyena, the contemporaries of the mammoth and the woolly rhinoceros in Western Europe.

But this is not the whole of the case: *we can trace the elephant, the rhinoceros, and the hippopotamus on the shores of the Mediterranean down to the beginning of the Christian era.* If this statement be true, the existence of the same animals in Europe at a recent period is not only rendered probable, but it would be a matter to excite surprise that they should not be found there. For why should Europe be free from great carnivores

and great pachydermatous animals, when they were found in all the other continents—in North and South America, in Asia and in Africa? Why should Europe constitute an exception?

The monkey is still found in Spain on the rock of Gibraltar. Remains of the African elephant have been found in a cave near Madrid; and Don Juan Vilanova y Piera, a Spanish archæologist, gives an account of the cave of Las Maravillas, in Valencia, where he found, at the depth of several meters, the bones of the extinct mammifers mingled with implements of the Polished Stone Age.* In the neolithic caverns of Gibraltar, explored by Captain Brome, we find again the bones of the spotted hyena, the lynx, ibex, serval, Barbary stag, and other African species. All of these animals inhabited Spain during the Second Stone Age. And now, if we cross the Straits of Gibraltar, we learn from the "Voyage of Hanno" (about 500 B. C.) that the expedition under his command, sent out by the Carthagenian Government, saw "herds of elephants" grazing at Cape Soleis, on the north-west coast of Africa. A little later Herodotus informs us that "the western parts of Libya abound with wild beasts—serpents of enormous size, lions, *elephants*, bears, etc."† Pliny, in the first century of our era, writes that "Africa produces elephants beyond the deserts of Syrtes, and in Mauritania,"‡ (Fez and Morocco.) Strabo states that above Mauritania, on the exterior sea, is the country of the western Ethiopians. "Iphicrates," he adds, "says that cameleopards are bred here, and elephants, and rhizeis, [rhinoceroses,] in shape like bulls, but in manner of living, size, and strength resembling elephants."§ And again: "Mauritania produces large serpents, elephants, antelopes, buffaloes, lions," etc.‖ And, again, he mentions that the Mauritanians dress themselves in the skins of lions, panthers, and other wild beasts, and their foot-soldiers, he tells us, "have for shields the skins of elephants."¶

On the other side of Europe, as has been now ascertained through the Egyptian and Assyrian inscriptions, it appears that the elephant was hunted in the valley of the Tigris as late as about 1130 B. C. We learn from the stele of Amenemheb, a military officer of the time of Thothmes III., translated by

* Congress Prehistoric Archæology, Norwich volume, 1868, p. 398.

† Book iv, § 191. ‡ Nat. Hist., viii, c. 11. § Strab., book xvii, c. 3, § 5.

‖ Ibid., § 4. ¶ Ibid., § 7.

M. Chabas, that this Egyptian monarch, (about 1500 B. C.,) in an expedition against Nineveh, captured in the chase one hundred and twenty elephants.* We learn again from M. Lenormant that in the twelfth century B. C., according to an inscription on the prism of Tiglath-pileser I., preserved in London, this monarch "killed ten elephants on the banks of the Khabour," (an affluent of the Tigris), and "captured four alive."†

On the black obelisk from Nimrud, in the British Museum, the Muzri (a people from northern Kurdistan—the upper Tigris) are represented as bringing to Shalmanezer II. (B. C. 858–823) the camel, the elephant, and the rhinoceros as tribute. We learn from these facts that the disappearance of the elephant from the Mesopotamian valley has occurred in historical times, and that in the Barbary States elephants, lions, cameleopards, and probably the rhinoceros, were common after the beginning of the Christian era.

A representation of the hippopotamus has been met with in a specimen of pottery obtained by Dr. Schliemann from the third (ascending) relic-bed at Troy—the bed immediately above the Trojan bed, which proves the existence of this animal on the coasts of the Hellespont about 1100 B. C.; and if on the Asiatic side, of course on the European side of these straits also. It was this *Asiatic* hippopotamus which is described in the Book of Job, just as it was the *Asiatic* crocodile, and not the Egyptian, which is described there also.

The hippopotamus is referred to in ancient Indian writings, and is expressly mentioned by Alexander the Great, in a letter to Aristotle, as existing in India; and the same fact is stated by Onesicritus.‡ It was found in the Delta of the Nile in Roman times, and the traveler Zerenghi killed two individuals near Damietta in the sixteenth century. Its bones have been also found in the river Chelif in Algeria.

No more need be added on this point I can only again express my astonishment that such facts are silently ignored by writers who urge the presence of this fauna in the palæolithic caves as their strongest evidence for the antiquity of that age.

As to the *change of climate* which is alleged to have taken

* Comptes Rendus de l'Academie des Inscriptions et Belles-Lettres, 1874, tome i, pp. 157, 178. † Ibid., p. 182.

‡ See Buffon, Nat. Hist., vol. vii, p. 453. London. 1812.

place since the reindeer lived in the South of France, I have only to remark that the remains of this animal have been found near London, with metal implements, and that it is admitted pretty generally that he was living in France in the Neolithic Age. If the reindeer, therefore, proves a much colder climate, it has not taken any very extended period to bring about the change which has taken place.

My space leaves me but little room to notice the *physical changes* which have taken place. They involve a movement of some of the (northern) European coast-lines amounting to, (ascending and descending,) perhaps, some four hundred feet. I would remark upon this that these movements of the crust of the earth were very active during the Glacial Period, and continued after the close of that epoch. The sea rose and fell on the coasts of Scotland and England during the Glacial Period twelve or thirteen hundred feet, and the elevations and subsidences of the land were repeated more than once.

There was one great movement of this sort (on a reduced scale as compared with those of the Glacial Epoch) in post-glacial times—at the time of the Palæolithic Flood.

We are not so much surprised at these disturbances of the crust of the earth when we learn that at Uddevalla, on the west coast of Sweden, the land has been elevated more than two hundred feet since a date which, according to M. Torell and Sir C. Lyell, "by no means reaches back to the Glacial Period"—as is proved by the sea-shells found at this height, which agree with species now proper to the fauna of the adjacent and more temperate seas.*

Again, at Södertalje, near Stockholm, a buried fisherman's hut has been found at the depth of sixty-four feet, covered by marine strata containing shells of the existing Baltic species. Sir C. Lyell says, "It seems impossible to explain the position of this buried hut without imagining first a subsidence to the depth of more than sixty feet, then a re-elevation." Several vessels of antique form, and (which Sir C. Lyell omits to mention) an *iron anchor and some iron nails*, were found near the hut.† We have thus (descending and ascending) a move-

* See Lyell's Principles of Geology, vol. ii, p. 192, Amer. ed.

† Lyell's Antiq. Man, p. 240. *Archiv. für Anthropologie*, August, 1875, s. 17.

ment of nearly one hundred and thirty feet since the iron anchor and nails mentioned were deposited where they have been found.

The north-east coast of the Island of Möen is another example. Here, according to M. Puggaard and Sir C. Lyell, the coast has been raised four hundred feet since the Glacial Period—and this, in this part of Europe, was considerably more recent than the Glacial Epoch of the Somme valley, as will be seen presently.

I would merely mention in addition, as examples of similar movements, the island of San Lorenzo, in front of Callao, where Darwin discovered, at the height of eighty-five feet above the sea, in a bed of modern marine shells, roots of sea-weed, bones of birds, ears of maize, plaited reeds, and some cotton thread; and, again, Hobson's Bay, Australia, the bottom of which, some years since, was ascertained to be rising at the rate of four inches in a year; and, again, the instance cited on page 373, *Recent Origin of Man*, near Nova Zembla, where the Gulf Stream Islands have risen from the sea one hundred and ten feet in three hundred years. Many other examples might be given; but these suffice to show that a movement of this sort of several hundred feet at the close of the Glacial Age cannot be regarded as very extraordinary, and affords no evidence of a great lapse of time since its occurrence. This point the reviewer alike passed over in silence.

There was one other point which he abstained from noticing, to which I challenge attention. This is the argument, in chapter xxxii of my book, for the recent date of the Glacial Age. That argument is this: Lyell and all the archæologists admit that no palæolithic implements are found in Denmark, Sweden, or Scotland, and that palæolithic man never penetrated these regions. The reason assigned is, that *the ice* had not retired from the north of Europe—the Glacial Age still lingered. The first traces of man in these countries are of the Neolithic or Polished Stone Age. Man advanced as soon as the retreat of the ice permitted him; *and this was in the Neolithic Age*. Therefore, the Glacial Age closed in Denmark during the Neolithic Age, which archæologists represent to possess an antiquity of six or seven thousand years; it is in reality not more than

thirty-five hundred years ago. The Glacial Age in the valleys of the Thames and the Somme had ended a short space earlier.

*We thus fix the date of the Glacial Age.* And I do not believe any reply can be made to this.

That remarkable epoch in the geological history of the earth closed certainly less than six or seven thousand years ago in the north of Europe. And there is probably good reason to believe that Mr. Lenormart is right in thinking that the tradition of it is preserved in the venerable records of the Zendavesta.

JAMES C. SOUTHALL.

---

## ART. III.—REV. WM. TAYLOR AND INDIA MISSIONS.

*Four Years' Campaign in India.* By WILLIAM TAYLOR. London: Hodder & Stoughton. New York: Nelson & Phillips.

THERE are certain great problems in modern missionary work in the light of which this book will be read, and the work of which it is a narrative will be judged. Christian missions to heathen nations are no longer to be considered as an outburst of "puritanical fanaticism," or as a mistaken but harmless benevolence, but rather as the highest manifestation of the "faith, the philanthropy, and the power" of the Christian Church. Of their ultimate success few persons well informed of their past history and present power and opportunities could be found to seriously doubt. Quite apart from the question of their steady and certain triumph, however, is the specific one, whether a general Christian "awakening" or "revival" is possible among great bodies of heathen people, or whether we may hope for sudden or simultaneous movements toward Christianity among them; and if so, at what stage of Christian endeavor, through what means and methods, and under what circumstances, or with what force and hope, may we use the phrase, "A nation shall be born at once?"

It was because of their hope to find some agency highly adapted to excite such general "awakening" that the India Conference of the Methodist Episcopal Church invited Rev. William Taylor to labor with them. After having worked with them and other missionaries in India, and subsequently independently of them—four years in all—he wrote this book,

which, he says, is "the first published report of a new soul-saving mission in a great heathen country, with specimen incidents and illustrations of the first three years of its eventful life."

The book has been more criticised than the man or his mission work. The "Indian Evangelical Review," for January, 1876, says: "As a Christian workman Mr. Taylor undoubtedly stands far in advance of many; as an historian, at least of his own labors, he falls as far behind." It says, "It is a most unfortunate production," and "regrets that he should have published it." The uncharitableness of the assertions and assumptions concerning other missionary agencies has been considered in bad taste, and as incongruous with Mr. Taylor's Christian professions and known general character. Our writer thinks the "flings" at other missions to be the equivalent of asserting that "their course has been one of failure, their results nothing, their policy a blunder." Exception has also been taken to the irreverence, as it appears to be to some persons, of some of the phraseology. How "God intends to run" this mission work, and "the Holy Spirit being allowed to test his Pauline methods," with much like phrase, is not acceptable to the taste of many people.

On the other hand, there has been much hearty commendation of, and great interest in, the book. To our own taste and judgment the publication of the detailed moral and spiritual history of persons who sought an interview with Mr. Taylor as a spiritual adviser is of very questionable propriety. Yet to many these may be a source of profit.

Incidentally this book treats—and treats pretty fully—of the manners and customs of the people of India; and is, herein, entertaining, instructive, and accurate. (For illustrations, see pages 90, 91, 95, 96, 105, etc.)

The book has the character of a journal of the author, of whom we may safely say that his simplicity, sincerity, self-denial, integrity, great faith, and devotion to the cause of Christ, have but rarely been questioned; while his tact, his dash, his courage, his perseverance, and his pluck, have attracted the attention and challenged the admiration of men who, besides being without appreciation of his preaching or regard for his piety, downrightly disliked his evangelistic methods. But however excellent, he is too unique to pass uncriticised. His

friends have defended his eccentricities and deficiencies by saying that "he is Taylor," and that "the culture which would remedy his glaring faults" might strip him of the "power to do the peculiar work which God has committed to his hands." There are few but will admit that his faults are of the head, and not of the heart or intention. His renown as a revivalist occasioned his being invited to India. He had seen a great "revival of God" in a half dozen of the West India islands; had, he says, twelve hundred colonists and seven thousand Kaffirs converted in his meetings in South Africa, and had the official report by others of the conversion of six thousand persons at his meetings in Australia.

While laboring in connection with our North India missionaries no such general results attended his efforts. If one may judge from the tone of his entries the review does not seem to have been wholly satisfactory to himself, for he thus summarizes: "A few hundreds of nominal Christians professed to find peace at our meetings, and also a small number of Hindus and Mohammedans, and God gave a fresh divine impulse to the work which thrills on with increasing power year by year." This is scarcely to be considered remarkable success.

There was, however, a great disparity between the other fields in which he had labored and that which he found in India. In those the populations were small, the territory limited, the Christian laborers relatively more numerous, and the people better instructed in Christianity. In the six West India islands on which he labored are five thousand acres of territory, containing a population of about a million, administered to spiritually by three hundred and eighty-six European and colonial missionaries, and among whom the Wesleyan Church alone reckoned some eighty thousand hearers. Religion was in a state of decline; the Wesleyans, he says, had in the six years preceding his visit struck from their Church records the names of six thousand Church members. There was opportunity for revival.

Old Cape Colony and its dependencies, in South Africa, contain twenty-five thousand acres, and have a population, including Zulus and Bechuanas, not reaching two millions, among whom are thirty-five thousand Church members, three hundred and fifty European ministers, and fourteen hundred lay agents —"a proportion of Christian laborers unequaled anywhere in

the heathen world. New South Wales comprises say three hundred thousand acres of land, with a population of but little more than half a million, three hundred thousand of whom are recognized "adherents" of Churches; the average attendance on Christian worship reaching a hundred thousand. An eminent authority says that there is here "a larger proportion of well-educated people than can be found among the same number of people in the British Isles." In the whole of Australia are eight colonies of English-speaking people, the vast majority of whom are Protestants.

How dissimilar from this India was may be seen at a glance. (1) Here were only six hundred foreign missionaries, with a proportionate number of native agents, in a population approaching three hundred millions, occupying a territory twenty-three times larger than England and Wales, and equal in area to all Europe, exclusive of Russia and Scandinavia. There were (2) the proclivities and prejudices of diverse races. Remnants of two race-waves of Turanian tribes, sustaining a relation to later invaders similar to that of the North American aborigines to the Anglo-Americans, are found in widely separated, and often remote, portions of India. Aryan, Mongul, Portuguese, Dane, French, and Briton have followed, and form at present a mosaic of twenty-one races and thirty-five nations. (3) More than a half hundred languages and dialects add to the hinderances of evangelistic labor. A hundred millions of the people of India are speaking Hindi and Urdu; thirty-six millions use Bengali; to Tamil Telugu and Marathi are to be assigned a population of fifteen millions each; while the Punjab claims but three millions less. Among those of lesser prominence the Canarese claims ten, to the Gujerati are given seven, and to the Oriya five, millions. (4) Diversity of forms of faith and worship add to the complications. Ten thousand Jews are in India. A hundred and fifty thousand descendants of the old fire-worshiping Geubre are present in the Parsee, the merchant prince of India. Seventeen millions engage in the dismal orgies and rayless rites of demonolatry and aboriginal nature-worship; forty millions are fired with the furious fanaticism of the false prophet of Mecca, and follow his green flag; and one hundred and seventy millions are molded by the principles and practices of Brahmanism. (5) The influence of the

Indian social organization is not to be discarded in its relation to Christian revival. Partly from religious causes, and partly owing to a highly artificial distribution of labor forces, there exist class divisions of society, which classes think and act with unparalleled compactness. These "castes" are hereditary, the parents and priests through infant marriages perpetuating the distinctions. Property is held by the family as a whole, and violation of caste usages is legal ground of disinheritance. The peace of the dead is dependent on ceremonial observances of the living, which may not be performed when class obligations are omitted. Such a system not only perpetuates institutions, but evils and errors as well. It does more. It destroys independence of action and individuality of thought. It incapacitates for personal assertion. The individual comes to have but little comprehension of the possibility or the duty of the desirability of other action than that of his class. There is but little room for conviction of personal sinfulness when conscience as well as conduct is communal.

Taken all in all—for we have but hinted at the bulk of hinderances to a Christian awakening or revival in India—we do not wonder that Brother Taylor says (p. 75) "the combinations of opposing forces in India probably exceed those of any other part of the globe." But the question still recurs: What is possible to Christian faith and effort in this direction? Taylor says: "The brethren got an idea that I would at once attack the masses in the street and mow them down like grass." Precisely so. This indicates just what it is all-important the Christian Church shall not allow to slip from its thought, and hope, and aim—to wit: the possibility of a simultaneous movement of masses of heathen toward Christianity. Taylor thought the obstacles we have enumerated, combined with the feeble force and low intelligence of a first generation of Christian converts from heathendom, and the antagonistic influences of unworthy representatives of Christian countries, resident in India, offered for the present insuperable obstacles to a general Christian awakening. He says: "We cannot expect very great results among the natives in the presence of a nominal, ineffective Church. If there were no such Church we might hope for immediate results among them; but now our only hope is to make the Church more effective."—P. 69.

Let us look, then, at the grounds of hope which remain for such Christian awakening in India.

First—for nothing strikes like a fact—India has already witnessed local movements of masses of people, such as it is desired should become general. Rev. Mr. Boerrusun is a Norwegian missionary laboring among the aboriginal tribes north-west of Calcutta, known as the "Santals." A few years ago he wrote: "The Lord is doing wonders here. During the last few weeks I have baptized upward of five hundred persons, and every day from ten to a hundred fresh candidates present themselves, and are eager to be taught further in the truths of the Gospel. Every one of them is an evangelist, doing all he can to get some one of his heathen brethren to share the blessing he has himself experienced." Many women "come as far as twenty to thirty miles, and the whole land of the Santals seems to be under the mighty influence." This same missionary, according to the "Lucknow Witness," in four months of 1872 baptized no less than fourteen hundred persons, converts from heathendom.

A hundred thousand Shanars, a devil-worshiping tribe in South India, have accepted Christianity, and their "revival" meetings have been attended with remarkable physical phenomena, such as whip-like cracking of the hair, violent jerkings, etc., similar to those witnessed in earlier times at camp-meetings in Kentucky and elsewhere. Three hundred Telugus were baptized by Baptist missionaries in December, 1870, while, in the midst of harvest, men and women turned out by hundreds to hear about Jesus." A general movement of masses of people toward Christianity has also been witnessed in the case of the Karens. These, and like instances of tribal movements, show the possibility of a great awakening in India. What has been may be, and we can but long for its coming. Here in the Santal, as in other cases, were numerical results of evangelistic labor amid India's "combination of opposing forces," and in many senses in the presence of the same paralyzing influences from a feeble Church as those found in the localities where Taylor labored in India. We concede a difference between these rude tribes and the burnished Brahminism and bannered Islamism of the Gangetic valley, but do not yield the logical force of the precedent. We say these more than suggest that like results are possible in other parts of India.

A second ground of hope for such general movement is found in a considerable and increasing force of Christian converts scattered over India. Relatively few, it is true, yet sufficient to show that Christianity may win its way among all; and to furnish an agency on which the Holy Ghost may move to make it a great spiritual factor in a general awakening.

Brother Taylor and others write much of apostolic success. It has been recently pointed out that equal if not greater success has already attended missionary labor in India. Nor let it be interposed that we have greater facilities than had they, for even that has been anticipated. The apostles found the Hebrew Scriptures already in the hands of their first converts, for these had been translated into Greek three centuries before, and thus there was a people prepared of the Lord, both Jews and Greeks. For the first hundred years the Gospel did not spread among those attached to the soil, but was mainly confined to the cities and towns, and only a few Gentiles were at first among the converts. In seventy years after the first preaching of the apostles (A. D. 100) it has been estimated that there were a hundred thousand converts. In India, seventy years after Carey's first baptism of a native convert, there were (in that land and British Burmah) seventy-three thousand native Christian communicants, and a nominal Christian population among the natives of over three hundred thousand.

If aggressive force is indicative of spirituality, this Christian body may point with hope to their more recent ratio of increase. Throughout India, exclusive of Burmah, between 1862 and 1872, there was an advance from one hundred and forty-eight thousand seven hundred and thirty-one, to two hundred and twenty-four thousand one hundred and sixty-one, that is, to the extent of sixty-one per cent. Within this decade the number of Telugu Christians advanced from twenty-three to six thousand four hundred and eighteen. In Chota Nagpore the growth was from two thousand five hundred and thirty-one to twenty thousand. Our own Methodist Episcopal Mission in North India advanced five hundred per cent. Protestant Christianity has spread more rapidly in India than did Brahminism, Moslemism, or Romanism in the East. A uniform increase equal to that of the past decade would afford a hundred and thirty millions of Christians in India in the year A.D. 2001.

Within the same decade Hinduism has increased but five per cent., leaving a net gain of Christianity over it of fifty-six per cent., which would show that the Church in India is to-day gaining on the world numerically as rapidly at least as in the most favored sections of America. We say it is in accord with precedent, principle, and faith, to hope that the Holy Ghost may move this body of Christians to simultaneous spiritual effort.

A third hopeful feature is found in a general state of expectancy favorable to Christianity. In no other country are there so many convinced of the truths of Christianity who are counted with the opponents of it, and in no other heathen country is there so general anticipation of the ultimate triumph of Christianity over other forms of faith. "Do not take so much trouble; our folks will soon become Christian even if left to themselves," said a Hindu woman in the zenanas of Calcutta to Miss Britain. "Only have a little patience, and all the Hindus will become Christians," said another Hindu woman to Mrs. Page. "We believe we speak the simple truth," said the "Lucknow Witness," "when we say that millions of natives are firmly convinced of this. We have found it an accepted belief in the most remote mountain hamlets where no European had ever penetrated, and we find it received as an inevitable event of the near future in every city and town of the plains." Rev. Dr. Waugh says: "A deep and widespread conviction seems to prevail, not only in cities, but also in the country places, among the villagers, and, indeed, throughout all classes, that a day of overthrowing of the old religions and effete faiths, of the breaking up of old forms, is at hand. The common people speak of the coming day of overturning, and seem not dismayed at its approach, but announce themselves as ready to join in the van, indeed are only awaiting its coming to break away from their present thraldom and bonds of caste." A company of educated natives, none of whom were Christians, met for five Sundays in succession in Calcutta recently to discuss the question, "Is it likely that Christianity will become the religion of India?" At the close a vote was taken, and it was unanimously declared in the affirmative. They seemed thunderstruck with the result of their own deliberations. One of the gentlemen, a head-master of a government school, got up and said, "Then what are we

here for?" This was echoed by all present. They broke up, and never met more.

He is a poor student of history who does not know what important factors in popular movements such a general state of expectancy among a people can become. Some day, perhaps not distant, there may be found in this the basis of a widespread Christian awakening. The uprising may come with a rush, and there may not be men enough to show inquirers the way.

The very air is full of restlessness and change. European education is breaking up old systems; English legislators are teaching the equality of man. Western medical science is displacing muttered incantations; forty millions of Hindus have tried the railway; the penny-post and telegraph are exposing idolatrous shams; twenty-six hundred vernacular and five hundred English books, one hundred and fifty-six native and sixty English newspapers, with thirty-one native and thirty European magazines—all the issues of a single year in India—show its literary stir. Multitudes of Hindu boys never become idolaters at all. "The age of hero-deification is already passing away," says the government report of Madras. A government officer reporting not as a missionary, but as a Roman consul might have done, says: "The magnificent temples erected in past ages are slowly succumbing to the destroying hand; new temples on a scale of grandeur equal to those of former ages are unknown . . . this is but a visible sign of the waning vitality of the religion itself. . . . The day is not probably far distant when a religious revival, a shaking of the very bones of Hinduism, shall occur."

Professor Max Müller wrote several years ago: "From what I know of the Hindus, they seem to me riper for Christianity than any nation that ever accepted the Gospel."

Added to all this—for it is allied with it—the Hindu social and religious disintegration points to the fact that as the Hindus are wont to think and act only in mass, this general breaking up favors the acceptance of Christianity by these disintegrated masses. The Presbyterian missionaries of Futtehgarh found in the Saadh a class of people whom no missionary had visited, thrown off from the Brahmanic community, following a leader who was instructing them in a religion

which was neither Hindu, Moslem, nor Christian, but was more Christian than any thing else. They sought and readily accepted Christian instruction. We have the record of like disrupted communities in Bengal, Northern India, and in fact quite extensively over the country, the leaders in many cases instructing the people to accept the teaching of the Christian missionaries. Here is a further force favorable to some general movement toward the Christian faith.

Lastly—for we must have done with this, though it might be extended indefinitely—there is the ground of hope from the development of native leaders. The modern missionary force has, through much discouragement, aimed to develop indigenous lead for its mission Churches. Nor have they wholly failed. At the fiftieth anniversary of the Sandwich Islands we are told that the orator was a man who narrowly escaped being buried alive by his heathen mother, and that he held an audience of three thousand persons for more than an hour by his eloquent address, delivered without note or comment. The Theological Seminary of the Karens has been left in the charge of natives, and suffered no loss. In the Jaffna College of Ceylon, and in the Tamil seats of learning, natives have been successful professors. Of one hundred and eighteen delegates at the Allahabad Conference twenty were native Hindus of various castes and languages. They sat side by side as peers with graduates of Oxford, Cambridge, Amherst, Williams, Yale, Princeton, Alleghany, and Dickinson colleges. Recognized leaders of religious reform have also arisen among the Hindus, such as Babu Keshab Chunder Sen, about whom the semi-Christian revolt against Hindu idolatry gathers.

Taking all these component facts together, what might not some Christian native leader, competent for the emergency, do in leading a general movement toward Christianity? It is always possible that from among the multitudes thronging the bazaars, dreaming in the jungle, pondering philosophical problems, some one may be arrested by a tract, instructed in the school, trained in the seminary, with a head like that of Loyola, and heart like that superstitious monk of Wurtemburg, who redeemed half Europe, and, dying, bequeathed to the world a Protestant Church and an open Bible—who, we say, with a head like that of Loyola, and heart stirred like that of

Luther, subtle with all the subtlety of the East, wise with all the practical knowledge of the West, shall be to his people what no foreign evangelist can ever become, the leader of a grand Christian reformation, revival, or awakening, which shall sweep from the Himalayas to Cape Comorin, and from sea to sea. One such Christianized Hindu might revolutionize all India. One such converted Moslem might reorganize half of Asia.

To say nothing of the supernatural force promised in prophecy, and looking only to human means, we ask, "If Mohammed were possible, why is this a dream?" Such is the combination of disturbing forces in India that one Turanian Peter the Hermit might break in pieces all Hindu systems, one Bengali Chrysostom might move and remold the mighty masses of the Ganges, one Tamil Whitefield might sweep Southern India with revival flame, one Indian Wesley might inaugurate on the plains of Hindustan a numerically mightier Methodism than Europe or America has yet seen.

But what is the relation of the work whose history is sketched in this book to other missionary work in India, and to the state of things we have sketched? Thus far we have treated only of the indications and forces within purely native society. There is, however, another element of power and hope, and to it Taylor turned, not with the supposition that it was ripe as a spiritual agency, but that by patient preparatory labor it might become so. As the Jews, scattered in all lands, speaking all languages, familiar with all local social usages, components or adjuncts of all communities, might, if converted to Christ, become at once a ubiquitous, indigenous missionary force; so one feels, in turning to India, that the sixty-four thousand Europeans and the ninety thousand Eurasians (so called because one parent is European) residing in that peninsula are so systematically distributed over India that, without any change in locality or occupation, they might readily become an almost ubiquitous missionary force, and a chief means of a general awakening.

As long ago as 1866, Bishop Cotton, of India, spoke of the causes which must continually add to the number of this community, "sharing our English blood and our Christian creed." He gave a graphic picture of their wide distribution in India.

Along the five thousand miles of trunk railway, with feeders and branches, are European observers, firemen, mechanics, and guards, with their families or without them, in considerable communities, smaller groups, or in isolated houses. Connected with the agricultural operations of the valley of Assam, the plain of Cachar, the beautiful Himalaya Districts of Kumaon and Kangra, with tea plantations and other industries, is an ever-augmenting foreign community. Added to these are government clerks, dependents, planted at intervals all over India; officers of coasting and river steamers; collectors of customs, as in the Salt Districts, ten or twenty miles apart, from the Punjab to Central India; tradesmen, surveyors, contractors; and below these of definite occupations and means of livelihood, fallen into reckless living, and found in the back slums of great cities like Madras, Bombay, and Calcutta, or wandering along the roads.

All these classes feel in greater or less degree a moral loneliness in India, and being without moral restraints and checks

where a large one is feebly occupied; and that a society which plants its missions in more places than it can find the force and funds to develop, is open to the charge of folly and pride.

William Taylor turned his attention to this class, and to all English-speaking peoples as well, not only with a view to their own salvation, but with the aim and the hope of their becoming a great evangelistic agency among the heathen. Much of the work, most of it in fact, is simply English work for English people, few natives having been reached, and its members being mostly from the middle class of European residents. "The first three years of its eventful history" afford us nothing conclusive by showing whether this method will be more successful than others have been in influencing the natives. There are some things plainly to be hoped for, prominent among which is the development of a large unpaid agency among Europeans in India. Few persons in estimating the result of foreign missions and their cost as compared with the same in home work, estimate the amount of voluntary labor and unreported contribution that goes to the latter, and its almost entire absence of the same from the foreign field.

The success of the scheme which Brother Taylor presses involves the development of like unpaid Christian labor in India among the foreign and Christian population particularly. Already this has supplemented ordinary agencies with a large amount of voluntary labor of lay agents, both European and native. In Bombay are a half dozen who preach in Marathi; in Madras "Lawyer Gordon" and other able European laymen preach in Tamil. A civil engineer, transferred from the Bombay Church to Hyderabad, holds "meetings," and speedily a Church of a hundred and seven communicants demands a pastor; while a regiment of soldiers carries the Methodistic flame from Poona to Kurrachee and Kotree, and Rev. F. Goodwin becomes pastor of a Church of nearly a hundred members. There are few probabilities, however, that the application of this voluntary force to educational work can be successful beyond the most elementary instruction.

One of the difficulties of the general scheme is found in the migratory character of nearly all the population among whom it is chiefly inaugurated within India itself, and the change by

retirement to Europe and substitution by other persons, who must in turn be "adjusted" as an agency to this work. The migration within India, it is true, may be the means of rapid ramification of this work; but that wide ramification may also discover a new danger to be cautiously guarded, for it will tend to the establishment of agents at points so remote from each other as to be not mutually supporting, or to admit of close organization or proper supervision in places where funds will not be forthcoming for the development of any but pastoral work to a few Europeans.

The attention of European and India Christians has been given to the importance of developing this Christian community, and Rev. Mr. Somerville and others have been sent to India as "revivalists," and what is called a "winter mission" has resulted in the sending of a few eminent workers to labor in India during the cool season. All this but shows that Brother Taylor's effort to reach the Europeans meets a recognized want, and none can do less than hope for it the best of results. It may yet so stir the English-speaking peoples of India as to make them a chief agency in India's redemption. It may be the fuse that shall fire, the force that shall combine, all else that we have shown to be in such marvelous readiness for general action.

A second of the chief topics with which the contents of this book are allied is benevolent, and, especially, missionary economics. This is presented in three or more aspects.

The first form in which it appears is one which we can little more than state. It is found in Brother Taylor's independently maintaining his family and meeting some portions of his individual expenses while conducting his evangelistic work. He relies on books, as Paul relied at times on his trade as tentmaker. This plan of work has had many illustrations on the foreign mission field. Miss Baxter of Hong Kong, Miss Aldersey of Ningpo in former years, Miss Whateley, daughter of the archbishop, laboring among the Fellahs of Egypt, and Mrs. Watson of Mount Lebanon, are noble examples of this self-abnegation in our own day. Many, very many converts from heathenism have exhibited a like devotion, though our space will not permit us to even mention eminent names. In the exhibition of general selfishness in the world, one can but admire this self-denying conduct.

We must, however, guard against an approval which implies acceptance of this as the chief method of conducting mission work. There must be some concert and organization which can distribute laborers in various fields as necessity may demand, and experience shall suggest to be wise. The general council of all Christian laborers which gives direction and proportion to labor, which finds its expression in boards of management, is a necessity to prevent "wrong missions to wrong places and among wrong peoples." Nor can the general Church be relieved of the claim on it for proportionate labor as expressed in systematic collections and institutions for training missionaries, and which in fact should pervade schemes of education of youth, projects of commerce, plans of government, and all other social and personal thought and action. These persons alluded to may be ensamples but not substitutes. As a rule, the call to go implies the call to send. The missionary spirit must pervade society, and show itself in all secular life. James I. and Charles I. proclaimed in 1662 that their special motive in encouraging the American colonies was their zeal for the extension of the Gospel. The seal of the Massachusetts colony was an Indian, with the Macedonian invitation, "Come over and help us!" These but illustrate the spirit which should pervade all forms of Christian life, personal and communal.

The second of these monetary features is the announcement of a "self-supporting plan" of conduct of mission work. It is very desirable that we get all the wisdom or inspiration possible on this topic, and we regret the apparent or real confusion of statement in the book on the matter. It is asserted that "one peculiarity of the work is that it is self-sustaining," (p. 130,) and we are told that Agra was ceded as a mission to the India Conference "provided they would conduct it on our self-supporting principles," (p. 328,) and he declares that "our mission Conference in the north" cannot "live on the principle" on which this is "to run," (p. 164,) and he expresses his belief that "God wishes to demonstrate the soundness," etc., of his "own Gospel methods of aggression, one principle of which is self-sustentation," (p. 164.) This is all plain enough, but presently we find a limitation of the term "self-support," and subsequently what seems to us the abandonment or denial of it.

1. "Our *principle* applies particularly to the support of ministers of the Gospel," (p. 156,) and "what I have pledged our India people for specially is the support of their ministerial workers," (p. 404.) Cawnpore is called "the first self-supporting mission in the Conference," though money was appropriated by the board of building, etc., (p. 46.) This is certainly not a sense in which the term "self-support" has been used, and would scarcely seem to justify so serious an announcement of the divine purpose to "demonstrate its soundness," etc.

The missionaries engaged in this work are in large measure pastors of European congregations, and much of their work is with English people. Were these Europeans to rely on American contributions for the support of their pastors it would be manifestly wrong. Yet it is only in this sense of pastoral support that the Cawnpore mission could be called "self-supporting," for it took no precedence in the amount of missionary moneys contributed locally over other missions. The second year of the Lucknow Mission (1862) the local contributions were $2,369, and those of Nynee Tal for the same year were $2,756. The second year of the Cawnpore Station as "self-supporting" its local income was $1,189. The same year (1874) Nynee Tal received $3,556, Shahjehanpore $3,979, Paori $2,506, and Bareilly $2,406 as local revenue. He seemingly modifies even this pastoral-support plan, for, on page 156, he illustrates it by "our Churches in America" which receive aid from the Missionary Society "for the beginning of work in their bounds too poor to start of itself," which logically would carry with it aid to support pastors "when too poor to start" that alone; which is, in fact, the case, as the work of our Missionary Society in the United States consists of the support of missionaries, more than one fourth of the entire ministry of the Methodist Episcopal Church being supported in whole or in part by the Missionary Society. [There are 10,923 itinerant preachers and over 3,000 missionaries at work in the United States.]

The Presbyterian Church has, perhaps, more than one fifth of its pastors, possibly one fourth, thus aided by its home missionary and sustentation funds. These have been considered to be judicious expenditures, but we suppose nobody ever thought of calling these "self-supporting" Churches. On all our Conference minutes they are registered as "missions."

2. When we read a phrase like this, "There are resources enough in India of men and money to run at least one great mission," (p. 156,) our next thought is that it is meant that whatever aid for pastoral support, or other purpose beyond what the specific Church or locality is able to furnish, is to be raised in India, and we are ready to accept that as explaining the "self-supporting principle." Such missions have been very successfully "run." One at Ghazeepore has been long in operation on this plan. Rev. Mr. Wilder conducted the Kalapoor Mission through twelve of the most expensive years of its successful life entirely on contributions of a local character.

Unfortunately, however, even this fails to adjust the phrases found in the book. We read that "one appropriation of funds from any missionary society would set upon us the brand-mark of existing Indian missions, and tend to bring us down to their dead level," (p. 164,) and it seems to confirm our view, but is at once followed by the announcement that it is "no infringement of self-support" to accept funds from individuals in other lands, or from any missionary society to any extent, (pp. 156, 157, 396, 397;) so that this "self-supporting" mission may secure its expenses from (1) the Churches; (2) "indigenous resources" of the country; (3) or by "foreign funds." There is much emphasis laid upon this order of application for money, but this would scarcely constitute it "self-supporting;" and as any body knows these are apt to be conducted simultaneously, the principle does not always appear prominently to be "self-support," nor do we see why the North India Mission "could not live" on this plan. It would better accord with these statements and with the facts if it were called a self-originated and self-helpful mission; for moneys have been raised in India "for work too poor to start of itself," and aid largely and freely solicited in Scotland and America for the Cawnpore school, and American aid given to the Calcutta Church; and it is probable that the work could be much more rapidly developed than now if it could have large contributions from our Missionary Society other than what it has had, though that has been no inconsiderable sum. Brother Taylor asks the Missionary Committee to send men, (p. 164,) which covers the *principle* of aid from them, and the work is by so much not "self-supporting."

There is some reason to fear lest our Methodist community

may receive the impression that our missionaries in North India have not been as careful to secure contributions in India as they might have been, and some danger that we will forget our obligations to the Europeans, and both heathen and Christian natives who have contributed to our work. Very much or most of the money for our Southern India work is contributed by the same class which has always from the first, and often in advance, aided our own and other missions in India.

We have seen it stated that as long ago as 1866 one sixth of the whole cost of Protestant missions in India was subscribed by people in India, and one fifteenth by native converts themselves. Rev. Dr. Mullens, in his statistical tables of India missions for 1871, shows that £50,000 sterling were annually contributed to the various missionary societies in India out of their official income, in the midst of their official labors, by men who were toiling in India to accumulate sufficient funds to enable them to retire to England, a fact honorable to the men, and decisive of the reality of the good being accomplished by the missions. He also shows that as early as 1861 natives in India connected with the various missions contributed $109,046 annually to this work.

Our own mission has had a remarkable record. At the very initiation of our India Mission, and "in advance" of the appointment of the missionaries, Europeans in India in 1858 (while the smoke of the mutiny was not yet cleared away) pledged Dr. Butler to contribute one half the cost of six missionary residences if the men could be sent to occupy them; a proposition which they met and extended to six more, and subsequently fulfilled in the case of every missionary residence in our field. In 1860 Dr. Butler wrote to our Mission Board that they had $30,000 worth of property in India, more than half of which money was raised in India, which he says does not show all they have done, for besides all else they have enabled us to support our schools without calling on the Board for funds. Well might he say: "We have asked and received aid such as no missionary society has ever realized in a foreign land and at the hand of strangers." In 1867 the contributions in India were within thirteen hundred dollars of being one half as much as the Missionary Society appropriated to India for that year. In 1865 the Bareilly District alone raised

$13,175 gold, of which Rev. Dr. Waugh says, "few districts in home conferences raise so large a sum, and some conferences report much less."

Nor was this a spasmodic benevolence, as the following will show. The amounts raised in India for our North India mission work, including property, press, school, preachers, itinerating expenses, etc., is for the years respectively as follows: For 1858, $2,125; for 1859, $6,228; for 1860, $6,922; for 1861, $7,306; for 1862, $8,573; for 1863, $9,310; for 1864, $14,718; for 1865, $21,344; for 1866, $19,585; for 1867, $16,555; for 1868, $23,085; for 1869, $22,585; for 1870, $24,478; for 1871, $28,837; for 1872, $27,373; for 1873, $23,003; for 1874, $25,444; for 1875, (estimated,) $25,000. Besides which there have been large contributions of property not herein included. These contributions, it will be remembered, were in British gold. It would be sufficiently moderate to place the cost of gold and exchange during five years of our war at one hundred per cent., and during the other years at twenty per cent., and thus this will be seen to approximate a contribution in our currency of half a million of dollars.

A somewhat careful estimate of the number of American missionaries on the field from the beginning till now will show that this sum would not only have paid all their salaries, but have left a very liberal margin for the support of native helpers.* Nor is our own Society exceptionally faithful and fortunate, for a summary of Mr. Scott Robinson's tables shows that the British Societies contributed to the Foreign Missions £900,000, and that more than £200,000 had been given by the missions themselves.

Brother Taylor says that appropriations to mission Churchse "in advance will, in most cases, supersede indigenous resources," (p. 397,) and "hinder, if not preclude, a healthy development" (p. 157) of the work; and "one appropriation of funds from any missionary society would set upon us the brand-mark of existing Indian missions, and tend to bring us down to their dead level," (p. 164.)

There are no persons more open to suggestive criticism, nor

* The average has been fifteen missionaries. If all received the salary of married men, counted at the early appropriation of $1,030, and the later one of $1,200, for a man and his wife, it would leave more than $150,000 surplus.

more ready to improve their methods, than foreign missionaries and the managers of such societies in the home boards. Such look with great eagerness to all opportunities to economize their funds, and reap the speediest and most permanent return from expenditures. They have experimented with almost all possible methods, and have not unfrequently made important changes in the same. We are not, however, of conviction that, with exceptional cases, circumstances, and localities, they have failed in prudent administration of their funds, when judged even by the tendency to develop indigenous resources on foreign fields among converts.

The native Churches of Hawaii have contributed, since 1870, more than seventy thousand dollars to carry the Gospel to the Marquesas Islands. One single Church sustains five foreign missionaries in the field, and some Churches contribute an average of four dollars and ten cents per member. There are fifty-seven Churches in the Sandwich Islands which sustain seventeen foreign missionaries.* The Micronesian Islands have twenty Churches with a thousand members who contributed in their monthly missionary concerts, in one year, one thousand dollars, and sent ten catechists to labor among a population entirely foreign to them.

Fifty years ago there was not a native Christian in the Friendly Islands; yet the Rev. Mr. Dare said at the Round Lake Camp-meeting, in 1873, that during each year, for two years previous, the native Churches there had contributed twenty-five thousand dollars for the support of the Gospel among themselves, and fifteen thousand dollars for foreign missions; thus supporting fifty-two ministers and nine hundred catechists. We have seen their contribution stated much higher on good authority. In Australia the native ministry is entirely supported by native contributions, and the Tongataban (Wesleyan) Circuit, at the last quarterly meeting of 1875, had one hundred pounds surplus after paying eleven ministers and all other demands. The Tonguese raise seventy thousand dollars for religious purposes, twenty thousand of which is for foreign work. Ko-thah-byu was the first Karen baptized. That was in 1828. There are now three hundred and forty

* Fourteen islands of the group with fourteen thousand Church members, gave forty thousand dollars in 1872.

seven self-supporting native Churches among the Karen Baptists. The London Mission of Hong Kong, China, has two hundred and sixteen members, who support, by voluntary subscription, two of their own native preachers, meet all Church expenses, and have a mission at Fanshau, founded by them without foreign aid, where they pay the salaries of a native pastor and a school teacher. Rev. C. H. Wheeler said in 1872: "Of the nineteen Churches about Harpoot, Turkey, fifteen are independent of foreign aid and the other four nearly so; while four other communities in which Churches will soon be formed already support their pastors, and six others where there are like prospects pay half the salaries, and in fifteen other communities the work of self-support has already begun." The mission Churches of the American Board in Asia contributed, in 1874, forty-five thousand dollars. When Bishop Kingsley visited China, in 1869, our Foochow Mission adopted the principle of estimating the ability of each circuit to support their Churches and pastor, and to make definite appropriation to meet the balance necessary for the support of the native preachers.

Nor is India wholly excepted from this general and satisfactory showing of the results of what Brother Taylor must consider to be "appropriations in advance," if they are to be found anywhere. The Basl Missionary Society in West India reports that "almost all heads of native families have an income of less than $5 per month, (to support say five persons,) and yet the communicants contribute on an average seventy-five cents per year. The London Missionary Society says of its missions on the Malabar coast: "Several of the Churches are self-supporting; the contributions have reached $7,000 a year, which, considering what is paid for labor in that country, is equal to $40,000 at least of our currency." The South India Mission of the Church of England Missionary Society contributed one year $13,582 gold. In Travancore the annual contributions per member were creditable, and in Madras the natives gave an average of seventy-eight cents, gold. Of Travendum Rev. J. Duthie said, as far back as 1866, that one thousand and sixty native Church members contributed during the year $1,146 50 for Church objects. This church is entirely self-supporting, and has for a number of years past paid the salary of

its pastor, two catechists, three school-masters, two Bible women, and one medical evangelist.

In our own Methodist Mission in North India the Amroha Circuit is presided over by a native preacher converted from Islam. The chapel and parsonage were paid for by the native Christians, and three years ago they contributed fairly toward their pastor's support. In 1873 Rev. C. W. Judd reported from Bareilly, "Almost all contribute something for the support of the Gospel in some way;" and from Budaon we read, "The membership is learning to give creditably for religious purposes." "Every year we shall put more men on the self-supporting column." Says Rev. E. W. Parker: "In a Quarterly Conference to-day (1874) a committee retired to determine the preacher's salary, and they will raise it." He also says, "The entire income of the native Christians not acting as preachers within the bounds of the entire India Mission does not amount to $6,000 annually." They say that whenever their preachers can be supported by the native Christians giving one twentieth of their entire income for this object they will withdraw all applications for assistance in that work.

In the Rohilcund District Conference, in December, 1873, there were eighty-two members present, who adopted an important paper setting forth that "such a thing as total dependence on foreign aid is unknown in any of our Churches," there being only partial dependence in any case. They say the profession of Christianity militates against them pecuniarily; that those capable of large business ventures, and who might thereby contribute largely, have been taken for mission work as evangelists, etc.; that the income of the majority of their number is per head scarcely a tenth of the lowest income of our American laborer; and that the tendency to improvement which Christianity provokes, increases their expenses without a corresponding increase at present of their income. They say though they support their pastors there are ten evangelists wanted for one pastor, and it is unreasonable to expect them to meet this expense. We might have shown the actual field of operations in the various missions have, with few exceptions, been greatly enlarged with but little increase of expenditure. In the case of the American Board between 1865 and 1875 the work increased forty per cent. and the cost but very little.

We do not see, taken all in all, that our Churches, mission boards, and missionaries, have any "occasion to distrust" their methods, or to be discouraged at the results of their labor.

We have not room to discuss the remaining economical questions raised in the book, which refer to the cost of missionary living, and the development of self-reliance and self-helpfulness of converts from heathendom. We regret that Mr. T. should say (p. 155) that a "social standing equal to that of an officer in the army" is considered essential to the success of a missionary, and propose that his preachers should "live on a subsistence allowance," as if that were exceptional economy. Living is exceptionally expensive in India, and yet the salaries of all the societies range from $1,000 to $1,200 for married men; in China from $800 to $1,000; in Bulgaria and Western Asia from $650 to $900; and for unmarried missionaries from one half to one third these amounts, sums which the most careful economy has proved to be only "subsistence allowance," and so proverbially below the salaries of Europeans in India as to give moral force to their teachings among the natives.

Our South India work, it is true, economizes by "supporting" only a celibate ministry as yet; but their work is only in a rudimentary state, and success and proper example and influence of the missionaries implies an increase of cost.

The spirit and purpose of the portion of the work which treats of "the Compound System," as he calls all efforts to help native converts temporally, we most heartily approve, though we deem his phrase unfortunately extreme. We cannot discuss the subject, but may hint that there are very many cases in which it would be impossible to "send them back to their friends and kindred," (p. 160,) or to remain in "whatsoever calling" they may have followed previously. For the full discussion of this theme we must refer our readers to the published Report of the Allahabad Conference, held in 1872. We can only illustrate our own assertion by the convert who has followed trade or arts connected with idol making or festivals of false deities, idolatrous sacrifices, and by instances where the form of taking possession of a legacy is connected with heathen rites, and the person is reduced to poverty if not obtained. As to returning them to their homes, etc., we may simply say, with the Indian Evangelical Review: "The course

he recommends is almost always simply impossible unless the young convert will either (in most cases) renounce Christianity, or else retain certain marks on his person or clothing which may be innocent in themselves, but which are always regarded by the people as the distinctive marks of the old religion."

No one system has, however, been found to be the best for all parts of India. There certainly have been evils connected with the methods of aiding persecuted converts, and those whose occupation is destroyed by their becoming Christians. But when gathered on co-operative farms or factories, such as our Panahpore Christian Village, they may become a light in the darkness about them ; the missionary may give them better and more systematic attention, their children can be gathered into schools; they are more removed from the debasing influences of heathendom and are afforded pastoral care, and religious social privileges, such as they cannot have when living alone, or in little groups of two or ten. Besides, these converts, weak and ignorant, set off in heathen communities, are poor representatives of the Christian light and knowledge, and often even of its power.

Another of the great topics of missionary policy which we have not room to discuss is the Church relations of missions. The India missionaries long since entered into an unwritten compact to occupy separate portions of India, for the purpose of avoiding conflict among their converts, and for the more speedy and thorough evangelization of the land. Our own Methodist Episcopal Church assumed the responsibility of Oudh, Rohilcund, etc. The large commercial cities were left free to all missionary workers by common consent. Brother Taylor's work in some sense outside of these great cities would seem to conflict with this compact if it should succeed in the conversion of many natives, because he has organized the Methodist Episcopal Church in each place for the converts. The Allahabad Conference, however, seems to have conceded that his work was exceptional, and they did not condemn this feature of it.

This leaves only the question of the bearings of this widely spreading Church in its relation to the India Church of the future. There are those who think that the organized sects of Protestants ought not to seek to reproduce their various ecclesiastical

systems and polity into missionary fields, but seek to develop an indigenous and united Church in each land. Mr. Isaac Taylor, in his "New Model of Christian Missions," would have all Christian Protestant missions under one leadership. The attempt is being made in Mexico to establish "The Church of Jesus," and in Italy and Japan the blending of the denominations in Church organization is being attempted. Thus far, however, the result seems only to be to add another "Church" to the many already extant in these lands. It seems impossible at present to harmonize all in this movement, however desirable it may seem to be in some particulars. Meanwhile we have the assurance that the reproduction of these various denominational forms in heathen lands may show the heathen the oneness of Christians notwithstanding trifling differences; may teach them how to conduct that controversy and conflict of intellect which unfolds truth as it could not otherwise be discovered. Besides, even could we harmonize as sects in formal organization, it would not prevent the recurrence of the same diversity of theological view among the converts from heathendom, as the views of Christian theology which the sects represent are imbedded in the Scriptures, as in human psychology and metaphysics. Sect-forms may, perhaps, be credited with one advantage. In presenting the various creeds and polities, they have forestalled the reproduction of other distorted presentations of Christian theology, and the systematic and thorough representation of historical theology, made by them, has given us the most remarkable, yea, most astonishing fact, that no new heresy has arisen in connection with modern missions.

Besides the general defense which could be made for Brother Taylor in thus organizing every-where the Methodist Episcopal Church for the care of converts, there are specific ones which we cannot, for lack of room, enumerate. We believe the whole Christian Church, which recognizes vital godliness as distinct from ritualistic righteousness, may well rejoice in this movement and organization of our South India Mission. Some bold general aggressive work of the Christian Church looking to the presentation of spirituality as opposed to formalism, seems absolutely demanded to save Protestantism in India among the foreigners and middle English-speaking classes. The Church

of England in India has, of late years, become "High-Church" in its tendencies to an alarming degree. The various dissenting bodies of Europe do not seem just now ready to organize, and conduct a general and strong counteracting movement in India. Hence the sympathy which our mission commands among these persons in India, and the attraction it presents to those within the English Church who appreciate spirituality as opposed to formalism and ritualism.

We cannot fail to recognize the relation of all that is done in India to the work of evangelization of Asia. "India redeemed, Asia is the Lord's," was the sentiment and belief of Bishop Thomson, with which we heartily sympathize, and which lack of space alone prevents our attempting to explain, illustrate, and demonstrate. God bless William Taylor and the Methodist Episcopal Missions of all India! God bless all the missions of all the Churches in all places!

## Art. IV.—ENGLISH AND AMERICAN METHODISM CONTRASTED.

As an exposition of Christian doctrine, the Methodism of Great Britain and the United States of America exactly coincides. Though separated, as we sometimes find them, by oceans, mountains, rivers, lakes, and prairies, the pulpits of the two great Anglo-Saxon families of Methodism invariably ring the same note. In each country the same triune God is adored, the same terrible apostasy is lamented, and the same glorious provision of divine mercy is offered for acceptance. In each country the distressed penitent is taught to look for relief, not to any meritorious works that he can perform or to any imaginary treasury of merit that fellow-mortals have accumulated for him, not to any sacerdotal efficacy lodged in certain officers of the Church, nor to any supposed virtue in the penances or sacraments which the Church may have enjoined, but to the "Lamb of God, which taketh away the sin of the world," and to him alone. In each country the believer is encouraged to expect the witness of the Spirit to his adoption.

and to strive for a state of grace in which his character and experience will be mature and complete. In each country he is comforted with the prospect of a future resurrection, and of a gracious recognition and approval at the bar of infinite justice; and in each country he is taught to anticipate, if faithful unto death, the eternal felicities of a world of unmingled purity, happiness, and glory.

But while these cardinal doctrines form the base of the theological structure of Methodism on both sides of the Atlantic, and are guarded with equal jealousy by each, there seems to have been, at least in former years, a lack of flexibility on the part of the Wesleyan Church in dealing with other views, some of which are not only outside of the denominational standards, but which are regarded by other evangelical Churches as matters which are open to further inquiry. Thus not many years have passed since a Wesleyan minister was expelled from the ministry for preaching what are understood as millenarian tenets. Within a still briefer period another shared the same fate for expressing in public the opinion that the offspring of sanctified parents partake of their moral purity; and only two or three years ago another was dealt with in a similar way, because he repudiated the class-meeting as a scriptural test of Church membership.

In each of these instances the accused parties displayed some pertinacity in the defense of their opinions, which, whether it arose from the strength of their convictions, or from carelessness as to their fate, certainly tended to accelerate their doom. A more liberal spirit, however, is now rapidly gaining ground in the British Conference, and in a few years these and similar acts of severity will be remembered with as little complacency as Calvin must have reflected on the burning of Servetus.

Regarding Methodism *as an ecclesiastical organization*, the points of diversity between the two branches are more numerous.

In the machinery of Wesleyan Methodism the class-meeting occupies a very eminent place. It is the primary cell from which the society, the circuit, the district, and the conference are evolved; it is the unit on which the whole fiscal economy rests; and, as has been intimated, it is the *sine qua non* of membership itself.

The importance attached to class-meetings by Wesleyan Methodists may be accounted for on historical grounds. Methodism was originally *a society in the Church of England.* It consisted of members of that establishment who failed to find in its formal services, and in the dry morality taught in its pulpits, that spiritual aliment which they required, and hence, while retaining their connection with it, availed themselves of the evangelical theology and devotional appliances provided by the Wesleys. By meeting in class such persons not only participated in that communion of saints which Scripture enjoins as the privilege and duty of believers, but afforded a sign that they concurred in the movement which the two brothers originated. Hence the class-meeting eventually became the test of membership—not in the Church, for many persons who disapproved of Methodism remained members of the Church of England—but the test of membership in the Wesleyan society; and though since then the relation which Methodism sustains to the Church of England has undergone a great change, especially since the "High Church" principles began to prevail in the latter, until Methodism shall openly renounce its association with it, and take its legitimate position as a distinct Church, the original test will probably retain its original significance.

American Methodism, on the other hand, commenced its astonishing career unfettered by tradition and unburdened by precedent. It adopted the class-meeting as a valuable means of grace, but regarded attendance on other means of grace, such as the ministry of the word and the sacrament, as of equal obligation.

In the ministry of Wesleyan Methodism, for reasons which will be afterward explained, the pastoral feature is to a great extent lacking. In order to supply this deficiency as far as possible, the preacher is expected to visit each class during the quarter, and after having heard the religious experience of those who are present, to give to each a ticket on which a passage of Scripture is printed, and on which the minister has written his own name and that of the member to whom it is handed. These tickets are the Church credentials of the holder. They secure admission to love-feasts, and similar social meetings; and as a new ticket is issued every three months, the possession of the one for the current quarter is a

sufficient guarantee that the holder of it is a recognized member of the body, in whatever part of the country he may happen to be. Though the distribution of these tickets involves a good deal of extra labor on the part of the preacher, the plan works well; and while objections have been raised against every other peculiar feature in the economy of Methodism, no one has ever assailed the ticket system. It possesses at least this advantage over the American method, that it requires every one who wishes to be considered as a member to come in contact periodically with the minister and Church members of the place where he then resides; and thus that anomalous state of things is rendered impossible in which a person may absent himself from the means of grace, withhold contributions for the support of the Gospel, and even live in a backsliding state, and yet claim membership with the Church on the ground that he has somewhere in his keeping a worn-out letter of dismissal, written months, or even years previously by some preacher of a distant conference in a remote region in the United States.

The duties of the *leaders' meeting* of the Wesleyan Methodist Society so closely resembles those which are discharged by the court of the same name in American Methodism, as to require no further notice.

The *quarterly meeting*, or, as it would be called in this country, the Quarterly Conference, is composed of the traveling preachers; the local preachers of three years' standing; the circuit, society, chapel, and poor stewards; the trustees and class-leaders; the superintendent preacher (or preacher in charge) taking the chair. At this meeting a circuit steward is annually elected, whose duty it is to keep the circuit accounts, to provide a comfortable and well-furnished house for the minister, and to welcome him on his arrival. He receives the moneys raised in the various societies, and pays the preacher the stipend which the circuit has fixed upon at previous meetings as its allowance. In some instances the receipts, when all accounted for, do not realize the sum agreed upon; but in such cases the circuit steward usually advances the deficiency from his own private resources, and such deficiency is regarded as a circuit debt. Gentlemen are usually elected to the office of circuit steward whose circumstances enable them to make such

advances without inconvenience; but should such circuit debt, after being carried to the following quarter, remain unliquidated, it is usual to assess the various societies in proportion to the average amount they pay in; and should this also fail, recourse is had to public collections, tea-meetings, lectures, bazaars, or some other method of raising money.

Such an officer as a circuit steward is not only considered honorable by the incumbents, inasmuch as it is a manifestation of the respect and confidence of the circuit, but is considered by the English preachers as exceedingly useful to themselves. In him, that authority which in America is divided among the whole board of stewards is centralized. Hence, the preacher on an English circuit is never exposed to the mortification, after "calling a meeting of officials," of finding himself the only one present. The circuit steward having authority during the interval between the preceding and following quarterly meeting to meet all legitimate claims which may be made upon the circuit, on arriving at a new field of labor he not only finds the lists of names, residences of members, and times and places of preaching, which his predecessor has left, but a "living epistle" in the person of the circuit steward, whose explanations elucidate all circuit matters far more effectually than writing can do, and whose hearty shake of the hand often helps to reconcile him to a field of labor which would be equivalent to what in the West would be considered as a "grasshopper district."

The division of circuits; the desirability of an additional preacher; the erection and enlargement of new places of worship; the examination and approval of local preachers; the examination of candidates for the ministry, and their recommendation to the district meeting, (as it is there called,) are all duties of the quarterly meeting; and although beyond its province, and severely censured by the stationing committee, many quarterly meetings of late have been in the habit of selecting and inviting preachers for the following year. This practice, which is becoming exceedingly prevalent, unless checked by wise legislation is likely at no distant date to be the source of trouble and perplexity, inasmuch as it is an assumption on the part of the laity of that liberty of choice which both they and the ministers voluntarily surrender when they give the

conference the power of appointing preachers to their fields of labor. The admission of the laity into conference, which seems likely to become a part of Wesleyan Methodist polity at no very distant period, will tend to rectify this evil, or at least deprive it of its most objectionable features.

The *district meeting* is second only to the Annual Conference in the power with which it is intrusted. It consists of all the traveling preachers in the district, whether on probation or in full connection. One day of the session, however, is open to circuit stewards, when purely financial business is transacted. In the district meeting charges against traveling preachers are examined and disposed of, applications for aid from distressed chapels and schools are considered, candidates for the itinerancy are approved or rejected, the numerical state of the several circuits ascertained and recorded, a representative to sit with the chairman of the district on the stationing committee at the following conference is elected, and a general examination is instituted respecting every department of the work within the bounds of the district.

There are two officers in whose prudence and general ability the efficiency of the district meeting mainly depend, namely, the chairman and secretary, both of whom are elected at the previous conference by the preachers in the district after the list of appointments has been finally read. It is the duty of the chairman to preside at district meetings, and to exercise a general oversight and superintendence over the whole work within the boundaries of his district; to attend quarterly meetings when invited to do so by the superintendent preacher of such circuit; to provide supplies for vacant charges; and should any emergency arise requiring the exercise of discipline in the interval between the district meeting and conference, it is his duty to call a minor district meeting, consisting of four ministers, two chosen by the accuser, and two by the accused, to try a preacher; and if found guilty, to suspend him until the ensuing conference, if deemed expedient.

It is the duty of the secretary of the district, as he is technically called "the financial secretary," to record the proceedings of the district committee; to obtain the various statistics from each circuit, and to arrange and tabulate them in such a way as to facilitate the business of the Annual Conference.

There are many advantages which Wesleyan Methodism derives from its district committee meetings. The advantage which the preacher in full connection derives from them are obvious. He thereby acquires a thorough acquaintance with the condition of every circuit in the district, and with the experience thus acquired is able to discharge the duties required of a minister more intelligently; he obtains an education which will qualify him for the office of a chairman himself, should it be conferred upon him; and if circumstances needing judicial investigation should occur, he can confidently expect that in the hands of persons who are in the district, many of whom are acquainted with the peculiarities of each point, a just and impartial verdict will be given. The advantage to the people consists in its inexpensiveness, and in its freedom from prejudice or partisanship. The chairman of the district, like the rest of his brethren, is appointed to a charge, and from it he derives his support; the slight traveling expenses which may be incurred by an occasional visit to another circuit being the only expense which the circuit he visits is expected to defray. The advantage to the chairman of the district himself consists in his being spared the toil and danger of constant traveling, and unnecessary visits to charges whose condition is such as to need no such interference. Considering that by the adoption of district meetings the General Conference has manifested a desire to approximate to the English system; considering that the political genius of the national government is in direct opposition to the centralization of power in the hands of individuals; considering the great expense which the system of presiding eldership entails upon the people; and considering the general dissatisfaction which prevails in the Methodist Episcopal Church on the subject, the time may not be far distant when the scaffolding of presiding eldership, which, however ornamental, adds no stability to the structure, and was only designed to be of temporary value, will be removed, and another appliance substituted bearing a close resemblance in its simplicity and effectiveness to that which from an early period has been tested by the Wesleyan Methodists of Great Britain.

The only court which remains to be noticed is the Annual Conference, the presiding officer of which is elected by the

assembled ministers at the commencement of its session. His term of office is for one year, and his duties during the sittings of the conference and during the following year correspond to those of the episcopacy in the American Church, except that he is not expected to be always traveling, nor to interfere in any way with the appointments of ministers. Furthermore, he is not relieved by his office from the labors and responsibilities of circuit work. It is usual, however, to appoint with him an extra preacher, (generally an unmarried man,) who acts as his secretary, and occupies his pulpit in his absence, and whose salary is paid out of the Contingent Fund.

The election of the president is immediately followed by the election of a secretary, who is permitted to select three or four assistants, and an equal number of letter-writers.

The general routine of business in the Annual Conferences of Wesleyan Methodism resembles in every respect that of the Annual Conferences of the Methodist Episcopal Church, except that in England, where General Conferences have not yet been adopted, the Annual Conference is invested with legislative as well as administrative functions. New regulations do not come into force, however, until they have been consented to by a majority of the quarterly meetings held during the ensuing year.

The "Legal Hundred" of Wesleyan Methodism consists of one hundred ministers, vacancies in whose number are filled up half by seniority and half by election. As all ministers in full connection who have obtained leave to be present from the district meetings have a right to vote in conference, the legal fiction is kept up merely to fulfill the conditions of the "poll deed," on which the property of Methodism in its places of worship rests, and to meet a possible contingency which might arise from civil commotion, or from the prevalence of some terrible disease, when it might not be prudent, or even practicable, for a larger number than a hundred ministers to meet in one locality.

The "appointing power" of Wesleyan Methodism rests with the whole conference. A stationing committee, consisting of the chairman of districts and the representatives chosen at the district meetings, meet a week previous to conference and prepare a rough draft of appointments, which is printed and cir-

culated freely among the preachers and the various circuits in the connection. During the sittings of the conference the committee is prepared to receive suggestions which may be made on either side, and which frequently lead to alterations in the list, after which it is read to the conference a second time. The stationing committee still pursue their toil, and toward the close of the conference the third reading takes place, after which no changes are made.

Complaints have been made in this country respecting the secrecy of presiding elders, and the hardship inflicted by it on the ministers at their disposal. The experience of the writer leads him to prefer the American system, supposing it to have such faults, which have been greatly exaggerated, to the English plan. The cases in which genuine merit is overlooked must, in the nature of things, be exceedingly rare. Of all genius it may be said that it "cannot be hid." And those in which it is suppressed and ignored through prejudice, or any other ulterior motive, it is charitable to hope are still less frequent. It is the interest of the appointing power to promote the welfare of Methodism as a whole, including the district, the circuit, and the preacher; and if the preacher is anxious that the right man should be in the right place, those who decide this matter are influenced by an equal amount of anxiety in the same direction. It has been observed that in cases where private influence has been brought to bear on the decisions of the cabinet the results have not been so satisfactory either to the preacher or the charge concerned as to encourage a frequent repetition of it. And though the finality involved in the American mode of appointment may sometimes press rather heavily on the preacher, there are serious evils which from time to time arise in English Methodism from a lack of it. Humiliating scenes have sometimes been witnessed in the English Conference when brethren have occupied its time and appealed to its sympathies in pathetic and tearful requests for better circuits on some purely personal grounds, and in cases where the incapacity of the petitioner would render a favorable reception of his plea destructive to the interests of the cause, all of which must have been exceedingly painful to the assembled brethren; and it seems to be the least of two evils, if such disappointments are inevitable, that any ebullition of

feeling arising from it should be confined to the privacy of the domestic hearth and the seclusion of the closet. Even if such appeals were partially successful, and, in consequence of them, a slight modification were made in the appointment in question, there would be room for the impression that a still more earnest appeal and a more persistent effort would have resulted in a still greater boon; and thus, while beginning by blaming his brethren, he would end by an equally futile condemnation of himself. On the other hand, the American preacher, knowing that after the stations are read off his destination is settled, soon settles down, and learns to look at the brightest side of that which is beyond his power to alter.

In the ministry of the "old country" the Presbyterian order alone is recognized, which is believed to include the diaconate and episcopacy. Junior preachers, who are on probation and have not been ordained, sustain the same relations, and discharge the same offices, as the deacons of the Methodist Episcopal Church. It is usual to appoint two or more preachers to each circuit, one of whom is *primus inter pares*, and is called the "superintendent." It is he who prepares the circuit plan, and fixes the times and places where his colleagues are to preach. Circuit business of every kind is usually taken to him to be disposed of, or is reserved for the consideration of the preachers' meeting, which is held weekly.

The charges of the English preachers are all circuits. Stations in the American sense of the term are unknown. Strenuous efforts have been made recently, on two or three successive conferences, by a body of trustees in London, whose chapel was at that time burdened with a heavy debt, to create a station, of which a well-known and eloquent preacher and lecturer was invited to become the pastor; but, though they made most lucrative offers, the conference firmly declined to depart from their established usage. By Wesleyans generally itinerancy is regarded as the glory of Methodism. By itinerancy they mean not simply that provision in their ecclesiastical economy by which the residence of the preacher in a particular locality is limited to a term of years, nor the fact that his destination is in the hands of an appointing power rather than his own choice. They understand by itinerancy the work of itinerating. They understand by itinerating the perambu-

lation of "the great iron wheel" in contradistinction to snugly squatting at the hub. They understand by itinerancy in ecclesiastical science what the theory of Galileo is in the science of astronomy—the theory which gives orbits to its luminaries "forever *moving* as they shine," instead of that of Copernicus, which limits them to one spot in the expanse of night. They conceive that any system which confines a preacher all the year to one congregation, though it may be Congregationalism, or Presbyterianism, or Episcopalianism, is not Methodism, and that when its ministers cease to be traveling preachers, or "round preachers," as they have sometimes been styled, they will have abandoned a feature in their work which, though regarded by other sects as a singular eccentricity, is the only implement by which the world can be "turned upside down."

Local preachers in England find their office to be no sinecure. Some are employed every Sunday, and some have nine or ten appointments during the quarter. In many circuits there are only two or three traveling preachers, while there are a score or more of preaching places to be visited, hence it would be impossible to fill the pulpits without lay assistance. But the co-operation they meet with from this quarter is cordially rendered, and as a whole very efficient.

With respect to the amount and the reliableness of income, the Wesleyan preacher has a great advantage over the ministers of the Methodist Episcopal Church. Few preachers in England receive a smaller allowance than £150, ($750.) If he has a family he receives an additional sum of £10 for each boy, and £7 for each girl. Besides this amount, which is considered as quarterage, his house rent, fuel, and medical expenses are paid for him; and as each circuit not only provides a house, but a sufficient outfit of furniture, thus, though constantly on the tramp, he is at least well cared for.

In the American Methodist Church, on the contrary, where a comprehensive and connectional system of finance is wholly lacking, the greatest disparities exist. While some preachers enjoy a larger income than the most favored Wesleyan preacher, the great majority are poorly provided for, and many, it is feared, are in circumstances of great need.

The following is a summary of the sums received for pastoral support by eighty-four circuits in a conference which has

been considered thriving and prosperous, omitting contributions for the support of presiding elders:—

| | | | | | | | |
|---|---|---|---|---|---|---|---|
| 4 paid | $1,000 and over. | | | 14 paid | $400 and less than | | $500. |
| 3 " | 800 and less than | | $900. | 14 " | 300 | " | 400. |
| 6 " | 700 | " | 800. | 14 " | 200 | " | 300. |
| 2 " | 600 | " | 700. | 14 " | 100 | " | 200. |
| 4 " | 500 | " | 600. | 7 " | less than $100. | | |

It may be objected that in consequence of the grasshopper "raid," the report of the last year's income can scarcely be considered as affording a fair view of the average receipts. The following table, therefore, is supplied, which covers the same ground for the previous year:—

| | | | | | | | |
|---|---|---|---|---|---|---|---|
| 7 paid | $1,000 and over. | | | 18 paid | $400 and less than | | $500. |
| 2 " | 900 and less than | | $1,000. | 14 " | 300 | " | 400. |
| 4 " | 800 | " | 900. | 16 " | 200 | " | 300. |
| 5 " | 700 | " | 800. | 2 " | 100 | " | 200. |
| 3 " | 600 | " | 700. | 2 " | less than $100. | | |
| 8 " | 500 | " | 600. | | | | |

Considering that in the whole conference referred to there are only thirty-four parsonages, and that in fifty circuits out of the eighty-four who gave in their reports there were fifty in which the preacher is required to pay house rent, and all other expenses whatsoever out of his income, the preponderance of ministerial comfort indubitably rest with the Wesleyan.

*As a financial scheme,* the chief source of supply in the Wesleyan Methodist Society is found in the contributions of the members in the various classes; the minimum sum which each is expected to contribute being one penny per week, and one shilling per quarter. Public collections are also made every three months at each preaching place, to afford those an opportunity of contributing to the support of the ministry who, though members of the congregation, are not members of the Society, and do not meet in class. There are every year an increasing number of cases, too, in which chapels become free from debt, and in such cases there is a surplus of income over expenses which is derived from pew rents, which is also brought to the circuit board and assists in paying the salaries of the preachers.

*The Auxiliary Preachers and Widows' Fund* was established for the purpose of affording a means of subsistence to preachers who through sickness or infirmity were laid aside

from their work, and their widows at their death. It is supported by contributions in the classes, each member being expected to pay at least sixpence annually for this object. According to the last plan sanctioned by the district meetings and conferences, supernumerary preachers receive annuities from this fund in the following proportion:—

| | | | | | | |
|---|---|---|---|---|---|---|
| Those who | have traveled | 12 | years are entitled to | £15 | annually. |
| " | " | 18 | " | 20 | " |
| " | " | 24 | " | 25 | " |
| | | 29 | | 35 | |
| " | | 34 | | 40 | |
| " | " | above 39 | " | 50 | |

Widows are entitled to the following sums, according to the years named above, namely: £10, £12, £15, £16, £18, £20, £24.

The gross receipts for the year 1871 amounted to £17,138 7s.

*The Contingent Fund* is also maintained by subscriptions in the classes. From this fund grants are made to circuits which would be unable otherwise to support a preacher. The traveling expenses of preachers who are moved long distances; the purchase of furniture for additional preachers' houses; the relief of special cases of affliction, such as protracted sickness, funerals, etc.; the support of supplies for circuits which may become vacant during the year, are all paid from this useful fund. Its receipts during the year 1871 were £25,787. 6s. 2d.

The chief features of diversity between English and American Methodism have now been pointed out. It is right, however, to observe that such diversity does not affect the prosperity of the common cause. Both can point to noble benevolent and educational institutions which they have reared. Both are equally interested in the rising race, and are putting forth strenuous effort to render Sabbath-schools more numerous and effective. Both are equally zealous in propagating the Gospel by domestic and foreign missions. Both are laboring to afford the rising ministry the advantage of instruction in theological seminaries; and by the princely gifts which from time to time are thrown into the treasuries of the Churches by the self-denying devotion which the biographies of each Church commemorates, by the fidelity and spiritual growth of the people who are brought under their influence, and by the constant extension of the boundaries of the spiritual Zion which is per-

ceptible on both sides of the Atlantic, it is evident that the love of Christ is the grand constraining principle in the hearts of each.

There are no human schemes, however carefully devised and conscientiously carried out, which are exempt from imperfection. But the instances are not rare in which what appears to be imperfections are in reality adaptations of providence. So it is with Methodism. Each branch has its own work, and God has conferred on each the implements most suitable for its performance. There is work for the brother with the faultless coat and snowy neckcloth and courteous bearing, who labors in a country where precedent exerts an enormous sway, and where the limits of society are nicely marked and rigidly guarded; and in a country out of whose mighty forests the seats of future empires are being hewed, and on whose boundless prairies the homes of nations are being prepared, there is work for men who, though comparatively careless of conventionalities, are laboring with a stout heart and willing arm. But they have one creed, one object, one Saviour, one eternal home; and by faith they may stretch their arms over the great deep, and grasp each other with the grip of genuine sympathy and affection, for they are brothers in toil, brothers in tribulation, and brothers in triumph.

## Art. V.—HUXLEY AND EVOLUTION.

*The Direct Evidences of Evolution.* Three Lectures in New York, September 18, 20, and 22, 1876. I. The Untenable Hypotheses; II. Circumstantial Evidence of Evolution; III. The Demonstrative Evidence. New York Tribune Extra, No. 36.

For the complete, authentic, and accessible form of the lectures cited above we are indebted to a phase of newspaper enterprise which is purely and creditably American. It is a pleasure to make acknowledgment of the great service rendered to science and literature in America by the cultured editorship of the New York Tribune, which discovers so large resources of "news" in the events and utterances of the world of science and letters.

The lectures themselves were widely heralded; every movement of the distinguished foreigner was made a sensation, and the whole country had been lifted to the tiptoe of expectation. The theme announced was one which had already agitated every thinking circle of two continents. Professor Huxley had long been distinguished as a bold leader in the advocacy of an hypothesis which required a reinterpretation of some passages of Scripture; and a vague expectation had been awakened that some sort of a skirmish between science and theology was impending.

It is fair to record the fact, however, that no conflict with the fundamental principles of religious faith was anticipated by any holding representative positions in science; nor were corresponding representatives of theological learning fearful, to the least extent, that any phase of science so sustained by evidence as to be generally accepted by the scientific, could contravene the accepted fundamentals of religious belief. The popular apprehensions existed, as they have always existed, in the minds of one class who have no adequate knowledge of the nature and force of scientific evidence, and of another class who rather enjoy the spectacle when theology gets a pelting, even if with mere "tufts of grass." Undoubtedly it is the depraved heart which prompts to a large share of the satisfaction felt in such a case; but there seems to be, also, a semi-humorous element in our nature which enjoys, as a mild sensation, any discomposure manifested by theology at being even unjustly accused of jealousy toward science.

It is fair also to record the fact that the three lectures of Professor Huxley do not contain a single expression avowing or intimating an atheistic belief; and all assertions to the effect that "he more than suggested that his aim was atheistic," have no other foundation than the opinion of their authors that the doctrine of evolution means atheism. On the contrary, Professor Huxley has expressed himself in such terms as to clearly indicate that he reserves a place for original creative agency. He says:—

Though we are quite clear about the constancy of nature at the present time, and in the present order of things, it by no means follows necessarily that we are justified in expanding this generalization into the past, and in denying absolutely that there

may have been a time when evidence did not follow a first order, when the relations of cause and effect were not fixed and definite, and when external agencies did not intervene in the general course of nature.

And again:—

My present business is not with the question as to how nature has originated—as to the causes which have led to her origination, but as to the manner and order of her origination. . . . This is strictly an historical question. . . . But the other question, about creation, is a philosophical question, and one which cannot be solved or approached, or touched by the historical method.

The first of the above quotations is not wholly unambiguous. It seems that the lecturer must employ the term "cause" in a physical rather than a metaphysical sense. He directs our attention to a time when the present order of nature had not begun to exist, and the orders of sequence of physical effects had not been ordained. He must have contemplated an adequate efficiency for the inauguration of the present order. In admitting the conception of a different order he at least implies the conception of a power superior to the present order, adequate to begin or end its existence. The second quotation means clearly that the evolution hypothesis may be established, and yet leave every person free to satisfy himself in reference to both the efficient and the final cause of evolution. It means that the theist may posit a Creator at the beginning. It means, we think, more than this. If natural history cannot reveal the nature of causal efficiency at the beginning of the series, it can no more reveal the nature of the efficiency which manifests itself at every term of the series; that is, the hypothesis of evolution authorizes the believer in imminent divine power to posit such power in every term of the evolution. If the lecturer recognized such legitimate inferences from his language, it is greatly to be regretted that he was not more explicit. It would, indeed, have been a departure from strictly scientific method, (in distinction from philosophical,) but it would have been a courtesy appreciated, if not deserved, by the religious public. If, however, a scientist chooses to disguise his opinions on a theological question, it is probably his right to do so. There may be, nevertheless, a degree of reserve amounting to an affectation. But, it is to be hoped, in any

event, that American dissentients from Professor Huxley's scientific or theological positions will afford him no ground to complain of contemptuous criticism and misquotation.*

Before proceeding to the consideration of the "Direct Evidences of Evolution," as presented by Professor Huxley, we desire to enter our dissent from some of his preliminary positions:

1. *The Miltonic conception of the creation is not entirely the biblical one.* Professor Huxley, in his first lecture, has presented us two "hypotheses" concerning the origin of the existing order of nature, which he pronounces "untenable." The first is the theory held by many of the Greek philosophers —though not by the greatest of them, Socrates, Plato, and Aristotle, nor by the Stoics and Eleatics, nor indeed by Xeniades, Democritus, and Epicurus—that the order of the world is eternal. The lecturer showed, as has been done time and again by others, that the succession of events in the past history of the world, as revealed by geological science, is such as *necessarily implies a commencement*—a beginning of its organic history, and a beginning of its cosmical history. The second "untenable hypothesis" is that of "creation." For the purpose of making known his conception of the "creation hypothesis," he assumes that which is set forth in the epic of John Milton; and, after presenting Milton's graphic though grotesque picture of the origin of animal forms, proceeds to show that it is not scientifically exact. This was no difficult undertaking, since there was probably not an intelligent person in his audience, or in the city of New York, who maintained that Milton's picture is a representation scientifically exact. It is doubtful if the poet himself regarded it as a literal history of events in detail. Milton employed a warm and productive imagination, and it might be affirmed in advance that the poet's pen would produce a picture whose exuberance of metaphor would prove eminently distasteful to cold and rigorous science.

But the lecturer attempted also to show that the Miltonic

* Those who feel curious to know more of Professor Huxley's theology may read the article entitled "School Boards" in "Critiques and Addresses." It may be noticed by the readers of Huxley's writings that he employs the word "theology" to signify a body of ecclesiastical principles and practices, and not the science of God.

*order* of creation is not sustained by paleontology. Well, if the language of Milton means and implies what the lecturer claimed, we must admit that the scientific record diverges. But what was the necessity of setting up poor old John Milton and knocking him down amid the jeers of such an audience? It would have been an equal feat to indict and convict old Bishop Burnet for the showing of his "Sacred Theory of the Earth." We can discover no explanation of this exploit, save the lecturer's belief that the Miltonic conception of creation "is that which has been instilled into every one of us in our childhood, and that it is generally accepted as the most consistent form of the creation theory." He does not pretend that in overthrowing the Miltonic theory the cosmogony of Genesis falls to the ground. He says expressly: "I do not for one moment venture to say that it could properly be called the biblical doctrine," and admits that such assumption would "be met by the authority of many eminent scholars, to say nothing of men of science, who, in recent times, have absolutely denied that this doctrine is to be found in Genesis at all." He does give us clearly to understand, however, that the Miltonic theory is untenable, "whatever the source from which that hypothesis might be derived, or whatever the authority it might be supported by." Just so far, therefore, as exegesis may be able to show that the Miltonic hypothesis, as set forth by Huxley, is a correct interpretation of Genesis, so far the lecturer disputes the biblical record.

Now, though we do not propose to enter upon an exegetical examination, we desire to record a denial that the Miltonic theory, as held up by Huxley, does represent the teaching of Genesis, or the views of well-informed scholars as to that teaching. We need not inquire whether the lecturer correctly sets forth the Miltonic ideas. It is what he sets forth that is so clearly antagonized by the facts of paleontology. We deny that Genesis, in giving us the creation of plants upon the "third day," means "the plants which now live—the trees and shrubs which we now have." * The language refers to that order of existence exemplified familiarly in "grass," and "herb," and "tree." Hence, it is not necessary to infer a second creation

* This subject receives additional elucidation from a table which we hope to present in a subsequent article.

of modern plants to which the record makes no allusion. We deny, again, that Genesis, in affirming the creation of terrestrial creatures familiarly exemplified in "cattle," "creeping things," and "beasts," has any reference to such an obscure, sparse, and incomplete terrestrial fauna as would be represented by a few snails, scorpions, and insects, breathing the air of Coal Measure times. Clearly, the fauna to which Genesis refers is a complete terrestrial fauna, eminently characterized by mammalia. Can Professor Huxley affirm that paleontology has found any "cattle" fossilized in our coal-beds? Now, a complete terrestrial fauna, such as included "cattle," did not appear until the period which geology has characterized as the "Reign of Mammals." Every geological tyro knows this. It is incorrect, therefore, to affirm that the biblical (or even Miltonic) "sixth day" must be held to begin "in the middle of the Paleozoic formations;" and hence the Bible does not raise a conflict with the facts by placing the advent of the cattle-fauna anterior to the advent of birds. We deny that the Bible declares the creation of "whales" upon the "fifth day," before the advent of birds. It proclaims the creation of *tanninim* (probably Enaliosaurs) and other marine creatures. We deny that the biblical scheme is to find its parallel—where Hugh Miller, Chalmers, Pye Smith, Silliman, *et al.*, sought for it disastrously—in that fraction of terrestrial history which has passed since the beginning of sedimentation. We hold that its reach is co-extensive with the scientific unfolding—from firemist to man. We maintain, finally, that the order of the biblical record is step by step parallel with the geologic; and that the method of origination depicted by Genesis is not at all incompatible with the hypothesis of evolution. We maintain, in fact, that the origination of new forms by descent is only creation by development; and while Professor Huxley's argument is good against the "creation-theory" which he holds up, it is the very foundation of another creation-theory more in accord with the sacred Scriptures.

2. *The evidences in support of the evolution hypothesis are not demonstrative.* We think Professor Huxley has been carried away by enthusiasm in affirming evolution inductively "demonstrated," or in any way demonstrated. The final conclusion is even beyond the reach of inductive evidence. The

data of induction may justify the conclusion that gently graduated series of animals have succeeded each other in past time; but this is no proof of a derivative relationship between them. The only possible inductive evidence of relationship would be examples of actual transition from species to species; but these, according to all observation, are facts of almost unparalleled infrequency, and, at best, are not of such observed frequency as to justify a generalization covering the whole field of life, past and present.

In spite of these exceptions to the breadth of Professor Huxley's claim, we are pretty strongly persuaded that the doctrine of derivative descent of animal and vegetal forms represents the truth. We have not been hasty to reach this conviction. We have pondered many a difficulty, and raised many a query; but we have seen old difficulties vanishing and new proofs perpetually arising. We have learned more of the wonderful resources of the hypothesis in explaining the current and the exceptional phenomena of life and organization.* We now think it is far safer to accept the hypothesis than to reject it. If it is safer for the scientist it is safer for the Christian. It is therefore time for him to seek how to co-ordinate his essential faith with the impending finality of science.

* Professor Huxley himself has undergone a similar change of opinion. In his address before the London Geological Society for 1862 he reviewed the paleontological evidences of progressive modification of types, and concluded with the following inquiry and answer: "What, then, does an impartial survey of the positively ascertained truths of paleontology testify in relation to the common doctrines of progressive modification, which suppose that modification to have taken place by a necessary progress from more to less embryonic forms, or from more to less generalized types, within the limits of the period represented by the fossiliferous rocks? It negatives those doctrines; for it either shows us no evidence of any such modification, or demonstrates it to have been very slight; and, as to the nature of that modification, it yields no evidence whatsoever that the earlier members of any long-continued group were more generalized in structure than the later ones."—*Lay Sermons and Addresses*, pp. 225, 226. In his address before the same society in 1870 he says: "When I come to the propositions touching progressive modification, it appears to me, with the help of the new light which has broken from various quarters, that there is much ground for softening the somewhat Brutus-like severity with which, in 1862, I dealt with a doctrine for the truth of which I should have been glad enough to find a good foundation. . . . When we turn to the higher vertebrata, the results of recent investigations, however we may sift and criticise them, seem to me to leave a clear balance in favor of the doctrine of the evolution of living forms, one from another."—*Critiques and Addresses*, pp. 186, 187.

It is not our purpose in this article to attempt any presentation of the facts which, in our judgment, as in that of the majority of scientific men, afford a strong balance of evidence in support of the doctrine of evolution through a material continuity. We may, however, indicate in a synoptical way the nature of the argument.

There is, first, what may be called the *geological evidence*. The discovered records of extinct life upon the earth, it must be admitted, are extremely defective, and offer many instances not in accord with the requirements of the doctrine, though there are no established facts irreconcilable with it. But there are two truths of prime importance which we must bear in mind: 1. The known record consists of but a few fragments of the actual history of extinct life. This is obvious when we consider how small a portion of the mass of fossiliferous rocks has been explored, and what rich discoveries continue to reward the exertions of geologists to extend their explorations. It is further obvious from the perishable character of organic remains subjected to the vicissitudes which the fossiliferous rocks must have undergone in the progress of the world's changes. 2. We have, in spite of these imperfections, a few instances of pretty complete graduation from type to type—as in the transition from reptiles to birds, and in the transition from the five-toed plantigrade quadruped to the one-toed and digitigrade horse; and in similar transitions to the type of the ox, the hog, the elephant, and the ape. Now, when we consider that it is a fact that every extension of our knowledge of extinct life shows a tendency to fill up the gaps which exist between known types, it seems reasonable to anticipate that if ever the lost record becomes completely restored, we shall be in possession of graduated series of forms leading from the existing highly differentiated types of life, back to some extinct forms; and that these extinct forms, instead of standing isolated, as many of them appear to stand, are similarly connected by gentle gradations, with forms still more ancient.

Next, we have the evidence of *variability of species*. Late researches have shown that it is much greater than had been generally supposed. Indeed, we are now acquainted with hundreds of cases in which forms that had been generally recognized as good species are found to be connected by inter-

diate forms. In fact the transmutations have recently been found to go so far as to constitute a passage *from genus to genus*. Thus, while the strongest geological evidence leaves us still free to deny any derivative relationship between the terms of the completed series of extinct forms, the established variability of animal forms, living and fossil, opens the way to believe that the serial terms revealed by paleontology have been genealogically connected.

Next we have the *embryological evidence*. This seems to us the most convincing of all; for it affords not only a picture of the succession of extinct forms, but it is a picture in which the successive terms are *known* to be derivatively related to each other. Trace any higher vertebrate—man himself, if you will—from a primitive condition in the ovum. How marvelous, how awe-inspiring is the unfolding! We have first the yolk, with its "germinative vesicle" and "germinative dot." Then both undergo a succession of segmentations, until there results a crowded mass of cells, ("morula," or "mulberry" stage.) Some of these dissolve, and the remainder arrange themselves as a hollow spheroid consisting of a single layer of cells ("planula" stage.) The single layer becomes double, with an opening at one pole of the spheroid, ("gastrula" stage;) and now appears a thickening on one side, in the midst of which is disclosed the "primitive furrow," afterward to be inclosed and become the spinal marrow. An enlargement is seen at one extremity; this is the forming brain; and the various segments of the brain appear as gentle swellings. At the opposite extremity is a tail. Transverse marks in the middle of the neural furrow indicate the approaching vertebral structures; while certain segments along the place of the neck are seen to receive blood-vessels from the provisional heart, and to sustain completely all the structural relations of the branchial, or gill arches in the type of fishes. Arms and legs bud out—as yet without digits, or they may be viewed as uni-digitate, like the limbs of *Lepidosiren*. Stumpy digits afterward appear, like those of the so-called *Cheirotherium* of Triassic times. The face goes by degrees through the conditions seen in low sharks, amphibious and higher vertebrates. Step by step the internal structures advance toward their destined forms, functions, and positions. Thus, by a process of repeated

differentiations, the complications and special adaptations of the higher vertebrate come into existence.

But what of all this? Very much, indeed. This marvelous evolution which we see the higher vertebrate pass through is *absolutely identical* with the embryonic history of every other animal down to a certain point in its development. Every animal begins in the egg, and the eggs (we exclude shell and other accessories) of all animals are completely undistinguishable in structure. Every animal, except some of the very lowest, presents us, in its development, the morula stage. Every animal, with a few additional exceptions, passes also through the planula stage and the gastrula stage. Thus every vertebrated animal presents us the same primitive furrow, the same cerebral enlargements, the same segmentation, the same caudal continuation, the same vascular area, the same one-chambered heart, the same branchial arches and blood-vessels, the same progressive changes in the development of the brain, the same mode of formation of the enteric and abdominal cavities, the same beginnings of the formation of the face. This identity in embryonic histories may be unexpected; it may be amazing; it may be humiliating; but there is nothing better established in science.

This is not all. There are living creatures which represent these successive stages of embryonic development. There are some so low that they never pass beyond the structure of the egg—simple cells, often, like some eggs, capable of movement by means of prolongations of their substance. There are some which attain to the morula condition, and then are adult. Others pass to the planula stage, and still others, to the gastrula. Certain worms (*Turbellaria*) represent a succeeding stage, as the Ascidians are believed to picture a still later one. Thus on, from *Amphioxus* and the lampreys to the sharks, Amphibians, Monotremes, Marsupials, and Lemurs, at the bottom of the order of four-handed animals, we discover living forms which stand forth in the museum of Nature as pictures of the embryonic stages of the highest vertebrate.

Finally, the embryonic series finds its parallel not only in the embryonic history of other animals, and in the adult forms of animals presented as we range up and down the scale of life, but the succession of extinct types, as far as we have read it, presents us with another parallel.

Now, while we *know* the stages of the embryonic series to stand derivatively related, it seems reasonable to infer that the corresponding forms in the realms of actual and extinct life are also derivatively related. It would appear, at first view, that the nature of the derivation is fundamentally different in the two cases; but even this does not impair the meaning of the fact that, in both cases, we have *a material continuity from form to form;* and this is all which evolution requires. On reflection, however, the mode of the continuity in the case of the embryo appears substantially identical with the assumed mode of continuity in the succession of geological types. Ordinary embryonic development proceeds through the multiplication and specialization of cells stimulated by the nutritive plasma in which they are bathed. Generative development begins in the multiplication and specialization of a cell stimulated by contact with a cell specialized spermatically in the same individual, or in an individual sexually different. Propagation, moreover, may be viewed as simply a mode of perpetuating or renewing an individual which is bisexual, either monœciously, as in lower animals and most plants, or diœciously, as in most animals and certain plants. The progress noted in the succession of extinct forms is assumed to have resulted from some influence exerted upon embryos in the progress of their development. The development accelerated or prolonged, would end in an organism more advanced. This would be a new specific form appearing as a stage of embryonic history; and though many generations may have intervened while the embryo was arriving at this new specific type, we may view these generations as simply nature's expedient to continue the being in existence, in spite of the wastes of physical life. So what seems, at first, a mere analogy, resolves itself into a profound biological identity.

The presentation of the facts which sustain the argument thus outlined must be waived for the present. But the question of evolution cannot be dismissed by the philosopher and the theologian even when it shall have been proved: 1. That geological history presents us universally, series of nicely graduated forms; and, 2. That these forms are all genetically related to each other, and that, consequently, all living forms are genetically connected.

Supposing both these positions well established, we have only reached the determination of a certain order of succession, and a certain derivative relation. We have not yet discovered the agencies through which the derivation is effected, and the conditions under which those agencies are operative. Nor have we discovered the efficiency which operates the agencies, and the mode of its activity; nor the reason why all these things are brought to pass as they are. In brief, after we have discovered *what* takes place, it remains to learn *through* what it takes place, and *by* what it takes place, and *for* what it takes place. These are the ulterior questions which were not touched by Professor Huxley in his lectures. He did not ignore them, but he waived them.*

We shall do no more than bring these remaining questions into view, in order that the reader may have a proper apprehension of the breadth of the theme.

I. What are the Physical and Physiological Conditions (approximate causes) of Variative Derivation?

It is in the domain covered by this question that the various theories of derivation have sprung up. At the outset, a fundamental discrimination must be made. There are the organic activities appropriating material within reach, and building the organism according to a certain pattern; and there are the external conditions in the presence of which these activities are carried on. Whatever influence the environment may exert, it can obviously be no more than a conditioning influence, since whatever is done with the organic structure, is done in the organism and through physiological processes. Now, whatever may be the nature of the forces acting within, it is conceivable that they may be conditioned or determined in their activity by the quality and quantity of food, water, air, and rest. These belong to the environment. Variations in the supply of these requisites depend on two classes of influences. These are the *natural* influences, arising from daily,

* He says: "The cause of that production of variations is a matter not at all properly understood at present. Whether it depends upon some intricate machinery—if I may use the phrase—of the animal form itself, or whether it arises through the influence of conditions upon that form, is not certain, and the question may, for the present, be left open.—Page 23, "Tribune" ed. "My present business is not with the question as to *how* nature has originated, as to causes which *have led* to her origination."—Page 19.

seasonal, periodical, and secular changes in the supplies, and from the movements and migrations of the animal. These variable factors have been taken into the account by the older transmutationists, Lamark and St. Hilaire, and by the later Darwinists. Then there are the *artificial* influences (as we may style them) arising from the contests of individuals for the possession of the requisites of life. This is the "struggle for existence," which constitutes the peculiar feature of Darwinian derivative doctrine. The effect of this struggle is always the survival of the fittest, and a consequent tendency to improvement. It is thus that the environment may condition the organic activities of animals that have come into the world, and entered upon the struggle for self-support. But the most impressible period of life is the embryonic. To what an extent must requisite supplies during ovarian and uterine existence condition the physiological activities which are making the being what it is to be. It is certainly quite conceivable that favorable conditions should so accelerate embryonic development that higher results should be reached at full term, or that unfavorable conditions should so retard development that lower results should be reached. This idea is the peculiar feature of the derivative theory of Cope and Hyatt. It seems really to have struck upon a more fundamental and productive cause of derivative variation than the struggle for existence. It accounts for regress as well as progress. It addresses itself to the tissue-making forces at the time when the foundations of the tissues are being laid, and not when the organic structure has been already cast in its mold.

But now, independently of all external conditions, it is conceivable that the organism may be the subject of an inherent and unremitting nisus—a tendency, in spite of obstacles, to accomplish certain results, and attain to fitter conditions. It is our own conviction that here lies the secret force which works out the multifarious phenomena of organic life. Such a nisus was appealed to by Lamark; and Professor Huxley has more than once hinted the probability that it is a potent factor in vital phenomena.

II. What are the Efficient Causes of Variative Derivation?

Plainly it may become shown that the mode of activity of the organism, either conditioned or unconditioned by the

environment, is the means through which the vital phenomena of the world are brought to pass, and we may still be ignorant of the efficient cause of that activity. Now, even though an indwelling and persistent nisus should appear to be the principal impulse to activity, we have to seek after the source of the impulse. Does it originate in the tissue in which it acts? Is it a product of the tissue? These are the bottom questions, the solution of which possesses the highest interest for theology. We do not propose to enter here into any argument; but for our part, it seems perfectly clear that the efficient cause of physiological changes is objective to the organism in which they are revealed. Our conclusion is grounded, first, on our necessary conception of efficient cause; secondly, on the discernment reflected in the mode of activity of physiological causes. Efficient—that is, primitive, original, real—causation is the direction of adequate efficiency, through appropriate instrumentalities (if needed) toward a preconceived and desiderated result. If any supposed cause acts in any other way, then it is itself an effect, and the real cause remains to be sought. If physiological force does not thus act, then, in tracing results to such force, we have not found their cause. Such may be the "causes" with which science deals, but they are not reason's causes. In this case, we have to seek for the volition and preconception and motive back of physiological force. But if physiological force does thus act, then volition and preconception and motive are revealed in every vital change. Thus we argue, even when force acts without adaptiveness. But vital forces act *with reference* to external conditions, and *with reference* to ideal concepts. Here is double proof, then, of intellectual discernments. Whatever results, therefore, are produced by the slow, perpetual activities of physiological forces, conditioned, to whatever extent, by the environment, are the results of an ever-present, discerning efficiency; and the more we see the organism molded to the environment, the more clearly we see reflected the intellectual element of that efficiency. If the existing world is the genealogical result of primitive conditions, then the efficiency which the cycles of the past have witnessed, in the transformation of successive terms, has been enlightened by intelligence, directed by choice and impelled by will. We cast our glances back over

the awful chasm of the cosmic æons, and contemplate it as the theater of the display of an infinity of miracles, revealed in an unbroken, sustained, adaptive, and all-embracing system of evolution.

III. What is the Final Cause of Variative Derivation?

We are properly reminded by the nescientists that we must not presume to know fully the motives which actuate an infinite will. At the same time we feel fully persuaded that no intelligence acts without some motive—not even an infinite intelligence; for motive stands correlated to intelligence as such, and not to the greatness of intelligence. We feel it, therefore, perfectly legitimate to inquire after the motives which have controlled divine activity in the ordering of the world. We shall not, however, elaborate the inquiry here. The natural reason can never divest itself of the conviction that complicated and slowly maturing results, which respond to the wants of sensitive beings, were designed so to respond. Among the wants of intelligent beings are appropriate *stimuli* to mental activity, and appropriate rewards for mental effort. One of the highest and noblest *stimuli* to mental activity is the hope of attaining to the higher laws or modes of change and succession in the natural world. The law of evolution discloses itself as the highest generalization of the phenomena of the cosmos. If we discover that this law involves not only an ideal, but a physical, continuity, we seem to have attained, in cosmical dynamics, to that unity which has been the aspiration of all science and all philosophy. This, then, is the highest possible disclosure of the Supreme Intelligence which nature can yield; and we shall expose ourselves to no just charge of credulity, in thinking such a revelation of the Supreme Mind to be one of the final causes of the all-embracing scheme of evolution by continuity.

The world and its parts may be compared to a stately dwelling; and the scientist who investigates its constitution and the mode of its origin, is like a visitor from some realm where houses are not built. This intelligent visitor studies inquiringly every accessible part. He catalogues the parts, as the naturalist catalogues the members of the animal kingdom. He discovers a unity in the conception of the edifice, and says that its style is "gothic;" as the zoölogist says the style of a large

portion of the animal kingdom is "vertebrate." But our stranger has never seen an edifice in process of construction, and he conjectures the method in accordance with which its features might have been originated and combined. Evidently, he says to himself, one method would be the full completion of each portion of the building before beginning another portion, as a mud-wasp builds its cell. At length, however, he discovers an edifice in process of erection; as the biologist studies the building up of an animal from the egg. An excavation is first made for the foundations; this is the "primitive furrow." The basement walls are raised around it; the sills and the floor-timbers are laid; these are the "protovertebræ." Next the side-walls are raised and the roof is closed in. Thus the most general features of the structure first appear. The places of partitions and stair-ways are indicated by rough timbers, and the plan of the house is outlined. As the work proceeds the rough timbers are covered with flooring and lath; then the walls receive coats of brown mortar, and, lastly, a white finish. Still remain the casings and moldings, and paint and varnish. Now the house is complete, and our gratified stranger concludes that the stately edifice, the cathedral, the town hall, were all constructed according to a method of "evolution." He has discovered the method, the order of succession of the parts. Now he knows that all buildings are constructed according to a law of evolution; as the biologist has learned in reference to animals, and the cosmologist in reference to worlds. But our stranger could not for a moment imagine that the method or law of construction did the work of construction, nor can the biologist hold that the law of evolution accounts for the existence of the animal. The work in the edifice has been done by mechanics, with the use of tools and machinery. These are the physiological activities which build up the tissues and members of the animal. These mechanics act under the bidding of another will, and, in this relation, they are only a part of the mechanism which performs the work. Their hands are not the prime cause of the building—they are not the real cause. The building would never exist if there were not a prime mover in the will of the proprietor. That will is the cause of the edifice. But this will has not ordered this structure without motive. Whatever the

motive—for residence, for display, for a monument, for some caprice, or for some motive undisclosed—there has been a *why* of his determination.

Thus, in the contemplation of the universe, it is the part of science to catalogue the phenomena and learn their mode and order of occurrence, and the physical agencies concerned in their production. But there are profounder inquiries propounded by reason, and deeper longings felt by the soul. After science has accomplished her last work in her especial domain, reason draws aside the vail which obstructs the vision of science, and discovers the Supreme Efficiency working in all things, and working out the welfare of sentient beings; and the soul arises and adores the God whose presence it before had felt, but now rationally cognizes.

## Art. VI.—THE CLASSICAL LITERATURE OF THE CHINESE.

The famous classical writings of the Chinese comprise nine works, treating of subjects kindred in their nature, and affording to the student of all ages a study of the deepest interest. Their authors and subjects will be briefly noticed before we proceed to speak of them collectively, our object being more particularly to show the unbounded and molding influences for good that these wonderful monuments of antiquity have exerted upon the Chinese race. To treat of the classics separately would necessitate the writing of nine volumes, so vast are the fields of thought traversed by each of them, so interesting the subject-matter, and so momentous and critical were the events and the times that conspired to produce these remarkable specimens of literature. To these classical writings this immense empire owes her existence and her present degree of civilization; and to them her millions have looked during numberless ages for guidance in their political policy and for instruction in their daily lives.

As will be seen from the brief digest of subject-matters below given, six of the classics are attributed to the sage Confucius, (552-479 B.C.) Although he did not, in reality, write the whole

of these six works, yet those which were originally written by others were so completely altered, remodeled, and rewritten, that Confucius is most justly regarded by the Chinese as the common author of the entire six. Furthermore, the subjects treated of by these original authors took such a tinge in passing through the mind of Confucius that they were no more the work of others; and it is by virtue of their Confucian character alone that these writings have become immortalized. The three remaining classics were written by Tseng Sin, Kung Kich, and Mencius, the most renowned among the disciples of Confucius.

These four sages, then, are the philosophers of China, the authors of the nine Classics, and upon their lips have hung, for twenty-four hundred years, the billions of this empire. Contemporaneous, in sacred Scripture, with Ezra; in history, with Cyrus; in the oratorical world, with Demosthenes; and in the philosophical, with Plato, Aristotle, Zeno, and Epicurus; we are constrained to wonder at the perfection and the original and practical character of the productions of the four philosophers, whose land it pleased God to place so remote from "the cradle of civilization." The nine Classics are named as follows: 1. The Book of Changes; 2. The Book of History; 3. The Book of Odes; 4. The Book of Rites; 5. The Spring and Autumn Annals; 6. The Great Study; 7. The True Medium; 8. The Confucian Analects; 9. Mencius.

The Book of Changes was composed in prison by Wen Wang about 1150 B. C., and is one of the most ancient books extant. It treats of general philosophy, and the First Cause as taught by Fuhhi. His institutes were founded upon the eight diagrams from which has been deduced a system of ethics. The work was completely rewritten by Confucius about 500 B. C.

The Book of History presents us with a history of China between the dates 2350 and 770 B. C. The internal evidence establishes the conclusion that Confucius acted as editor of documents existing in his day; but the precise alterations that these ancient writings underwent in his hands cannot now be ascertained.

The Book of Odes is one of the most ancient collections of odes extant. There is nothing of an epic character in the work, nor even any lengthened narrative. The book contains

about three hundred odes, and the internal evidence clearly assigns their composition to the period included between the dates 1765 and 585 B. C. The several authors of these poetic effusions are unknown. The work was compiled by Confucius, who, finding the odes current among his countrymen, embellished and versified them. Their prosody is unique. Most of them are composed in lines consisting of four syllables, each syllable being a word, as Chinese is a monosyllabic language. Although this is the regular meter, yet poetical license permits frequent departure therefrom; and we find lines numbering from one to eight syllables, but no more. The quatrain is the favorite verse; but we also find stanzas consisting of from two to seventeen lines each. The rhyme is peculiar and varied. Thus we have stanzas of from two to twelve lines rhyming in succession; stanzas of from four to twelve lines rhyming alternately; stanzas of entirely irregular rhyme; and also a few in blank verse. These departures from the quatrain, however, only enhance the beauty of the poetry, which would otherwise become somewhat tedious. The odes were sung in China as the compositions of the earliest European poets were sung in ancient Greece. Their style is simple and their subjects various; and they represent, in the purest manner, the habits of thought of the ancient Chinese.

The Book of Rites was written by an ancient prince, named Chou, who drew his materials directly from the lips of Confucius, thus acting, in reality, as the amanuensis of the sage. The work gives directions for all actions of life, referring not only to the external conduct, but being interspersed with excellent observations regarding mutual forbearance and kindness in society, which are regarded as the true principles of etiquette.

The Spring and Autumn Annals is an historical work written by Confucius himself, and is so named because "its commendations are life-giving, like spring, and its censures life-withering, like autumn." It contains a congeries of historical incidents extending from 802 to 560 B. C.

The Great Study was written during the fifth century B. C. by Tseng Sin, one of the most eminent of the disciples of Confucius. It is a genuine monument of the Confucian school, and its author faithfully reflects the teachings of his master. The argument of the work is briefly summed up in four heads:

The improvement of one's self; the regulation of a family; the government of a State; and the rule of an empire.

The True Medium was composed by Kung Kich, the grandson of Confucius, and its date is about 390 B. C. The work has a noble, independent character, and is well worthy of being treasured in the library of the world's classics. Its plan is to illustrate the nature of human virtue, and to exhibit its conduct in the actions of an "ideal man of immaculate propriety," who always demeans himself correctly, in which alone consists true virtue.

The Confucian Analects consist of dialogues held between Confucius and his disciples, and were compiled by the sage himself. The date of the work has been fixed at about the beginning of the fifth century B. C. Its aim is to exhibit the duties of political government as those of the perfecting of one's self, and of the practice of virtue by all men.

Mencius consists entirely of the conversations held between the sage Mencius and the princes and grandees of his time. It was written by Mencius himself, and its date is about 330 B. C. The object of the work is to tranquilize the empire, to rectify men's hearts, and direct their minds to heaven.

Such, in brief, are the subject-matters of the classics. A careful perusal will show that the nine works are imbued with the same spirit for the amelioration of man. The subjects and aim being thus collateral, it will be as unnecessary as impossible for us to enter upon the fields presented by each of the works, for they are too vast for treatment in a review. It is proposed, therefore, merely to take a general survey of the classics, and to show in what a wonderful degree these writings have benefited a third part of the earth's population. The unbounded admiration felt for the classics and their remarkable authors has caused these writings to become still more famous from the unequaled influence they have exerted in the formation of the Chinese character. They are held in great veneration for their antiquity and their excellent philosophy. Scholars commit them to memory, and writers quote largely from this inexhaustible source; for the arguments, illustrations, and sentiments are all but unexcelled.

These remarkable bequests of antiquity have not only had the most practical effect upon the manners and life of the Chi-

nese, but they have furnished them with a model of government to which they have scrupulously adhered for more than two thousand years. The six Central Boards in Pekin, as well as the system of Government throughout the empire, are founded upon and modeled after the plans enjoined in the Classics. The religion of State is founded upon them, and the people are instructed from their earliest childhood in all the details they contain respecting conduct toward the aged, their rulers, and their parents. A critical examination of the works will discover the molding principles which operate on Chinese youth from earliest years. Nor is it difficult to account for the wonderful influence which the Classics have had upon the Chinese character. Those who are most aware of the excellences of the precepts and the incomparableness of the dogmas are those who have had experience in the tortuous dealings of the human heart, and have the power to enforce obedience upon their juniors. By the time these latter are qualified to take their place in the upper rank of the social system, habit leads them to exercise their sway over the rising generation in the same manner, and thus it is that the teachings of the Classics have been perpetuated.

The works are replete with the practical observations which distinguish the writings of the sages, and their principal object in writing them was to compare the misgovernment and anarchy which characterized their own times with the excellent and peaceful reigns of the ancient monarchs, and thereby to enforce those principles of good government on which they consider the welfare of the State to depend. The writings are interspersed with examples of ancient imperial ordinances, mandates addressed to the high ministers of State, plans and instructions prepared by statesmen for the guidance of their sovereign and the princes, imperial proclamations admonishing the people, and vows taken before God by the monarchs when going out to battle. The principles of administration laid down are founded on a regard for the welfare of the people, and would, if carried out in their perfection, insure universal prosperity. "If the exemplary ruler would teach and govern his people, let him employ eulogism and authority. Let him rather not execute the laws against criminals than punish an innocent person. Let him render his children virtuous, and

preserve them from whatever can injure life and health. A virtue that delights in preserving the lives of the subjects gains the hearts of the people."

The seeds of all things that are valuable in the estimation of the Chinese are found in the Classics. They form the basis of their political system, their history, and their religious rites; and from them are evolved the principles of their "tactics, music, and astronomy." Here we have expressions drawn either from the recesses of feeling or descriptive of the state of public affairs, unexpected metaphors and illustrations, exemplary precepts of government, and clear intimations of the knowledge of the one true God; which, together with the acknowledged antiquity of the works, encircle them with a lasting interest. Upon a careful perusal of these ancient writings, one cannot but be convinced that these Chinese moralists, though destitute of any adequate knowledge of the one true God, began at the right place in their endeavors to reform their countrymen, and that they did not fully succeed was owing to causes beyond their reforming power. They displayed remarkable originality of thought, inflexibility of purpose, and extensiveness of views, and are among the greatest men Asia has ever produced. Their writings not only prove them to have been masterly dialecticians, but show the shrewd insight they had of the character of their countrymen when they began as reformers and teachers by reviving the instructions of the ancients, and then gradually merging these into their *own* views. Had they acted otherwise, their moral teachings would have been lost entirely. Their writings abound in irony and ridicule directed against vice and oppression; and, clothed in their *reductio ad absurdum* garb, they sweep every thing before them.

The characters of the four sages present remarkable exceptions in the Asiatic world, and they were ready to sacrifice every thing to their principles. "I love life," says Mencius, "and I love justice; but, if I cannot preserve both, I would give up life and hold fast justice." Again: "Although I love life, there is that which I love more than life—goodness: although I hate death, there is that which I hate more than death—wickedness." In native vigor and carelessness of the reproaches of their compatriots, they closely resembled the more eminent disciples of our Lord. These philosophers divided

mankind into three classes: Those who are good *without* instruction, those who are good *after* instruction, and those who are bad *in spite of* instruction. Their estimate of human nature is high, they believing that it was originally good, and that "all men have compassionate hearts—all feel ashamed of vice." They exhibited the nature of human virtue in the conduct of an ideal man, who, having arrived at self-completion, conducts to the completion of other men and things. "He descends to nothing low or improper. In a high station, he feels no contempt for his inferiors; in a humble situation, he fawns not upon his superiors. He corrects himself and blames not others. He satisfies completely all the requirements of duty in the various relations of society and government. He murmurs against neither heaven nor man. Hence, he dwells at ease, entirely awaiting the will of God." This is their standard of excellence; but, alas! unattainable by human strength *alone.*

Among the leading features of their philosophy are subordination to superiors and upright dealing with our fellow-men. Political morality must be founded on private rectitude. Filial duty, reverence for the ancient books and rulers, and adherence to old usages, are duties of prime importance. Their philosophy recognizes uprightness as the basis of all things, and harmony as the all-pervading principle of the universe. When there are no movements of the passions, this is equilibrium or uprightness; when the passions have been moved and they all act in due degree, this is harmony. When uprightness and harmony have been extended to the utmost, the universe will be at rest; and when they exist in perfection, there will result sincerity. Sincerity is *absolute* when *intelligence* results from *it*, and *acquired* when *it* results from *intelligence.* Sincerity conducts to self-completion, and possesses all the qualities which can be predicated of heaven and earth.

Man has received his nature from heaven; and, the nature being moral, conduct in accordance therewith constitutes what is right and true. By virtue of this moral nature, man becomes constituted a law to himself; over it he requires to exercise a jealous watchfulness; and, as he possesses it, he becomes invested with the highest dignity and power. A strict accordance therewith is called the *path*, and the regulation of the path is called *instruction.* The path of duty is to be pursued

every-where and at all times, while yet the secret spring is in the Heaven-conferred nature. "The path is not far from man. If man tries to pursue a path that is far from him it cannot be *the path.* When man cultivates to the utmost the moral principles of his nature and exercises them on the principle of reciprocity, he is in the path. Do to others nothing that you would not have them do to you."

Man is *by nature good.* If the heart be once rectified, little else will remain to be done; and then it is that we recognize the *goodness* of the nature. Man is born for uprightness; and, since the nature of man is good, there are in him the natural principles of righteousness, benevolence, propriety, and apprehension of moral truth. The several passions and affections, which are distinct both from benevolence and self-love, in general contribute and lead us to public good as really as to private. There is, furthermore, a principle of reflection in man, by which he distinguishes between, approves and disapproves, his own actions. Man follows his nature to a certain degree, but not entirely; his actions do not come up to the whole of what his nature leads him to; and he often violates his nature. There is no part of himself which a man does not love; and as he loves all, so he must nourish all. In order to determine whether his manner of nourishing be good, let him decide *by reflection where* it should be applied.

The immense love of the philosophers for humanity dominated over all their other sentiments, and has made of their philosophy a system of social perfectionating which has never been equaled. It sets forth the higher and more extensive principles of moral science which come into use in the conduct of government. Its object is "to illustrate illustrious virtue, to love the people, and to rest in the highest excellence." The method reaches from the cultivation of the person to the tranquilization of the empire; and the intermediate series involves the investigation of things, the completion of knowledge, the sincerity of the thoughts, the rectifying of the heart, the cultivation of the person, the regulation of the family, and the government of the State, culminating in the empire tranquilized.

The object of government is to make its subjects good and happy. Rulers should love the people, governing only for the

good of those over whom they are exalted by Heaven. They have no divine right but what springs from the discharge of their duty. The insisting on personal excellence in all who have authority in the family, the State, and the empire, is a great moral and social principle. This excellence must be rooted in the state of the heart, and be the natural outgrowth of sincerity. "As a man thinks in his heart so is he."

In the administration of government the ruler is exhorted to cultivate his own character, to honor men of virtue and talent, to love his relatives, to respect the great ministers, to treat the whole body of officials in a kind and considerate manner, to cherish the mass of the people as children, to encourage all classes of artisans, to show indulgence toward men from a distance, and to affectionately cherish the princes of the empire. Hence are evolved five duties of universal application: Those between sovereign and minister, husband and wife, father and son, elder and younger brother, and friends. These are carried into effect by the three virtues—knowledge, benevolence, and energy; and the one thing by which these virtues are practiced is sincerity, which is benevolence by which a man's self is perfected, and knowledge by which he perfects others.

Filial duty figures prominently in the administration of government, and holds the highest place in the list of virtues and obligations. It is the root of virtue and the stem from which instruction in moral principles springs forth. Its observance is inculcated upon children from their earliest years, and hardly can a blacker crime be conceived of than disobedience to parents. Filial duty commences in attention to parents, is continued through a series of services rendered the State, and is completed in the reflection of glory upon our ancestors by the honorable elevation of ourselves. "When ministers disregard the monarch, then there is no supremacy; when the maxims of the sages are set aside, then the law is abrogated; and so they who disregard filial duty are as though they had no parents. These three evils prepare the way for universal rebellion."

The will of the people is the supreme power in the State, and the relation between ruler and people is clearly referred to the will of God. Heaven having produced the people, appointed for them rulers and teachers, in order that they should

be assisting to God. Heaven gives the empire, but Heaven does not speak. It therefore evinces its will only by man's personal conduct and his conduct of affairs; therefore Heaven sees and hears according as the people see and hear. These principles, as exemplified in the classics, are indisputable; but their application must be attended with difficulty. The sentiments, however, have operated powerfully to compel the good behavior of the rulers of the empire for more than two thousand years, and the government of China would, were it not for them, have been a grinding despotism. The people are feared by their rulers on account of the great popularity and justice of these expressions, for in them it is claimed that the people are ready and anxious to be governed by a good ruler. "If the ruler be righteous the people will flock to him, and, though he wished to abdicate, he could not."

The two chief elements of benevolent rule are that the people be made well off, and that they be educated. When the people have been made numerous through righteous government, then enrich them; and when they have been enriched, then teach them. Upright rulers will secure peaceful administrations, by which the first step is attained; admirable regulations for agriculture and commerce are then proposed, by the faithful carrying out of which the second step is attained, and with this attained the people are fitted to profitably devote themselves to learning, which they could not do were their lives embittered by miserable poverty. And as these ancient philosophers proceed in their discussion of these two elements, and gradually develop the principles involved, we are astonished to find that their minds comprehend, especially in the latter one, what was not advocated by minds of our own prided civilizations until twenty-four centuries later.

The classics abundantly confirm the conclusion that the ancient Chinese had a knowledge of God, who frequently appears in them as "The Ruler of the Universe," "The Supreme Ruler," "The Great and Sovereign God," and "The Bright and Glorious God." He appears especially as the Ruler of men, giving them all things that they can desire. In producing the multitudes of the people he gives to them a good nature: but few of them are able to keep it so. He is perfectly just, and will of himself injure no one. He combines

omniscience, omnipresence, and omnipotence. He watches particularly over the conduct of rulers, while they reverence Him and administer their high duties in his fear, and with reference to his will, taking his ways as their pattern. He maintains them, smells the sweet savor of their offerings, and blesses them and their people with abundance and general prosperity. When they become impious and negligent he punishes them, takes from them the throne, and appoints others in their place. Sometimes he appears to array himself in terrors, and the course of his providence is altered. The evil in the State is ascribed to him. He is called unpitying. But this is his strange work, in judgment, and to call men to repentance. He hates no one, and it is not he who really causes the evil time; that is a consequence of forsaking the old and right ways of government. Sacrifices were offered to God by the sovereigns in praise, supplication, and thanksgiving. They were preceded by fasting and various purifications. Libations of fragrant spirits were made, and the victims correspond to what we find were offered to God in the Bible times.

While the ancient Chinese thus believed in God, and thus conceived of him, they believed in other spirits under him. These frequently made their appearance on earth, and some of them were good and some evil.

A belief in the immortality of the soul has been a characteristic of the Chinese from their first appearance in history. Many persons, who had led holy lives, are represented as being "on high, bright in heaven, ascending and descending on the right and left of God." Though the Chinese have always believed in a future state, yet it is portrayed as a future for the better, for these ancients appear to have shrunk from the contemplation of an eternity of woe. They believed, however, that in the future the felicity of souls would depend upon their probationary lives; those who had led the holier lives being nearer the throne of God, while the evil-doers would be further from the throne, and enjoy a felicity diminishing in proportion to the wickedness of their lives.

As moralists, the writers of the classics stand almost unequaled. In their view of human nature, there is nothing contrary to the teachings of our Christian Scriptures. It does

not cover what we know to be the whole duty of man, yet it is defective rather than erroneous. They had no means of obtaining an adequate knowledge of God or of the fall of man; nevertheless God is always spoken of as the Supreme Ruler of the universe, through whom all things have been, are, and will be, and in whom are involved the divine personality and supremacy. They were without the light which revelation sheds on the whole field of human duty, and the sanctions which it discloses of a future state of retribution. They, therefore, indicate no ardent wish to penetrate futurity and ascertain what comes after death.

Compared with the precepts of Greek and Roman sages, the general tendency of these writings is good; while in their general adaptation to the race and the society of the Orient of their times, they exceed even those of western philosophers. Instead of dealing exclusively in sublime and unattainable descriptions of virtue, these sages taught rather how the common intercourse of life was to be maintained, and in this respect their writings are distinguished from those of all philosophers in other countries. The classics have, furthermore, exerted such an incomparable influence over so many billions of minds, that the works of Greek and Roman genius appear *merely* as monuments of literature, while these writings of China's sages are invested with an interest which no book but the Bible can claim. One of their most remarkable features is their entire freedom from any description or language that can debase or vitiate the heart. The classics of the Hindus, Greeks, and Romans teem with glowing narrations of amours and obscenities; and the purity of the Chinese classics in this respect is most remarkable. Their moral tone is unexcelled, and there is nothing in them that will not bear the most scrupulous perusal.

The period that gave birth to the classics was one of great turmoil—one of social and political demoralization. Wars were rife between the several States into which the empire had become divided, and degeneracy and disintegration pervaded all of them. The sages, therefore, wrote their works because "the world was fallen into decay, and right principles had dwindled away." They directed their maledictions particularly against vice among the rulers of the people who thus

came to fear the books on account of their popularity, and were consequently compelled to administer their rule in a far less tyrannical manner than they otherwise would have done. The morals of the empire were, at this time, in a deplorable condition. The teachings of a system of philosophy resembling, yet worse than, the epicurean had been commenced by the philosopher, Yang Chu, the substance of whose writings was: "Let us eat and drink; let us live in pleasure; gratify the senses; get servants and maidens, music, beauty, and wine. When the day is insufficient, carry it on through the night. For the being ends at death."

This system of philosophy had gained a footing, and was rapidly hurling the empire to destruction. Rulers and people grasped eagerly after its seductive teachings; and, in the course of a few years, China witnessed some of the most licentious times that have marked a nation's history. Then fell emperors; then came wars from within and without, and pestilence. The land was drenched in blood, and the empire was divided into innumerable States, carrying on an endless warfare with one another, when suddenly there glimmered through the dreadful darkness of those times the teachings of the classics. Their immortalized philosophers traveled over the country doing good among the people; rebuking the warring princes; exhorting to virtue and a unity of the empire; to purity in private and public life; yet always preserved from the wrath of princes by the reverence for them that was rapidly taking hold of the people. Benevolence, righteousness, propriety, and fidelity were inculcated. A bulwark of human nature formed for virtue was raised up. The current was stayed. The empire became united. Ameliorating influences pervaded society; and the philosophers of the classics did all that men, without an adequate knowledge of God, could have done to improve their fellows. The people were directed into the paths of truth and duty, and the empire was passed on for twenty-four hundred years further; and here she stands, wrapped in reverence at the feet of those philosophers to whom she owes her greatness and her existence, and lost in admiration at the tones of those voices that have come down through twenty-four centuries.

The classics are as remarkable for their beautiful solemnity

and lordly composition as they are for their intrinsic worth as moral guides. The great sages and philosophers have here condensed the grandest utterances of their wisdom, and the severest lessons of their virtue. The pathos of some portions of the works will draw floods of tears, the agony depicted in other portions will cause the reader to tremble in terror; while the calm, gentle flow of still other portions will bear him into a peaceful sea of oblivion, where he remains entranced until the waves of recollection wash him back upon the shores of reality. Lessons of virtue and morality are blended with exhortations to rulers and people to clothe themselves in humility, to search diligently after learning, and to repose in the pure excellence of virtue. "Grieve not that men know you not, but rather be grieved that you are ignorant of men." "Learning without reflection will profit nothing; reflection without learning will leave the mind uneasy and miserable." "Without virtue, both riches and honor are like the passing cloud. No man esteems virtue as he esteems pleasure." "The perfect man is never satisfied with himself; he that is satisfied with himself is not perfect." "Sin in a virtuous man is like an eclipse; all men gaze at it and it passes away. He mends, and the world stands in admiration of his fall."

The good that has been wrought by these writings is almost incredible; and when we consider that they were in those ancient times intrusted to silk and tablets of wood, bamboo and stone, and that they were so miraculously preserved from destruction during the long reign of the infuriated emperor, Chin Shih Huang, who issued the proclamation for the burning of the books and the destruction of the *literati* in 212 B. C., we are constrained to believe that a designing Providence alone permitted them to be transmitted to posterity unimpaired. They have been cherished by the emperors, the national historiographers, and the imperial music masters. They have promoted the cause of good government and virtue; they give us faithful pictures of the politics of the country and the social habits of the people, and, above all, they have exerted a wondrous influence for good throughout the masses of the empire. At their antiquity we gaze in astonishment, and their primitive beauty binds us fast in admiration. They echo through myriad ages the customs, lives, trials, joys, and fortunes of the

most ancient nation in existence in its integrity, and cast rays of light upon centuries when the world was slumbering. But is there no dark side to this picture? Has the government of China been perfect during the past two thousand years, or have her masses been renowned for their virtuous manners? Has her civilization not remained almost stationary for twenty-four centuries? Has she not been lashed by intestine wars? Have no foreign hordes swept through the land? Have no dynasties risen and fallen in seas of blood? Has the history of any nation been so crowded with battles, sieges, and massacres as China's? Alas, that we cannot answer these questions as we could wish! And why? The philosophers of the classics were without the divine writ. They had no means of obtaining an adequate knowledge of the living God. The Redeemer had not yet sacrificed himself for lost humanity, and their minds were not enlightened by the splendor of the revelation.

The authors of the Old Testament were possessed of a living knowledge of the Supreme Being; the authors of the New Testament were flooded with the light of revelation. The Almighty, in his infinite mercy, has cast our lot among Christian nations. Are the governments of those nations perfect? Have their millions attained to the pure excellence of virtue? Have sanguinary wars, in which very brothers have gloated in each other's kindred blood, been wanting? What then? Do we assume that man is no better off for having received the will of God? or do we venture to compare that precious writ with the writings of the sages? The Bible reflects the mind of God. In it we trace his grandeur and his simplicity, his exaltedness and his condescension. In his wondrous love for fallen man the Almighty has here revealed his will. He has sacrificed his only Son, and, having placed before us the standard, he leads us onward step by step toward perfection. But men are prone to sin, hence the evils that befall us. In exact proportion, however, as we follow his teachings and throw ourselves upon him, we are blessed and prospered. Hence it is that Christian countries have progressed so far beyond the civilization of China.

Until within a very few years China has been without the Bible. Her classics have been the sole guide of her masses,

and men being prone to sin, many evils have befallen the empire. Her civilization has remained stationary, for she has been without the revivifying influences of the Gospel. Her philosophers submitted excellent plans and ideals, but for the execution of and compliance with them they depended upon human strength alone. On account of this, then, it was that they failed in bringing their countrymen up to the standard of our Christian civilization. Not that we would say that they could have done better than they did, for we believe they could not. Destitute as they were of the divine word, they did all that could have been done by unaided mortals to improve their fellows. They reared a monument of filial piety, mutual forbearance, improvement of self and fellows, human virtue, ideal government, private and public rectitude, uprightness, sincerity, morality, and humility; then drew their fellow-men by cords of family affection, kindness, and benevolence to gaze upon it through the vista of righteousness, propriety, knowledge, energy, peace, purity, fidelity, truth, duty, and religion. What else was wanting to give life to this vast fabric? Nothing but the moving spirit of the Almighty and the permeating influences of the Gospel.

The missionaries of the cross are at work, but the field is boundless. Occasional spires point heavenward, as ships upon the deep. A few thousand have been saved from among these twenty score of millions. The field is too vast for the number of the laborers. The progress is slow, almost discouraging; but the energy and perseverance of these self-sacrificing philanthropists in a measure atone for the fewness of their numbers. They have left home, friends, familiar scenes, Church endearments, their native civilization, and all the Christian influences under which they have been brought up, to sacrifice themselves for the Redeemer's cause in this distant land. In their devotedness they travel through the interior, scattering the words of salvation broadcast, and, at the risk of their lives, lifting up their voices in the multitudes and pointing toward the bleeding cross. And how many have nobly perished with that immortal, "Father, forgive them; for they know not what they do," upon their lips! Would that Christian nations would redouble their efforts and send more such laborers to this field to bring to these perishing millions the Bread of Life, and rescue

them from an eternal death! Let the lands of our nativity exert themselves to make some slight recompense for the innumerable blessings which a merciful Father has showered upon them, and strain every nerve to hasten the glorious time when salvation shall be within the reach of all. *Then* will the huge idol of Chinese superiority and superstition be shattered; *then* will China take her place in the family of occidental civilizations; *then*, clothed in righteousness, will she sit at the feet of Jesus; and *then* will a new generation of thinkers arise, to whom the classics will be a study, but not a guide.

## Art. VII.—THE THIRTY YEARS' WAR.

Although peace had been secured to the Protestants of Germany, by the treaty of Augsburg, in 1555, the state of the country was still unsettled, and new disturbances were anticipated. The Papists, who had lost so much ground, were waiting the opportunity to recover something back; while the Protestants were intent on keeping all they had gained, and on making, if possible, further encroachments.

Charles V. was succeeded by his brother Ferdinand, and he by his son Maximilian, both of them amiable and upright rulers, who were disposed to observe their treaty obligations, and to regard their subjects, whether Protestants or Catholics, with kindness and impartiality.

Rudolph II., son of Maximilian, was a different character. He was a bigoted Catholic and a persecutor, who involved himself and his house in great trials, and died leaving little of imperial authority except the name. He was succeeded by his brother Matthias, who had long been in contest with Rudolph, and had taken from him most of his dominions. But *his* reign was not peaceful or prosperous, and having no direct heir to succeed him, the government descended to Ferdinand of Gratz, another branch of the Hapsburg family, known in history as Ferdinand II. He was crowned at Frankfort in 1619. He had before been appointed, though not inaugurated, king of Bohemia. The Bohemians were unwilling to accept him as their king, and chose in his stead the elector palatine, Fred-

erick V. But Ferdinand succeeded in driving Frederick into exile, and was at length acknowledged king of Bohemia. This Ferdinand had been educated by the Jesuits, was guided chiefly by their councils, and was, for long years, a principal cause of the troubles which affected Germany.

The Thirty Years' War originated in Bohemia, in 1618, a little previous to the commencement of Ferdinand's reign. Its origin was on this wise: By the existing laws, as understood by the Protestants, they had a right to build new churches, not only in their own provinces, but wherever they were needed throughout the kingdom. In accordance with this right, two churches were erected in the year 1617, one of which was torn down by the Catholics, while the other was closed, and its proprietors imprisoned. An appeal was made to the existing authorities; but these, so far from restraining the aggressors, the rather encouraged them, and Ferdinand, though not yet king of Bohemia, was very severe upon the Protestants.

Enraged by these proceedings, a convention of Protestant delegates assembled at Prague in May, 1618, determined to preserve their own rights, and to take vengeance on their enemies. In this assembly were several Catholics, and among them two, Martinitz and Slavata, who, by various oppressive acts, had made themselves particularly obnoxious. These the Protestant delegates seized, and hurled them out of a three story window. The men were not killed, but a great excitement followed. Anticipating a retribution, the Protestants flew to arms, and, under direction of Count Thorn, took possession of every city in Bohemia which was not occupied by the imperial troops. They had a brave ally in the person of Count Ernest of Mansfeld, who came to their assistance with three thousand men.

Count Thorn advanced with his army upon Vienna, and fired even upon the imperial castle, where Ferdinand had taken up his quarters. The situation of Ferdinand at this time seemed almost desperate. His enemies talked of confining him in a convent, and training up his children in the Protestant faith. But his own firmness did not forsake him; and he was speedily and unexpectedly relieved by the arrival of a body of imperial cavalry. Count Thorn was obliged to retire; and Fer-

dinand hastened to Frankfort, where he was chosen emperor of Germany, as before stated, in 1619.

Sad for Bohemia was the punishment which the new emperor and king soon inflicted on it. Forty-eight of the Protestant leaders were taken prisoners on the same day, and twenty-seven of them were condemned to death. Their property was confiscated, as well as that of many others, among whom was the brave Count Thorn. By degrees the Protestant clergy were all driven out of Bohemia, and an order was issued that no person should be tolerated there who did not adhere to the Catholic religion. It is stated that thirty-thousand families were at this time forced to leave the country, the most of whom went to Saxony and Brandenburg.

To all human appearance, the contest now seemed to be about decided. Bohemia was subjugated, its late king was dethroned and in exile, and Ferdinand had every thing in his own way. But Count Mansfeld was still left to the Protestants, who was an efficient helper, and who employed his forces somewhat independently, as Providence might direct. In a short time he had collected an army of twenty thousand men, and was able to confront Count Tilly, whom the emperor had left to keep the field. Mansfeld did not attempt, however, to recapture Bohemia, but marched his forces into other parts of Germany. In connection with Christian, Duke of Brunswick, he spread desolation among the Catholic bishops on the Rhine. After devastating the Rhenish provinces, they marched together into Holland, and joined the brave Netherlanders in their struggle against the Spaniards.

It now seemed as though peace might be restored to Germany if the victors were inclined to act with moderation. But Ferdinand had no thought of halting in the midst of his revolutionary movements. He considered himself as called upon in Providence (to use his own language) "to crush all the seditious factions which had been stirred up chiefly by the heresy of Calvinism;" and he recognized in the success which had thus far crowned his efforts an intimation that God was with him. He succeeded, at this time, in getting one more vote in the college of electors, which placed the majority in the hands of the Catholics.

In these circumstances the Protestants, not being able by

their disjointed efforts to maintain their ground against the Catholics, chose Christian IV., king of Denmark, for their commander in chief. He promised them effective assistance, and England did the same. On the other hand, the emperor found a powerful helper in Albert of Wallenstein, a man of vast wealth and unbounded ambition, who, encouraged by the stars, in which he had great confidence, thought himself able to carry the whole country with him. He attached himself to the emperor, and marched with a troop of cavalry, raised at his own expense, to assist him in an expedition against Venice. For this and for other services Wallenstein received, in 1622, the territory of Friedland, in Bohemia, together with the title of duke. He also purchased about sixty estates of the Bohemian nobility, which had been confiscated after the battle of Prague, and thus made a great addition to his wealth. He soon had an army of no less than fifty thousand men, to be employed in the service of the emperor. But as it had been raised and equipped at his own expense, he had it under his entire control.

Wallenstein was born to command. His eyes were bright and piercing, and his figure proud and lofty, so that his very appearance inspired reverence and awe. In the autumn of 1625 he marched with his new army into lower Saxony. Count Tilly, though engaged in the same cause, was afraid of him and refused to join him. In 1626 he defeated Count Mansfeld on the bridge of Dorsey, and this able defender of the Protestants soon after died. In the same year died his friend, the Duke of Brunswick, and thus were the Protestants deprived of their two ablest generals. At the same time, the king of Denmark, who had been appointed their commander in chief, was able to do but little for them. He was not born to be a military leader, and in the same year was defeated by Tilly, and lost all his artillery. In the following year (1627) Wallenstein marched against him, and drove him out of Germany. It was now seriously contemplated to dethrone him, and appoint Ferdinand king of Denmark.

Meanwhile the army of Wallenstein had increased to one hundred thousand men, and the princes of Germany—even the Catholic princes—were afraid of him. Tilly hated him, for he monopolized for himself all the fruits and the credit of the

joint victories. The emperor himself was no longer able to control him. He lived in a style of pomp and splendor exceeding that of the greatest monarchs, while thousands of wretched beings around him were literally dying of starvation. At the same time, he brought heavy accounts against the emperor for sums which he had advanced in prosecuting the war. His charges amounted to more than three millions of florins, which the emperor being unable to pay, he made over to his proud ally the territories of the duke of Mecklenburg in consideration of the debt. Wallenstein thus became a prince of the empire.

From Mecklenburg Wallenstein turned his eyes to the neighboring province of Pomerania. He wished to get possession of the city of Stralsund, that he might establish a garrison there. But the citizens of Stralsund refused to receive him; and, being assisted by the kings of Denmark and Sweden, they were able to make a formidable resistance. This moved the wrath of the imperious warrior, and he is said to have given utterance to the following oath: "If Stralsund be linked with chains to the very heavens, I swear it shall fall." He was unable, however, to take the city, and having remained before it several weeks and lost twelve thousand of his men, he was obliged to abandon the object and retire.

At this time the king of Denmark desired peace; and, contrary to all expectation, Wallenstein advised the emperor to grant it. The probability is that, being now a prince of the empire, he did not wish to destroy further the power of the German princes. A very advantageous peace was concluded in 1629, by which the king of Denmark recovered all his lands, without being obliged to bear the expenses of the war. But this peace was of short duration, and could hardly be called a peace while it continued. The Roman Catholics thought the opportunity too favorable to be neglected, and resolved to push their claims as far as possible. They demanded of the Protestants the restitution of all the ecclesiastical benefices of which they had taken possession since the treaty of Passau in 1552, and the emperor decided that their claims must be granted. "At this order," says a distinguished historian, "the Protestants were completely paralyzed; while the more short-sighted of their enemies hailed it with delight." It produced, as we shall see, not only the greatest confusion, but unutterable calamities all

over Germany. To enforce it the two grand armies of the emperor were kept in the field, and continued their depredations on friends and foes. Wallenstein's army in particular, which had always lived on plunder, caused so much disaster and ruin, that the emperor himself could no longer shut his eyes or his ears against it. His brother, Leopold, wrote him a long letter giving him a most harrowing description of the pillage, the conflagrations, the murderous outrages, and other shameful oppressions which the army inflicted upon the peaceful inhabitants. Such testimony overbalanced all the arguments which the friends of Wallenstein had hitherto urged; and at an assembly of the electoral princes, in the summer of 1630, it was demanded that he should be deprived of the chief command, and to this the emperor was obliged to consent. To the surprise of all, the haughty Wallenstein submitted to the order. He had learned from the stars that it was now time for him to retire. He quietly withdrew to his duchy of Friedland, there to await the progress of events in Germany.

The period on which we are now advancing introduces us to one of the noblest monarchs and bravest warriors of the seventeenth century—Gustavus Adolphus, king of Sweden. In 1611 he succeeded to the Swedish throne; and, influenced partly by injuries received from the emperor and from Wallenstein, partly by compassion for his suffering and all but prostrated brethren—the Protestants of Germany—but more, perhaps, by what he regarded as his manifest destiny in Providence, he declared war against the emperor Ferdinand. On the 24th of June, 1630, he landed on the coast of Pomerania with fifteen thousand Swedes. No sooner had he touched the shore than he dropped on his knees in prayer, and his example was followed by his whole army. With but small and limited means, he had undertaken a mighty enterprise; and how could he succeed in it but by the help of the Almighty? By the Catholics of Germany his coming was regarded with indifference, and even contempt. He was called "the petty king of the north," and "the snow king, who would soon disappear under the rays of the imperial sun." Even the Protestant princes of the empire seemed quite undetermined as to the manner of receiving their new ally. Some were afraid, and dreaded the vengeance of the emperor; some were jealous

of all foreign interference; while others preferred to remain faithful to the existing government, rather than incur the hazard of a change. In vain Gustavus urged them all to unite with him. "Our situation," he said, "is like that of a vessel in a storm. In such case it does not suffice for a few only to labor for the general safety, while the rest fold their arms and look quietly on. If we would succeed we must all work together, and each must perform with his might the particular part assigned to him." But the Protestants in general possessed no such spirit of earnest union, nor did they exhibit that conscientiousness of purpose which was so needful in their circumstances.

Gustavus, being reinforced by a large number of enlisted troops, advanced with rapid marches through Pomerania, beating and putting to flight all the imperialists that stood in his way. He was anxious to press forward to Magdeburg, a Protestant city, which was already besieged by the forces of Count Tilly; but he was hindered by the indifference and opposition of Protestants, until the enemy were successful and the city was lost. And in the sack of this city were witnessed some of the more terrible incidents of the Thirty Years' War. Men, women, and children, the aged and the young, all were massacred alike. Infants at the breasts of their mothers were seized, stabbed, and hurled into the flaming ruins of the city. This scene of horror continued from ten o'clock in the morning until night, nor would Tilly give orders even then that the butchery should cease.

After the capture of Magdeburg, Tilly was very anxious to have a drawn battle with the king of Sweden; but Gustavus was not ready yet. He wished first to restore his cousins, the banished dukes of Mecklenburg, to their rightful possessions, which had been taken from them and given to Wallenstein, and in this he was successful.

Tilly next turned his eyes upon the rich province of Saxony, and advanced upon Leipsic. This brought the elector of Saxony to his senses. He had hitherto stood aloof from Gustavus, but now he joined him without reserve. He entered into an alliance offensive and defensive, and united his army to that of the king. The battle of Leipsic immediately followed, in which Gustavus was victorious. It was a hotly contested

struggle. Tilly lost seven thousand of his men, and came very near losing his life.

This victory was of great importance to the king of Sweden every way. It gave him confidence and strength, and established his reputation as a warrior throughout Europe. From this time he pressed forward more boldly and rapidly, achieving in his progress one continued triumph. The most important cities fell into his hands, some of them voluntarily, and others after a slight resistance. Tilly, though still at the head of an army much more numerous than that of the king, was unwilling to attack him. But after a time he was forced into a battle in Bavaria, where he was mortally wounded and lost his life. The greater part of Bavaria now fell into the hands of Gustavus, and the elector was forced to seek refuge in Ratisbon. The Saxons meanwhile had entered Bohemia and taken Prague.

Ferdinand had now lost the fruits of a twelve years' war. And, worse than this, he found himself threatened even in his patrimonial estates. This was a crisis for which he was in no way prepared. It came upon him like a thunder-clap. In these circumstances he saw but one means of extrication, and that was the recall of Wallenstein.

Nor was this an easy task. This proud man, offended and indignant at being dismissed from the service, now lived in mortified retirement, though in great splendor, brooding over the past. He received the emperor's deputies coldly, and it was only after the most earnest persuasion that he consented to raise for his imperial master an army of thirty thousand men, and of these he was to have the sole and supreme command. He also received additional largesses and promises from the emperor—enough to satisfy his almost boundless ambition.

Wallenstein's first exploit was to recapture Prague, and drive the Saxons out of Bohemia. Joined by the duke of Bavaria, he next made an advance upon Nuremberg, one of the most considerable places in the possession of Gustavus. Here both armies intrenched themselves, each intending, by disease and famine, to force the other to quit its stronghold. Tired of the delay, and sick of the distress and ruin which he saw around him, Gustavus at length abandoned his position, and marching

with sound of trumpet past the enemy, who dared not attack him, he retired into Bavaria.

Wallenstein now left his encampment, set fire to it, and marched into Saxony. The king hastened to meet him and afford relief, and reached Nuremberg on the 11th of November. The good people welcomed him as a deliverer from heaven, and even offended him by the fulsomeness of their adulations. "I fear," said he, "that God will punish me for the folly of these people. It seems as if they were making an idol of me."

As the weather was becoming cold, Wallenstein did not think it advisable to commence hostilities before spring. Gustavus, however, had no thought of delay. He advanced immediately to Weissenfels, and on the 15th of November took his position in front of Wallenstein's army, near Lutzen. On the morning of the battle a thick fog covered the plain, and the Swedes sang Luther's celebrated hymn, "A mighty rock is our God;" also a hymn composed by the king, "Fear not, thou little flock." After a short prayer, when the sun was just emerging from behind the clouds, the king mounted his horse and said, "Now onward! May our God direct us! Help me, O God, this day to fight for the glory of thy name!" Then throwing aside his cuirass, with the words, "God is my shield," he led his troops at once to the front of the imperial army, which was intrenched on the paved road leading from Lutzen to Leipsic. Here occurred one of the most deadly fights that ever took place in the history of the world. I have no time or inclination to trace the particulars of it. Suffice it to say that the Swedes were left in possession of the field, but their beloved monarch lost his life. Owing to his short-sightedness, he was led to advance too near to a squadron of the imperial horse, where he received a shot in the arm and another in the back. With the exclamation, "My God! My God!" he fell from his horse, and was dragged by the stirrup some distance on the ground. His corpse was not discovered till the next day, when it was found so disfigured by the hoofs of the horses, and covered with blood issuing from eleven wounds, that it could hardly be recognized. It was carried first to Weissenfels, and thence, by the desire of the queen—who had followed her royal consort into Germany—it was removed to Stockholm, where it was buried.

Thus passed away, in the thirty-eighth year of his age, Gusta-

vus Adolphus, one of the best and bravest soldiers and sovereigns that ever lived. His courage was the result of his faith. He trusted in God, prayed to him, and gave him the glory of all his achievements. In this respect he resembled Joshua, David, Judas Maccabæus; and, in more recent times, the prince of Orange, Oliver Cromwell, and our own Washington. The Germans do well to honor the memory of their great deliverer. A worthy monument marks the spot where he fell; the day of his death is devoutly celebrated; and a society for the spread of the Gospel, bearing his name, is scattering its blessings throughout the earth.

Gustavus Adolphus did not live to close the war in Germany; but he inflicted blows which hastened its termination, and is worthy to be regarded as, under God, the Protestants' deliverer. After his death the Swedish Council, to whom was intrusted the guardianship of his daughter, resolved to continue the war, and appointed his friend, Chancellor Oxenstiern, to fill his place.

Wallenstein, who might have availed himself of this critical moment to push the war to a conclusion, was mysteriously inactive. He busied himself, through the winter, in trying and executing some of his principal officers to whom he attributed the loss of the late battle. He then recruited and reorganized his army; but instead of marching against the Swedes he went into Silesia, where he captured old Count Thorn, one of the early leaders in the war. But instead of executing him, as every one expected, he gave him his liberty.

Bavaria was at this time hard pressed by the Swedish generals, and Wallenstein was entreated to hasten to its relief, but he declined doing so. Indeed, the old man was half dead with the gout, and had become an object of suspicion to the emperor, and of hatred to the German princes generally. A conspiracy was secretly formed against him, and he was murdered at the house of the burgomaster of Eger in the winter of 1634. His vast estates were confiscated after his death, a portion being given to his enemies, but the greater part retained by the emperor.

Ferdinand, son of the emperor and king of Rome, was now placed at the head of the imperial army, and for a time he met with some success. He attacked the Swedes in Franconia and

defeated them. Twenty thousand of their troops were slain or captured, and among the latter was one of their generals. This was a stunning blow to the Protestants. Several of the Protestant princes, the elector of Saxony among the rest, made their peace with the emperor, hoping in this way to obtain some relief from their sufferings.

But divine Providence still guarded the cause of truth, and relief at length came from a quarter where it was least expected. The French minister, Richelieu, had long observed with satisfaction the misfortunes of the house of Austria, and the moment, he thought, had now come when he might vend his services to the Protestants of Germany at a profitable rate. While he was torturing and destroying the Huguenots of France, he would cripple the emperor by granting assistance to the Protestants of Germany. Accordingly he made a treaty with Chancellor Oxensteirn, regent of Sweden, by which efficient aid should be afforded. By the help of French money an army was raised, and placed under the command of the duke of Weimar. The Swedes had a brave leader in field-marshal Bannier, who attacked the Saxons—now the allies of Ferdinand—and entirely defeated them. The time had come, too, when Ferdinand himself, so long the principal disturber of Germany, must retire from the scene. He died on the 15th of February, 1637, at the age of fifty-nine, and was succeeded by his son, Ferdinand III.

From this period the war in Germany presents but a continuation of gloomy, disheartening scenes; for, wanting, as it did, a leader of noble genius, and influenced, as its agents were, by motives merely personal and selfish, its whole character assumed an ignoble and mercenary appearance. The duke of Weimar, who was at the head of the Protestant forces, made some important conquests along the Rhine. But he did not live long to enjoy them. He died, under a suspicion of poison, in 1639, at the age of thirty-five.

Efforts had been made for several years to bring about peace, but without success. Richelieu enjoyed seeing Germany cut to pieces by its own people, and encouraged the Protestants to carry on the war. Bannier, the Swedish general, had been committing terrible devastation in Bohemia, but he died in 1641. He was succeeded by Leonard Torstenson, who, though feeble

in body, was, next to Gustavus Adolphus, the most active and talented of any of the generals in this war. He had a series of successes over the imperial troops in Silesia and Moravia, and in one instance approached so near to Vienna as to make the emperor's capital tremble. In the autumn of 1642 he attacked the Austrian commander, Piccolomini, at Leipsic, and entirely defeated him. This was the greatest battle fought in the last period of the war.

In the spring of 1644 the Swedes advanced again into Germany, and defeated the imperial general, Gallas. In the following year Torstenson defeated the Austrian troops in Silesia, capturing one general and killing another. His victorious army now marched upon Vienna, and threatened its capture. But the health of Torstenson failed, and he was obliged to give up the command of the army.

He was succeeded by Gustavus Wrangle, who continued the war with success. He was assisted by a French army under Turenne and Condé. They subjected the whole of Bavaria, so that the elector was constrained to give up further hostilities. Several other of the German Catholic States were led to follow his example, and the emperor was left almost alone to contend with his enemies. The allies were preparing to follow up their successes, when the ears of all concerned were rejoiced with the happy news of peace from Westphalia.

Negotiations had been in progress for several years with a view to peace, but difficulties were encountered which it was hard to overcome. The foreign nations which had interfered, particularly the French and the Swedes, presented their claims, and these must be adjusted. Then the possessions of the several German States, and their relations to the empire, which had been much disturbed during the long struggle, came under discussion and must be settled. But the most difficult subject of all, that which had originated and protracted the war, was that of religion. There need have been no war, and it might have subsided at almost any time, if the Catholics had been willing to concede to the Protestants their religious liberty and rights, and these, in the end, they were obliged to concede. The decrees of the peace of Augsburg, passed in 1555, (and which were ample,) were eventually renewed. They were as follows:—

"1. The Protestants who follow the Confession of Augsburg shall, for the future, be considered as entirely exempt from the jurisdiction of the Roman pontiff, and from the authority and superintendence of Romish bishops.

"2. They are at perfect liberty to enact laws for themselves relating to their religious sentiments, discipline, and worship.

"3. All the inhabitants of the German empire shall be at liberty to judge for themselves in religious matters, and to join themselves to that Church whose doctrine and worship they think the purest and the most consonant to the spirit of pure Christianity.

"4. All those who shall injure or persecute any person under religious pretexts, or on account of their opinions, shall be proceeded against as enemies of the empire, invaders of its liberty, and disturbers of its peace."

It was further ordered in the new treaty of Westphalia that the Protestants should retain all the ecclesiastical property in lands and churches which they possessed in 1624; also, that no sovereign prince should oppress any of his subjects whose faith differed from his own; and that the imperial council should be composed equally of Protestants and Catholics.

By these regulations the peace of Westphalia became a fundamental law of the empire, and under it the minds of the people were gradually and generally tranquillized. The Protestants had gained all that they contended for, and the Catholics were obliged to sit down defeated and discouraged.

In this same memorable year (1648) the independence of the Dutch Republic was acknowledged in the treaty of Munster, and all claim of sovereignty over it, on the part of Spain, was forever relinquished.

## Art. VIII.—SYNOPSIS OF THE QUARTERLIES AND OTHERS OF THE HIGHER PERIODICALS.

### *American Quarterly Reviews.*

American Catholic Quarterly Review, January, 1877. (Philadelphia.)—1. The Liberalistic View of the Public School Question. 2. Pantheistic Theories of Soul. 3. The Bismarck of the Eighteenth Century. 4. Symbolism of the Cosmos. 5. Fashions and Principles in Poetry. 6. Can the Immateriality, Spirituality, and Immortality of the Human Soul be Demonstrated? 7. A Partisan Assault upon the Catholic Church.

Baptist Quarterly, January, 1877. (Philadelphia.)—1. Doctrinal Contents of Christ's Teaching in the Synoptical Gospels. 2. Modern Evolution Theories. 3. Comparative Religion. 4. The Life of Dr. Norman Macleod. 5. Baptist Doctrine and the Pulpit. 6. Life and Teachings of Sophocles.

National Quarterly Review, December, 1876. (New York.)—1. The Monism of Man. 2. The Influence of Geographical Position on Civilization in Egypt and Greece. 3. Lord Macaulay and his Writings. 4. The Comedies of Plautus. 5. Curiosities of Ancient French Jurisprudence. 6. The Physiology of Lunar Light. 7. The Ancient Scythians and their Descendants. 8. The Bombastic Element in Education.

New Englander, January, 1877. (New Haven.)—1. Chinese Immigration and Political Economy. 2. As to Roger Williams. 3. The Inward and the Outward; or, the Concrete in Nature, Morals, and Art. 4. Science in the Pentateuch. 5. The Folly of Atheism. 6. John Stuart Mill. 7. Woman's Voice in the Church. 8. Anderson's Histories of Foreign Missions. 9. Horace Bushnell. 10. The New Philosophy of Wealth.

New England Historical and Genealogical Register, January, 1877. (Boston.) 1. Sketch of the Life of the Hon. Millard Fillmore. 2. Probable Parentage of the Rev. Hugh and Messrs. John and Matthew Adams. 3. A Yankee Privateersman in Prison, 1777–9. 4. Notes on American History. 5. Hollis, N. H., in the War of the Revolution. 6. The Star Spangled Banner. 7. Record of the Boston Committee of Correspondence, Inspection, and Safety, 1776. 8. Services of New Hampshire during the Heroic Age of the Republic. 9. Memoranda from the Rev. William Cooper's Interleaved Almanacs, 1728–30. 10. Seals from the Jeffries Manuscripts. 11. Documents from the Gerrish Manuscripts. 12. Marriages in Pembroke, Mass., Solemnized by the Rev. Thomas Smith. 13. The Slave Trade in Massachusetts. 14. Records of Hull, Mass. 15. Record-Book of the First Church in Charlestown, Mass. 16. Thomas Hale, the Glover, of Newbury, Mass., 1635, and his Descendants. 17. Letter of the Secret Committee of Congress to Silas Deane in France, 1776. 18. Descendants of John Alger, of Boston. 19. Abstracts of the Earliest Wills in Suffolk County, Mass. 20. List of Innholders, etc., in Boston, 1714.

Southern Review, January, 1877. (Baltimore.)—1. The Four Gospels. 2. Women of the Revolution. 3. Louis IX., King of France. 4. The Graphic Arts. 5. Vindication of our Philosophy. 6. A Matron and Maid of Greek Romance. 7. Terms of Communion. 8. The Rose in Poetry. 9. Bishop M'Tyeire's Decision.

Quarterly Review of the Evangelical Lutheran Church, January, 1877. (Gettysburg.)—1. Bishop Butler and his Sermons. 2. The Denial of the [illegible] 3. Semi-Centennial Necrological Address. 4. The Organic Structure and Prerogatives of Primitive and Apostolic Churches. 5. Our Present Knowledge of the Sun. 6. Confession. 7. The Origin of Life, or the Germ Theory. 8. The Mission of the Church. 9. Lutheran Church Polity.

BIBLIOTHECA SACRA, October, 1876. (Andover.)—1. The Origin of the Concept of God. 2. Theological Education. 3. An Exposition of the Original Text of Genesis i and ii. 4. Implements of the Stone Age a Primitive Demarcation between Man and other Animals. 5. Horae Samaritanae; or, a Collection of Various Readings of the Samaritan Pentateuch compared with the Hebrew and other Ancient Versions. 6. Governmental Patronage of Knowledge. 7. Natural Basis of our Spiritual Language. 8. The Slavic Races and Panslavism. 9. Dr. P. Asmus on Indo-Germanic Natural Religion. 10. John the Baptist. 11. Professor Max Müller and his American Critics.

In article third it is maintained, with a good deal of ingenuity, that the *tohu* and *bohu* of the first chapter of Genesis, rendered "without form and void" in our translation, does not describe a chaos or a nebula, but solid ground. By an induction from all the passages in which the words are used it seems to be shown that they signify *desolation* and *emptiness;* and not only this, but a *desolation* of a land once occupied with structures, and an emptiness or vacancy of a land once occupied with inhabitants, a "*de-structure ing* and a de-people-ing." The inference is that the "creation" of the primitive work was a recreating or renewing. The earth had been occupied by previous races. The writer does not in the present article indicate at what point in geological history this repeopling took place, or what the nature of the previous inhabitants. We may remark that Delitzsch and others maintain that the notices in scripture of the fallen angels indicate such inhabitants, and they trace the desolation of the earth to their sin.

In the fourth article Dr. Thompson emphasizes the fact that the appearance of implements in the strata of the earth marks the distinct appearance of man on the stage.

"There is no instance on record of any animal making an implement for a special use or end. There are animals and birds that use the materials of physical nature with much ingenuity and skill in building their houses and nests. It is enough to instance the intelligence of the beaver in adapting stone, wood, earth, and water to his wants, and in surmounting the obstacles to his task in some less favorable site. There are tribes of *Simiae* that use stones and sticks for cracking nuts or as weapons of defense. But all this is far removed from the making of implements for a purposed use. The beaver chooses his stones, and breaks or twists his sticks; but he never shapes a stone with which to cut and shape a stick. The chimpanzee takes a stone to crack a nut; but he takes it up a stone, and lays it down again a stone; he never shapes it

to a hammer, fits it with a handle, to be reserved for this special use. The baboon throws a stone to wound or frighten his enemy. He never shapes the stone to a spear-head or a battle-ax, to be kept by him for the service of war. No animal goes beyond using the crude material that nature furnishes. He may use this skillfully and well, adapting it to his own necessities; but he does not improve upon nature; does not change the form of her crude material, making of this an instrument for higher ends; does not make an implement in the sense which we attach to that word in the hands of man. Hence the implement is a line of demarkation between man and other animals."

But since it may be objected that advanced apes may have made tools and have been destroyed by developed man in the rivalry of life, the following reply is given:—

"In the present state of scientific knowledge there is no tangible evidence of the existence of any such higher kind of apes. The links between the highest known species and man must have been many and long, but no trace of these has yet been found. True, this is a merely negative reply. But the existence of such species of apes is a pure *assumption* based upon analogy. Now the want of *data*—that is to say, negative evidence—is logically valid against an assumption. Since, then, the links of connection are wanting, this anthropoidal pedigree of man must be held in suspense as only an hypothesis. Darwin presents it with his accustomed modesty. But Haeckel goes so far as to say, 'We must necessarily come to the conclusion that *the human race is a small branch of the group of Catarrhini, and has developed out of long since extinct apes of this group in the Old World.*'"

The reviewer does not indicate at what geological era the implements first appear. Probably he puts the era far earlier than we should. His argument is, therefore, good against the deduction of man from the lower animals, but not for the Hebrew or Septuagint date of the origin of man.

The Bibliotheca Sacra has lately contained two very able articles on Darwinian Evolution, by Rev. George F. Wright, balancing the argument, but giving the preponderance for evolution. Yet man's creation might have been a miracle just like the incarnation and the deeds of Jesus.

NORTH AMERICAN REVIEW, January, 1877. (Boston.)—1. Points in American Politics. 2. Daniel Deronda. 3. Richard Wagner's Theories of Music. 4. Bret Harte. 5. The Triumph of Darwinism 6. The Eastern Question.

March-April, 1877.—1. The Electoral Commission and its Bearings. 2. Demonology. 3. Christian Policy in Turkey. 4. William Henry Seward. 5. English Arctic Expedition. 6. Poetry and Verse-making. 7. The Insurance Crisis. 8. The Centenary of Spinoza. 9. The Silver Question.

The venerable North American has ceased to be a Quarterly! It seems, also, to have ceased to be the political organ of what John Randolph piquantly called "The House of Braintree," the Adams family. The change is manifested in the first number by the fact that the political article comes from the hand of Richard H. Dana, Jun.

---

## *English Reviews.*

BRITISH AND FOREIGN EVANGELICAL REVIEW, January, 1877. (London.)—1. Mahommed and Mahommedanism. 2. Genesis and its First Four Chapters. 3. The Fruit of the Vine in Palestine. 4. John of Barneveld and the Synod of Dort. 5. The Moral Argument for Christianity. 6. Vatican Influence in the Sixteenth Century. 7. The Doctrine of the Westminster Confession on Scripture. 8. Unitarian Christianity in Creed and Worship.

BRITISH QUARTERLY REVIEW, January, 1877. (London.)—1. Julian's Letters. 2. The Poetry of the Old Testament. 3. Alexander Vinet. 4. Priesthood in the Light of the New Testament. 5. Herbert Spencer's Sociology: its Ground, Motive, and Sphere. 6. Guizot's History of France. 7. The Servian War.

LONDON QUARTERLY REVIEW, January, 1877. (London.)—1. The Turkish Power —its Origin, History, and Character. 2. Roman Catholic Literature in China. 3. Indian Pantheism. 4. Charles G. Finney. 5. The Hidden Life in the Colossian Epistle. 6. Arctic Heroes. 7. The Anglo-American Churches of the United States. 8. George Eliot and Comtism.

LONDON QUARTERLY REVIEW, January, 1877.—1. Letters and Papers, Foreign and Domestic, of the Reign of Henry VIII. 2. Old Norse Mirror of Men and Manners. 3. Dr. Carpenter's Mental Physiology. 4. English Policy in South Africa. 5. Geographical and Scientific Results of the Arctic Expedition. 6. A French Critic on Milton. 7. Mohammed and Mohammedanism. 8. A Ramble Round the World. 9. The Eastern Question and the Conference.

WESTMINSTER REVIEW, January, 1877.—1. A Ministry of Justice. 2. The Warfare of Science. 3. The Factory and Workshop Acts. 4. The Life of the Prince Consort. 5. The Turkish Question: Russian Designs and English Promoters of them. 6. John Locke. 7. The Financial Difficulties of the Government of India.

CONTEMPORARY REVIEW. Eleventh Year. Strahan & Co., Paternoster Row, London.

### NOTES TO ARTICLE FOURTH.

As Catholicism in Maryland is constantly quoted as a case of toleration, the following article was furnished by Mr. E. D. Neill to test the history. After quoting Cardinal Wiseman's

boast and Bancroft's eulogistic history of the supposed toleration, Mr. Neill first gives

*A Biographical Notice of Lord Baltimore.*

If we would understand the principles of the Maryland Charter, it is desirable to know something of the man in whose interest it was framed. Sir George Calvert, the first Lord Baltimore, it is said, was the son of a respectable Yorkshire grazier. At an early age he became a student of Trinity, Oxford, and in February, 1596-7, graduated. His talents, industry, and executive force quickly gave him position under Sir Robert Cecil, the efficient Secretary of State. He had just attained manhood when, in 1606, he represented Bossiney, Cornwall, in Parliament. About the year 1608 he was made clerk of the Privy Council, where he attracted the attention of the pedantic as well as coarse-mouthed King James; and in 1612 assisted his royal master in writing the tractate against Vorstius, the successor of Arminius in the University of Leyden.

Five years later he was made a knight, and in 1619 he became a Secretary of State, and thus learned much relative to the colonization of America.

As early as April, 1619, he informs the Virginia Company of London that the king wishes to transport a man suspected of deer-stealing, and the following November is in earnest consultation with the members relative to the speedy dispatch of fifty convicts in Bridewell to the new settlements on the banks of the James River.

After meeting with considerable opposition because he was the king's secretary and a non-resident, he was in 1626 elected a member of Parliament for Yorkshire. The session began January 30, 1620-21, and from the first day he stood up as advocate of the royal prerogative, in opposition to Pym, Coke, and other leaders of the party of the people. It was at this period, before he became a Roman Catholic, that he began his Newfoundland plantation.

In the year 1622 the death of his wife, and the marriage of his eldest son, Cecil, to Anna, the beautiful daughter of Arundel, a Roman Catholic earl, caused the formation of new associations, which had a potent influence upon his future. From that time he grew more intimate with Gondomar, the Spanish, and Tillieres, the French embassador, and was much occupied in preparing articles of agreement for the marriage of Prince Charles with the Infanta of Spain. When this plan failed Calvert became increasingly unpopular with the majority of Parliament, and it was necessary for the king to make him less prominent. "Secretary Calvert," says a letter written on August 7, 1624, to Sir Dudley Carleton, "droops and keeps out of the way."

A royal favorite a few months later, he was permitted to sell his secretaryship, and about two weeks before the death of James I. was created Baron of Baltimore, with a grant of land in the county of Longford, Ireland. Goodman, once the Protestant

Bishop of Gloucester, after he joined the Church of Rome, writing of Calvert, said:—

"As he was the only secretary employed in the Spanish match, so undoubtedly he did what good offices he could therein for religion's sake, being infinitely addicted to the Roman Catholic faith, having been converted thereto by Count Gondomar and Count Arundel, whose daughter Secretary Calvert's son had married."—Pages 617–619.

Omitting his attempt to colonize Newfoundland, we trace

*His Landing in Virginia.*

He found John Pott, a Master of Arts and physician-general, the acting governor, and probably the same person who with him and Thomas West, afterward the Lord Delaware, had in 1605 received the degree of A.M. at Oxford. As he desired to settle, the colonial authorities offered to Baltimore the usual oath of allegiance, which he declined. The Virginia officers report to the council in England:—

"According to the instructions from your lordships and the usual course held in this place, we tendered the oaths of supremacy and allegiance to his lordship and some of his followers, who, making profession of the Romish religion, utterly refused to take the same, a thing which we would not have doubted in him, whose former employments under his late majesty might have insured a persuasion he would not have made a denial of that, in point whereof consists the loyalty and fidelity which every true subject oweth unto his sovereign. His lordship offered to take the oath, a copy whereof is included; but in true discharge of the trust imposed upon us by his majesty, we could not imagine that so much latitude was left for us to decline from the prescribed form, so strictly exacted and so well justified and defended by the pen of our late sovereign, king James, of happy memory."

Baltimore's determination to dwell in Virginia was not dampened by this rebuff, and he proceeded to England to confer with his friend Charles I. The Duke of Norfolk, the brother of his son Cecil's wife, the same year contemplated a settlement, and the Virginia Legislature, in acknowledgment of the intention, created the present county of Norfolk. In 1631 Baltimore obtained a grant of land south of James River; but the opposition of Francis West, who was Lord Delaware's brother, and others, was so decided that it was canceled. He still persevered, and in 1632, just before his death, was promised a charter for lands alleged to be unoccupied by Englishmen north and east of the Potomac River.

When Charles I. asked what the country ceded should be named, Baltimore said that Carolana, a good name, had been already given to the province of Attorney-General Heath. "Let us then," said the king, "name it after the queen. What think you of Mariana?" He was reminded that this was the name of the Spanish historian who taught that the will of the people was greater than the law of tyrants. Still disposed to compliment the

queen, the king then said, "Let it be Terra Mariæ," which is translated Maryland.—Pages 619-620.

*No Toleration in Baltimore's Charter.*

When we examine the Maryland charter it is found to contain *neither the elements of civil nor religious liberty*, but to be just such an instrument as the friend of James and his son Charles would wish.

To him and his successors is given full and absolute power to ordain, make, and enact laws, with the advice, assent, and approbation of the freemen of the province; but they could not meet without his permission, and until they met he was empowered to make wholesome laws. He had authority also to appoint all judges, justices, and constables.

*There is not a line in the whole instrument which indicates toleration in religion.* In all charters of that age granting lands in uncivilized countries there is a reference to the extension of Christianity. The Virginia charter of 1606 was given by King James, to use its words, because

"So noble a work may, by the providence of Almighty God, hereafter tend to the glory of his Divine Majesty, in propagating of the Christian religion to such people as yet live in darkness and miserable ignorance of the true knowledge and worship of God, and may in time bring the infidels and savages living in those parts to human civility, and to a settled and quiet government."

The instructions to the first Virginia expedition conclude thus:

"Lastly and chiefly, the way to prosper and achieve good success is to make yourselves all of one mind for the good of your country and your own, and to serve and fear God, the Giver of all goodness, for every plantation which our heavenly Father hath not planted shall be rooted out."

In the Maryland charter there is only a slight reference to the extension of Christianity, and that is a transcript of the Carolana charter of 1629:—

| CAROLANA. | MARYLAND. |
| --- | --- |
| "Whereas our trusty and well-beloved subject, Sir Robert Heath, our Attorney-General, being excited with a laudable zeal for the propagation of the Christian faith." | "Whereas our beloved and right trusty subject, Cecilius Calvert, Baron of Baltimore, etc., being animated with a laudable and pious zeal for extending the Christian religion." |

But the Maryland charter, while recognizing Christianity in general terms, *confined its development within the Church of England.* The proprietary had the patronage of all Churches, "*and of causing the same to be dedicated and consecrated according to the ecclesiastical laws of our kingdom of England.*" This examination clearly proves the error of those who assert that by this charter "equality in religious rights not less than in civil freedom was assured."

We will now proceed to consider the inaccurate statements concerning the first company of Maryland settlers.—Pages 620-621.

*His Maryland Colony was chiefly Protestant.*

It was not until the autumn of 1633 that Cecil, Lord Baltimore, gathered a company to begin a plantation.

On October 29 one hundred and twenty-eight persons were on board of the *Ark* at anchor near Gravesend, and to them Hawkins, the searcher for London, administered the oath of allegiance. This vessel of three hundred and fifty tons, and the *Dove*, a pinnace of fifty tons, sailed in November, with about three hundred persons, including the crews.

At the Isle of Wight, where there was not a close watch, they stopped, and here came on board the Jesuits, Andrew White and John Altham, *alias* Gravener, with two associates, John Knowles and Thomas Gervase, as assistants. White was over sixty years of age, but still vigorous. Gravener and Gervase had both been members of the Jesuit college at Clerkenwell, which had been broken up by the English authorities. Before the vessels reached Chesapeake Bay, Cecil, Lord Baltimore, on January 10, 1633–34, writes to Wentworth:—

"I have, by the help of some of your lordship's good friends and mine, overcome these difficulties, and sent a hopeful colony into Maryland, with a fair and favorable expectation of good success, however, without any danger of any great prejudice unto myself in respect that many others are joined with me in the adventure. There are two of my brothers gone, with very near twenty other gentlemen of very good fashion, and three hundred laboring men, well provided in all things."

This statement is very different from that of modern historians. Grahame magnifies "very near twenty gentlemen," both Protestant and Roman Catholic, into "about two hundred gentlemen, of considerable rank and fortune, professing the Roman Catholic faith." Bancroft, more guarded, says, "Two hundred people, most of them Roman Catholic gentlemen, and their servants."

The number that took the oath of allegiance, and other facts, prove that from the first the colony *was chiefly Protestant.* On the voyage twelve died, but only two confessed to the Jesuits, and acknowledged that they were Roman Catholics.

The two commissioners of the colony were Thomas Cornwallis and Jerome Hawley. They were the leading minds—men of experience. Cornwallis, described in a pamphlet of that day as "a noble, right valiant, and politic soldier," was the son of Sir William, and grandson of Sir Charles, once embassador to Spain. He was the father of the Rev. Thomas Cornwallis, rector of Ewarton, Suffolk, whose son and grandson also became presbyters in the Church of England. This Cornwallis, of Maryland, was also the ancestor of the gifted and learned authoress of "Small Books on Great Subjects," Frances Cornwallis, who died in the year 1858. Hawley was the brother of the governor of Barbadoes, and was then made treasurer of Virginia.

Leonard Calvert and his associates reached the mouth of the

Potomac in March, 1634, and the *Ark* and the *Dove* stopped for a few days at an island.—Pages 621, 622.

*Maryland Itself was Protestant.*

Maryland had already been explored, and to some extent occupied. About the year 1619 Ensign Savage explored the Chesapeake Bay. Fuller, in his "Worthies of England," states that Edward Palmer, of Leamington, who died before 1625, resolved to found an academy in Virginia, "in order whereunto he purchased an island called Palmer's Island," which was in that bay, near the mouth of the Susquehanna River. Kent Island, in the same bay, was represented in the Legislature of Virginia before Calvert's arrival. The waters of the Potomac also had for years been resorted to by New England vessels. Henry Fleet, a Protestant, had for ten years established trading posts at Indian villages, and Calvert, in the pinnace, went up the river to ask his advice. Fleet came back with him, and recommended Yoacomaco as a place for settlement, an Indian town, one of his old posts. Hither the colonists came, and, before the first of April, all had landed, and the town was henceforth called St. Mary.

At an early period Lord Baltimore and the settlers came into collision. Like their Virginian neighbors, they enacted in their Assembly a body of laws, and sent them to England for his approval, but he showed that he had the same views as to the rights of the people as when a leader of the king's party in Parliament, and rejected them. He courteously upheld the position of James I.: "It is the king that makes the laws, and ye are to advise him to make such as will be best for the commonwealth;" and pointed to the monarchical power of originating all the laws vested in him by the charter.

It was not until 1638 that they were allowed to have another assembly to advise and consult on the affairs of the province. It met on the twenty-fifth of January, and the Rev. John Lewger, formerly a rector of the Church of England, now a Roman Catholic, lately arrived, appeared as the first secretary of the province.

Laws, prepared by Baltimore, were presented, and the independent colonists refused to receive them, and the body dissolved. In February they came together again, and Cornwallis led them in opposition to Governor Calvert, and they decided to separately consider each law proposed, and it was at last resolved that all laws should be read three times, on three several days, before a vote was taken, and declared their wish that all bills for acts should emanate from a committee of their own body.

Lord Baltimore, finding he could not exercise the arbitrary power claimed, in 1639 called a third assembly, and they emphatically declared that the colonists of Maryland were to have all the liberties Englishmen had at home, and then adopted the statute of England that "Holy Church shall have all her rights and

liberties." The holy Church was that of the charter, *the Church of England.*"—Pages 622, 623.

*Machinations of the Romanists.*

The political agitation seemed more prominent than the religious, because no Church of England ministers accompanied the colonists.

The only ecclesiastics appear to have been those already mentioned. They were active, devoted servants of their order. They taught that there was no salvation outside of the Church of which the Pope was the visible head. With the governor in sympathy, they could not have had a more desirable field, and they used their opportunity. Even the Indians were influenced by their teachings. They relate the following story in their narrative lately printed by the Maryland Historical Society:—

The chief of the Piscataways, who lived but a few miles below the present city of Washington, the capital of the Republic, told Father White that he dreamed that he saw his dead parent worshiping a dark and *hideous spirit;* then appeared a ludicrous demon, accompanied by one Snow, "an obstinate heretic from England." At length Governor Calvert and Father White came, in the company of a beautiful god of exceeding whiteness and gentle demeanor; and since that time, said the Indian warrior, he had been drawn by the cords of love toward the black-robes, the Jesuits. The interpretation of the dream was plain. The hideous and repulsive spirit was heathenism, the ludicrous demon was Protestantism, the tender divinity of exceeding whiteness was Romanism. The "obstinate heretics" were not satisfied with the condition of things, and as early as December 26, 1635, at a meeting of the Privy Council at the palace of Charles I., Archbishop Laud being present, it was reported that one Rabuet, of Saint Mary, had declared that it was lawful to kill a heretic king, and that public mass was held in Maryland.

But the Jesuits did not abate their zeal. Their Journal says:—

"On Protestants as well as Catholics we have labored, and God has blessed our labors, for of the Protestants who came from England this year [1637–8] almost all have been converted to the faith, besides many others, with four servants that were bought for necessary use in Virginia; and of five workmen we hired, we have in the meantime gained two."

When the news reached England of the open violation of the laws by the Jesuits there was a good deal of indignation at their tampering with the religion of the colonists, and it received the attention of Parliament.

In the remonstrance of the House of Commons on December 1, 1641, presented to Charles I. at Hampton Court, the complaint was made that he had permitted "another State molded within this State, independent in government, contrary in interest and affection, secretly corrupting the ignorant or negligent professors of religion."

After this Lord Baltimore acted as if he thought the zeal of the Jesuits was without knowledge, or ashamed of his friends, for on March 7, 1642, quite in the intolerant spirit of that age, he wrote these words:—

"Considering the dependence of the State of Maryland on the State of England, unto which it must as near as may be conformable, no ecclesiastic in the province ought to expect, nor is Lord Baltimore nor any of his officers, although they are Roman Catholics, obliged in conscience to allow such ecclesiastics any more or other privileges, exemptions, or immunities for their persons, lands, or goods, than is allowed by his majesty or other officers to like persons in England."

The next year also he sends to Boston and invites the Puritans to settle in Maryland, but none accepted the offer.—Pages 623, 625.

*The Real Authors of the Act of Toleration were Protestants.*

After Charles I. was imprisoned Lord Baltimore began to curry favor with the dominant [Puritan] party in England, and he displaced the Roman Catholic governor of Maryland, and appointed William Stone, of Virginia, a strong Protestant, and a friend of Parliament, in his stead. The new governor entered into negotiations with the Puritans of Nansemond, who consented to settle in Maryland upon the conditions that they should have liberty of conscience, and choose their own officers. Soon after they arrived on the shores of the Chesapeake Bay, in April, 1649, the Legislative Assembly met and passed the memorable Act of Toleration, embodying the spirit of "that golden apple, the ordinance of toleration," passed by Parliament, to which their former pastor, Harrison, alludes in a letter to Governor Winthrop.

It has generally been supposed that Lord Baltimore prepared the act, but in the statement of his case, published at London in 1653, it is distinctly asserted that this and other laws *were first enacted in Maryland, and were not engrossed and approved by him until August*, 1650.

The members of the Assembly of 1649 *were largely Protestant, and the majority Puritan.* Hammond, a Baltimore partisan, asserts that it consisted of Puritans and other Protestants, and "*a few papists.*" The Assembly of 1649 also "overhauled the oath of fidelity," says another writer of the day, and added a clause that liberty of conscience should not be infringed.—Pages 626, 627.

From all this it appears that Baltimore was under a Protestant sovereign; that the toleration act was passed by Protestants; and that Baltimore had no hand in its passage, but signed it in England because he could do nothing else. Baltimore was the pet and tool of Charles I., and deserves no reverence from mankind. Thus ends the romance of "Catholic toleration in Maryland."

## *German Reviews.*

THEOLOGISCHE STUDIEN UND KRITIKEN. (Theological Essays and Reviews.) 1877. Second Number. *Essays:* 1. KOESTLIN, State, Law, and Church in Evangelical Ethics, (Second and concluding Article.) 2. WIESELER, A few Remarks on the Roman Documents in Josephus, (*Antiq.*, 12, 10, 14, 8, and 14, 10.) *Thoughts and Remarks:* 1. TOLLIN, Servetus' Dialogues on the Trinity. 2. KOENIG, The Remainder of the Works of Baruch. *Reviews:* 1. ACHELIS, The Sermon on the Mount, (Die Bergpredigt nach Mathäus und Lukas, Bielefeld. 1876.) reviewed by SCHMIDT. 2. KOEHLER, Irvingism, (Het Irvingisme,) reviewed by SCHWARZ. *Miscellaneous:* 1. Programme of the Haag Society for the Defense of the Christian Religion. 2. Programme of the Teyler Theological Society at Haarlem for 1877.

The article by Professor Köstlin on "State, Law, and Church," concludes the interesting discussion on the limits of State jurisdiction. It treats especially of the right and duty of the State Government with regard to social life and to religious denominations. In our own country only one aspect of this question —the rights claimed for the State with regard to public instruction—has enlisted the national attention, and is rapidly increasing in importance, many being even inclined to look upon it as one of the great political questions of the future. In some countries of Europe, and especially in Germany, two other questions constitute at present the subject of most exciting controversies. The one is the demand of the Socialists, that the State Government should take charge of all the material labor to be performed within the State, execute it by means of an immense common capital, distribute it among individual citizens according to their individual capacities, and reward every individual according to his merit. In the United States the Socialists as a party are almost unknown. The great newspapers hardly take notice of them, and at the political elections they do not yet make their appearance as an organized party. In Germany the entirely unexpected strength developed by the social democracy at the new election of a German Reichstag, in January, 1877, has thus far been the greatest sensation of the present year in the political world. In no less than thirteen districts they elected their candidates by a majority of all the votes cast, and in a still larger number their candidates polled the largest vote next to the successful candidate. In the kingdom of Saxony the aggregate votes received by their candidates by far exceed the vote cast for the candidates for any of the other parties. The outlook

appears sufficiently critical to induce distinguished writers of all political and religious parties to give at length their views on the condition of society, on the improvement of the situation of the laboring classes, and on the aversion of the great dangers which, in the opinion of many, threaten to subvert the entire fabric of the present society. The recent German literature on this subject is quite considerable, and the extracts given from some of the principal works by Professor Köstlin very interesting. Among the more important works of this class are Schmoller, "On some Fundamental Questions of Law and Political Economy," (1875;) Treitschke, "Socialism and its Patrons," (1875;) Martensen, "Socialism and Christianity," (1875;) Meitzen, "The Joint Responsibility of the Educated and Wealthy Classes for the Welfare of the Working Men," (1876;) Geffken, "Socialism," (1876;) Thiersch, "On the Christian State." None of these writers sympathize with the political and atheistical radicalism of the socialist party. Some, however, make to them the concession that on the part of the State Government more might and should have been done in behalf of the poorer, and, in general, of the laboring classes; and that the State Government may greatly extend its spheres of action in this direction. A distinguished Protestant theologian, Bishop Martensen, of the Lutheran Church of Denmark, goes so far as to demand that the State from time to time fix the laborers' wages, and adopt suitable measures for restricting the undue power of capital. This wish relative to capital Professor Köstlin regards as quite reasonable, but he finds fault with Martensen for not showing how the State can realize it, and he believes that all that the State will ever be able to do will be little in comparison with what Christian capitalists can and should do. As regards the relations between State and Church, Professor Köstlin, as may be expected, favors the continuance of a union between Church and State as it now exists in most of the European countries, though he deems the establishment of ecclesiastical self-government, by means of Church synods, for the regulation of all questions of a religious character, as indispensable for the preservation of the evangelical Church. The recent literature on this subject is also extensively quoted and thoroughly reviewed.

In addition to the Book of Baruch, which is one of the Biblical Apocrypha of the Old Testament, there are now known to theologians two works bearing the name of Baruch, which belong to the class of so-called pseudepigraphal books. The one is the *Apocalipsis Baruchi*, which was published in 1871 by Fritzsche, in an appendix to his *Libri Apocriphi Vet. Test.;* the other is "The Remainder of the Words of Baruch," which Dr. E. König, of the Thomas School of Leipsic, has translated in the present number of the "Studien" from the Ethiopic. It appears to be the first translation into any of the modern languages. The Ethiopic translation was for the first time published by Dillmann, in 1866, in his *Christomathia Æthiopica;* and a Greek version, in 1868, by Ceriani in his *Monumenta Sacra et Profana.* A careful comparison of the Ethiopic and Greek versions, made by Dr. König, showed considerable difference, and made it probable that the Ethiopic version resembled the original (which is as yet unknown) more than the Greek. As the publication of these two pseudepigraphal books does not go back farther than 1866, neither of them could be mentioned in the first volume of M'Clintock and Strong's Cyclopedia, (articles Apocrypha and Baruch,) which bears date of 1867, but the printing of which was begun even before 1866.

The review of Köhler's work on Irvingism, (*Het Irvingisme,* Hague, 1876,) by Schwarz, is an interesting contribution to the recent history of Irvingism, or, as it is officially called, the Catholic Apostolic Church. This remarkable sect was first introduced into Holland, in 1863, by a German minister, Schwartz of Berlin, who had been appointed "apostle of the Netherlands" by the Berlin prophet, Henry Geyer; while an English apostle, Woodhouse, who differed from Geyer's views on the continuance of the apostolate among the Irvingites, excommunicated him. The sect soon gained in Dr. Isaac Capadose, the son of the celebrated Jewish convert Capadose, an able and influential representative. Capadose resigned a high office in the colonial ministry, became, in 1865, priest, and in 1868 angel-evangelist. Though a number of members have since been gained, congregations of any importance have only been organized in Hague and Rotterdam. (Köhler estimates their total number at five hundred.) Chiefly owing to

the indefatigable zeal of Dr. Capadose the sect has recently gained a footing also in Denmark, though their number is unknown, as the members are advised to remain nominally connected with the Lutheran Church, although on joining the Irvingites they must look upon the State Church as the "synagogue of the antichrist." In the country of its origin (England) the sect appears at present to make no progress. In March, 1851, it numbered thirty-two Churches and four thousand nine hundred and eight adherents. Since then no reliable statistics have been published. In Prussia the sect had, according to the latest statistical reports, seventy-four congregations and five thousand and seventy-nine members. The congregation in Berlin numbers nine hundred persons, and has two chapels.

ZEITSCHRIFT FUR KIRCHENGESCHICHTE. (Journal for Church History. Edited by Dr. Theodore Brieger, Professor of Theology at Marburg. Third Number.) *Researches and Essays:* 1. HARNACK, On the So-called Second Epistle of Clement to the Corinthians. (Second Article.) 2. GASS, Contributions to a History of Ethics; Vincent of Beauvais and the Speculum Morale, (First Article.) 3. RITCH, On the Two Principles of Protestantism. *Critical Reviews:* Works on Church History published in 1875. III. History of French Protestantism. By Th. Scott. *Miscellaneous:* 1. DUMMLER, Jewish Proselytes in the Middle Ages. 2. TSCHAKERT, Pseudo-Labarella's "Capita Agendorum," and their True Author. 3. LENZ, An Ecclesiastical Political Work on Reform from the Œcumenical Council of Basel. 4. BENRATH, On the Letter supposed to have been written by Melanchthon to the Venetian Senate. 5. Two Letters of Dr. Eck published by E SCHULTZE. 6. EUBAXIAS, Statistical Report of the Church of the Kingdom of Greece.

The third number of this Journal for Church History will greatly strengthen the high reputation which this new representative of German Theology has already acquired. The titles of the articles as quoted above attest their interesting character, and the names of the authors are a sufficient guarantee for their intrinsic value. The critical review of entire sections of the recent literature on Church History continues to be specially interesting. The article in the present number does not strictly confine itself, as the heading announces, to works published in 1875, but treats in an exhaustive manner of all the recent literature on the subject. The Reformed Church of France is uncommonly rich in documents relating to her early history, as the discipline of the Church directed each Church to record all ecclesiastical occurrences of importance. The careful and extensive study of these documents in modern times is chiefly due to an excellent Protestant Society, the *Société de l'histoire*

*du Protestantisme français*, which was founded in 1852, and has always counted among its directors a number of distinguished men. Among the present members we find, among other distinguished authors, the names of Charles Waddington, Maurice Block, the best statistician of France; F. Schickler, Jul. Delaborde, Jul. Bonnet, H. Bordier, Charles Read, E. Sayous. The society causes, at its own expense, researches to be made in libraries and archives, publishes inedited manuscripts and valuable works which are out of print, and proposes prize questions which have led to the completion of a number of valuable works, as for instance, "A. Court: *Histoire de la Restauration du Protestantisme en France, au xviii siècle d'après des documents inédits*, by E. Hugues, Paris, 1872. This society has given an interesting outline of its history in the treatise, *Notice sur la société de l'histoire du Protestantisme français*, 1852–1872, (Paris, 1874,) and it possesses an excellent organ in the monthly *Bulletin historique et literaire*, (vol. 24, 1875,) which is edited by its secretary, Jules Bonnet. The society also possesses a library which was founded Nov. 10, 1865, and contains by far the best collection of books, (now more than 7,000,) engravings, German reviews, manuscripts, medals, photographs, etc., relating to the history of Protestantism in France. The society has recently begun a new and enlarged edition of one of the chief works produced by French Protestants, the "France Protestante" of the brothers Haag. An account of this new edition has already been given in a former number of the Methodist Quarterly Review. The publication of three other important works is contemplated by the Society, a history of French Protestant literature, a French Protestant bibliography, and a geography of French Protestantism, all of which are greatly needed, for the immense abundance of material on individual localities and persons makes the compilation of general works all the more difficult. Even a comprehensive and exhaustive history of French Protestantism is still wanting, as the well-known work by the late Professor De Felice, *Histoire des Protestant, de France*, (sixth edition continued from 1861 to the present day by Professor Bonifas, of Montauban, Toulouse, 1875,) is only a compendium; and the greatest work on the subject by the late German General Von Polenz (*Geschichte des Französischen Calvinismus bis zur Nationalversamm-*

*lung im Jahre*, 1789, 5 vols., Gotha, 1857–1869) has not been completed. After this account of the *Société de l'histoire du Protestantisme français* and its literary activity, the author of the critical review enumerates a very large number of works published in France or Germany relative to the history of French Protestantism. Many of them are only of local interest, and we can only notice briefly some of the more important ones. Of the excellent edition of the complete works of John Calvin which is published by Professors Baum, Cunitz, and E. Reuss of Strassburg, vols. 13 and 14, containing the letters of Calvin from 1548 to 1553, appeared in 1875. A work on the reformation in Geneva before Calvin, by Pietschker, (*Die Lutherische Reformation in Genf*, Cöthen, 1875,) is of importance, as a Protestant reply to the Catholic work by Kampschulte on Calvin (Leipsig, 1869) was generally felt as a great want. A posthumous volume of the celebrated work by Merle D'Aubigné (*Histoire de la Reformation en Europe au temps de Calvin*, tom. vi, Paris, 1875) treats of the appearance of Calvin in Geneva, the disputation in Lausanne, the banishment of Calvin and his colleagues, his marriage with Idelette de Bure, his controversy with Sadolet, and his approaching return to Geneva. The history of the principal Protestant colleges is treated in a series of articles published in the *Bulletin*, (1873, 1875,) by Gaufres; the history of the Reformed pulpit orators, and chiefly of J. Saurin, in a work by Berthallet, (*J. Saurin et la predication Protestante jusqu'à la fin du regne de Louis XIV*., Paris, 1875;) the history of Alexander Vinet, the greatest Protestant theologian of French Switzerland, in a work by Rambert, (*Vinet, histoire de sa vie et de ses ouvrages*, Lausanne, 1875.)

## *French Reviews.*

REVUE CHRETIENNE, (Christian Review.) September, 1876.—1. E. DE GUERLE, Edgar Quinet, (First Article.) 2. E. DE PRESSENSE, The Bible and Conscience. 3. FRANK PUAUX, Some Remarks on Germany.

October, 1876.—1. ROSSEEUW ST. HILAIRE, Groen van Prinsterer. 2. E. DE GUERLE, Edgar Quinet, (Second Article.) 3. F. LICHTENBERGER, The New Temple of Strasburg, (First Article.)

November, 1876.—1. STAFFER, The Essenian Sect. 2. PENEL, Primary Instruction in Paris. 3. F. LICHTENBERGER, The New Temple of Strasburg, (Second Article.) 4. H. S., The Day of the Innocents at Westminster Abbey.

December, 1876.—1. BOUVIER, Esaie Jaso. 2. CH. WADDINGTON, Bonnet's "Last Accounts of the Sixteenth Century." 3. F. LICHTENBERGER, German Chronicles.

January, 1877.—Pressensé, The Philosophical and Religious Crisis. 2. E. W., Macaulay. 3. Recolin, A Reception at the Academy.

February, 1877.—1. BONNET, Reminiscences of Augustin Thierry. 2. REY, John Stuart Mill, (Third Part.) 3. F. PUAUX, Paris and Montauban, (First Article.) 4. F. LICHTENBERGER, German Chronicles.

In the preface to the number of December, 1876, the editors announce that during the next year (the twenty-fourth of its publication) it will publish articles from E. de Pressensé, on "The Actual Mission of Protestantism," "A Christian Worship at Alexandria at the Time of Origen," and on "Christian Doctrines;" from Eug. Bersier, on "Final Causes," according to the book of M. Janet; from E. de Guerle, on "Charles de Remusat;" from Ruffet, an historical essay on "Bernardino of Ochino;" from Sabatier, on "Baur and the Tübingen School;" from Staffer, an essay on "Judaism at the Time of Jesus Christ;" from Francis de Pressensé, on "Lord Palmerston and the Eastern Question;" from Jules Bonnet, on the "Reminiscences of the Last Years of the Life of Augustin Thierry." Articles have also been promised by Ernest Naville, Lichtenberger, Ch. Waddington, A. Matter, F. Puaux, and other contributors whose names are familiar to the regular readers of the "Review."

M. Penel, in the November number, gives an interesting abstract of an important work on "Primary Instruction in Paris and the Department of the Seine," by M. Gréard, one of the Inspectors General of Public Instruction. A census taken in 1873 showed that there were in Paris 105,331 children from two to six years, and 186,693 children from six to fourteen years, or, in all, 292,024 children from two to fourteen years. On the other hand, the number of children registered

in the *salles d'asiles* and in the public and free schools was 184,646. Supposing, therefore, that from 1873 to 1874 the school population remained about stationary, it would follow, from a comparison of the two figures just quoted, that there were 107,378 children between the ages of two and fourteen who did not attend either any school or *salle d'asile*, and the number attending the one or the other class of educational institutions was 184,646. From this number we must, however, deduct 10,112 pupils of schools who are older than fourteen years, and thus the actual attendance of the schools and *salles d'asiles* was reduced to 174,534, and the aggregate number of children not attending any of these institutions is found to be 117,490. This apparently very large number of illiterate children fortunately admits, however, of very large deduction. There are 11,147 pupils of lyceums, colleges, and free secondary schools; and, contrary to the general supposition, a very large proportion of these pupils are the children of Parisians. The number of children who receive private instruction at home is estimated at 45,500, and the number of those who attend irregularly, and are not included in the school register, at 28,000. The aggregate number of these three classes of pupils being 84,647, the number of children from two to fourteen years receiving no instruction would be 32,843. Of these, 14,527 are children from two to six, and 18,316 children from six to fourteen years. Although a considerable number of children still remain without any instruction, the seating capacity of the public *salles d'asiles* and the public schools is still insufficient for all the children registered, the latter exceeding the former by 38,886. Great efforts are, however, now made by the municipal government of Paris to remedy this want, and by comparing the school statistics of Paris with those of other large cities, as Geneva, Vienna, Dresden, Washington, and New York, M. Gréard shows that Paris can already stand a comparison with a number of these cities. The progress made since 1830 is astonishing, and it may be hoped that under the wise administration of the present Minister of Public Instruction, M. Waddington, the efforts made by the advocates of educational progress will be successful. M. Gréard, the Inspector General of public schools, whose work on primary education in Paris has called forth this article of

the "Christian Review," deserves a prominent place among the promoters of public education. Besides the work already mentioned, he has published a very useful collection, in three volumes, of all the French laws, decrees, etc., relating to primary instruction, under the title, *La Legislation de l'Instruction Primaire en France, depuis* 1789, *jusqu'à nos jours.* (Paris, 1874.) The first volume contains, in chronological order, the legislation from 1789 to 1848, the second that from 1848 to 1874, and the third a very complete analytical table, giving the substance of all the laws in alphabetical order.

## Art. IX.—FOREIGN RELIGIOUS INTELLIGENCE.

### THE CHURCH OF GREECE.

A theologian of the national Church of Greece, A. Papalukas Eutaxias, who has studied theology at one of the German universities, communicates to the *Zeitschrift fur Kirchengeschichte* an interesting account of the condition of his Church. As reliable information on the Eastern Churches is by no means abundant, we extract from this article the most interesting facts:—

A new epoch for the Church of Greece began to dawn as early as the beginning of the present century. The oppression by the Turks had somewhat relaxed, and the favorable opportunity was at once seized to improve the condition of the Church. In the preceding centuries the examples of theological learning among the higher clergy had been isolated; but now, after a certain authorization had been obtained from the Turkish Government to establish schools of a higher grade in the large towns, the cases of ignorance became rare. The war of independence proved a great turning-point. The Church of Greece regarded it as her first task to provide for a better education of the clergy, and (as efficient measures for the immediate education of the entire clergy could not at once be taken) especially for that of the higher clergy, the bishops and the itinerant ministers who were to assist the former. A first attempt made by the Government of Capodistrias to establish a seminary on the island of Paros failed. During the reign of King Otho I., in 1837, the University of Athens was founded, which contained among its faculties one of theology, which soon shaped itself, so far as circumstances would allow, after the model of the faculties of Protestant theology of Germany. Since then the bishops and the itinerant clergy have been chiefly taken from the ranks of the students of the theological students of the University of Athens. This practice of the Church of Greece was imitated by the Greek Church of Turkey, as soon it received a higher degree of liberty through the Hatti-Sherif of Gulbane, (1839,) and the Hatti-Humayum, (Feb. 18, 1856.) As there were not sufficient resources for found-

ing a complete university, the Church had to content herself with the establishment of two theological seminaries, (Θεολογικαὶ Σχολαί,) the one upon the island of Khalke, not far from Constantinople, the other at Jerusalem. Unfortunately, both resemble more the Roman Catholic seminaries of France, Belgium, and Italy, than the Protestant schools of Germany. These two seminaries, likewise, are chiefly intended for the education of the higher clergy, and in one respect the Church in Turkey has even gone ahead of that of Greece, as an ecclesiastical canon expressly provides that for obtaining the office of a bishop it is indispensably necessary to have studied in one of the seminaries, or, at least, to have as good knowledge of theology as the graduates of the seminaries. For the lower clergy neither the Church of Turkey nor that of Greece has as yet made sufficient provision. The former is only now meditating to establish for this purpose ecclesiastical seminaries wherever it is practicable. The Church of Greece is already in possession of a few, but as yet very little has been accomplished by them. The earliest of these schools was the "Ecclesiastical Rizarrian School" at Athens, so called because its foundation is due to the liberality of the brothers Rizaris. This seminary was followed by three other "sacerdotal seminaries," (Ἱερατικαὶ Σχολαί,) one upon the continent of Greece, in Khalkis, one for the Peloponnesus, in Tripolis, a third for the islands, in Hermopolis, upon the island of Syra, to which more recently one has been added upon the island of Corfu—all erected and supported at the expense of the Government. All of them resemble the Roman Catholic seminaries of the Middle Ages, which have also been taken as models in Russia. The best among these seminaries, the Rizarrian school, has recently received considerable improvement, for which it is chiefly indebted to the indefatigable zeal of its present director, the learned Archimandrite Socrates Koliatzos, who several years ago made a journey through western Europe, especially Germany, in order to make himself thoroughly familiar with the condition of the theological schools. It must, however, be admitted that, in spite of all these efforts, a notable improvement of the scholarship of the lower clergy has not yet taken place. The number of pupils of the theological schools who actually enter the priesthood is still very small. The principal reason for this must be found in the lamentable financial situation of the lower clergy. For the higher clergy the Government provides fixed salaries: for an archbishop, about 300 marks (1 mark=23.8 cents) a month; for a bishop, 250 marks; for an itinerant minister, 150 to 160 marks—sums which are small enough, if compared with the revenues of the bishops of other European countries, but which are, nevertheless, sufficient to make their financial position tolerable. But no provision has on the part of the State Government been made for the lower clergy, who wholly depend on the fees received for their ecclesiastical functions. As these are utterly insufficient for the support of a family, (in the Church of Greece the habit prevails to appoint only married clergymen as parish priests,) the priests are compelled to carry on some business in addition to their cle-

ical office. In most cases this is agriculture. The pupils of the sacerdotal seminaries show, therefore, a great inclination to prefer to the thorny office of priest another career which promises them a more comfortable and more profitable position in life. The lower clergy has, therefore, to a large extent to recruit itself from the ignorant classes of the people. Their ignorance is, however, at present much more dangerous to the Church than it was formerly. Even the small amount of learning which the priests possessed formerly, and which was generally limited to Bible history, the catechism, and the study of the liturgical functions, sufficed for the modest claims of their congregations. Now anti-ecclesiastical, and, in general, anti-christian and irreligious doctrines have been widely disseminated throughout the land by the many young Greeks who have been educated in western Europe, and against these influences an ignorant clergy is entirely powerless. Infidelity threatens, therefore, to undermine the whole basis of the Church, if the Church does not succeed in obtaining the services of a thoroughly educated clergy. More fortunate the Church of Greece has been reviving theological scholarship in her midst. A large number of young men have been sent to Germany to study at the Protestant universities; and these students now occupy several episcopal sees, and almost all the professorships of the Rizarrian school, and of the two theological schools in Turkey. They have not only fostered the study of theological science, but have also advocated the introduction into the Greek Church of such institutions of the German Protestant Churches as appear to be compatible with the character of the Greek Church. Thanks to this influence of German Protestantism, the Church of Greece already possesses an interesting theological literature. The oldest professor of theology at the University of Athens, Dr. Constantinus Kontogenes, is the editor of an excellent theological journal entitled the "Evangelical Preacher, (Εὐαγγελικὸς κήρυξ,) and has published an outline of Hebrew Archæology, an Outline of an Introduction into the Old and New Testaments, a Patrology, (in two volumes,) and a Manual of Church History, of which thus far only the first volume has appeared. To the late Dr. Panagiotes Pempotes, professor of theology and court-pastor of the Queen of Greece, the Church is indebted for manuals of the Biblical History of the Old and New Testaments, of Dogmatic Theology, of Ethics, and of Liturgics, all of which exhibit a great depth of thought and lucid arrangement. Of the younger theological professors of the University of Athens, one, Dr. Nicholas Damala, has begun a very thorough work on the literature of the Greek Church relative to the New Testament; while another, Dr. Anastasius D. Kyriakos, has published a very valuable compendium of Church history. A work on the Church law of the Church of Greece has been published by John Papalukas Eutaxias. Another work by a Greek theologian, the first complete edition of the Epistles of Clement of Rome by Dr. Philotheus Bryennius, now Metropolitan of Serres, (in Macedonia,) made last year a sensation in the theological circles of all Christian countries, and has already been noticed in the Methodist Quarterly Review.

## Art. X.—FOREIGN LITERARY INTELLIGENCE.

### GERMANY.

A new "Bible Work for the People" (*Bibelwerk fur die Gemeinde*, Leips., 1876) has been begun by Professor R. F. Grau, who has already made himself known by several works as a theologian of the strictly orthodox school. As its title indicates, it is especially written for non-theologians. The New Testament will be completed in two volumes. It contains, besides the revised Lutheran translation, a twofold series of explanations, namely: 1. A series of notes on the language and the sense of the text; and, 2. A free reproduction of the contents in a language adapted to the understanding of the people.

Professor J. Bachmann has published the first volume of a comprehensive work on the life and writings of Dr. Hengstenberg, (Ernst Wilhelm Hengstenberg, Gutersloho, 1876.) Another theological biography is a life of the late Professor G. F. Oehler by Jos. Knapp, (Tübingen, 1876.) Professor Oehler was a prominent theologian of the kingdom of Wurtemberg. His two principal works, a theology of the Old Testament and a manual of symbolic theology, (a comparison of the doctrinal systems of the principal divisions of Christendom,) were published after his death, the latter by Professor Joh. Delitzsch. Professor Delitzsch also died before the work was issued, and the revision of the work was completed by Professor Franz Delitzsch, the father of the reviser.

An Introduction to the Old and New Testament, by Dr. Kaulen, (*Einleitung in die heil. Schrift Alten u. Neuen Testamentes*, Freiburg, 1876,) is recommended, even in the journals of Protestant theology, as one of the best recent publications of Roman Catholic theology. The same praise had been bestowed upon a former work of the author, on the history of the Vulgate, which appeared in 1868. His present work constitutes volume ix of the *Theologische Bibliothek*, published by the well known Catholic publishing house of Herder in Freiburg.

A work published under the title *Nach Rechts und nach Links*, (Towards the Right and Towards the Left, Leips., 1876,) by one of the oldest and most prominent theologians of Protestant Switzerland, Alexander Schweizer, Professor in Zurich, gives interesting information on the theological controversies of the last thirty years.

## Art. XI.—QUARTERLY BOOK-TABLE.

### *Religion, Theology, and Biblical Literature.*

*Philosophy of Trinitarian Doctrine:* A Contribution to Theological Progress and Reform. By Rev. A. G. Pease, Rutland, Vt. New York: G. P. Putnam's Sons. 1875.

Mr. Pease is a Congregational clergyman, who, being exiled from the pulpit by years of ill health, has taken refuge in his study, and the present he describes as the first-fruits of his studious labors. He is a subtle, though sometimes fanciful, thinker, and a graceful writer. He is not "orthodox" according to the Edwardian standard; he is a free thinker within the sympathy of the Evangelic Church. He seems rather Arminian, we might say Coleridgian, than Calvinistic; and on the Trinity his doctrine would, perhaps, square more nearly with the personal views of Athanasius himself than with the utterances of the so-called Athanasian creed.

He holds the doctrine—the doctrine of Arminius, John Wesley, and Richard Watson—of the co-eternity, co-divinity, consubstantiality, but not co-equality of the Son to the Father. The Son is divine by an eternally derived divinity. The son is the eternal divine Son of an eternally producing Father. And he truly shows this to have been the doctrine of Athanasius himself; but if we rightly apprehend him, he supposes that this doctrine is lost at the present day, and that now, as formerly, Athanasius is "Athanasius contra Mundum." And in one or two respects this, perhaps, is true.

In the days of early Christianity, and earlier, it was a great problem: *How can the Infinite produce the finite?* Between cause and effect there must be a congruity; but nothing is more incongruous, more out of possible community with each other, than the Infinite and the finite. The separating abyss is itself infinite, and cannot be crossed by any wing, or spanned by any bridge. The same impossibility is asserted in our own day among skeptical philosophists, and is at the bottom of their denial of the possibility of creation, rejection of theism, and outcries about anthropomorphism. The true infinity of this separating abyss became more and more perceptible to the Hebrew mind after the captivity in the vast plains and under the clear skies of Babylon, enlarged its conceptions of the true vastness of infinity, and enabled it to feel what it meant when it called God *omnipresent.* Then the very *Name* of God became so solemn that the true vowels of the word Jehovah were lost in perpetual silence. It was then that the conception of the Logos gradually came into thought.

This conception culminated among the cultured and philosophic Jews of Alexandria, by whom the problem, if not the solution, was bequeathed to the Neo-Platonists of the second and third centuries. It culminates most specifically in the writings of Philo. This conception it is which St. John, in the first chapter of his Gospel, appropriates and defines to Christian use, by applying the term Logos to Christ, and then throughout his Gospel picturing Christ as Logos. The author of the Epistle to the Hebrews, evidently a reader of Philo, in his first chapter, prefers the term Son, but presents simply a varying phase of St. John's doctrine.

The true successor on this point of St. John, and of the writer of Hebrews, is Athanasius. It was his view that Christ, the eternal son, solved the great problem, and bridged the infinite abyss. A congruity, effective of causation, was established by him between the Infinite and the finite. Creation had its pathway opened, and a universe was possible. Athanasius then saw that the Son must not be, like that universe, a created thing. He must be a middle term between the Infinite and the creation. Says Neander, (quoted by Mr. Pease,) "If we consider the connection of thought and ideas in the doctrinal system of this father, we shall doubtless be led to see, that, in contending for the Homo-ousion, he by no means contended for a mere speculative formula, standing in no manner of connection with what constitutes the essence of Christianity; that, in this controversy, it was by no means a barely dialectic or speculative interest that actuated him, but in reality an essentially Christian interest. On the holding fast to the Homo-ousion depended, in his view, the whole unity of the Christian consciousness of God, the completeness of the revelation of God in Christ, the reality of the redemption which Christ wrought, and of the communion with God restored by him to man. 'If Christ,' so argued Athanasius against the Arian doctrine, 'differed from other creatures simply as being the only creature immediately produced by God, then he could not bring the creature into fellowship with God, since we must be constrained to conceive of something still intermediate between him, as a creature, and the divine essence which differed from him, something whereby *he* might stand in communion with God; and this intermediate being would be precisely the Son of God in the proper sense. In analyzing the conception of God communicated to the creature, it would be necessary to arrive at the conception of *that which requires nothing intermediate in order to communion with God; which does not participate in God's essence as something foreign from itself, but which is itself the self*

*communicating essence of God.* This is the only Son of God, the only being who can be so called in the proper sense. The expressions Son of God and divine generation are of a symbolical nature, and denote simply the communication of the divine essence."—P. 35.

Mr. Pease prosecutes this doctrine to results which he does not attribute to Athanasius, and yet we suspect are truly Athanasian. If the Son be the middle term between God and creature, then the Son is the conduit of life from God to man. And then God, the Son, and man form what he calls a vital "organism." The life of God is in the Son, the life of the Son is in, or rather, *is* the spirit of man. Hence says Christ, "As the living Father hath sent me, and I live by the Father, even so he that eateth me shall live by me." "Because I live ye shall live also." "He that believeth on me shall never die." Mr. Pease, assuming that these phrases of life and death, scattered through the Gospel of John, refer to the conscious life and death of the spirit, attains the conclusion of "conditional immortality." Christ is the vine, and we are the branches, and separate from the vitality of the vine the branch perishes. Hence the doctrine not so much of annihilation as of cessation. The being perishes by the limitations of his own nature. Thus read, the Gospel of John bears a new aspect. But Mr. P. is aware that an exegetical battle is necessary over the meaning of the words life, death, perish, before this reading is established.

Whether Athanasius really held the doctrine of "conditional immortality," and whether he attained it by the same route as above described, Mr. P., who claims to have studied that author, doubtless knows better than we. But Mr. Hudson, in his scholarly work, "Debt and Grace," furnishes a remarkable extract from that illustrious father, which sounds very much like it.

On the doctrine of Original Sin the writer appears to be Coleridgian. The following extract from Coleridge is so related to the discussions of the hour that we present it to our readers:—

"We have the assurance of Bishop Horsley that the Church of England does not demand the literal understanding of the document in the second (from verse 8) and third chapters of Genesis as a point of faith, or regard a different interpretation as affecting the orthodoxy of the interpreter; divines of the most unexceptionable orthodoxy, and the most averse to the allegorizing of Scripture history in general, having adopted or permitted it in this instance.

"And, indeed, no unprejudiced man can pretend to doubt that if in any work of eastern origin he met with trees of life and of knowledge, or talking and conversable snakes, he would want no other proof that it was an allegory he was reading, and intended to be understood as such. . . . It cannot be denied that the Mosaic narrative thus interpreted gives a just and faithful exposition of the birth and parentage and successive moments of phenomenal sin, that is, of sin as it reveals itself in time and as an immediate object of consciousness. And in this sense most truly does the apostle assert that in Adam we all fall. *The first human sinner is the adequate representative of all his successors.* And, with no less truth may it be said that it is the same Adam that falls in every man, and from the same reluctance to abandon the too dear and undivorceable Eve, and the same Eve tempted by the same serpentine and perverted understanding which, formed originally to be the interpreter of the reason and the ministering angel of the spirit, is henceforth sentenced and bound over to the service of the animal nature, its needs and its cravings, dependent on the senses for all its materials, with the world of sense for its appointed sphere: *Upon thy belly shalt thou go, and dust shalt thou eat all the days of thy life.* I have elsewhere shown that as the instinct of the mere intelligence differs in degree, not in kind and circumstantially, not essentially, from the *vis vitæ*, or vital power in the assimilative and digestive functions of the stomach, and other organs of nutrition, even so the understanding in itself, and distinct from the reason and conscience, differs in degree only from the instinct of the animal. It is still but *a beast of the field*, though more subtle than any beast of the field, and therefore, in its corruption and perversion, *cursed above any*, a pregnant word," etc., etc.

---

*The Book of Psalms.* A New Translation, with Introduction and Notes, Explanatory and Critical. By J. J. STEWART PEROWNE, D.D., Fellow of Trinity College, Cambridge, and Canon of Llandaff. From the third London edition. 8vo., 2 vols., pp. 534. Andover: Warren F. Draper, 1876.

Two noble commentaries of the Psalms have recently been issued from the Andover press: that of Murphy, briefly noticed in a former Quarterly, and this of Perowne. Valuable as the former of the two is, the present work is the more elaborate and complete. Both are the results of thorough scholarship, are written in the style of attractive literature, and are carefully adapted to the wants of the merely English reader and the critical Hebrew scholar. With an express view to this double end, Dr. Perowne places

his philological discussions at the end of the Psalm, while the running notes, which are clear, spirited, and copious, are enjoyable by the reader who has never nibbled a Hebrew root.

Dr. Perowne's Introductions at the commencement of the work are fresh and rich. The topics are: David and the Lyric Poetry of the Hebrews; The Use of the Psalter in the Church and by Individuals; The Theology of the Psalms; The Position, Names, Division, and probable Origin and Formation of the Psalter, and the Inscriptions of the Psalms. The Psalms are lined in poetic form.

It was the rare lot of David the King to be first chorister of the Jewish and Christian Church through thousands of years. He is pre-eminently the Psalmist, often giving name to the whole collection. He had followers who were largely his imitators, though none his equals, in the psalm book of Israel. And his psalm book, more than any other book, has united the Jewish and Christian Church in one spirit, flowing down through the hearts and voices of the people of God in successive generations. Those emotions of the human spirit that belong especially to the region of the spirit are so deeply and truly expressed, that, as Athanasius says, a man "reads as if they were his own words, and he who hears them is pricked at the heart, as if he had said them himself." "Nowhere," says Luther, "will you find more happily or more significantly expressed the feelings of a soul full of joy and exultation, than in the Psalms of thanksgiving, or Psalms of praises. For there you may look into the hearts of the saints, as you would into paradise or into the open heaven, and note with what wonderful variety there spring up here and there the beautiful blossoms, and the most brilliant stars of the sweetest affections toward God and his benefits. On the other hand, nowhere will you find described in more expressive words, mental distress, pain, and grief of soul, than in the Psalms of temptations or lamentations, as in the sixth Psalm, and others like it. There death itself, hell itself, you see painted in their proper colors; there you see all black, all gloomy, in view of the divine anger and despair. So likewise when the Psalms speak of hope or of fear, they so describe these feelings in their own native words, that no Demosthenes, no Cicero, could express them more to the life or more happily."

From the Jewish Church the Christian Church learned to sing, and David is here still our king. Reverently to him, we call our efforts not *psalms*, but *hymns*. We have shaped the hymn to an

exacter rhythm and rhyme; we have invented instruments of great power; new ages and new institutions have added great new themes; but still we go back with ever new delight to the fountain of David. Here is no imitation, but inspiration itself. No wonder that the best talent and richest learning of the Church should rejoice in the work of giving to the world fresh editions of the old anthology to bring its original power to bear on the public mind of our own day.

The chapter on the theology of the Psalms embraces, among other points, the Messianic and the Imprecatory Psalms. There is in the Psalms a king higher than any earthly king; there is a just man more perfect than any human just man; there is a prophetic sufferer who endures agonies as a representative of Israel: these are not in the Psalms united in a single individual, and they remain a problem until Christ comes and unites them all in himself. Yet Dr. Perowne denies that each entire Psalm is Messianic. It is only in the superhuman traits in the human individual subject that the Messiah is shadowed. Hence he denies that the Psalmist's confessions of sin are Messianic, and justifies his denial on the unsuitableness of such confession to the sinless one, and especially upon the fact that such passages are never applied to Christ in the New Testament. The solution that some have given, namely, that these confessions are attributed to Christ, not personally, but as the representative of sinners, he peremptorily rejects. Upon the Imprecatory Psalms there is, we think, a right interpretation which he does not give. "Vengeance is mine, saith the Lord;" and if there be an inspired personator of divine justice, would not his Psalms be imprecatory? Is it not the wrath of the Lamb that says, "Depart, ye cursed?" Is there not a deep truth roughly expressed by Henry Ward Beecher when he said, "I go as heartily with David when he curses and swears, as I do when he prays?" Some years since Professor Park furnished in the "Bibliotheca Sacra" an article showing how the voice of modern civilization, condemning the barbarous war of the Sepoys against England in India, was expressed in the imprecations of David.

And even while we are writing, England and Europe are turning with disgust from the political apologies made by Disraeli for the cruelties of Turkey toward her Christian subjects, and demanding the expulsion of the Turk from the soil of Europe. David represented in a dark period the cause of a pure theism, the hope of a Messiah, in whom rested the future civilization of the world and the redemption of the race. His enemies were the obstacles

of advancement, the sons of darkness, the real foes of God and man. And even in the New Testament the picture of the Messiah riding forth to conquer the world (which we view as symbolizing the same battle of Christian civilization through the Christian ages) has strokes of equally vindictive severity. (Rev. xix, 11–21.) Terrible is the hostility of goodness against badness; and terribly does it become avenged under the government of Jehovah.

We have from Dr. Perowne a few paragraphs on the use of the divine names, Jehovah and Elohim, upon which theorists have built their systems, dividing the Psalms into Jehovistic and Elohistic, and assigning them in accordance to different ages and sources. Dr. Perowne says: "No probable explanation of this phenomenon has yet been given." Does it, in fact, need any explanation? Suppose some critic should take the Methodist Hymn Book and separate the hymns that speak of Jesus from those that speak of Christ and from those that speak of God, and classify them into Jesusistic, Christistic, and Godistic, would the "phenomena" need any "explanation?" We apprehend that all the "phenomena" would be found requisite for constructing just as plausible theories as ever came from an Ewald or a Colenso, based on the use of Hebrew divine names in the Old Testament.

We see no valid reason for conceding the existence of Maccabean Psalms. That the canon was closed with the close of the prophetic period, when Malachi uttered its last syllable, is the ancient and true ground. All attempts to invalidate that great signal fact in which the Jewish Church, the New Testament, and the early Christian Church so well agree, we promptly discard as neology and pseudo-criticism.

---

*The Epistle to the Romans in Greek:* in which the Text of Robert Stephens, third edition, is compared with the Texts of the Elzevirs, Lachmann, Alford, Tregelles, Tischendorf, and Westcott, and with the chief Uncial and Cursive Manuscripts; together with References to the New Testament Grammars of Winer & Buttmann. By HENRY A. BUTTZ, Professor of New Testament Exegesis in Drew Theological Seminary. 8vo., pp. 42. New York: Nelson & Phillips. Cincinnati: Hitchcock & Walden. 1876.

This, the first-fruits of Prof. Buttz's scholarly labors in New Testament Greek, is also the first production of a Greek text from either of our three leading theological seminaries, and the first specimen of a Greek book ever, we believe, issued from a Methodist press in England or America. It is a noble, if not a very large, commencement.

Its ample title-page explains its character. It intends to furnish a method and a means for laying a thorough foundation in original

New Testament study. This will, indeed, be sought only by the few even of our well-read ministry; but that few are to be warmly valued in their place, and supplied with every facility for prosecuting their studies to perfection. The immediate purpose of the work is to supply a class-book for the seminary. And, if it prove an encouraging success, the entire New Testament, in some similar form, will be carried to completion and issued from our Book Rooms.

We trust in the accuracy of the Professor's eyes as a proof-reader, and so believe in the perfect accuracy of the text. The type is clear and strong, but not sufficiently new. As a first attempt it is, we believe, creditable and hopeful; but it will not yet quite stand comparison with the Andover issues. Warren F. Draper's Greek and Hebrew cannot be surpassed, because they are about perfect. But, if our press prosecutes the work, our publishers expect to surpass all but the unsurpassable.

---

*The Life and Writings of St. John.* By JAMES M. M'DONALD, D.D., Princeton, New Jersey. Edited, with an Introduction, by the Very Reverend J. S. HOWSON, D.D., Dean of Chester. 8vo., pp. 436. New York: Scribner, Armstrong, & Co. 1877.

This is a learned and elaborate work, intended to perform the work for St. John which Conybeare and Howson's volumes did for St. Paul. It is very largely a fresh commentary upon the Gospels and a complete commentary upon the writings of the Apostle. The author places the date of the Apocalypse in the time of Nero, and gives an exposition of its visions after a theory of his own. It is finely illustrated with twenty-five maps and cuts. Without indorsing all the author's opinions, we accept his book as a valuable contribution to Christian literature, and as a standard work upon the life, character, and writings of the illustrious subject.

---

*A Commentary on the Holy Scriptures: Critical, Doctrinal, and Homiletical.* By JOHN PETER LANGE, D.D. Edited by Philip Schaff, D.D. Vol. vii of the Old Testament, containing Chronicles, Ezra, Nehemiah, and Esther. New York: Scribner, Armstrong, & Co.

This volume completes the Historical Books of the Old Testament, written during the period of the reconstruction of the theocracy, after the return from exile. CHRONICLES is annotated by Dr. Otto Zöckler, and translated, with additional notes, by Dr. Murphy, of Belfast, Ireland, author of Commentaries on Genesis, etc. EZRA is by Dr. Schultz, of Breslau, translated by Dr. Charles A. Briggs, of Union Seminary, New York. NEHEMIAH is annotated by Dr. Howard Crosby, Chancellor of the University of New York.

ESTHER, by Dr. Schultz, is translated and edited by Dr. James Strong, of Drew Seminary. Dr. Strong has translated the frequent Latin citations, added the Textual and Grammatical notes, enlarged the list of exegetical helps, and furnished an excursus of the Apocryphal additions to Esther, and another on the liturgical use of the book among the Jews. Dr. Schaff cheerily descries the close of his monumental work. "The remaining three," he tells us, "of the twenty-four volumes of this Commentary are in the hands of the printer, and will be published at short intervals."

---

*The Apologies of Justin Martyr.* To which is appended the Epistle to Diognetus. With Introduction and Notes by BASIL L. GILDERSLEEVE, Ph.D., (Gött.,) LL.D., Professor of Greek in the Johns Hopkins University, Baltimore. 8vo., pp. 289. New York: Harper & Brothers. 1877.

This is one of the select Douglas Series, which we have repeatedly noticed and welcomed in our Quarterly. The series is judiciously selected and admirably edited. Professor Gildersleeve's Introduction is finely written. The Epistle to Diognetus, though not Justin's, is a favorite with Christian scholars; and we are gratified that the Professor did not "resist the temptation to insert it."

This volume will be followed by the Confessions of Augustine, edited by Prof. Crowell, of Amherst, and by Chrysostom, prepared by Prof. D'Ooge, of Michigan University.

---

## *Philosophy, Metaphysics, and General Science.*

*Norse Mythology;* or, The Religion of our Forefathers, containing all the Myths of the Eddas, Systematized and Interpreted. With an Introduction, Vocabulary, and Index. By R. B. ANDERSON, A M., Professor of the Scandinavian Languages in the University of Wisconsin. Author of "America not Discovered by Columbus," "Den Norske Maalsag," etc. Second Edition. 8vo., pp. 473. Chicago: S. C. Griggs & Co. London: Trübner & Co. 1876.

Professor Anderson is a thorough enthusiast on the subject of Norse Mythology, and claims to have made in this volume the first complete and systematic presentation of it in the English language. He believes in Odin and Thor and the whole Gothic pantheon. He thinks the Norse system grander and nobler than the Greek, though they are "twin-sisters," while the Roman is little more than imitation. Even Shakspeare could accomplish but little until he had broken his "Roman chains" and let loose the spirit of Gothdom which was in him. He holds that in the Eddas are to be found abundant themes for the poet, the painter, and the sculptor, and is rousingly indignant that Teutons shall seek their subjects among the loathsome nudities of Greek art rather than in the pure and chaste Odinic myths. And, truly, here is a broad

field for an original genius whose soul and hand can unite in putting the old Norse Sagas into enduring marble.

A full introduction of a hundred and fifty pages prepares the way for an exhibition of the Norse mythology by a discussion of some questions that naturally arise in the mind of a student. Professor Anderson holds to an original Teutonic mythology, common to all the Teutonic peoples before their migration from South-eastern Russia, which, variously modified by the changed conditions of life in Norway, Sweden, Denmark, England, France, Germany, and Iceland, lived and flourished until Christianity uprooted and destroyed it every-where except in Norway and Iceland. "It is in Icelandic alone," says Max Müller, "that we find complete remains of genuine Teutonic heathendom. . . . Iceland was discovered, peopled, and civilized by Norsemen in the ninth century; and in the nineteenth the language spoken there is still the dialect of Harold Fairhair, and the stories told there are still the stories of the Edda, or the Venerable Grandmother." That Odin and Balder and Thor must die was a part of the system: the missionaries had only to proclaim that they were dead to give them the Gospel, and at the same time leave them the grand poetry of their old faith.

The body of the work is in three parts, the first entitled "The Creation and Preservation of the World;" the second, "The Life and Exploits of the Gods;" and the third, "Ragnavok and Regeneration." Here the system is fully unfolded, and illustrated by numerous and full passages of the Eddas.

But, as among the Greeks, so was it with the Norsemen. The nobler souls among them believed in an *unknown God*, whose name they might not speak, and who was the Great Supreme. And an inquirer into the origin of the system will doubtless find that to its originators it was simple poetry in which nature and its forces were personified, and that afterward, God being forgotten, these imagined persons were endued with life and actuality, and became objects of reverence and worship.

Professor Anderson is fully master of his subject, and will prove a most pleasant companion and guide to those who will consult his pages.

---

*Principia of Political Science.* Upon a Reverent, Moral, Liberal and Progressive Foundation. By R. J. WRIGHT, Professor of Ethics, Metaphysics, and Church History in the Christian Biblical Institute. Third Edition, Revised. 8vo., pp. 432. Published and sold by R. J. Wright, Tacony, Philadelphia. 1876.

The author of this thoughtful work was led by the events of the recent rebellion to a searching and extended study of political and

social questions, resulting in the projection of a series of volumes, of which this is the first. It is, we believe, the first attempt at a broad scheme of Social Science based upon truly American and Christian principles. While it is not at all likely that the plan here laid open will ever be adopted, except, perhaps, on a very limited scale, there are given many important suggestions which ought to have great weight with thinkers of all classes. It is certainly an advance to take the science out of the hands of infidels, professional politicians, and mere physical scientists, and to insist that any true exposition must base it upon a foundation which is metaphysical and moral, as well as physical and secular. In essential characteristics, therefore, Mr. Wright differs from Comte, Carey, Paley, Spencer, and Mill, while Fourier's ideal is impracticable. He also differs from all previous writers in his theory of the Six Units, namely, that human society, and, therefore, Social Science, consists of six fundamental elements, or Units—Individual, Family, Social Circle, Precinct, Nation, and Mankind. The problem is to so order and harmonize these units in their relations one to another, that the greatest prosperity and happiness of each and all shall be secured. The four Books, entitled respectively Introduction, Precinct, Nation, and Corporation, constitute an elaborate discussion, with much valuable information, rendering the volume an important contribution to political philosophy.

*The Geographical Distribution of Animals.* With a Study of the Relations of Living and Extinct Faunas, as elucidating the past changes of the Earth's Surface. By Alfred Russel Wallace, author of "The Malay Archipelago," etc. In two volumes. With Maps and Illustrations. 8vo. New York: Harper & Brothers. 1876.

To Mr. Wallace belongs the honor of having anticipated the fundamental principle of Darwinism, and some have claimed that to him rather belongs the main honor. But with genuine modesty he defers to his superior, and speaks with a tone of almost *allegiance* to the man who has given the idea of genetic evolution an almost epochal importance. If these two stately volumes shall be able to bear a similar relation to the eleventh and twelfth chapters of Mr. Darwin's "Origin of Species," as Mr. Darwin's "Animals and Plants under Domestication" does to the first chapter of that work, his highest ambition is satisfied. Both are men of genius in earnest pursuit of scientific truth, both are men of pure moral character, and both write in a style of transparent and fascinating simplicity. To Mr. Wallace belongs the honor of not being cheated by his science out of his religion, or daunted by association from a free and bold assertion of his unshaken faith in God.

The volumes present us with a distinct step of advancing science. Zoology has heretofore ranged over the animal forms that meets our eye upon the earth's surface, has analyzed their peculiarities, and made attempts at classification. It has made us acquainted with existing animal life. Paleontology has dug into the earth's surface to find what has existed in past ages, and has exhumed a wonderful variety, a rapidly increasing variety, of related primordial forms. Uniting the results of these two fields of investigation, we attain a new completeness of zoological science. With more or less confidence we pronounce upon the great genera. We find the geological starting-point where a given genus commences existence, and trace a rude biography. We trace, with some distinctness, how and where it grew; we note its means of spreading over the surface of the earth of its time; we ascertain the extent of its prevalence, the greatness of its predominance, and its present prospect of prosperity and power. We look at an individual dog and think how surely he is descended by a long pedigree of *canidæ* from a far-gone geological age. If antiquity is nobility, he is the aristocrat, and man the plebeian.

The volumes are regal in size, type, and illustrations. The maps and pictures are beautiful, and richly suggestive.

## *History, Biography, and Topography.*

*The Mikado's Empire.* Book I. History of Japan, from 660 B.C. to 1872. A.D. Book II. Personal Experiences, Observations, and Studies in Japan, 1870–1874. By WILLIAM ELLIOT GRIFFIS, A.M., Late of the Imperial University of Tokio, Japan. Crown 8vo., pp. 625. New York: Harper & Brothers. 1876.

Did Professor Griffis, in this magnificent volume, only lay open to the world the history of the old Japan which, for ages, had so persistently shut itself in from the knowledge of mankind, he would have made an important contribution to literature, and won for himself a lasting honor as well. But the new Japan that has shaken off the burdensome yoke of centuries, and is struggling to build itself up in the freer, grander life of the Western civilization, is doubtless the more interesting to us, partly because of the Asiatic peoples she is our nearest neighbor, yet chiefly because of our instinctive sympathy with every genuine effort of men or nations to improve their condition. Professor Griffis has had ample opportunity for the research and observation requisite for accurate delineation and statement. For six years he was in constant intercourse with intelligent Japanese. The present Japanese Minister at Washington, and also the President of the Imperial

University of Japan, were among his pupils at New Brunswick, New Jersey. He was the organizer of the Scientific School at Fukui, at the end of a year was transferred to the Imperial College at Tokio, and for three years and a half was in constant intercourse with the most cultivated and scholarly men of the nation. The old feudalism was in full force when he went to the country, so that he was a witness of the mighty changes accomplished by the revolution.

Japan is no longer a *terra incognita.* Our geographers have hitherto misled us in giving to the main island the name of the empire. "Dai Nippon, or Nihon, means Great Japan," and is the name given by the natives to the entire empire; while the name of the largest island is Hondo, and not "Niphon," as most foreign writers give it. Upon its 150,000 square miles, two thirds of which is mountain land, dwell 33,000,000 of people, whose real character has, until recently, been almost unknown. Even Commodore Perry, in 1853, was cheated into treating with the general of the mikado, believing him to be the emperor himself; but he never saw "the august sovereign of Japan," any more than the mikado ever saw the presents sent him by the United States. The two emperors, one spiritual and the other secular, were a fiction. "There never was but one emperor in Japan," says Professor Griffis; "the shogun was a military usurper, and the bombastic title 'tycoon' a diplomatic fraud."

Japanese history has its twilight of fable, yet the historic period proper is of twenty-five centuries' duration. Shintoism, the ancient national religion, differs not much from the ante-Confucian Chinese. "Its principles, as summed up by the Department of Religion, and promulgated throughout the empire so late as 1872, are expressed in the following commandments: '1. Thou shalt honor the gods and love thy country. 2. Thou shalt clearly understand the principles of Heaven and the duty of man. 3. Thou shalt revere the mikado as thy sovereign, and obey the will of his court.'" It became corrupted by Buddhism and Chinese philosophy, and largely supplanted by the former, but the reformers of the day are attempting to restore it in its original purity. This ancient paganism which made the mikado the descendant and representative of the gods, is seeking a union with the revolution which has proved him a man. It cannot succeed. New Japan must become Christian or fail. Not with such Christianity, however, as was introduced into the country by the Jesuits in the sixteenth century, leaving no trace of good influence upon the

moral life of the people, and is to-day every-where at war with the principles of the nineteenth century.

Our author very carefully exhibits the influences which led to the revolution whereby the mikado was brought out from the seclusion of centuries and made the real sovereign of the nation. The ancient feudalism was suddenly broken down, and an entirely new system inaugurated. What the outcome will be is as yet an unsolved problem, yet the fact that three millions of the population are in school is full of promise. The whole of this story of the mikado's labors to perform his oath, voluntarily made in 1868, that "intellect and learning should be sought for throughout the world, in order to establish the foundations of the empire," is very full of interest, as is, indeed, the entire volume.

---

*Memorials of the Wesley Family.* Including Biographical and Historical Sketches of all the Members of the Family for Two Hundred and Fifty Years; together with a Genealogical Table of the Wesleys, with Historical Notes, for more than Nine Hundred Years. By GEORGE J. STEVENSON, author of the "Methodist Hymn Book and its Associations," "City Road Chapel and its Associations," "Sketch of the Life and Ministry of C. H. Spurgeon," "The Origin of Alphabetical Characters," etc. 8vo., pp. 550. New York: Nelson & Phillips. 1876.

Doubtless the reader of the three goodly octavos of the Rev. L. Tyerman's "Life and Times of the Rev. John Wesley, M.A., Founder of the Methodists," said, or thought, as he closed the last volume, "This is all; nothing more can be written about the Wesleys." But lo! here comes another goodly octavo, plethoric with matter, much of which will be new even to the readers of Tyerman. The author tells us how he came into possession of the materials which form the basis of his work. By the last will of John Wesley all the letters and papers relating to his family were left in the custody of Rev. Henry Moore, who kept them safely till his death, in 1844, but made no use of them, and, perhaps, never even examined them. Mr. Moore's executor placed the papers in the hands of Mr. Stevenson, and the richness of the materials therein contained, and the recent discovery of other letters and documents connected with the Wesleys, impelled him to undertake a biographical sketch of every member of the Epworth family.

It seems that the Wesleys were what would be called, even in England, an old family. Almost a thousand years ago (A. D. 938) there was a Guy of Welswe, in Somerset, who was made a thane, or baron, by Athelstan, a Saxon king of England. The family name assumes various forms as the history proceeds: Weiswe, Welswey, Westley, Wellesley, Wesley, and Westleigh.

The genealogical table exhibits a formidable array of titles and dignitaries, civic, military, and ecclesiastic.

The biographies proper begin with the Rev. Bartholomew Wesley, who was born about the year 1595, and died in 1680. He was rector of Catherton, Dorsetshire, in 1640, with a parsonage, four acres of land, and the tithes of the parish, the whole income being worth £13 10s. To this was afterward added the "living" of Charmouth, two miles distant, which added £22 to his stipend. But he lived in troublous times. The Puritans, under Cromwell, overthrew the monarchy, and established a republic, which lasted eleven years, and then monarchy was restored. With the restoration came new laws, establishing High Church prelacy, and binding Church and State in closest alliance. In 1662, an Act of Uniformity made it unlawful for any man to receive or hold any ecclesiastical office unless he had been ordained by a Bishop, assented to every thing in the Church prayer book, and believed in the divine right of kings. Bartholomew Wesley was one of the two thousand clergymen who at once abandoned their churches and parsonages rather than submit.

His son, John Wesley, the grandfather of the founder of Methodism, was born in 1636, and died in 1678. He was educated at Oxford, entered the ministry, and in 1658 became vicar of Winterhorn—Whitchurch, in Dorsetshire. Unlike his father, when the Act of Uniformity was passed, he quietly submitted, and yet fell into disrepute among the clericals of his times, because of the "irregular" methods of labor into which he was led by his zeal for the salvation of souls.

His son was Samuel Wesley, the rector of Epworth, the father of a still more famous son, whose name is now familiar to the world. Biographies, more or less extended, are given of the various members of the Epworth family. Samuel Wesley, his wife Susanna, their seventeen children, and six grand-children. The Wesleys seem to have been all very decided characters, and their historian does them justice. The work is well written, clear, candid, truthful, free from the vice of over-laudation, and equally free from the opposite vice, the peculiar blindness which sees nothing in the sun save the spots. In the department of literature to which it belongs, the book is one of the best.

---

*The Chinese in America.* By Rev. O. GIBSON, A. M. 12mo., pp. 405. Cincinnati: Hitchcock & Walden. 1877.

We, Caucasians, have a vast deal of trouble with the "inferior races," races "guilty of a skin not colored like our own," but

which persist in carrying a black, a red, or a yellow visage, much to our disgust and contempt. We punish the black-face by kidnapping, enslaving, and robbing him of his earnings; we punish the red-skin by breaking treaties, driving him from his lands, and administering butchery; we punish the yellow-skin by first compelling him to admit our incursions into his territories, and then maltreating him because he comes into ours.

The yellow race in our country has found a very worthy patron and defender in Mr. Gibson. His head and heart are nobly consecrated to his work, and he has found it very easy to furnish a very interesting and valuable book on the Chinese and the Chinese question. His enthusiasm for his clients does not prevent his delineating them in duly discriminating colors. And then the ease with which he exposes the villainy with which the Chinese have been treated, the slanders with which they have been assailed, and the preposterousness of the panic which fools and knaves have tried to raise about the danger of their immigration, is all very edifying and instructive. The real source of all this tumult is the jealousy of the Irish papists, led on by their priests, and aided by demagogues especially of that political party whose tool and master at once the Irishry are.

We came near saying in our first sentence of this notice that "we" *Christian* Caucasians are the inflicters of these wrongs on this "inferior race." But Mr. Gibson's book furnishes us the fact that the true Christians are the true friends of poor Chinaman. When set upon by the mobs and mobocrats of San Francisco, Chinaman has learned by experience that his true friend is the "Jesus man." When a base city government passes oppressive enactments, he hurries for counsel to the "Jesus man." When a hapless woman flees from the house of prostitution into which she has been entrapped, she calls loudly and persistently for a "Jesus man." When a Jesuit priest delivers a violent harangue against these pagans, pagans learn with grateful surprise that the "Jesus man" has furnished a sweeping exposure of Jesuit falsehood, and beg the "privilege" of paying for the publication of an edition. The issue of this work is a favor to both races. What possible excuse is there for the falsehood, the cruelty, and the panic in regard to this race, when it is clearly shown that the whole immigration does not amount to more than about one hundred and fifty thousand?

Mr. Gibson shows that the Chinamen have been a great advantage to the Pacific coast. Without them the great national work

the Pacific Railroad, could not have been built. They have created many industries, which but for them would have had no existence. We confess, too, that our own sympathies are with our own housewives. When florid-faced Bridget overrides our faithful housekeepers with her captious arrogance, and dusky Dinah becomes too lazy or proud to go "out to work," we know no reason why Chinaman has not a right to step in.

---

*The First Century of the Republic;* a Review of American Progress. 8vo., pp. 506. New York: Harper & Brothers. 1876.

This volume consists of seventeen essays by as many authors, each of whom is an expert in the field which he traverses. As the title indicates, the aim of the work is to show what the American people have accomplished during the first century of their history as an independent nation. Our institutions rest upon two great principles, one of which had little support in historic precedents, and the other was almost an absolute novelty. These two principles are, First: That government is safest in the hands of the people, the masses, whose will should dictate its form, shape the legislation, and secure the enforcement of the laws. Secondly: That the Church and the State should be totally separated. These two constitute the basis of the boldest achievement ever deliberately and of set purpose tried. As the new nation began its first century, many a bird of ill omen flew between us and the sun, croaking dismally of failure. The apologists of hereditary rule predicted universal anarchy and confusion. The advocates of State Churches charged us with a neglect of religion, and mourned over a nation destined speedily to become irreligious, if not wholly atheistic.

It is but justice to ourselves and to the world that the results of our great experiment be set forth. This is well done in this goodly volume. The topics discussed are Colonial Progress, by Eugene Lawrence; Mechanical Progress, by E. H. Knight; Manufactures, Hon. D. N. Wells; Agriculture, Prof. W. H. Brewer; Mineral Resources, Prof. T. S. Hunt; Commerce, E. Atkinson; Growth of Population, Hon. F. A. Walker; Monetary Development, Prof. W. G. Sumner; Union, T. D. Woolsey, D.D.; Education, Eugene Lawrence; The Exact Sciences, F. A. P. Barnard, D.D.; Natural Science, Prof. T. Gill; Literature, E. P. Whipple; Fine Arts, S. S. Conant; Medicine, A. Flint, M.D.; Jurisprudence, B. V. Abbott; Humanitarian Progress, C. L. Brace; Religion, J. F. Hurst, D.D.

Under these heads every thing bearing on the progress of a people finds somewhere a place. The summing up of the century is very gratifying to an American. We are glad that this work has been written, and by able hands, writers whose established reputation guarantees the accuracy of the statements which they make. Charged as we were with venturing upon a dangerous experiment, and even if dangers still threaten our future, our past is entitled to this vindication. Let every American read it for the strengthening of his political faith, and for its rich stores of varied information.

---

*Viking Tales of the North.* The Sagas of Thorstein, Viking's Son, and Fridthjof the Bold. Translated from the Icelandic. By RASMUS B. ANDERSON, A.M., Professor of the Scandinavian Languages in the University of Wisconsin, and Honorary Member of the Icelandic Literary Society, and Jón Bjarnason. Also, Tegnér's Fridthjof's Saga. Translated into English. By GEORGE STEPHENS. 12mo., pp. 307. Chicago: S. C. Griggs & Co. London: Trübner & Co. 1877.

Professor Anderson's excellent work on the Norse Mythology is very appropriately followed by this volume of saga-translations, thus giving us a few complete illustrations of the system which in the former is so fully stated and interpreted. American readers have hitherto been dependent upon European publishers for this kind of literature, but the issue of this volume by an enterprising Chicago house marks the inauguration of a new era.

The Saga is properly a narrative prose composition in popular and colloquial form as it would be recited and handed down from grandsire to grandson. Some of them are strictly historical, while others of an older date have grown in the telling, as modern stories often do, and taken on a semi-mythical form, and others are purely fabulous. Yet even these last are found to present great truths of the Norse religion; the divine expressing itself in human thoughts and acts, and the human in aspirations and struggling for the divine.

The Saga of Thorstein Vikingsson belongs to the fictitious class, and is doubtless true to Icelandic medieval thought and feeling. The Saga of Fridthjof the Bold is a semi-mythological story, supposed to be based on some popular tradition. Its chief characters are descendants of personages who appear in Thorstein's Saga, to which it is, therefore, in a certain sense a sequel. It belongs to the twelfth or thirteenth century. These two sagas are held to be among the best of their literature. The reader is introduced into a new world of thought and feeling, but with the aid of an ample Glossary he soon comes to be very much at home.

The Fridthjof's Saga by Bishop Tegnér, the celebrated Swedish

poet, draws its materials from the sagas above mentioned, which Professor Anderson would have us regard as two introductory chapters to "this gem," as he characterizes it, "among modern poetical productions." Of the eighteen or twenty English versions of it, its author pronounced that of Professor Stephens to have been the most successful in reproducing the fundamental spirit of the original. It is worthy of the wonderful admiration it has evoked, and in its present form will contribute to enhance the interest now gathering around the Norse literature.

---

*Proceedings of the International Convention for the Amendment of the English Orthography.* Held at the Atlas Hotel, Philadelphia, Pa., August, 1876. 8vo., pp. 48. Published by the Spelling Reform Association, 15 South Seventh-st., Philadelphia; 13 Tremont Place, Boston; 35 Park Row, New York.

Next to the work of revising the English Bible, no movement is more important or more needed than the revision of our English orthography. When scholars like Professors Whitney, March, and Haldeman are aroused to the work there is some hope of its accomplishment. The same absurd conservatism opposes both revisions. An insensibility to the injury of the existing evils, and of the great benefits of a revision, locks the great mass of even thoughtful men into apathy and ignorance, and very many display an irritability and contempt at the very mention of the topic, which even ignorance cannot excuse.

An alphabet, varying so very little from the present as to make the change not difficult, might be so framed *as to make but one mode of spelling a word possible.* The result would be that instead of requiring a year or so for a child, with the most painful brain labor, to learn our capricious orthography by pure memory, the work might be accomplished in a few weeks far more perfectly than is now done in one's entire life. The expense in our public schools of learning to read would be reduced one half, and thus millions be saved to the country.

Another result would be the easy diffusion of the English language through the world. No language is more simple in its structure, or easier to learn to speak; but an impassable embargo is laid upon its diffusion by its impracticable orthography. A foreigner is obliged to learn how each individual printed word is pronounced, and, in spite of all defiance of rule, to retain it by sheer memory. With an easy revision—easy if there were but the unanimous will—there is no language now spoken which is so fair a candidate for universality as the English.

If our professors and literary men generally desire to vary the

monotony of daily routine with a philanthropic hobby, which may do a great good in the world, the spelling revision is an enterprise quite suited to gentlemen of their complexion. Our colleges, if united on the subject, could bring the work to a completion. The association now existing, embracing many veteran reformers, will rejoice in their aid.

---

*Old Tales Retold from Grecian Mythology in Talks Around the Fire.* By AUGUSTA LARNED, author of "Home Stories," and "Talks with Girls." Fifteen Illustrations. 16mo., pp. 498. New York: Nelson & Phillips. Cincinnati: Hitchcock & Walden.

The attempt of Miss Larned to render some features of the old Greek mythology intelligible and attractive to young people is highly commendable, connected as it is with historic and poetic literature, and her chosen method of conversations with a bright group of young nephews and nieces, invests the study with added interest. Twenty-six delightful evenings purport to have been spent in this way, until the whole Grecian Pantheon is pretty well explored. But these stories of gods and goddesses had an origin and a meaning, and the discussion of these points really goes back to the origin of all idolatry. Doubtless what was at first pure poetry personifying the forces of nature, came in times of ignorance and departure from Jehovah to be regarded as actual truth, and the powers thus personified as actual beings to be reverenced and feared. Once started on this track the progress to the most abominable idolatries was rapid.

We do not quite agree with Miss Larned in all her interpretations of the Greek mythology, nor in the view she takes of it as a religious system. It had no tendency to lead men to God, but the reverse. It could not be a preparatory school for the Gospel, as we understand her to teach; nor do we think that in its light any found the invisible Jehovah, as the Introduction seems to say. It led away from him and shut him from their vision. The Greek philosophy, on the other hand, was such a preparative; but it first rejected, as false and perverting, the whole system of fable.

---

*Forty Years' Mission Work in Polynesia and New Guinea, from* 1835 *to* 1875. By Rev. A. W. MURRAY, of the London Missionary Society, author of "Missions in Western Polynesia." 12mo., pp. 509. New York: Carter & Brothers. 1876.

This is a minute and instructive picture of the real work of missions. In November, 1838, the author, with his wife and nine other missionaries, sent by the London Society, embarked on a small merchant vessel, and after a weary voyage of seven months landed at Tutuila, one of the Samoan, or Navigator's Islands. This group is

nine islands lies in the Pacific Ocean, about two thirds of the way from California to Australia, and nearly in a line between them. They have a population of, perhaps, thirty-five thousand, who in 1835 were utter savages, with the addition of a few white men, escaped convicts from Botany Bay, who were more depraved and dangerous than the heathen themselves. Here Mr. Murray lived and labored for thirty-five years, and was then appointed missionary in New Guinea, an island directly north of Australia, where he remained five years.

The story of these forty years is told with no remarkable vivacity or force, yet, as we judge, fully and faithfully. The romance of the enterprise vanished with the first sight of the degraded men and women whom they had come to save, and for the moment some of the missionaries felt that they had undertaken a great work without counting the cost. Still, they went on with their labor, and gained the victory. We commend the book to all who deem themselves called to go forth to the foreign field, and to all who are interested in it.

It is a motley history of good and evil, successes and failures, conversions and defections, war and peace, joy and sorrow, but of heroic endurance on the part of Christian men and women, and with all the ebbs and flows of the tide, of steady progress in the direction of civilization and Christianity.

## *Literature and Fiction.*

*Frithjof's Saga.* A Norse Romance. By ESAIAS TEGNER, Bishop of Wexiö. Translated from the Swedish by THOMAS A. E. HOLCOMB and MARTHA A. LYON HOLCOMB. 12mo., pp. 213. Chicago: S. C. Griggs & Co. London: Trübner & Co. 1877.

The English version of this celebrated poem by Professor Stephens, of the University of Copenhagen, as it appears in Professor Anderson's "Viking Tales of the North," has been mentioned in our notice of that work. We have in the present volume another version of it, and the first complete one by American translators. With no attempt to speak of its merit as a translation, we can well understand the worthiness of any honest effort in behalf of a poem which has appeared in many editions and styles, thrilled all Sweden, been translated into most European languages, and set to music as well. According to Bayard Taylor, none of the previous English versions have been satisfactory to Swedes; but this one, from its fidelity to the original measures, the feminine rhymes, and the alliteration, has an apparent promise of better success.

But, passing the questions of accuracy and comparative merit, the poem as here given is full of beauty and power, and must certainly rank with the grandest productions of modern times. Its purpose is to portray the old heroic age of the North, using the ancient tradition as a foundation only, and making Fridthjof, the high-minded and brave, the representative of a people and an epoch. One almost feels the fresh north wind as he reads, purifying and invigorating to both climate and character; and he will assuredly incline more to a reverential fear of Odin and Balder than of Zeus and Apollo.

---

*Lectures on Courtship, Love, and Marriage.* An Infallible Guide to a Happy Home. By WESLEY SMITH, author of "A Defense of the M. E. Church," "Smith on Baptism," "Our National Affairs," etc. 8vo., pp. 444. New York: Printed for the Author by Nelson & Phillips. 1874.

Mr. Smith is a piquant and original, though not a very classical, writer. His work abounds in fresh suggestions drawn from life. The evils he reprehends need check, and the principles he lays down should be the guide of life in the important and delicate matters he discusses. We recommend its perusal to the classes for whom it is written.

---

## *Periodicals.*

*President Hayes' Inaugural Address.*

We congratulate the country on the election of President Hayes.

He is A STATESMAN OF UNIMPEACHABLE PURITY AND COMMANDING ABILITY. In his varied experience in the Army, in Congress, in the Executive Chair, and in the ordeal of a Presidential canvass, he has stood peerless and spotless, without fear and without reproach. Office has sought him, he has never sought office. Early in the canvass calumny undertook to assail him for a moment, but so elastic was the rebound upon the calumniator that even political lying was hushed into silence, if not into shame. Through the whole canvass his stainless purity and lofty independence were nobly maintained at every point. How mortifying a contrast to all this is exhibited by the base intriguer of Gramercy Park, the corruptest man, personally and politically, ever offered as candidate to the highest office in the nation's gift, with the single exception of Aaron Burr! As to President Hayes' ability, it is an amusing thing to hear taunts of his incompetency from that party, three of whose popular presidential candidates he beat in three successive elections to the executive chair of his own

State. Thurman, Pendleton, and Allen, three mighty Democratic chieftains, were in succession laid low by Rutherford B. Hayes, who is a nonentity! What nonentities must these three beaten competitors themselves be! and what a mass of imbecility the party must be whose mightiest men are demolished by said imbecile.

HE IS THE CHOICE OF A LARGE MAJORITY OF THE RIGHTFUL VOTERS OF THE COUNTRY. This stands unquestionably true whether the Commission was impartial in its process or not. If that Commission could have gone with an omniscient eye to the bottom of the case, if it could have ascertained how every free, unintimidated, uncheated voter, black as well as white, would have cast his free suffrage, it would have found that *not only Florida, South Carolina, and Louisiana were for Hayes, but that Mississippi, Alabama, and Georgia also, were for Hayes.* His opponents clamor very vociferously about "fraud" in Louisiana; but they can never drown their own consciousness that the most stupendous fraud, which has made the word "bull-dozing" a popular technic in our language, underlies every other fraud. However deep the Republican fraud there may have been, below its lowest deep is a lower depth of Democratic villainy, which aimed to crush the real Republican majority of legal voters in that State. The Republican frauds, if any there were, were the counteractive wrong against that far greater and previous wrong. The net result was right.

In our free North the majority for Hayes was, if we rightly recollect, two hundred and fifty thousand. And that body of free northern Republican voters is peerless in its intellectual and moral character. It is that body which, without invidious sectional comparison, we may fearlessly say is the nucleus of the nation: the *élite*, whose wealth, intelligence, enterprise, moral tone, and true Protestant Americanism, give character to our nation at home and abroad. To that body is opposed here in the North the unintelligence and the depravity that constitute the disgrace and danger of our great Republic. And yet the corrupt leaders of this corrupt mass are vociferating that General Hayes is "fraudulently elected," that he is "a minority President!" It is a bold and base untruth. If you speak of the wealth and moral worth, General Hayes is the choice of the great body of this true worth of the country. If you speak of mere *numbers*, withdraw the bull-doze and the white fraud, and *General Hayes is the choice of an overwhelming majority of the legal voters of the country.* President Hayes is the nation's rightful choice.

THE GOOD AND TRUE MEN OF BOTH SECTONS SHOULD UNDERSTAND EACH OTHER, AND UNITE THEIR FORCES. Smaller in number, yet embracing many of the noblest spirits of the earth, is a nucleus in the South between whom and the above-named moral *élite* of the North there is a true affinity, and there should be unity. The rebuke administered by the high-toned Democrats of the South to the treasonable, yet cowardly, threats of Northern Democrats in the late canvass, brings us a cheering proof that there is in the Southern heart a true allegiance to our national Union. The true aim of all true national patriots at the present time is to eliminate sectional issues from our political contests. A solid South against a solid or nearly solid North is a national danger and misfortune. In such a contest the South, unless clearly right, will be the usual loser. The single State of New York, usually Republican, could in the last contest have elected Hayes against a completely "solid South."

To our call for "a parley" on this subject in our last Quarterly, the "Southern Christian Advocate" responded in a candid notice of that number. It assents, if our recollection is accurate, to "a parley" provided we dismiss the Negro from discussion. That we can most cheerfully concede as our part of the compromise of peace, conditioned, of course, on a correspondent concession from the Southern side. That required Southern concession is simply that *the Negro be treated in a Christian manner.* Nor will we be exacting in our definition of this *Christian manner.* Nay, we will agree that the following definition, by Governor Drew of Florida, a Southerner and Democrat, shall be the standard. We take it from his late message to the Florida Legislature:—

The general dissemination of knowledge is a fundamental principle in a representative form of government, based upon universal suffrage. The sentiment that education and other privileges are suited to the few and not to the many, is not of this land of freedom, but is of foreign birth and monarchical parentage.

The very existence of our republic depends upon the intelligence and moral sentiment of those who exercise the right of suffrage. The experience of all civilized nations has demonstrated that it is cheaper to build school-houses and maintain schools, than to build poor-houses and jails and support paupers and criminals. Those opposed to free schools claim that it is unjust for the taxpayer to furnish means to educate the children of the non-taxpayer. Is it a greater hardship to pay tax to establish schools and to prevent crime, than to pay a greater tax to build penitentiaries and punish criminals? The public free school system is no longer an experiment in those States where it has long been established and its successful operation fully demonstrated.

Now that a very large constituent element of our population is released from bondage and intrusted with the power of the ballot, a system of free schools has become a means of self-preservation. To educate the colored race, and fit them to exercise the privilege of voting intelligently—to perform all the sacred rights

of freemen, to enjoy their liberty, to become wise and good citizens—imposes upon us a task to perform, a responsibility from which we cannot escape. Then let us set about the work cheerfully.

The adoption of that platform, Negro education and the honest observance of the Fifteenth Constitutional Amendment, will give the Negro a walking paper out of sectional discussion.

---

*The Wesleyan Methodist Magazine.* January, 1877. Large 12mo., pp. 80. London: Wesleyan Conference Office, City Road. Price, sixpence.

This, the oldest extant of Methodist periodicals, has attained its centennial year, and chats to us in a lively way its autobiography. It is just one year younger than our own American nationality. It is, under a changed name, the historical continuation of the Arminian Magazine, established by Wesley himself in 1778. The Magazine for January thus gives account of its own birth:—

"The Arminian Magazine" was originated by Mr. Wesley, in the year 1778, principally as an engine of polemical theology. It was much more a sword than a trowel. The preface to the first number announced it as designed to take the place of "The Christian Magazine," which had collapsed, and to oppose "The Spiritual Magazine" and "The Gospel Magazine," which had sprung up in its place. It was born armed, out of the busy brain of Wesley. Its controversial design was proclaimed in its title—"The Arminian Magazine." The preface was not merely a manifesto, but a distinct declaration of war. The very poetry—for a time composed almost exclusively by the Wesley family—was principally directed to polemical purposes: its muse, like an Amazon, preferring the trumpet to the lyre. Mr. Wesley did not leave it to win a market solely by its merits, but printed it "by subscription." It was to contain eighty pages, (the same number as the present,) its price being one shilling. It in fact only contained fifty pages—the first number forty-eight. It announced its resolve to admit neither news nor politics. Methodism had long felt the need of a literary organ of its own. For nearly forty years before he consented, Wesley had been "desired" to publish such a periodical. He and his brother were the conjoint editors, but for the first two years the ardent and poetic Thomas Olivers was the tryingly incompetent sub-editor, or "corrector of the press." Reviews were excluded, because the candid, conscientious, humble-minded Wesley would "not be bound to read over all the present religious productions of the press," and *scrupled* his own sufficiency for the work; and, it seems, knew no one to whom he could confide the reviewing department. (Pp. 1, 2.)

Then we are thus told how Wesley inserted some light literature, and how the straight-out Methodists did not like it:—

One very noteworthy point, and highly characteristic of Wesley, is that he admits, after the first few numbers, a considerable proportion of merely sentimental poetry, refined and elegant, but with not the slightest infusion of positive Christianity. A signal instance of this was the filling fourteen pages, of forty-eight, with Prior's metrical love-tale, *Henry and Emma*. In answer to the outcry against this, he admits that it is "not strictly religious," yet vindicated its insertion on the ground of its exquisite sentiment and diction, and the facts that "there is nothing in it contrary to religion, nothing that can offend the chastest ears, and that many truly religious men and women have profited thereby." Certainly it contains nothing un-Arminian. Wesley evidently held that if elegant entertainment is of the very essence of a *magazine*, nothing is out of place, even in a religious, a *Methodist* Magazine, which can powerfully please, without polluting or per-

verting. As to literary aliment, he seems to have adopted the old dietetic maxim, "Whatever does not poison fattens." Few will dissent from Wesley's judgment that *Henry and Emma* is "one of the finest poems in the English tongue, both for sentiment and language;" but to characterize it as "not *strictly* religious," is scarcely to give an exact description of it, since the only religious element it contains is purely pagan. Had it been produced by one of the popular poets of our own day, and sent to *Good Words*, its late illustrious editor would doubtless have inserted it with artistic illustrations; perhaps not without a momentary demur at its classic heathenism. The lamented Guthrie would certainly have forbidden it the "Sunday Magazine," and the Religious Tract Society would have deemed it hardly suitable for the "Leisure Hour." But by publishing a metrical romance side by side with the Life of an Early Methodist Preacher and one of his own letters on Christian Perfection, he definitely, though not definitively, acted on the principle adopted by most modern religious periodicals. On the other hand, by the strong, and not surprising, protest which the Methodists made against its appearance under such auspices, they both definitely and definitively rejected and discarded from Methodist literature the unreligious novel, whether in prose or verse. A religious novel, Wesley's very imperfectly expurgated edition of "The Fool of Quality," under the quieter title, "Henry, Earl of Moreland," published the very next year—a highly sensational anticipation of "Tom Brown's School Days," combined with a sort of mildly religious "Vanity Fair"—had a quite sufficiently wide, warm, and long-lasting Methodist popularity.

It is clear that the demur of the Methodists generally to the insertion of "Henry and Emma" in their Magazine was not to its purely imaginative character, but to the absence of the religious spirit. In any case, Wesley himself held the same view of the marvelous creative faculty with which the human imagination is endowed, which his brother Charles held as to music: that it

"—Alas! too long hath been—
Why should a good be evil?—
'Listed into the cause of sin,
Press'd to obey the devil."

The well-intentioned novel to which Wesley stood godfather he left to the care of the conference. It bore the imprimatur of the Methodist Book-Room, and was entered on its catalogues during a full generation after Wesley's death. It was immeasurably inferior in tone and tendency to the writings of Mrs. Charles, "Sarson," and "Ruth Elliott," and its prurient descriptions of scenes of vice were very perilous to young people of ignitible imagination. (Pp. 2–4.)

In 1804 Joseph Benson, "the most powerful popular preacher of the day, and next, perhaps, to Coke, the foremost man in Methodism,". was appointed chief editor, with three assistants. This plentiful supply of aid implied that "the office was meant to be, to some extent, a canonry, leaving him ample leisure for the writing of his Commentary." Even in those early days an editor was allowed—nay, provision was made for him—to be a commentator.

Benson retained the editorship until his death in 1821, and was succeeded by "the topmost man in conference," Jabez Bunting. "The great Methodist leader at once initiated a 'new series' of the Magazine. The word *Wesleyan* is prefixed to *Methodist* on the title-page." Who abolished the original "Arminian" we are not informed, but it was unwisely done. It was quite a heroism in Wesley to unfurl the name of Arminius at the head of his craft. That illustrious name even those who held the great

theologian's doctrines did not yet dare to properly revere and honor. And we regret that this true and noble successor of Wesley's original monthly has not borne its hereditary name.

The following eloquent paragraph describes the spirit in which the Magazine was first established:—

> The first point that strikes one is the controversial—one might rather say, the chivalrous—aspect, accoutermentand bearing of the Magazine of Methodism. Never did knight of the ages of romance, after holy vigils and solemn rites, ride forth more gallantly to redress wrong and champion civilization and religion than did the "Arminian Magazine" come "pricking o'er the plain" to confront and confound error, evil, and the powers of night. It did not merely stand in the lists, challenging all comers with lance in rest; but its bugle-blast smote with defiant resonance against the strongholds of godlessness and misbelief, and it drove *full tilt* against the giant heresies, the monster mischiefs, and the stalking specters of the age. Is there less need now than then of valor for the truth upon the earth: of earnest contention "for the faith once delivered unto the saints?" Is our latter-day unbelief, is our current error, less insolent, less confident, less seductive, less determined, less subtle, less equipped? Assuredly these are no times for a faithful witnessing Church to suppress or soften its trenchant testimony for "the truth as it is in Jesus." The present humor of unbelief is to compliment Christ out of his divine authority; to rob him, on the one hand, of his redeeming mediatorship, and, on the other, of his rights as a Revealer and a Ruler; to reject his sacrifice on Calvary in favor of his Sermon on the Mount; or to hail him as a Redeemer, and repudiate him as the sternest of all Denouncers of impenitent unbelief.

Though a centenarian, the Magazine is still young, and ready for another century. Those of our readers who wish to maintain a communion with English Methodism will scarce find a fitter medium than this fresh and living periodical.

## *Foreign Theological Publications.*

*Christliche Glaubenslehre vom Methodistischen Stand-punkt,* (Methodist Dogmatics.) By A. SULZBERGER, Ph.D. Bremen and Frankfurt. 1876.

Methodism is not destined to be long without a plentiful supply of systems of Dogmatics. The one able, elaborate work of Watson has well sufficed us for the whole crystallizing period of our existence. But in the nature of the case it could not suffice us forever. Self-respect, if no higher imperative were needed, would prompt us to show that we have not yet passed out of our period of productiveness into that of stagnant old age. And this "would" is in fair way of rapidly becoming an abundant "is." Already two of our German scholars have published in the German tongue the first-fruits of profound dogmatic study. And our three American preachers' Seminaries are following in the wake of the German. So that very soon we shall be able to see whether, indeed, we still possess throughout the whole Church a close dogmatic unity, or whether, as assumed by the Princeton Review

for October, 1876, we are suffering under "doctrinal flexibility" with a "drift in some directions toward Broad Churchism."

Dr. Sulzberger is in advance of his competitors in getting the main body of his Dogmatics before the public. In the January issue of this Review for 1873, we briefly noted the appearance of his Introduction (of some 189 pages.) We now have before us the whole work (680 small octavo pages) except the Eschatology, which, the author promises us, shall not be long in appearing.

The work of Dr. Sulzberger will not fall dead from the press. His constituency of German Methodist preachers requires the book, even were there no other call for it. But there are also two other calls for it;—to acquaint foreign theologians with the views of Methodism, and to enrich our English Methodist doctrinal teaching with the scientific rigor and soundness of recent German investigation. All three of these ends Dr. Sulzberger has kept steadily in view. His work is simple, practical, thorough. It is faithfully Methodistic, abundantly corroborating itself from Wesley, Fletcher, Watson. It is catholic and broad, using richly the great thoughts of the Fathers, as also those of Nitzsch, Sartorius, Ullmann, Hagenbach, Stier, Müller, Tholuck, Rothe, Martensen, Schaff, Pressensé, Whedon, Nast, and others. It is also eminently historical, briefly and clearly tracing the progressive development of the several doctrines.

After an elaborate introduction (150 pages) Dr. Sulzberger distributes his subject-matter into these four parts:—

I. Of God as Creator, and of the relation of the creature to God.

II. Of God as Redeemer, and of the redemption of man.

III. Of God as the Accomplisher of salvation, and of salvation itself.

IV. Of the last things, or eschatology.

The sections in Part First run thus: Theology, the Knowledge, the Existence, the Essence, the Attributes of God, the Natural, the Moral Attributes; the Trinity, Analogical and Metaphysical Explanations, Scripture Proof; the Divinity of the Father, Son, and Spirit; History of the Doctrine of the Trinity; Creation, the Mosaic Account, the Providence of God; the Creature, Angels, the Nature of Angels, Good and Bad Angels, Satanology; Primitive Man, the Fall, Depravity, the Stages of Sin, History of the Doctrine. Part Second has these sections: God's Purpose of Redemption, Preparation, Christ the Theanthropic Redeemer, his true Humanity, his Sinlessness, the Incarnation of the Logos, the Unity of the Theanthropic Nature of Christ, Scripture Proof, Histo-

ry of the Doctrine; the Relation of Christ's Work to his Person, his Prophetic, his High Priestly Office, History of the Doctrine of the Atonement, the Twofold Condition of Christ, his Resurrection, his Ascension. Part Third is discussed in these sections: Soteriology, Prevenient Grace, the Gift and Influence of the Spirit, the Relation of the Influence of the Spirit to Man's Freedom, the Order of Salvation, Calling, Enlightening, Awakening, Conversion, Repentance, Faith, Justification, Regeneration, the Witness of the Spirit, Sanctification.

This outline shows how thoroughly the field is covered. Whether the classification has not too much of characteristic German subdividing is an open question. We regret it as a more pardonable fault to divide too little than too much; as nothing tends more to confusion in theology no less than in metaphysics, than the discussing of the various phases of *one* thing as if they were different things.

Let us glance at some of the positions of Dr. Sulzberger: How to reconcile absolute divine foreknowledge with creatural freedom is a very difficult problem. Two ways out of the difficulty have been, either to suppress the foreknowledge, or to deny the freedom. Cicero did the former; the Stoics, the latter. A few mediæval scholastics and the modern Socinians follow Cicero, saying that God knows free creatural actions only when they actually take place; but this undermines the dogma of foreknowledge. Origen, Augustine, Anselm, Wesley, Schleiermacher, Nitzsch, unanimously hold that God foreknows the free *as* free.

The trinity is not a mere historical, transient, economical distinction, but is grounded in the eternal essence of God.

Creating is the bringing into existence of that which previously did not exist. Creating was not a necessary, but a free act of God. The assumption of a necessary creation leads inevitably to Pantheism. A necessity of creating cannot be inferred from God's *need* of an object to love. What God has needed for his love, he has already from eternity generated out of his own essence, namely: the eternal Logos.

To what end did God create the world? Two one-sided answers have been given. Calvinists say, solely for his own glory; eudæmonists say, solely for the happiness of the creature. The true answer co-ordinates both of these answers into one.

The process of creating has not gone on from eternity, but began definitely in a "beginning." (We regret to see Dr. Sulzberger answering the very natural query: What had God been doing

in the vast eternity before the beginning of the world? with the poor witticism of Luther: He had been sitting in the woods, cutting rods for impertinent questioners.)

God's sustaining or preserving of the universe is not, as old dogmatizers hold, a continued creation (*creatio continua*). For creating is bringing forth out of nothing. Preservation can here mean only a supporting, developing, and modifying of that which already *was*.

The laws of nature are ordinances of God, which he freely can and does change when the higher interests of moral creatures require it. God's government over nature is determinative; over moral beings, directive; over evil beings, permissive.

Inherited depravity is not personal guilt. No one is, or can be, justly damned because of his ancestor's sin.

Jesus Christ passed through the ordinary human development, from infant to child, to youth, to man. As child, he was ignorant of that which, as boy, he surmised; and as youth, he distinctly saw; and as man, he fully comprehended. In proportion as he grew up to full self-consciousness, he became also conscious of his relation to the Father; and in proportion as he grew in comprehension of the world, he grew also in comprehension of his unique, holy, and redeeming relation to humanity.

What is the nature of the person of Christ? To say that the divine Logos imparted omnipotence, omniscience, etc., to the human nature which he assumed, is to reduce his humanity to mere appearance. To say that he possessed all these divine attributes, but forwent their exercise, is also to deny the truly human nature of Christ. To say that while Christ, *as* the omnipotent and omniscient God, upheld and governed the world, he yet, *as* man, grew up from ignorance to knowledge, and learned obedience in a truly human manner, is to so destroy the unity of his person as to justify Dr. Nast in declaring that such a view is hardly better than ancient Nestorianism. Such a separating of the attributes of the theanthropic Mediator is not found in the New Testament. On the contrary, every dividing of the Redeemer into two *egos*, the one the exalted Logos, and the other the humble man, is directly contrary to clear Scripture. Modern orthodox theologians find a more satisfactory view in the *kenosis* that is involved in the text: "The Word became flesh." Christ did *not* lay aside, nor forego to use, his divine attributes, but he simply manifested them in a truly human manner. Even as when a man quits the light of day and goes into thick darkness, he does not lose his

power of vision, so the Logos did not *lose* his divine powers when he descended into the limitations of human nature. Such a *kenosis*, says Luthardt, as relates to the mere earthly condition of Christ, is indispensable to a truly human life in Jesus.

The atonement consists in the fact that Christ, the sinless One, freely took upon himself the consequences of sin. His death was not inflicted upon him by a few Jews and Romans, but was, in fact, the culminating work of the collective sinfulness of humanity as a whole. It is neither the passive suffering by itself, nor the active obedience, that atones, but both together. The value of Christ's death of suffering lay more in its quality than in its quantity. The intensive element of his passion lay in the *feeling* of abandonment by the Father. Every form of Jewish and heathen sin had conspired against him. Between him and the Father, the sin, the darkness of the world, had thrust itself, and had thus paralyzed his *sense* of blessedness. But the suffering which he endured was foreign to his nature. What he suffered was, therefore, the absolute pain of sin, but *not* its punishment. *He suffered, but he was not punished.*

Conversion and regeneration are not identical. Conversion is that act of the sinner whereby, under the continued activity of the Holy Spirit, he, with an earnest will-effort, and with his whole heart, turns away from sin and cleaves to God. Its conditions are, repentance of sin and faith in God through Christ. The sinner cannot be converted against his will, nor without his personal participation in the work. Regeneration, on the contrary, is a divine act attendant upon conversion, whereby the fruitful germs of a holy development are implanted into the repentant soul. The *modus* of this implantation, Mr. Sulzberger frankly admits, is beyond his comprehension; but the fact he holds fast to, under the testimony both of Scripture and of experience.

On the whole we regard this dogmatic attempt as a clear success. The author is admirably conservative, admirably judicious, admirably clear. He has wisely resisted the temptation to over self-reliance, and to hasty innovations. He is a safe guide for the young preachers of our widely-extended German Methodism. And we are not sure but that it would have a healthy effect to dress him up in English, and publish him alongside of the more ponderous works which are soon to issue from our English-American press. L.

## *Miscellaneous.*

*Indian Missionary Directory and Memorial Volume.* By Rev. B. H. BADLEY, of the American Methodist Mission. Large 12mo., pp. 279. Lucknow: American Methodist Mission Press. London: Trübner & Co. 1876.

This is a catalogue of all the missionaries who have labored in India, with very brief biographical notices of many of them. It begins with the first Danish Mission, in 1705, and extends to the present time. We count no less than twenty-eight missionary societies who have contributed laborers to this vast field, from various nations and denominations. It thus furnishes an outline and a reference book, but with little of the attractions of a history.

*Sermons on Living Subjects.* By HORACE BUSHNELL. 8vo., pp. 468. New York: Scribner, Armstrong, & Co. 1877.

*Epochs of Ancient History.* The Triumvirates. By CHARLES MERIVALE, D.D., Dean of Ely. With a Map. Pp. 248. New York: Scribner, Armstrong, & Co.

*Central Africa:* Naked Truths of Naked People. An Account of Expeditions to the Lake Victoria Nyanza and the Makraka Niam-Niam, West of the Bahr-el-Abiad, (White Nile.) By Col. C. CHAILLE LONG, of the Egyptian Staff. Illustrated from Colonel Long's own Sketches. 8vo., pp. 328. New York: Harper and Brothers. 1877.

*A Princess of Thule.* A Novel. By WILLIAM BLACK, author of "The Strange Adventures of a Phaeton," "Madcap Violet," "A Daughter of Heth," "The Maid of Killeena," "Green Pastures and Piccadilly," etc. 8vo., pp. 464. New York: Harper & Brothers. 1877.

*A Ride to Khiva.* Travels and Adventures in Central Asia. By FRED BURNABY (Captain Royal Horse Guards.) With Maps, and an Appendix containing among other information, a series of march routes, compiled from a Russian work. 8vo., pp. 403. New York: Harper & Brothers. 1877.

*Weavers and Weft;* or, "Love that hath us in his Net." By Miss BRADDON, author of "Lady Audley's Secret," "A Strange World," "Bound to John Company," "Dead Men's Shoes." 8vo., pp. 91. New York: Harper & Brothers. 1877.

*The Golden Butterfly.* A Novel. By the Authors of "Ready-Money Mortiboy," "When the Ship Comes Home," etc. Pp. 167. New York: Harper & Brothers. 1877.

*Annie Warwick.* A Novel. By GEORGIANA M. CRAIK, author of "Mildred," "Sylvia's Choice," "The Cousin from India," "Miss Moore." Pp. 104. New York: Harper & Brothers. 1877.

*The Sun-Maid.* A Romance. By the Author of "Artiste," "Victor Lescar," etc. Pp. 145. New York: Harper & Brothers. 1877.

*Madcap Violet.* A Novel. By WILLIAM BLACK, author of "The Strange Adventures of a Phaeton," "Princess of Thule," "A Daughter of Heth," "Kilmeny," "The Monarch of Mincing Lane," etc. Pp. 259. New York: Harper & Brothers. 1877.

*Dancing as an Amusement, considered in the Light of the Scriptures, of Christian Experience, and of Good Taste.* 8vo., pp. 79. By BOSTWICK HAWLEY, D.D. New York: N. Tibballs & Sons. 1877.

*Liver Complaint, Nervous Dyspepsia, and Headache:* their Causes, Prevention, and Cure. By M. L. HOLBROOK, M.D., editor of the "Herald of Health," author of "Parturition Without Pain," and "Eating for Strength." 8vo., pp. 141. New York: Wood & Holbrook. 1876.

Lightning Source UK Ltd.
Milton Keynes UK
UKHW052306041218
333416UK00027B/398/P

9 781330 532973